THE MASTER ARCHITECT SERIES VI
John Portman and Associates

Selected and Current Works

THE MASTER ARCHITECT SERIES VI
John Portman and Associates

Selected and Current Works

First published in Australia in 2002
by The Images Publishing Group Pty Ltd
ACN 059 734 431
6 Bastow Place, Mulgrave, Victoria, 3170
Telephone (61 3) 9561 5544 Facsimile (61 3) 9561 4860
Email: books@images.com.au
Website: www.imagespublishinggroup.com

Copyright © The Images Publishing Group Pty Ltd 2002
The Images Publishing Group Reference Number: 337

All rights reserved. Apart from any fair dealing for the purposes of private
study, research, criticism or review as permitted under the Copyright Act,
no part of this publication may be reproduced, stored in a retrieval system
or transmitted in any form by any means, electronic, mechanical,
photocopying, recording or otherwise, without the written permission
of the publisher.

National Library of Australia
Cataloguing-in-Publication data

John Portman and Associates: Selected and current works.

Includes index.
ISBN 1 8760 706 1.

720.973

Edited by Steve Womersley

Designed by The Graphic Image Studio Pty Ltd, Mulgrave, Australia

Film separations by SC (Sang Choy) International Pte Ltd, Singapore

Printed by Everbest Printing Co. Ltd. in Hong Kong/China

Contents

6 Introduction

Selected Works
14 **Selected Works**
16 Peachtree Center
18 AmericasMart
20 Inforum
22 Hyatt Regency Atlanta
26 Westin Peachtree Plaza Hotel
28 Atlanta Marriott Marquis
32 SunTrust Plaza
38 SunTrust Plaza Garden Offices
42 SunTrust III
44 Embarcadero Center
52 Renaissance Center
54 Marina Square
60 Shanghai Centre
66 Capital Square
68 Il Porto Vecchio
72 Shandong Hotel & Conference Center
76 Tomorrow Square
84 Nile Center
86 Le Meridien Hotel
88 Moscow Centre
90 Gateway City
94 Shanghai Daewoo Business Center
98 Chong Qing
100 Zhong Xing City
102 New Asia Center
104 New Ci Hou Plaza
108 Silver Tai World Trade Center
112 Shanghai Art Center
116 Facilities for the Airport Terminal Complex—Jing An
118 Huading Mansion
120 Guangzhou Daily Cultural Center
124 Songdo Daewoo Town
130 Parcel 8
132 Jin Mao
138 Lot 6
140 Sampoerna Tower

142 New York Marriott Marquis
146 The Pan Pacific San Francisco, (formerly The Portman Hotel)
152 The Regent Singapore
156 Westlake International Hotel
160 Hotelero Business Monterrey
162 'W' Hotel and Residences
164 Westin Hotel Charlotte
166 Village of Schaumburg Convention Center, Performing Arts Theater, and Convention Headquarters Hotel
168 Westin Hotel
170 East Seaport Apartment and High Rise Hotel Addition
172 Bank of China
174 Bank of Communications
180 Great Park
182 BSD New Town
184 Hsinchu Regional Master Plan
186 Dream Lake Mountain Villas
188 George W. Woodruff Physical Education Center
190 R. Howard Dobbs University Center
194 University/Olympic Apartments
196 Nursing, Health Science and Outreach Complex
198 Gwinnett Center Academic Building
202 Indian School of Business
208 Rockefeller Center Promenade
210 Entelechy I
214 Entelechy II
220 Furniture

224 **Firm Profile**
226 Principals Biographies
232 Collaborators and Consultants
234 Chronological List of Buildings and Projects
238 Bibliography
248 Awards/Exhibitions
252 Acknowledgments/Photography Credits
254 Index

Introduction

'To create space that enhances the quality of life is architecture's greatest gift to the community it serves.'

The 1990s exhibited significant activity in both the volume and variety of architectural projects undertaken by John Portman & Associates. By solving unique problems pragmatically, yet with vision and creativity, the body of work of John Portman and his firm now spans the world. This book is a compilation of work that attempts to contribute to an enhanced quality of life for both individuals and communities.

John Portman & Associates strives for an architecture that is more than just the design of a building, but rather the creation of 'a place for being'. Its challenge is to combine design excellence with economic feasibility, incorporating creative ideas to produce viable projects that put people's needs, both physical and spiritual, first and foremost.

Many factors influence the work and form the basis of the firm's design philosophy. Vision, creativity, and an entrepreneurial spirit are basic ingredients. Ideas, though sometimes bold, are always underpinned by pragmatics as the architecture attempts to focus on each project's contribution to the community it serves. Moreover, the architecture strives to consciously uplift people through an enhancement of the human condition.

Headquartered in Atlanta, the firm's early projects were geographically close. The largest endeavor was Peachtree Center. This commercial complex is still expanding, and now covers 14 blocks in Atlanta's central business district. From its inception, Peachtree Center stabilized Atlanta's downtown to protect it from the national tide of urban decay, neglect, and abandonment. It became the centerpiece of a thriving trade and convention industry, expanded the job base of the city's most vulnerable employment sector, and helped to transform Atlanta from a gracious Southern town into a growing international city. Peachtree Center began in 1960 with the Atlanta Merchandise Mart. Its central downtown location was a pivotal factor in the subsequent development of hotels and convention facilities that ultimately put Atlanta among the top tier of convention destinations in the U.S.A..

Peachtree Center was conceived as a new urban business center. To achieve this goal, Portman and his staff, of necessity, began by learning more about the economics that drive the engine of real estate development. Portman then took the controversial position of acting as architect/developer for a few of the firm's design projects. His resultant development knowledge and ownership interests gave the firm a unique perspective on the economic aspects of the design process as it resolved how to turn visionary ideas into practical realities. This broad knowledge base has been useful in providing added value to independent clients.

Peachtree Center was the firm's entrée into large mixed-use urban design. With it, a new open-ended urban form had begun. John Portman & Associates concentrated not on building new cities or suburban enclaves, but rather on building from within and transforming the urban structure of an existing American city. To do so, two of the many criteria they initially focused on were the impact of design on the scale of the city and the need to make buildings more environmentally friendly in order to enhance human lifestyle. Understanding the human response to space, nature, and light became and continues to be integral to the work. Nature and space—both external and internal— are indigenous to the firm's architectural philosophy.

To explore some of the new concepts, Portman used his own homes, Entelechy I and II. The first, completed in 1964, embodies many of his early design concepts. Here we first see 'controlled explosion', a new way of defining architectural space. Twenty-four massive hollow columns form the house's order. Each column is composed of eight perimeter arcs that can come and go, depending on spatial and structural need. The space within is opened to a variety of uses and new scale dynamics—order and variety—are simultaneously achieved.

From this probing approach came the idea for the modern atrium on a massive scale. The first such project was the Hyatt Regency Atlanta. This hotel revolutionized the hospitality industry and brought international recognition to the architect and arguably moved modern architecture to a new awareness of spatial possibilities.

In the Hyatt Regency Atlanta, the traditional form of the tightly confined city hotel was changed. The architecture figuratively 'exploded' the new 800-room hotel, opening it up for a totally unique guest experience. The 22 room-floors were pulled apart to create a large enclosed central space. The elevator cabs were taken from their shafts and transformed into an experience in their own right; as the glass cabs moved through

Introduction continued

space they provided changing views and became a large kinetic sculpture in the great space. Atop the building, a destination was provided in the form of a revolving restaurant overlooking a rapidly changing skyline. This made the hotel a public amenity for its guests as well as the community. Initially, during its construction many hotel operators rejected this new approach, but one did not. With the backing of the Pritzker family, the Hyatt Regency Atlanta opened in 1967. By creating a new hotel experience, it immediately placed the then small Hyatt Hotel Company at the leading edge of the hospitality industry and provided the thrust that established its now global presence. The hotel likewise won world recognition for the Atlanta-based architectural firm.

Another major milestone transpired on the West Coast of the United States. As Peachtree Center continued to evolve in Atlanta, Portman and his associates turned to a San Francisco urban renewal project that provided the perfect opportunity to implement a new lifestyle focused on human values in urban planning. Embarcadero Center, a five-block mixed-use complex, transformed a run-down warehouse district into one of the city's most successful people-oriented commercial developments, subsequently winning the Urban Land Institute's Award of Excellence for Large-Scale Urban Development in 1984.

In Embarcadero Center, as in Peachtree Center, one sees a major effort at re-creating the American city, with use and enjoyment by the people as a core value. Traditional street-level retail activity is expanded to multiple levels that are linked from block to block by pedestrian bridges, plazas, and promenades. The complex is pedestrian-oriented with a strong emphasis on urban landscaping and art in the public realm. People are drawn from Embarcadero Center's high-rise office towers, the convention hotel, and the adjacent residential apartments into shops and restaurants that link the development. There are a variety of spatial experiences, from tranquil to dynamic. The cafes and restaurants that open onto the smaller courtyards are intimate and cozy. By contrast, Justin Herman Plaza's large park-like space is the city's gathering place and is filled with outdoor activities. Indoors, the large asymmetrical atrium lobby of the Hyatt Regency provides magnetic appeal that draws people of all ages to enjoy the exciting spatial experience. The success of Embarcadero Center led to an additional three-block expansion in 1985, wherein the adjacent Federal Reserve office building was renovated and a fifth office tower and second hotel were added to the complex at the opposite end from the Hyatt Regency and Justin Herman Plaza.

The importance of Embarcadero Center is not that of any single building, although each stands strong in its own right, but it is how well they work together to enhance the city with a vastly improved human experience. This philosophy goes beyond Embarcadero Center, and extends into the broader context of looking at the city as a whole.

John Portman & Associates participates in numerous master planning projects, from Atlanta and San Francisco to Shanghai, Taipei and other cities around the world. Planning with human values is the first step in the architectural process. As each decade unfolds, the planning and architecture of John Portman & Associates reflects an evolution in its relationship to time and place. Yet, consistent with its evolution, the architecture always attempts to connect with how people respond to their architectural experience—how the buildings make them feel, how the space lifts their spirits—a people-conscious approach.

Since all people are more alike than unalike, the architecture attempts to transcend national borders by striving for universal human appeal. The 1970s began the expansion of the firm's work that is now as extensive overseas as it is in the States. The first international venture was in Brussels, Belgium. Drawing on the firm's experience with the trade marts in Atlanta, Portman designed and co-developed the Brussels International Trade Mart that opened in 1975. From Europe to the Mid-East, the architectural firm worked on major mixed-use complexes.

Jack Portman, John Portman's son, after graduating from Harvard, joined the firm and took a leading role in its international activities. Soon after establishing an office in Hong Kong in 1978, major commissions followed for condominiums in Hong Kong, and hotels and mixed-use projects in Singapore, Kuala Lumpur, and Jakarta.

When China first opened its doors to the West, Portman was one of the first to enter. From prior experience in Southeast Asia, Portman's respect for the indigenous cultures of Southeast Asia was a given. Jack Portman has taken the firm forward in building new

Introduction continued

business relationships in China. The first project was the design of a mixed-use complex for a Chinese client in Shanghai. The client unfortunately had difficulty in securing the financing to build it and approached Portman to join in partnership to secure the necessary project financing and provide development expertise in addition to the architecture for the project. The firm successfully brought into being Shanghai Centre, the largest foreign mixed-use project at that time in China.

Shanghai Centre drew on many years of Portman experience in creating successful urban centers. It was designed to provide all the services needed by the international business community as it established operations in China. The complex includes a hotel, apartments, offices, retail space, exhibition space, and a Broadway-type theater. At the time, the city's infrastructure was still weak, so the complex incorporated state-of-the-art telecommunication systems and back-up systems for mechanical and electrical requirements. Construction was a challenge as the project team strove to acknowledge traditional Chinese methods while at the same time dealing with the political circumstances of Tiananmen Square. Still, Portman's commitment to China prevailed. Shanghai Centre opened in 1990 and has been acclaimed for its local acceptance, architectural design, and exceptional economic success. Lessons learned in designing and executing Shanghai Centre continue to benefit clients on many of the firm's other large-scale, mixed-use projects in Asia.

John Portman & Associates' international work continues to expand. Offices are now open in China, Poland, and India. Clients in many high-density cities have responded well to the architectural approach that creates a 'place for being' in the midst of the congested city: culturally sensitive places that are designed for life—livable yet stimulating.

As a pioneer in mixed-use architecture, John Portman & Associates specializes in projects that combine multiple functions in one complex. Recently, some of its most challenging work has been in China. Arguably, one of Shanghai's most distinctive new towers is Tomorrow Square, a structure which addresses the Chinese desire for expressing the hopes and aspirations of the Chinese people in the 21st Century and evokes the desire for a forward looking yet pragmatic statement. The tower's functions are stacked vertically, creating a new, unique form on Shanghai's skyline. The architecture remains true to the creation of space that attempts to uplift the human spirit. On a smaller scale, Shanghai's Bank of Communications represents another project that is multi-functional. In the province of Jinan, the firm's design of the Shandong People's Hall and Hotel provides the provincial government with a landmark governmental complex that also serves as a regional conference center. In Hangzhou, the new Westlake Hyatt Hotel seeks to capture the beauty of the scenic site while integrating retail, residential, and commercial functions with those of the surrounding business community.

John Portman & Associates continues its on-going activities in educational institutional design. The individual character and fabric of a campus is not unlike a city and is a logical adjunct to the talent and experience of the firm. The college campus presents many of the same issues that arise with urban design: individual buildings seen in the context of the whole campus; traffic and circulation; and importantly, the multiple functions often expected to occur within a single structure. Recent fusion of academic activities has given the firm an opportunity to investigate new concepts relating to university design, to campus life, and its educational purpose. Planning on both a large and small scale continues as an indigenous part of the firm's work. Of note are the latest projects being designed for the Indian School of Business in Hyderabad, India and Gwinnett University Center in Lawrenceville, Georgia, the new college campus for the University System of Georgia.

Spanning the globe, projects are underway in Eastern Europe, including a new hotel under construction in Warsaw, and others in the preliminary planning and design stages. Though still headquartered in Atlanta, technology has enabled expedited service to places previously thought remote. The architectural staff itself is a diverse group of talented people from many countries and mirrors cultures where the firm works. Each is chosen for his or her talent, expertise, and commitment to the highest standards of quality in design and service.

Introduction continued

Through the years many architects working with Portman have contributed to the success of the firm. At the core of the firm's practice is enthusiasm, a curiosity about and a search for new ideas, a reverence for quality, a profound interest in human values, and always a respect for human scale.

Architecture – Sculpture – And the Soul of a Man

True art forms are born from within the integrity evolved from conditions naturally—an entelechy. Economy of means to ends producing non-arbitrary genuine form is the true fountain of youth in art. This holds for architecture and sculpture both independently and in union. Architecture and sculpture can both be elevated to a higher realm by their impact on each other when properly fused.

Architecture, perhaps not in a pure sense because of its technical and functional requirements, is sculpture. Its form and materials are similar to sculpture in their consideration. In some instances the architecture can approach pure sculpture, as in Eero Saarinen's TWA terminal at New York's Kennedy Airport, and for sculpture any vain attempt to live in this environment would appear futile. It would be sculpture within sculpture. This has been one of the chief criticisms of Frank Lloyd Wright's Guggenheim Museum. The architecture is so powerful, the sculptor feels inadequate to compete. Some have argued that architecture should be a simple, flexible background for living. This seemingly simple definition is much too thin, for architecture is itself first an art and as with all art must deal with the spiritual aspects of man. True architecture is unity with integrity of entity—space poetically enclosed. Architecture's raison d'être is space. How this space is achieved is what architecture is all about. Space must underlie all architectural meaning, and all other aspects such as structure, materials, and equipment are mere tools and must also be subordinate. Great architecture must be a complete entity through total consideration of parts emphasized in their natural and proper relationship.

The role of sculpture in architecture is counterpoint. The synthesis of architecture and sculpture must be fused into a state of unity and harmony wedded by space. Space, the substance of architecture, is also the substance of sculpture. Sculpture, when incorporated in architecture must have the quality of the thing within itself, yet be completely dependent and a part of the architecture. My feeling is that sculpture should be honestly presented as a work of art, not to be confused with the anatomy of the building. Its position, scale, form, color, and finish should be controlled by the building in such a way that the statics created reveal both in a harmonizing entity in unity. This is to declare void the traditional idea of bas relief carved on the carcass of the building, which infringes upon the dignity of the intended art as well as the building, much as the distasteful practice of tattooing defaces the human body. All special art forms, whether painting, murals or sculpture, should be emphasized as adjuncts to the architecture, retaining the integrity of both.

Architecture should create the space—sculpture command it, if used at all. In command, the sculpture can create the very essence of feeling, for if it is great art, it lives and its being permeates the space and enters the soul of man. Neither architecture nor sculpture should try to compete with each other, for when in union, the whole should be in repose, not conflict. Great architecture and sculpture never startle but have their innate quality in the genuine—born of depth. The aspiration toward the infinite is their task expressed by every means available to man. Great art in perfect harmony—architecture, sculpture, painting, music, philosophy—is the way to the greatest salvation man can have on this earth.

John C. Portman, Jr.

14

selected works

Peachtree Center

Design/Completion 1958 to present/1960-2001
Atlanta, Georgia
Portman Holdings
1,765,000 square meters
Concrete, stone, and glass

Peachtree Center is currently the architect's largest mixed-use complex. It is an evolving project that now spans 14 blocks in the heart of Atlanta's business district and provides a variety of activities and amenities to produce an enhanced lifestyle. The complex strives to satisfy pedestrian-friendly needs and is comprised of 10 office buildings, three large convention hotels, three trade mart buildings (AmericasMart), a retail mall, a large health club, and integral parking. An additional office tower is now in the design stage.

Peachtree Center was the first of the firm's urban planning activities to recognize the need for a new and unified urban fabric to stop the exodus of people from the eroding central city. As it has unfolded over a period of more than 40 years, each building is related to the other and to the original architectural fabric. The buildings were designed to recognize scale, form, and texture.

The site for Peachtree Center straddles a north–south ridge, falling off to the east and west. This opened up the opportunity for multi-level public spaces with pedestrian bridges linking the complex and freeing visitors from the congestion of vehicular traffic below. Retail activity and other amenities are on levels beneath the major towers to expand the complex's public arena in a logical continuum. Plazas and parks, both interior and exterior and abounding with major sculpture, open from street-level to bring elements of art and nature into the environment.

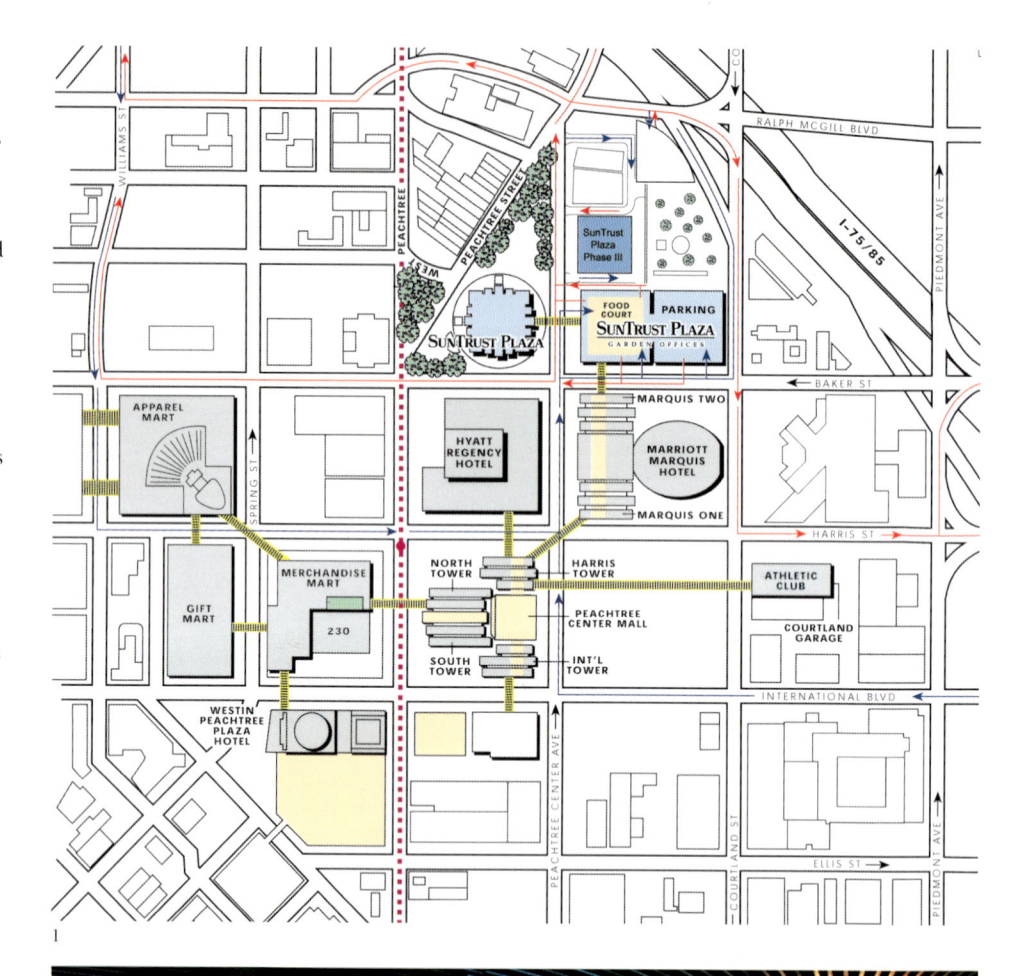

1 Site map of Peachtree Center Complex
2 Interior of Midnight Sun restaurant
Opposite:
　View looking north of Peachtree Center

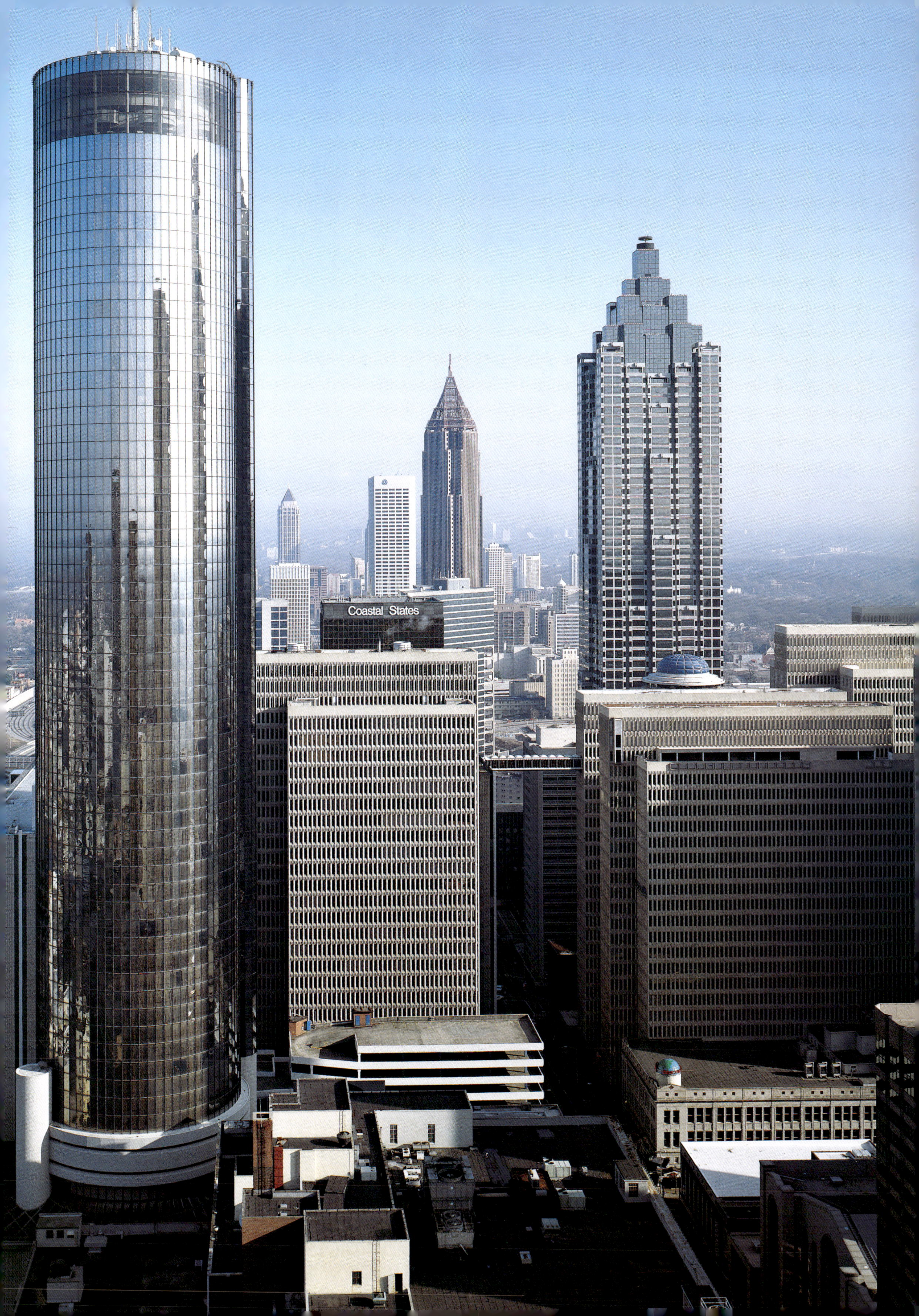
Coastal States

AmericasMart

Peachtree Center
Design/Completion 1958-1989/1960-1992
Atlanta, Georgia
AmericasMart Ltd.
483,270 square meters (without Inforum)
Concrete, metal paneling, and glass

1   Northwest view of Gift Mart
Opposite:
   Interiors of Merchandise Mart

AmericasMart is a major component of Peachtree Center. This vertical wholesale complex, closed to the public and open to the trade only, is comprised of three buildings connected by multiple bridges: Merchandise Mart, Gift Mart and Apparel Mart. The first phase of Merchandise Mart initiated the development by generating a significant base of new commercial activity for the city. The economical, low-budget, 22-story, 92,940-square-meter building has straightforward floor plans to maximize interior showroom space. Demand for space doubled its size in 1968 and later added another 55,750 square meters in 1985.

When the need for more space drew the apparel industry into its own building in 1979, the architect took a different approach. The 139,400-square-meter, windowless concrete structure turned inward, using a fan-shaped atrium lighted from above to provide space for large fashion shows and to establish strong visual connections between the showroom floors. A stage and seating area are at the atrium base. The original architectural and structural design anticipated a future vertical expansion to double the size of the building.

The 22-story Gift Mart was also a response to industry demand. To meet the challenge of limited available land adjacent to Merchandise Mart, Gift Mart was designed over and around an existing parking structure. Horizontal bands of reflective glass contrast the first two marts yet echo materials in the nearby Inforum and Peachtree Plaza Hotel.

1

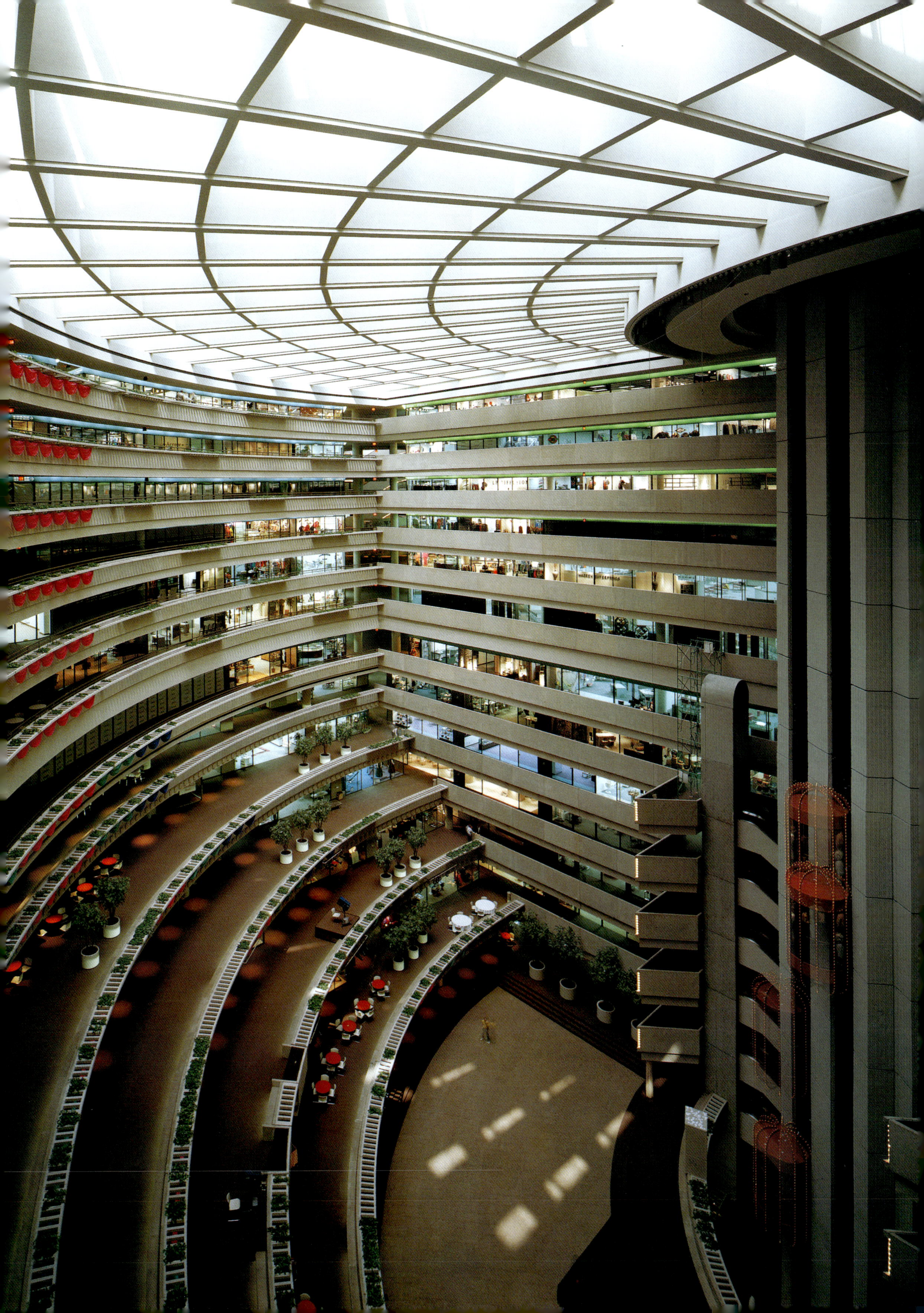

Inforum

Peachtree Center
Design/Completion 1986/1989
Atlanta, Georgia
Equitable Properties
139,400 square meters
Concrete and glass

1   Skyward interior view
2   North view
Opposite:
    Lobby

Inforum demonstrates the versatility of the Peachtree Center design concept. The building was originally intended to be an integral part of the AmericasMart complex. Two large enclosed pedestrian bridges link the building's exhibition level to that of the adjacent Apparel Mart. The lower levels provide meeting and conference rooms, a 600-seat theater and underground parking. The upper levels were designed for showrooms serving computer-technology products.

The large floor plate of the square building is situated around a north–south axial rectangular atrium that affords excellent office or showroom conditions for companies requiring expansive space on a single level.

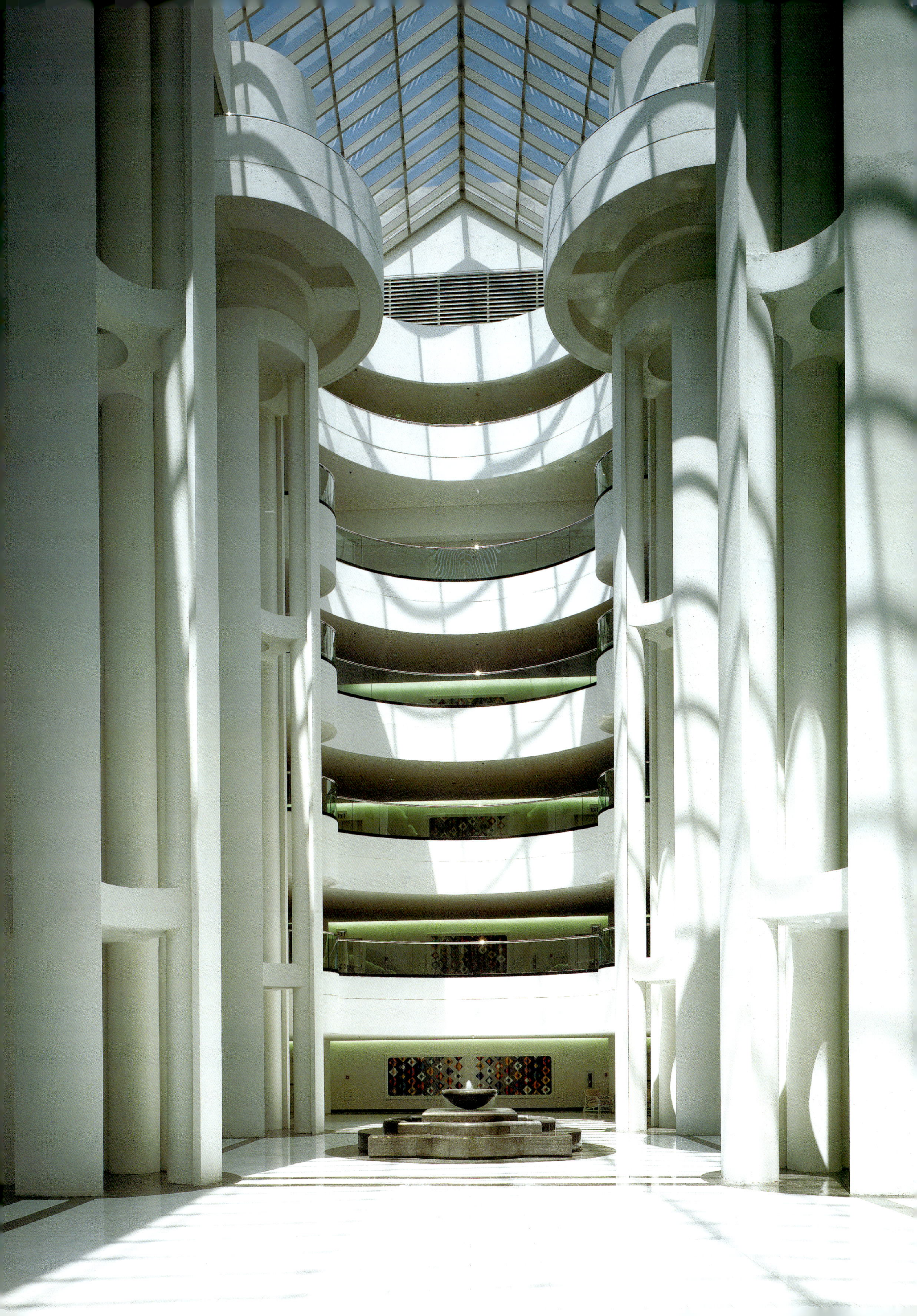

Hyatt Regency Atlanta

Peachtree Center
Design/Completion/Addition 1965/1967/1982
Atlanta, Georgia
Peachtree Baker Corporation
78,000 square meters
Concrete, metal, and glass

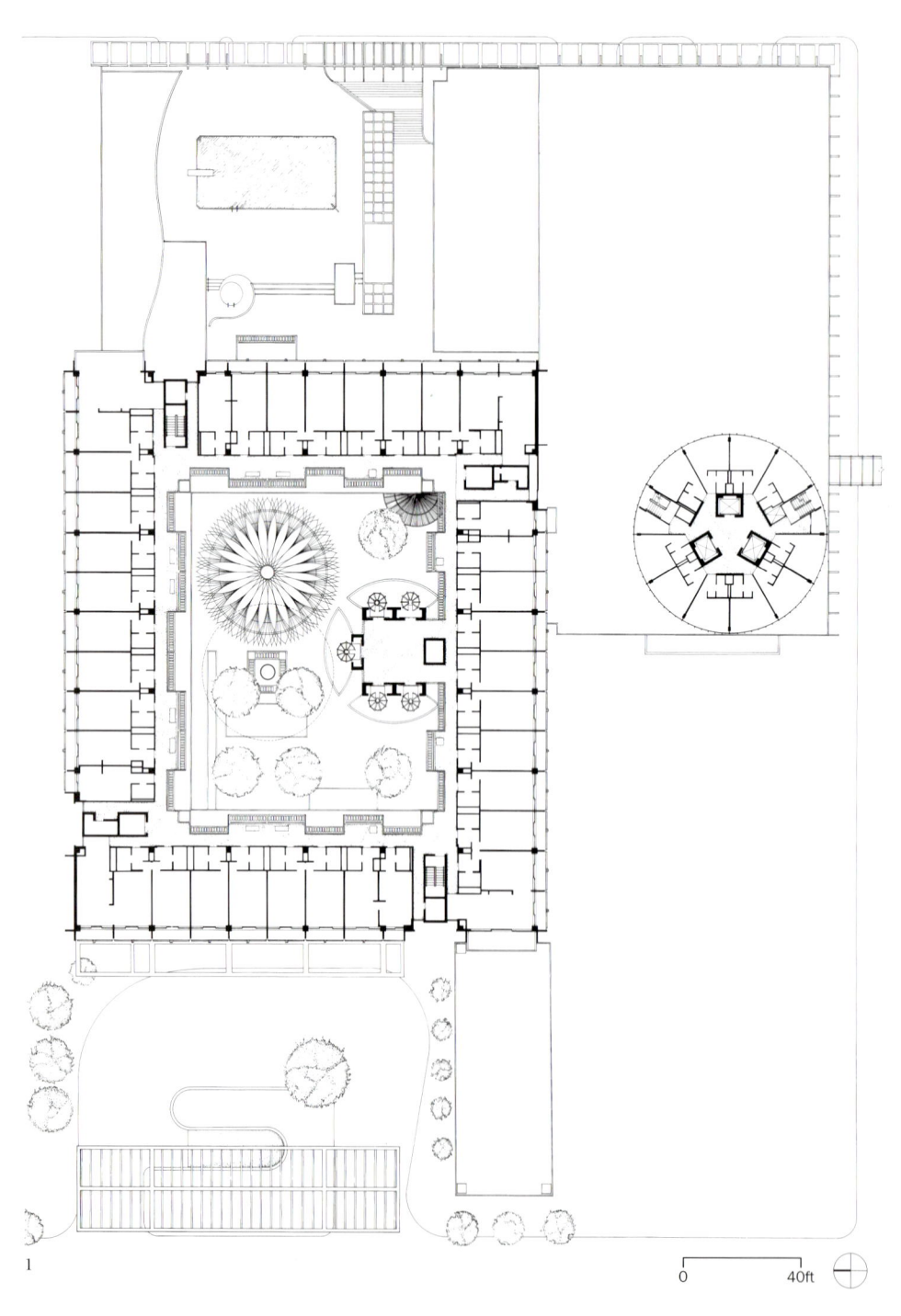

The Hyatt Regency Atlanta was Portman's first hotel, and it introduced the atrium concept on a major scale to contemporary hotel design. The hotel was conceived as a totally new guest experience: the antithesis of the traditional, tightly confined double corridor hotels. The design goal was to open the interior space to create an uplifting, dynamic environment: a space that would attract out-of-town visitors and the local community to its restaurants, bars, and cafes.

The 22-story concrete structure figuratively 'exploded' to create the huge, skylit atrium. With natural light, sculpture, trees and water, the interior resembles a large outdoor piazza bordered by a sidewalk cafe. The glass elevator cabs were pulled from their enclosed shafts, and travel vertically like a kinetic sculpture to the revolving dome-shaped restaurant atop the hotel.

The original 800-room hotel pioneered a new genre of hotel architecture as it addressed issues of affordable construction, safety, and most importantly the ability to create a unique 'sense of place' within a new urban architectural form. The success of the original project quickly spawned an expansion of two adjacent towers, adding 200 and 350 rooms respectively.

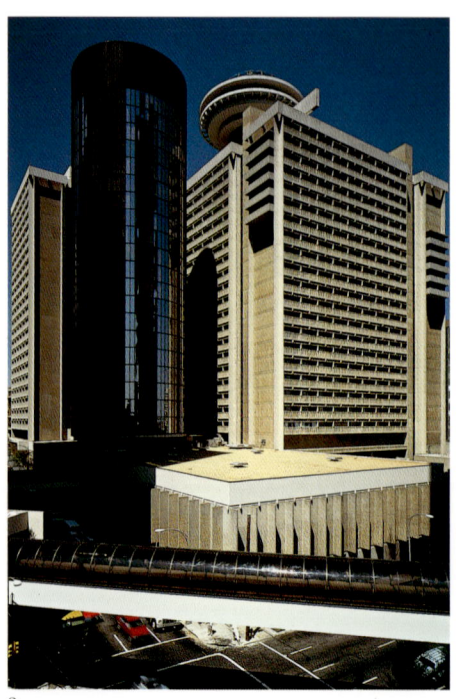

1 Site plan
2 View from northwest
Opposite:
    East view

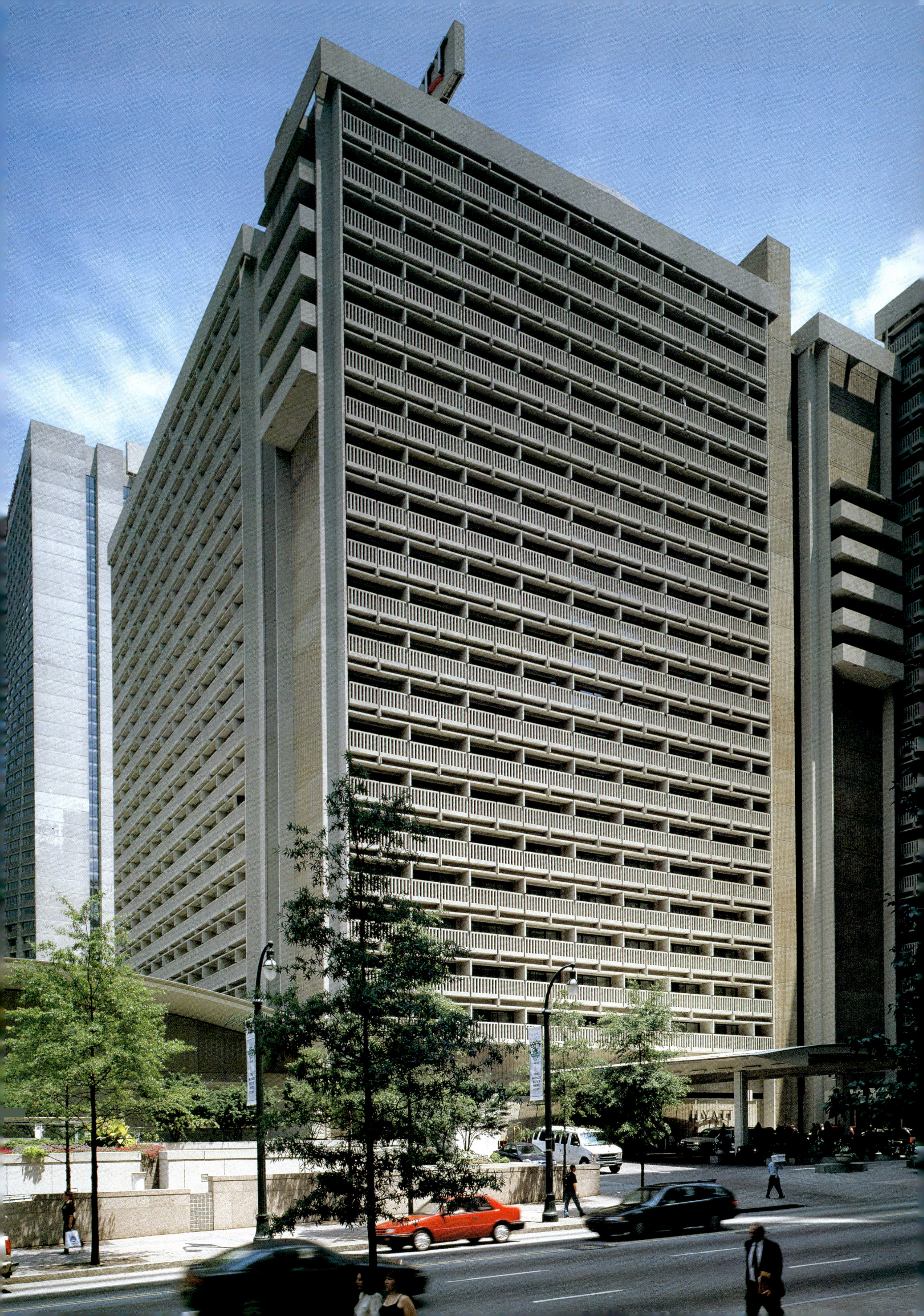

4   South view
5   Atrium
6   Lobby
7   Section

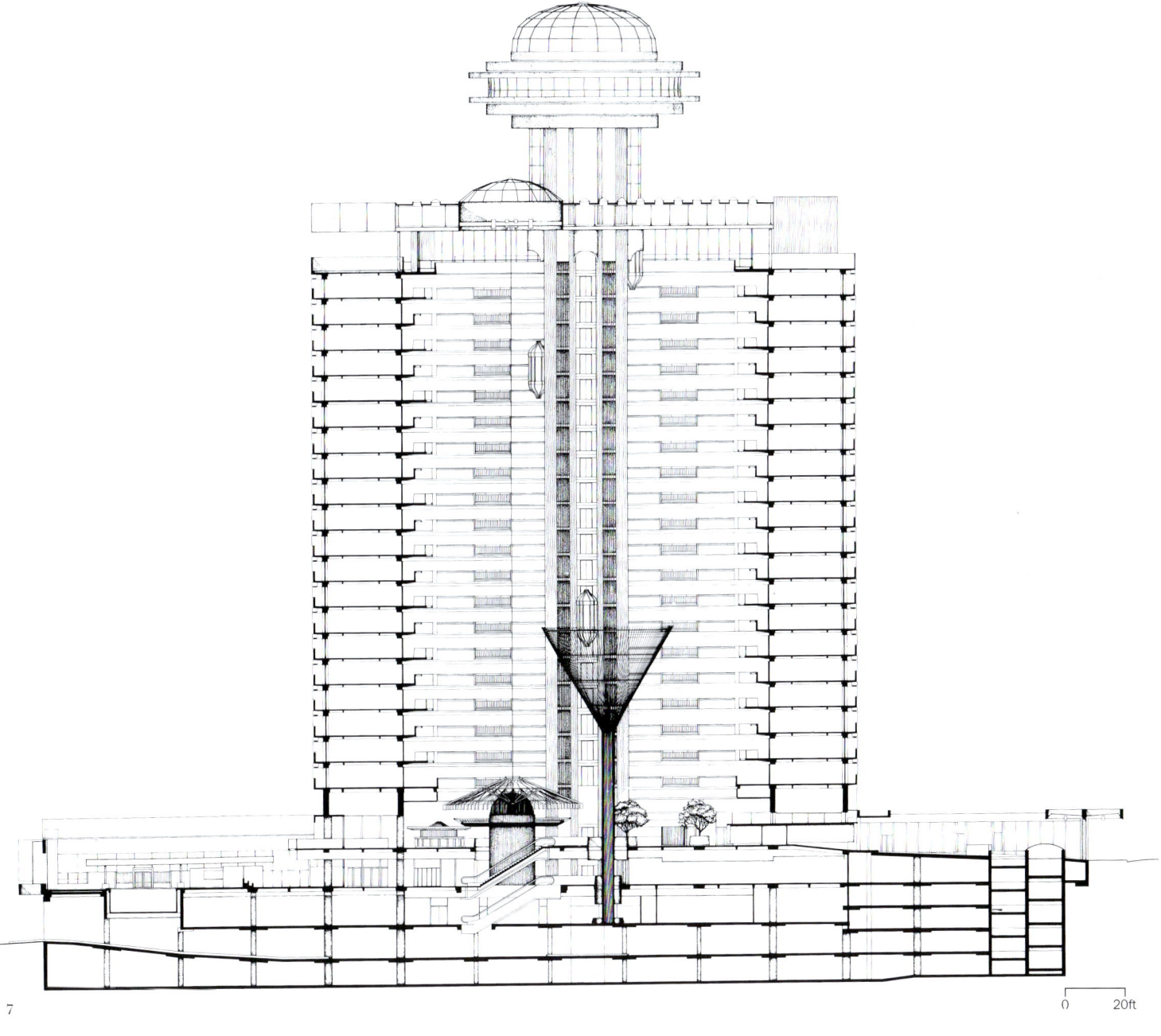

Hyatt Regency Atlanta 25

Westin Peachtree Plaza Hotel

Peachtree Center
Design/Completion 1974/1976
Atlanta, Georgia
Peachtree Hotel Company
102,193 square meters
Concrete, metal paneling, and glass

A major convention hotel on a long, narrow, sloping site presented numerous design challenges, including the need to create a unique yet different guest experience from the Hyatt Regency Atlanta only one block away.

To address these issues, the architect designed a podium base from which rises a glass-clad, 73-story cylindrical guestroom tower, which is topped with a multi-level revolving restaurant that affords spectacular views of the city. The rooftop restaurant is accessed by exterior glass elevator cabs, and is a destination for both out-of-town visitors and the local community.

The site necessitated entrances from different levels: a major entrance on the Peachtree Street ridge to the east and a motor lobby entrance on the lower west side of the ridge two levels below. The seven-story podium encompasses a multitude of public activity areas for the 1,100-room hotel, from registration to meetings, dining and recreation. The architect, mindful of the importance of open space, again 'exploded' the base of the hotel around the core that supports the tower to create a dynamic, five-level, 90-foot skylit lobby. Art and elements of nature, including trees and water, were integral to the original design. Simple concrete forms met the stringent financial criteria, yet were dramatically molded to create a dynamic space.

1 Section through public space
2 Lobby
Opposite:
   View from SunTrust Plaza

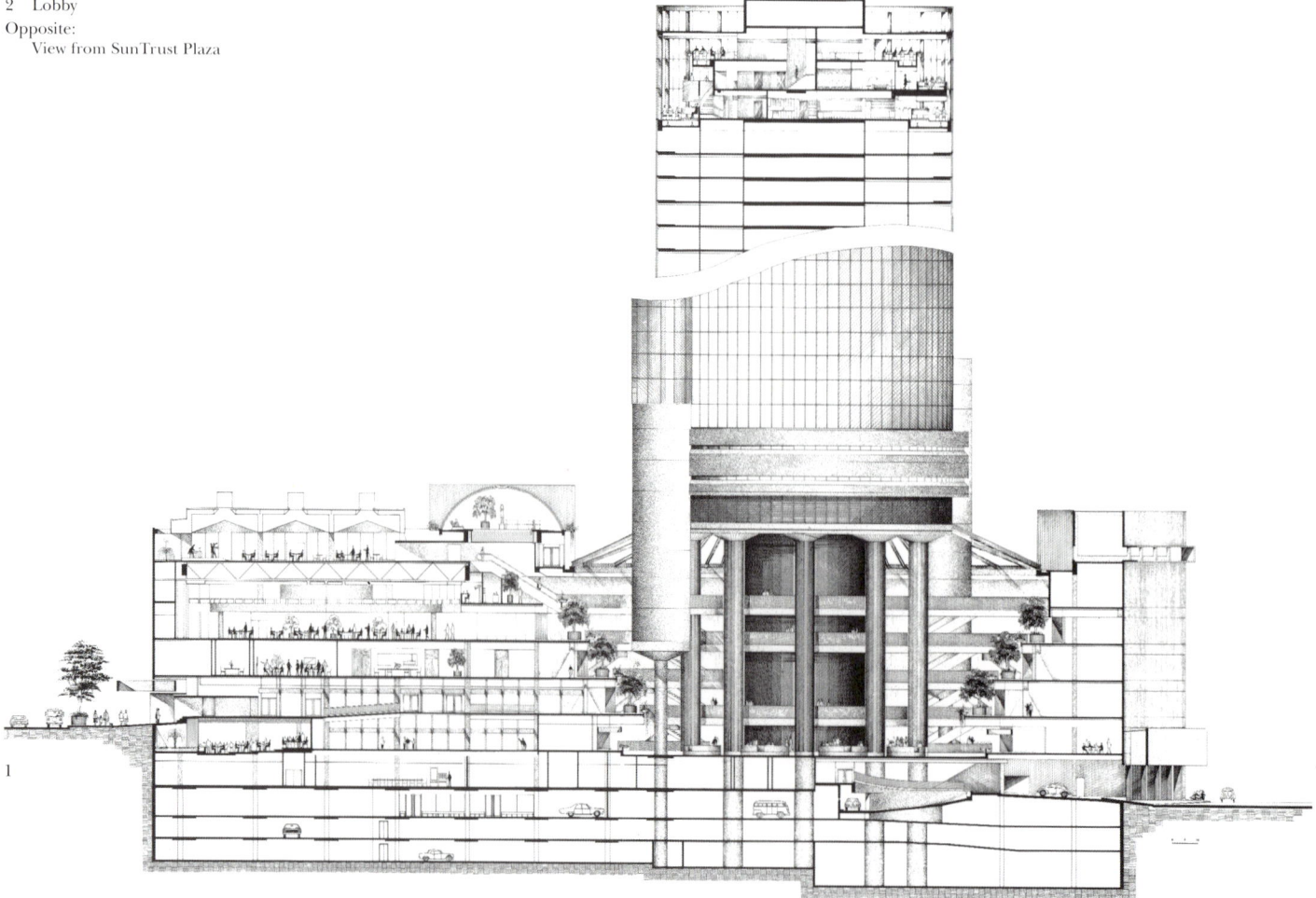

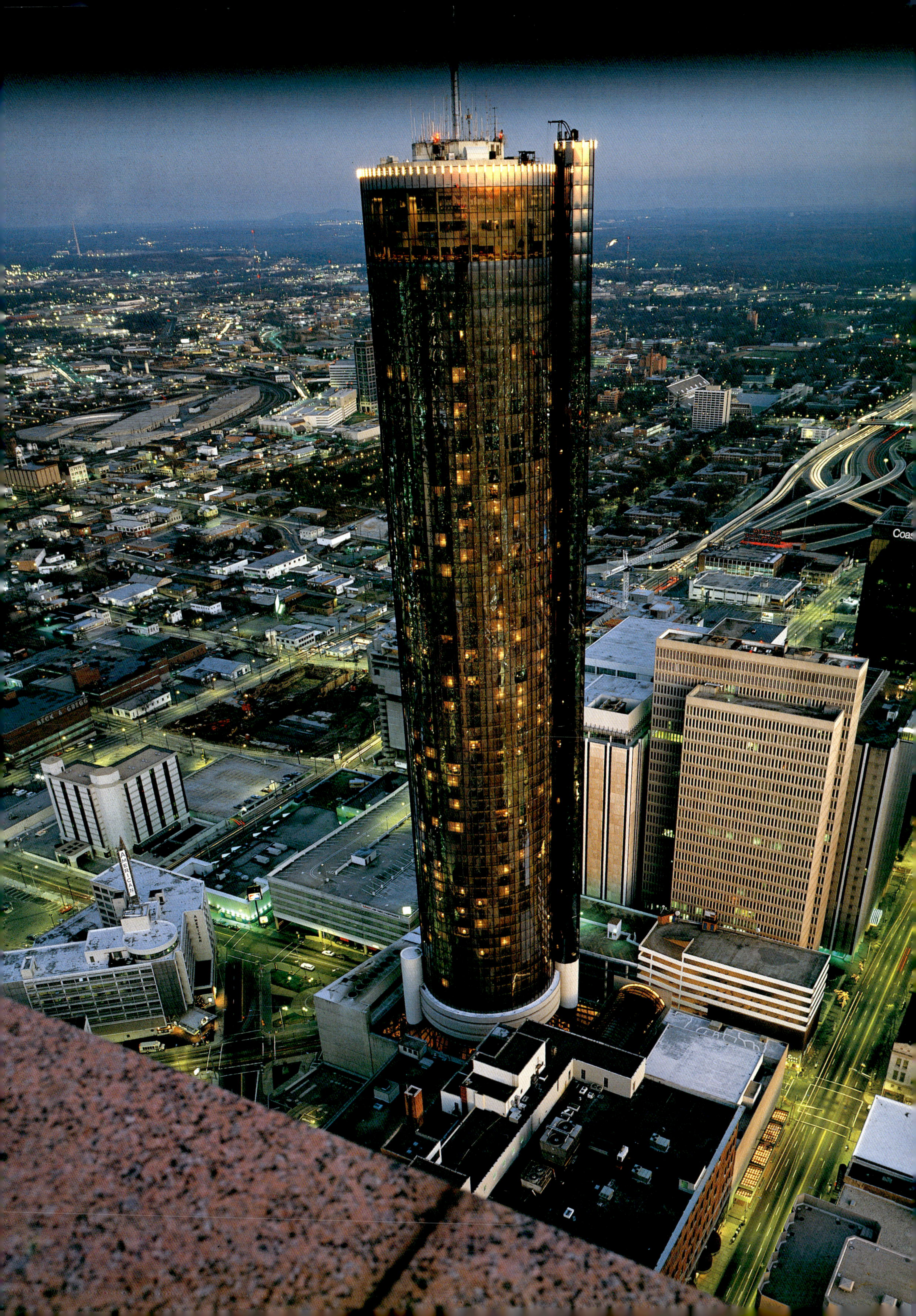

Atlanta Marriott Marquis

Peachtree Center
Design/Completion 1982/1985
Atlanta, Georgia
Marriott Corporation
48,000 square meters
Concrete, stone, and glass

1 Site plan
Opposite:
 Upward view

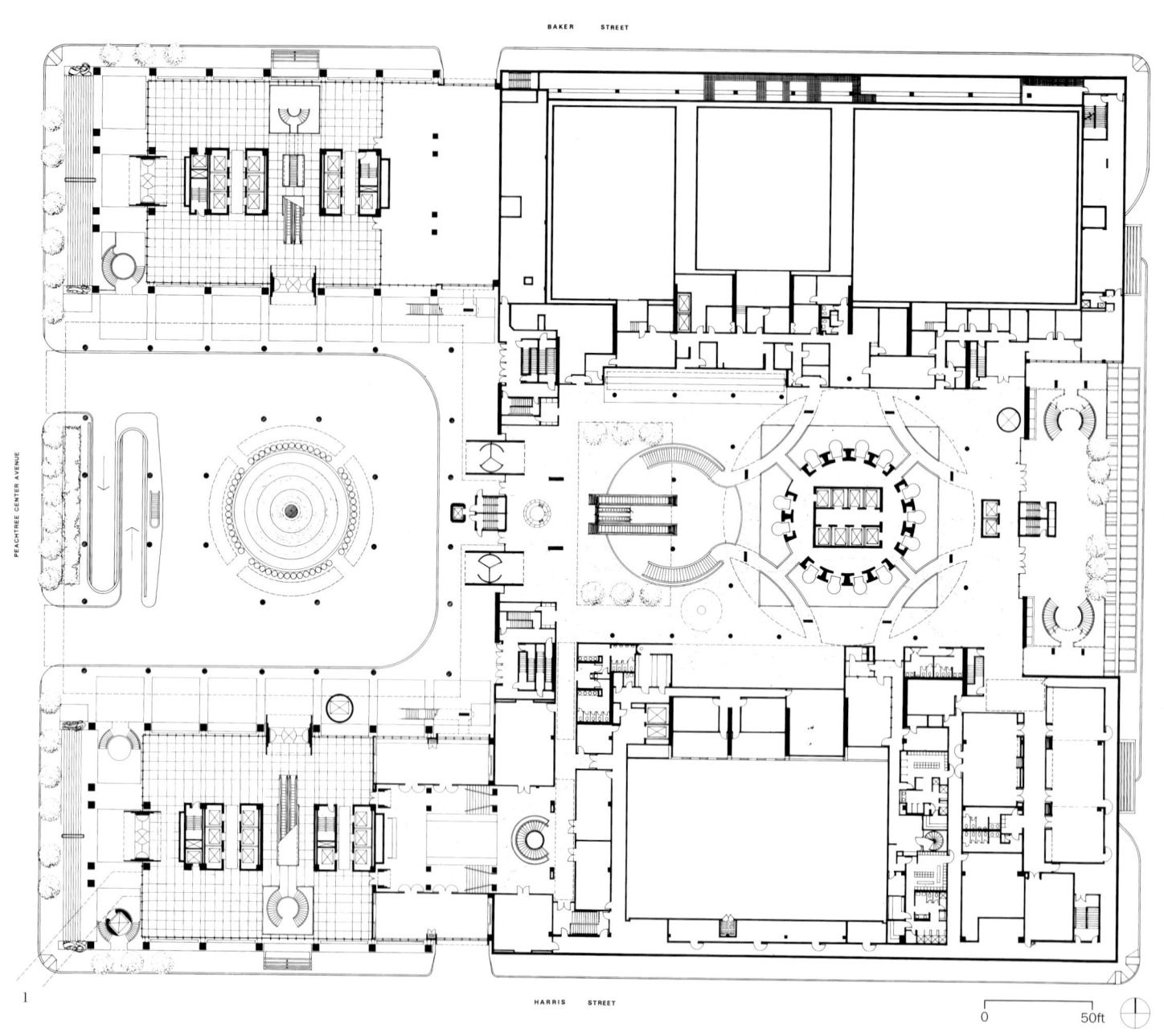

The design of the 1,675-room Atlanta Marriott Marquis took interior space to new heights. Situated in the center and occupying most of a city block, its parabolic concrete form rises from a large rectangular podium base.

The 53-story convention hotel is organized vertically to contain public activities within the podium, reserving the sculptural tower for guestrooms and suites. The podium incorporates an exhibition hall, conference center and two large ballrooms. From the covered motor lobby, guests proceed to registration prior to ascending escalators to the dramatic garden level lobby. From here, the atrium rises 515 feet, tapering from the sweeping curvilinear form into the smaller linear configuration of the upper concierge levels. Above the atrium level, the guestroom floors vary to conform to the building's parabolic shape. Guests are transported by glass elevator cabs, and experience dynamic and ever-changing views.

The lobby takes on the feel of a European piazza. Trees, plants, and fountains create a park-like environment in which one finds a variety of restaurants and cafes tucked into smaller, more intimate spaces. Pedestrian bridges connect the atrium lobby on the upper level of the podium with the office towers and other components of the Peachtree Center complex. Within a few blocks, the cluster of three Peachtree Center hotels (Hyatt Regency Atlanta, Westin Peachtree Plaza, and Atlanta Marriott Marquis) reflect a 20-year evolution using interior urban space to uplift the spirit and enhance the guest experience.

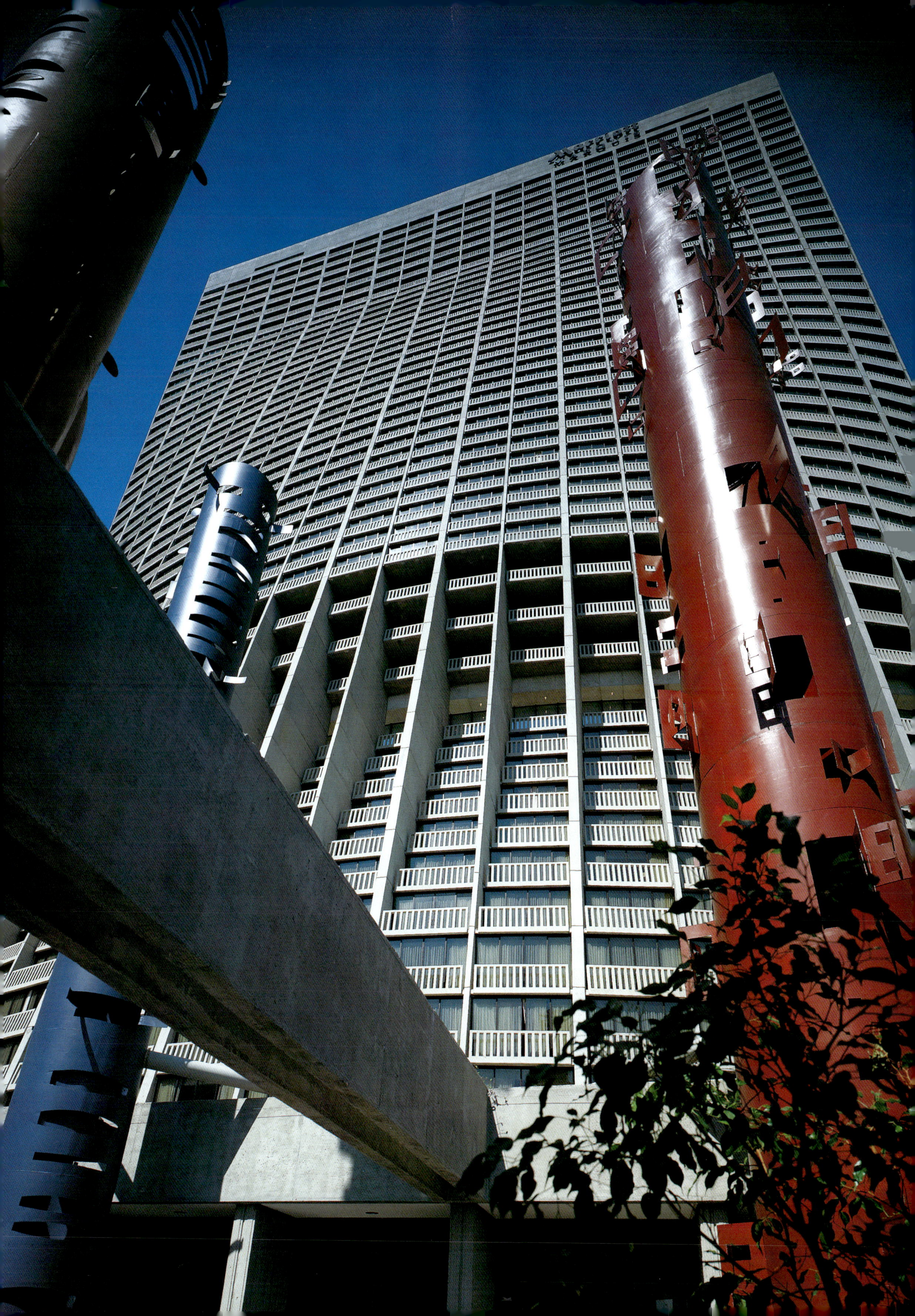

3

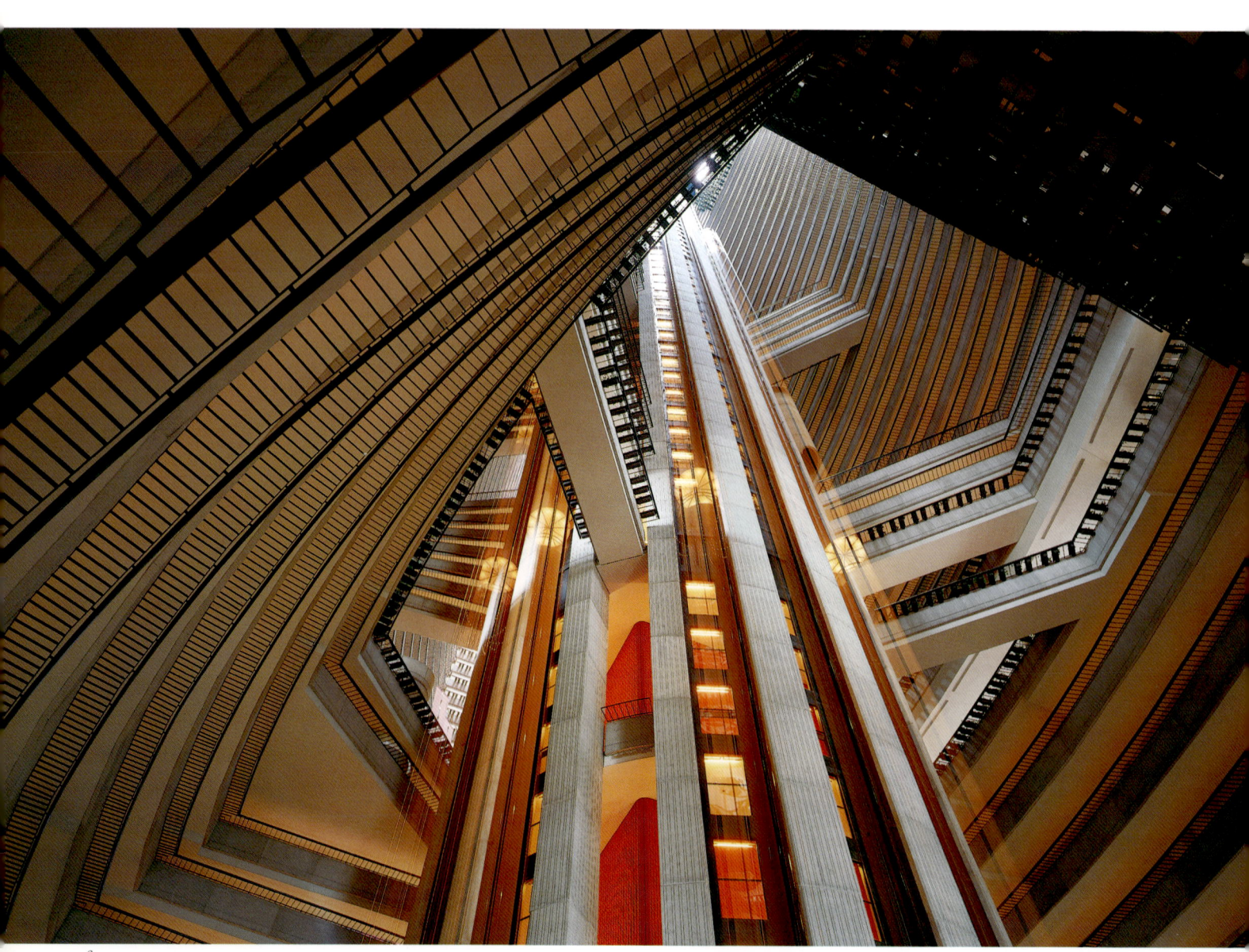

4

5

6

3 & 5 Lobby
4 Lobby bar
6 Upward view of lobby
7 Section

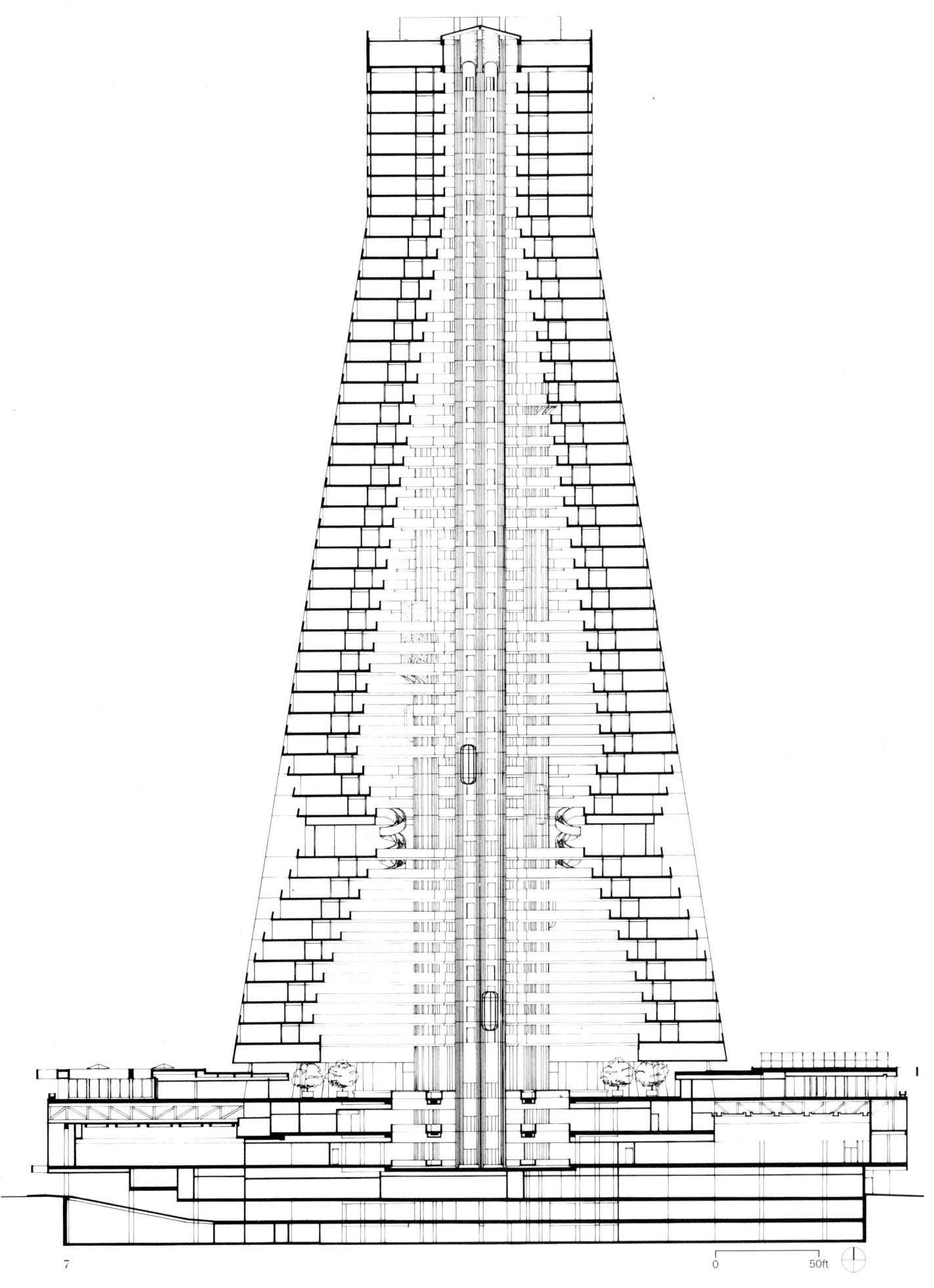

Atlanta Marriott Marquis

SunTrust Plaza

Peachtree Center
Design/Completion 1988/1993
Atlanta, Georgia
SunTrust Plaza Associates LLC
130,100 square meters
Concrete, stone, and glass

1 Site plan
2 Pedestrian walkway from Garden Offices
3 Ground floor exterior arcade
Opposite:
  View from north at night

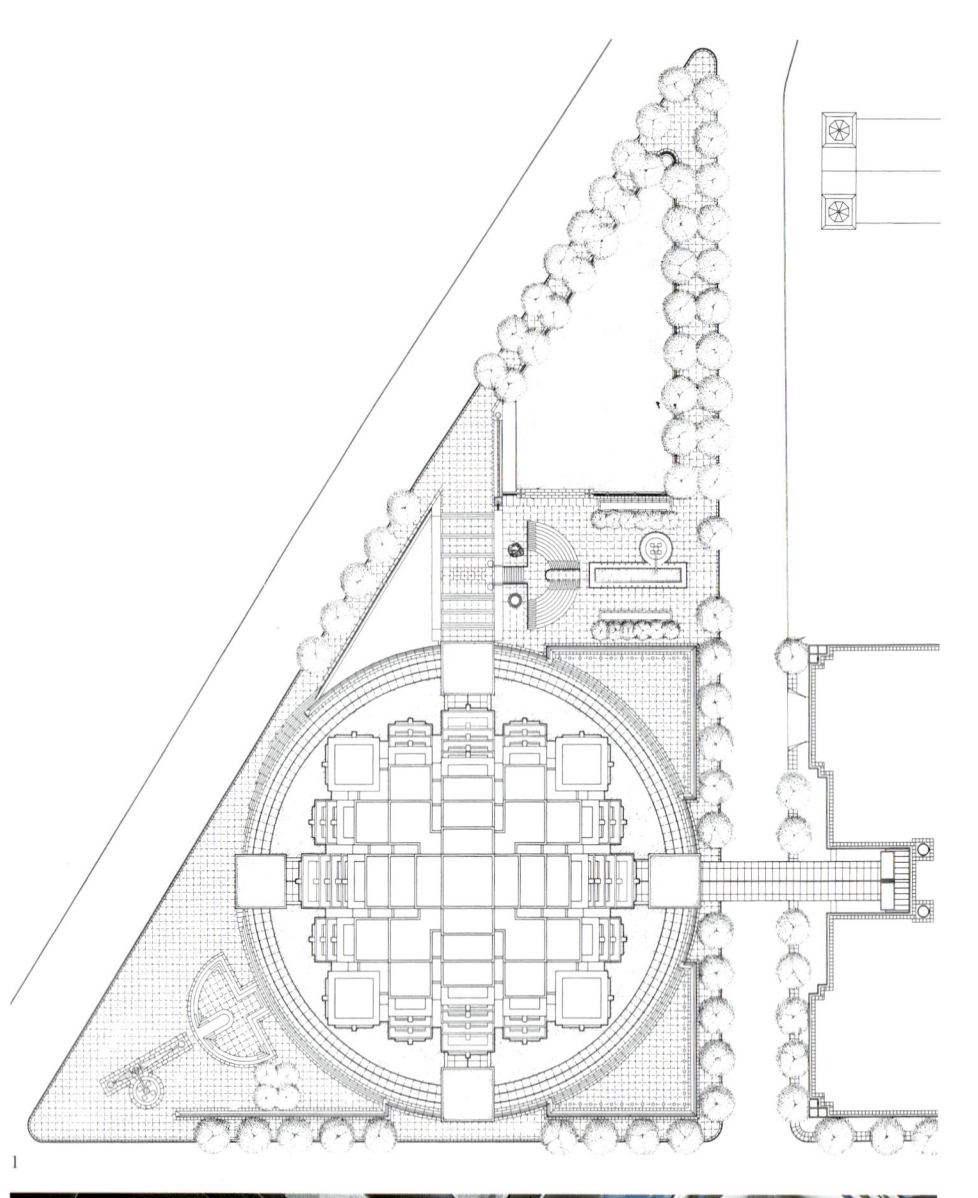

This 60-story office tower is a major icon on Atlanta's central business district skyline. The goal was to construct a major corporate headquarters building with interior and exterior space providing street life, green space and amenities that would enhance city life and anticipate future development.

The 842-foot tower is a signature building, anchoring the north point of Peachtree Center. The geometry of the building acknowledges the forms of Peachtree Center. The facades are a rich granite with gray glass reinforcing the tower's faceted sculptural form. The plan is basically square in form with alternating office projections stepping in and out, with recessed sections on each side to form and provide many corner offices per floor.

The site's sharp elevation afforded the architect the opportunity to establish four major entrances into a 62-foot-high lobby, each from a different street level and each offering a distinct sense of arrival. On the upper main street level, a balcony encircles the cylindrical elevator core and overlooks a major sculpture gallery designed for public enjoyment. Outside on the upper exterior plaza level a glass and steel canopy covers the walkway, encircling the tower. The exterior plazas and green space act as a public sculpture garden for the community to enjoy.

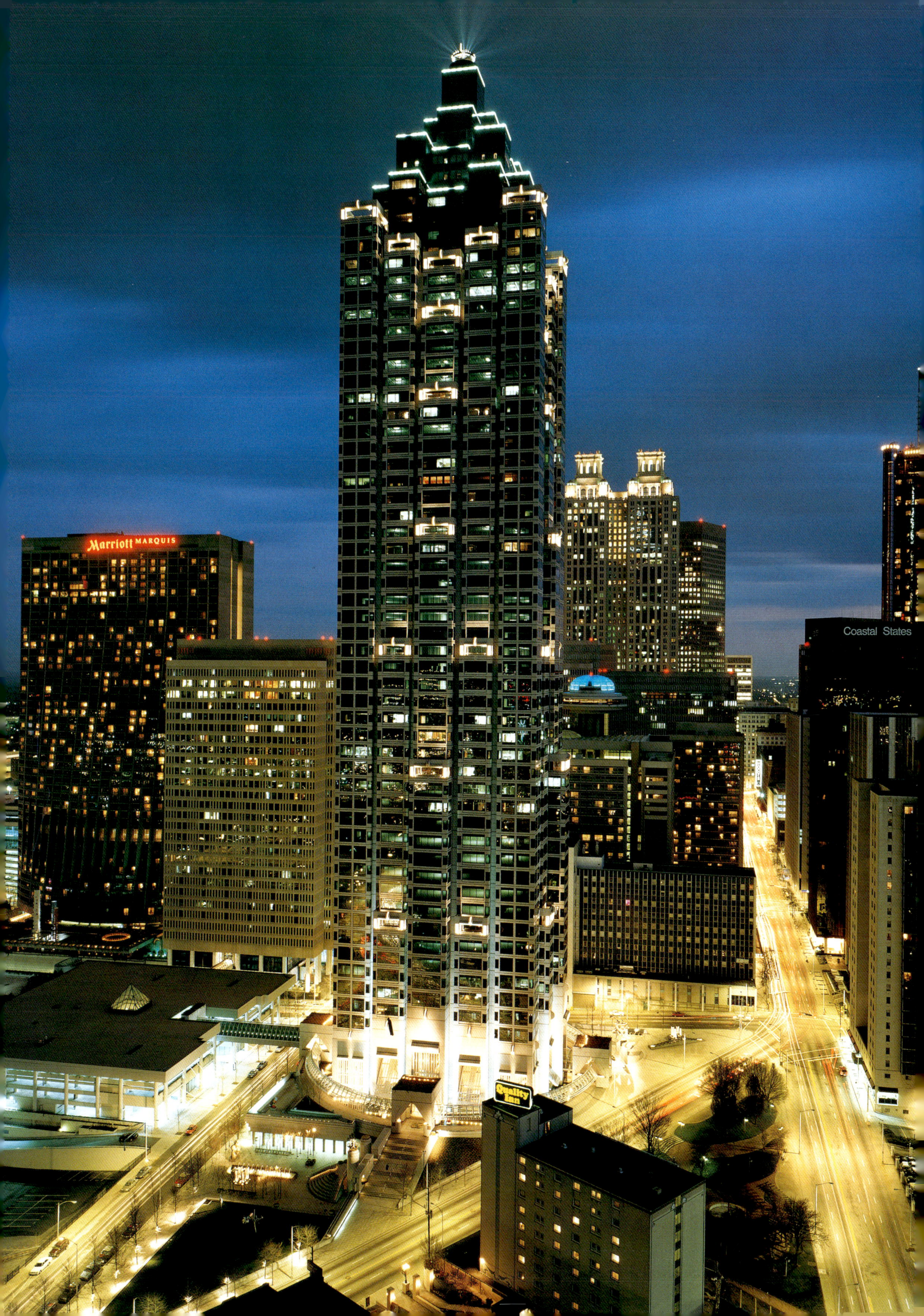
Marriott MARQUIS
Coastal States
Quality Inn

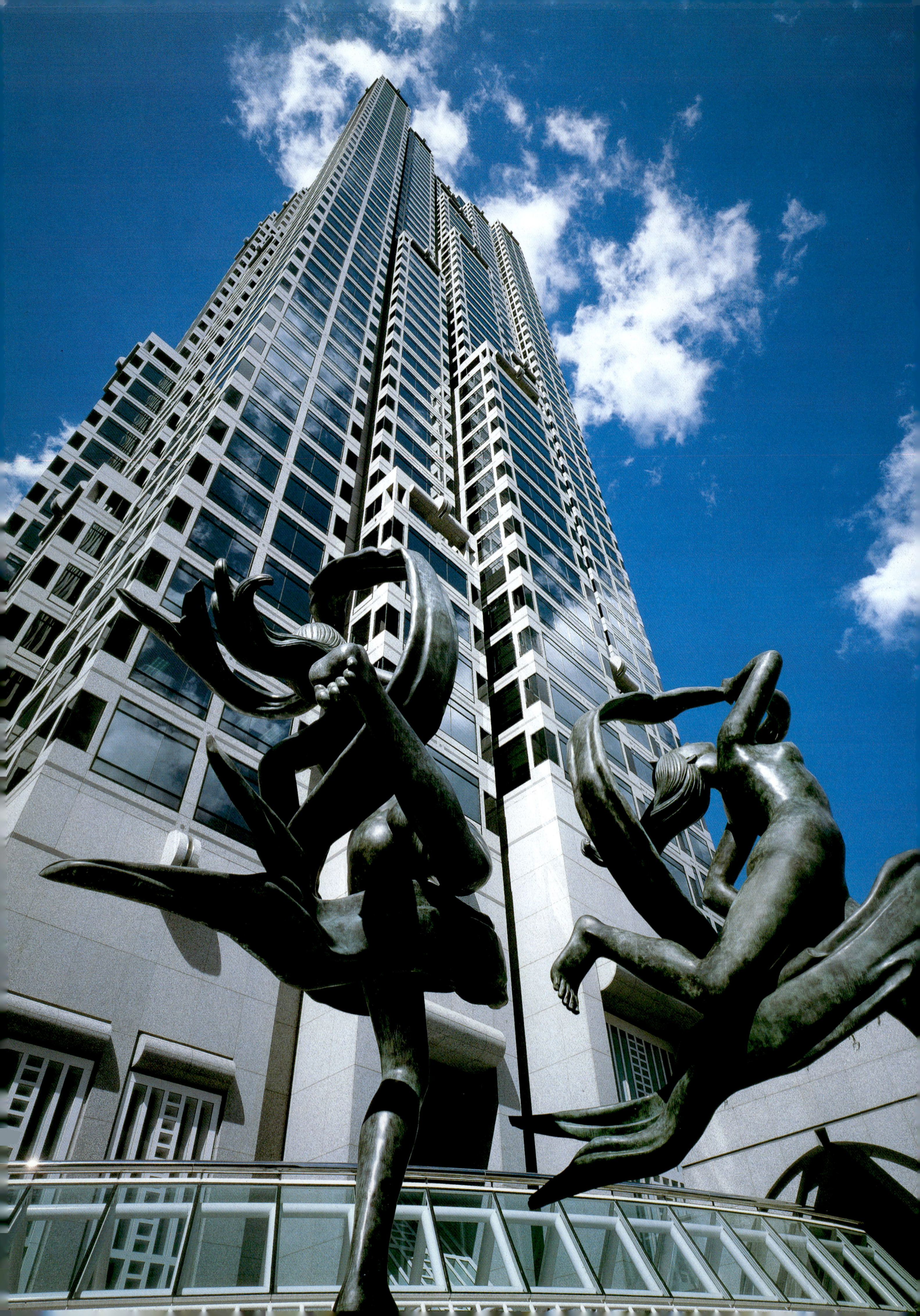

6

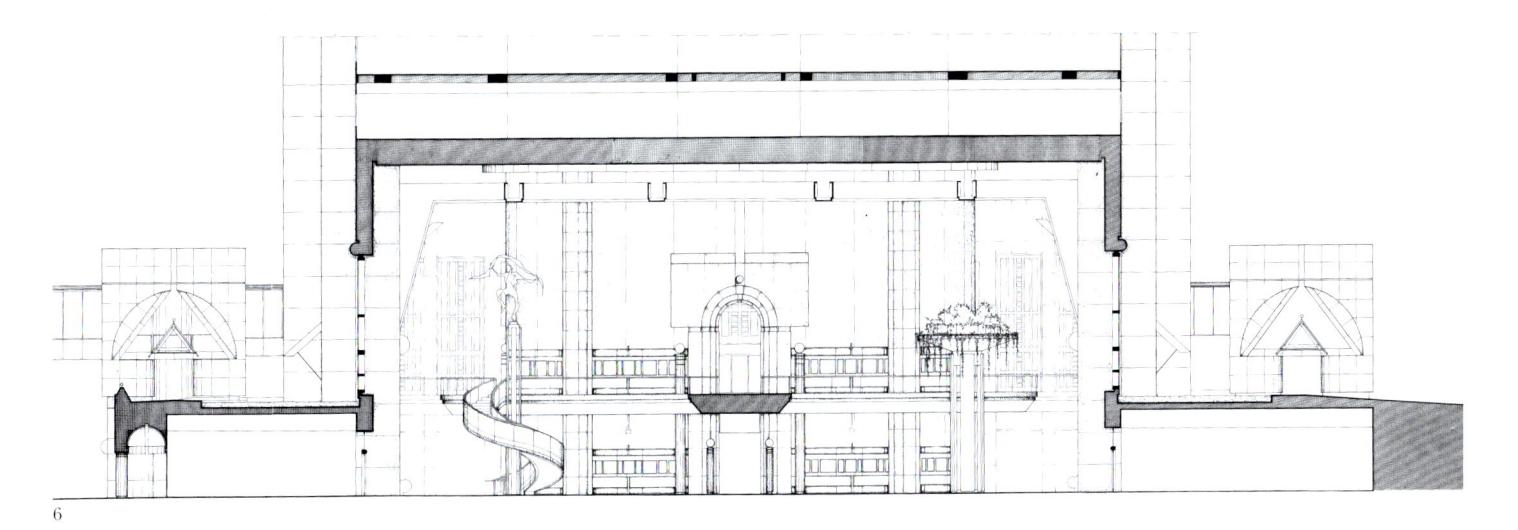

7

Opposite:
  Skyward view with *Ballet Olympia* sculpture by Paul Manship
6 Ground plaza section
7 Lower lobby
8 Pedestrian plaza at night
9 Spiral staircase in lobby

8

9

SunTrust Plaza   35

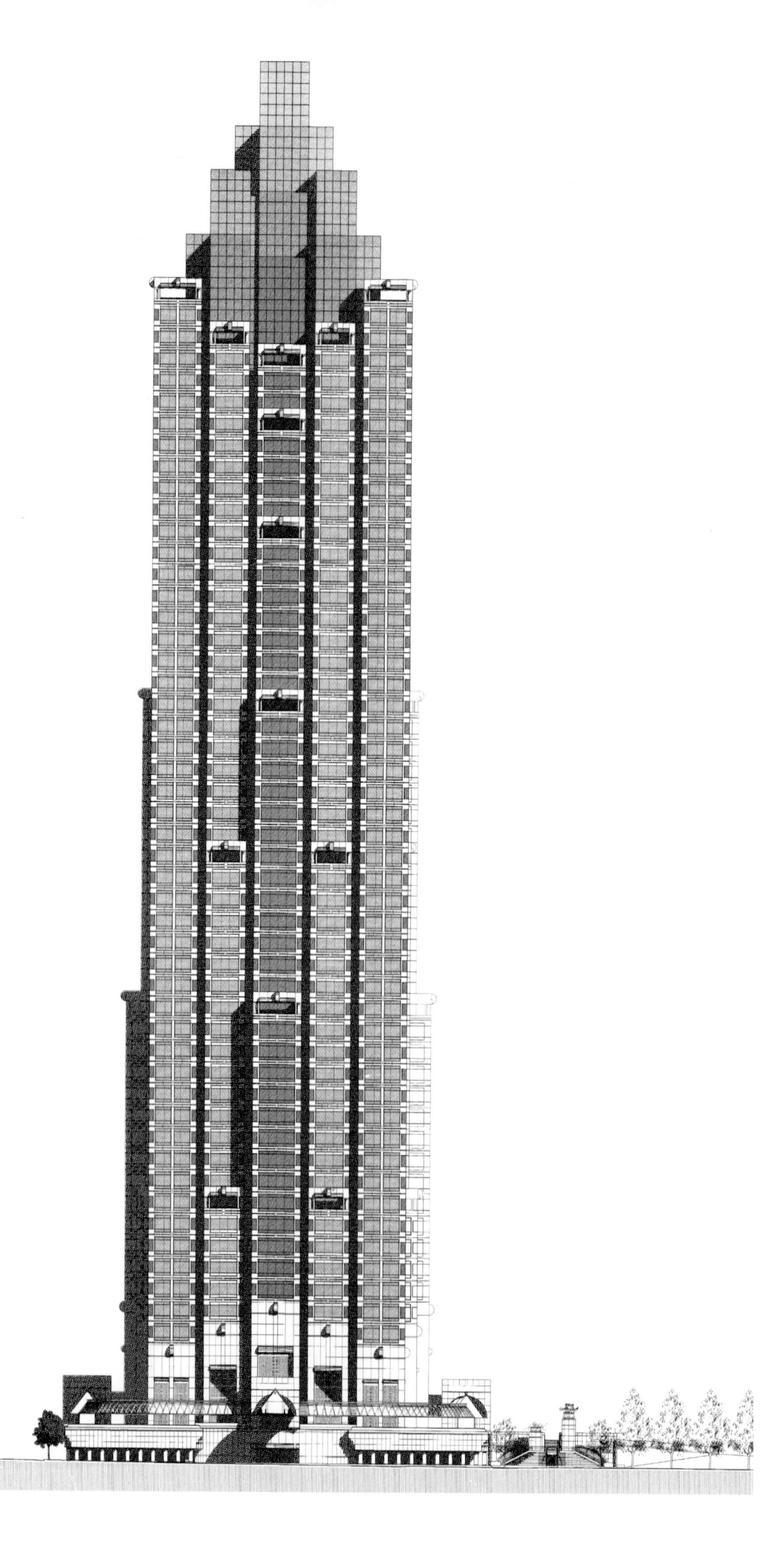

10 Elevation
Opposite:
   View from northeast

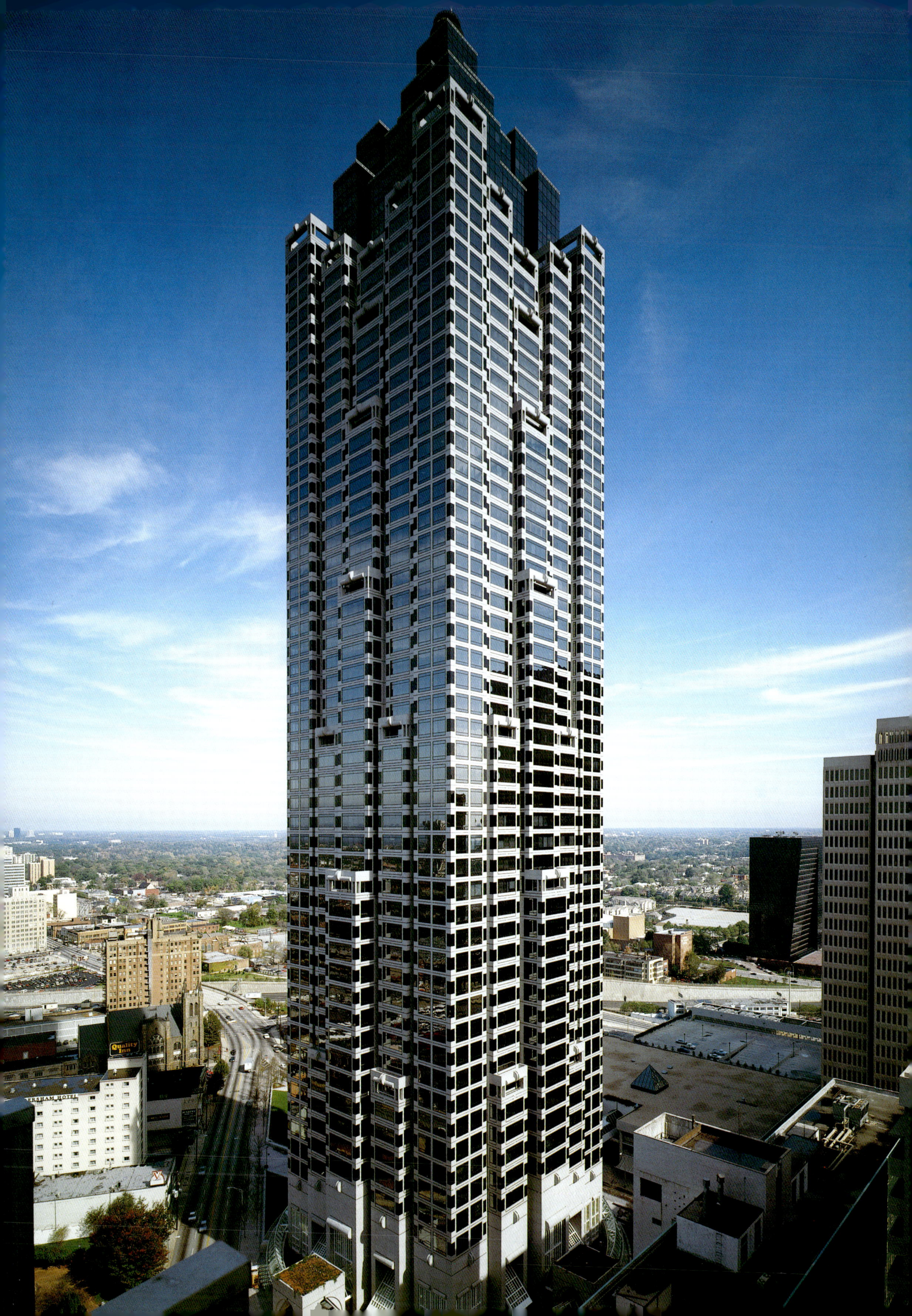
Quality Inn

SunTrust Plaza Garden Offices

Peachtree Center
Design/Completion 1998/2000
Atlanta, Georgia
SunTrust Plaza Associates LLC
55,760 square meters
Concrete, metal paneling, and glass

The design of the SunTrust Plaza tower anticipated expansion of additional office space. The adjoining 3,300-car parking deck, which was constructed with the tower, was structurally designed to accommodate a six-story addition. Initially the top level of the parking deck was used as retail space and a large food court with seating around a landscaped fountain. Pedestrian bridges linked the space to offices and hotels in other parts of Peachtree Center. The parking structure also helped retain the totally pedestrian orientation for the tower as all service functions to the tower are accessed through the deck via a tunnel to the service level.

The expansion was constructed seven years after the tower, and provides larger floor plates in the Garden Offices to address the needs of tenants requiring different operational layouts than those in the tower yet wanting proximity to Peachtree Center and the prestige of SunTrust Plaza. The lobby for the Garden Offices is on the bridge level with the food court. One can access the offices' long rectangular atrium lobby from the lobby or from the street level office entry. The garden atrium enables the office floors to share the beauty of the lobby below.

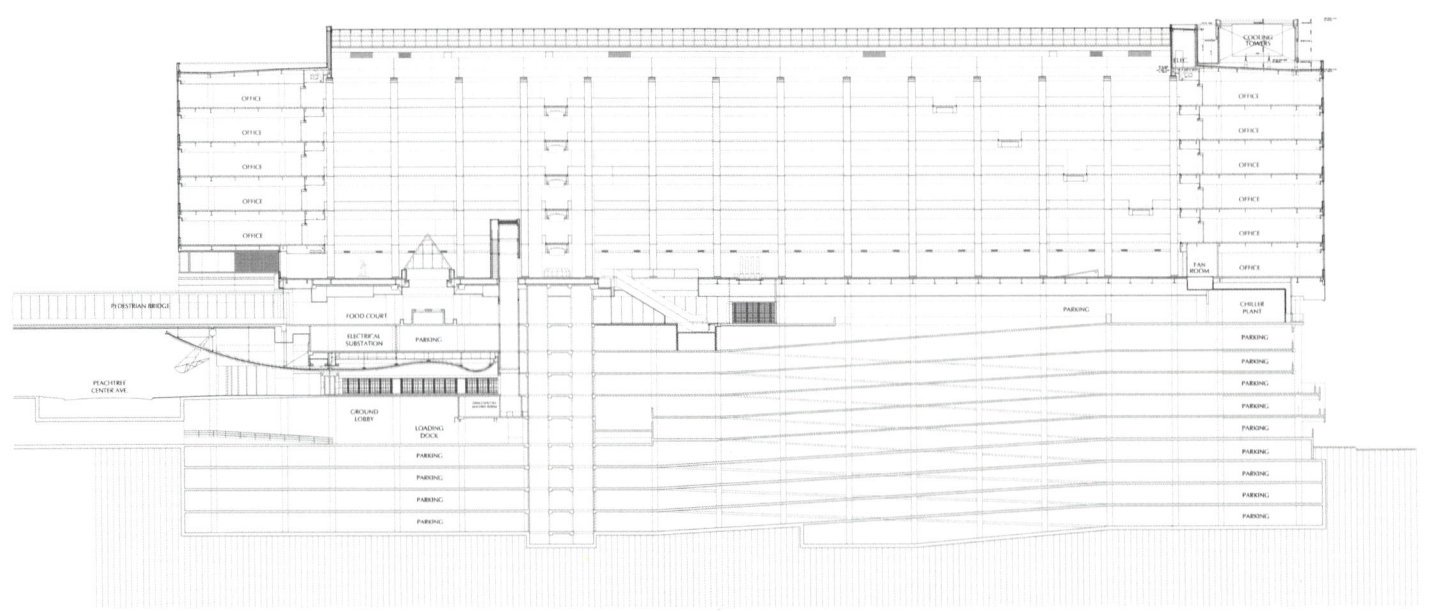

1 Lobby looking west to east at night
2 Section looking south
3 Atrium
4 Fountain in atrium

SunTrust Plaza Garden Offices 39

5

5 View looking south
6 Skylight in atrium
7 Upward view from atrium to tower

SunTrust Plaza Garden Offices 41

SunTrust III

Peachtree Center
Design/Completion 2001-2002/2004
Atlanta, Georgia
Portman Holdings
70,000 square meters
Concrete, stone, and glass

1   Rendering of lobby
2   Rendering of street level view from west
3   Rendering of street level view facing south
Opposite:
   Exterior view facing southwest

SunTrust III is the third quality component of the SunTrust office complex at the northern end of Peachtree Center. It is designed to complement the 60-story SunTrust Plaza tower and park across the street and to create an effective transition between the adjacent SunTrust Plaza Garden Offices and the historic church opposite. The smaller scale of the church and the desire to maintain the views for tenants in the Garden Offices were significant factors in the design.

The office building is raised 140 feet on eight square columns. A plaza of monumental proportions that opens beneath the offices is carefully designed to provide a friendly environment for office workers and the public. A circular core in the center of the space has been designed with pools, fountains, trees, and seating. At the rear is a glass structure that provides an elegant restaurant. Major works of art and a vine-covered arcade (or promenade) along the street reduce the massive space to an inviting human scale. From the grand street plaza and level entry lobbies, one can access the 26 levels of offices above and parking below. Bridges also give direct access to parking beneath the adjacent Garden Offices.

The tower's curtainwall exhibits sophisticated simplicity to enhance Peachtree Center. The tower's roof has two levels of penthouse offices in a garden setting. A cylinder the size of the core rises above the tower and is cut at a diagonal to provide for mechanical specifications and skylights for the penthouse offices while also providing a distinctive skyline symbol.

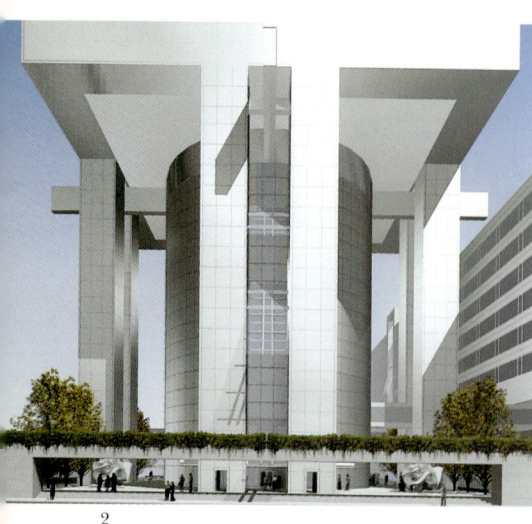

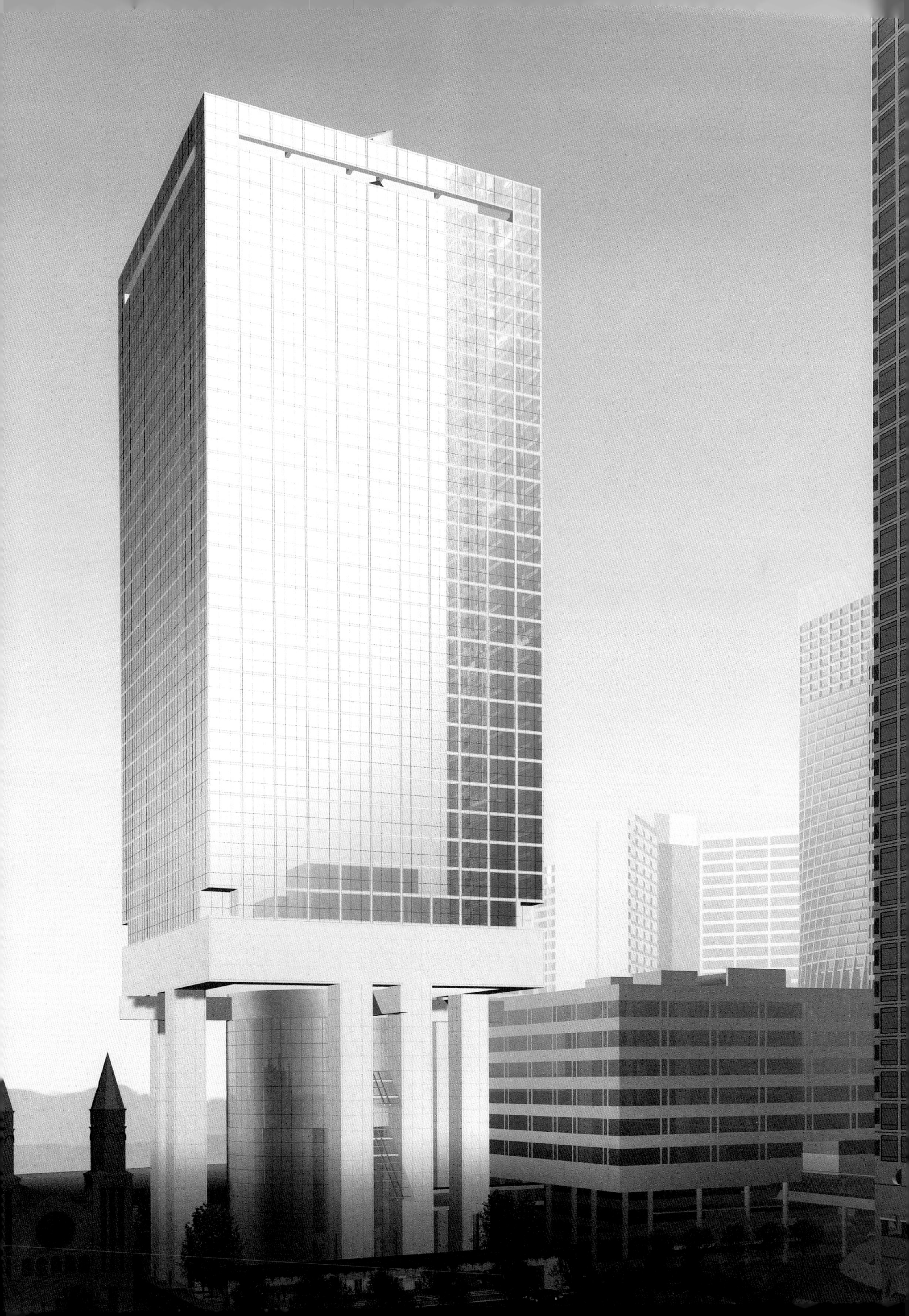

Embarcadero Center

Design/Completion 1968-1985/1971-1989
San Francisco, California
Embarcadero Center Associates
397,493 square meters
Concrete, stone, and glass

1 Skyward view from pedestrian plaza
2 Site plan
Opposite:
    Aerial view overlooking west tower

The award-winning Embarcadero Center is the commercial component of a major urban renewal project that renovated the former Federal Reserve office building and transformed a run-down warehouse district into a prototype for an urban people-oriented mixed-use development. Built in phases, the eight-block site comprises five office towers and two hotels, one with 800 rooms, the other with 360 rooms. The hotels are linked by a multi-level pedestrian retail spine that runs perpendicular to the bay and down the middle of the site, terminating at the large Justin Herman Plaza. The project is designed to support and unify pedestrian activity and to promote community gatherings while separating public functions from the private activities of the office workers and hotel guests.

The first hotel, the Hyatt Regency San Francisco, is adjacent to the plaza that has become a major urban park near the bay. The hotel was built to coincide with the opening of the plaza and was constructed out of sequence with the office towers. To draw people to the initially isolated site, the design needed to be not only functional but also memorable. Its wedge-shaped form steps back to further open the plaza to the bay, creating a magnificent public gathering place. Within, a 17-story atrium provides a second dramatic space for people to gather. The second hotel, built 14 years later at the opposite end of the complex, complements the first and serves the business traveler at a smaller scale, and provides transient housing as people anchors at both ends of the project.

Landscaped plazas and bridges along the pedestrian spine link the three levels of retail space that connect the high-rise office towers to the hotels and the Justin Herman Plaza. Small urban parks, sidewalk cafes, and an abundance of art provide a respite from the traffic congestion of the surrounding city.

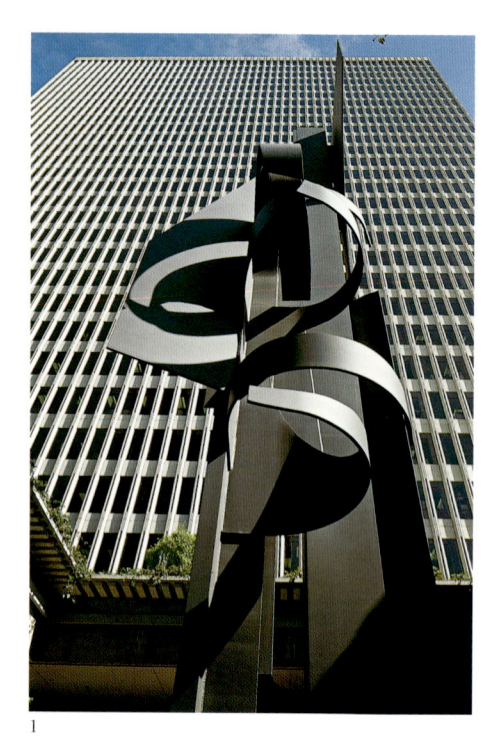

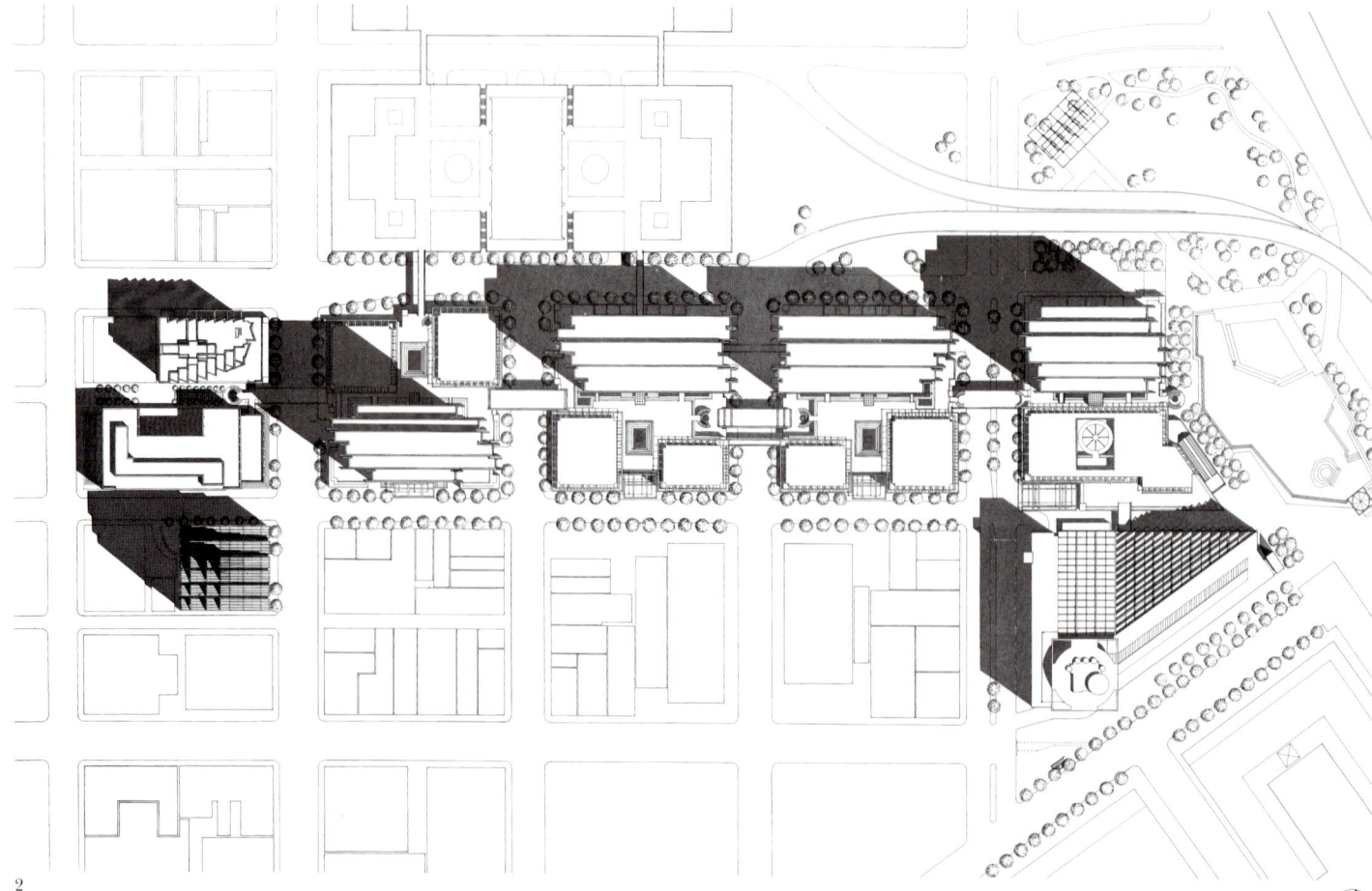

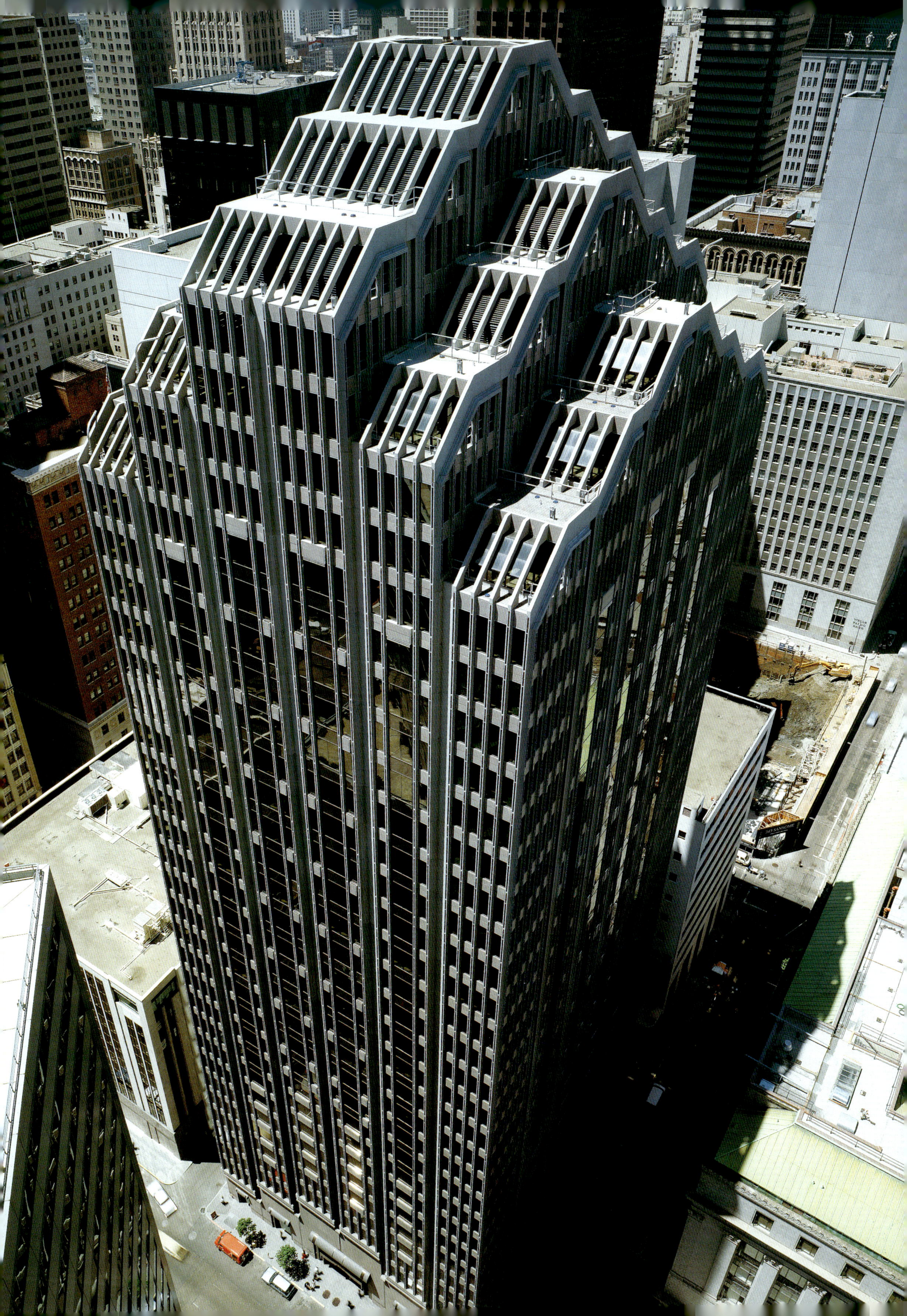

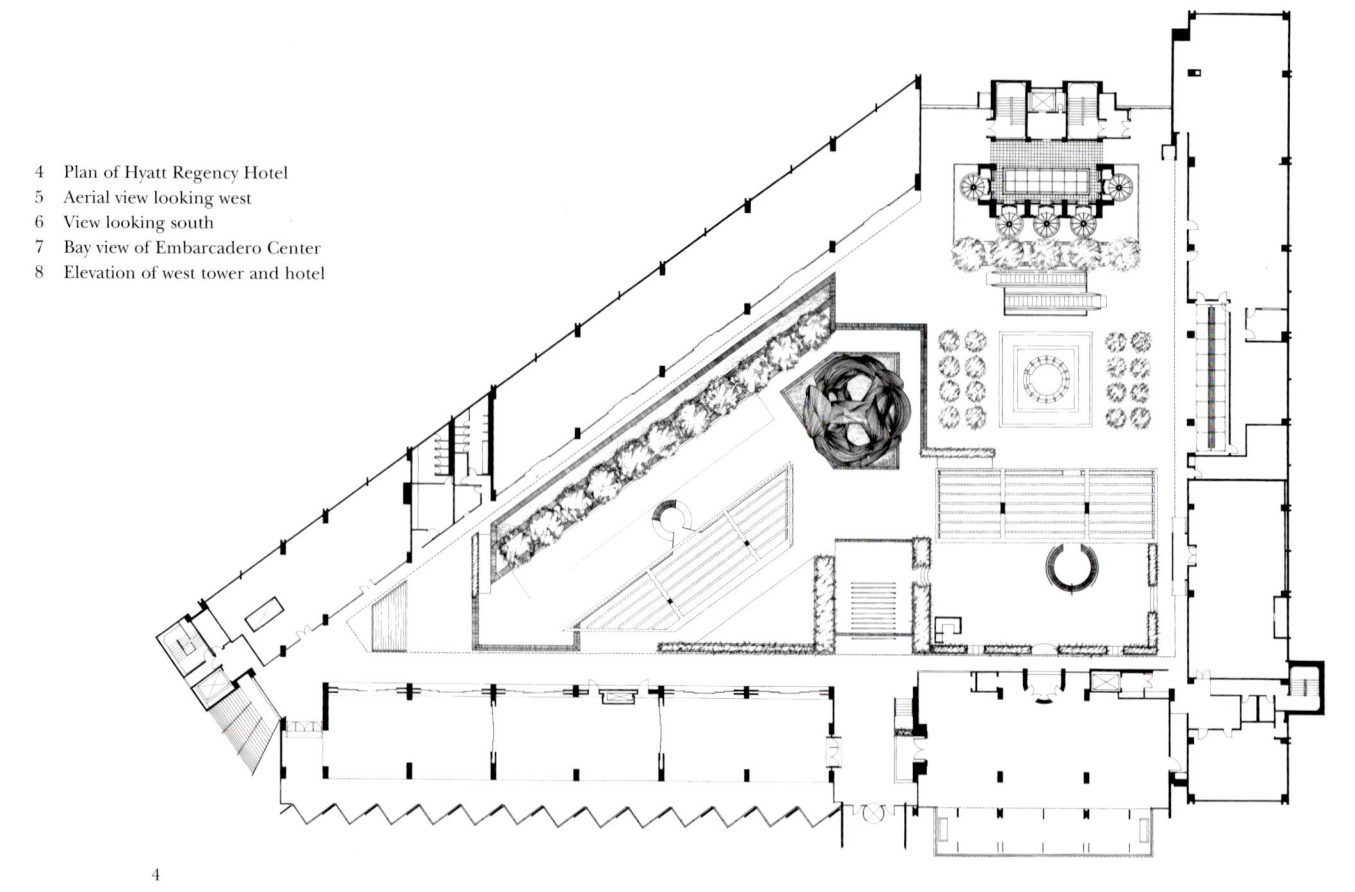

4 Plan of Hyatt Regency Hotel
5 Aerial view looking west
6 View looking south
7 Bay view of Embarcadero Center
8 Elevation of west tower and hotel

Embarcadero Center 47

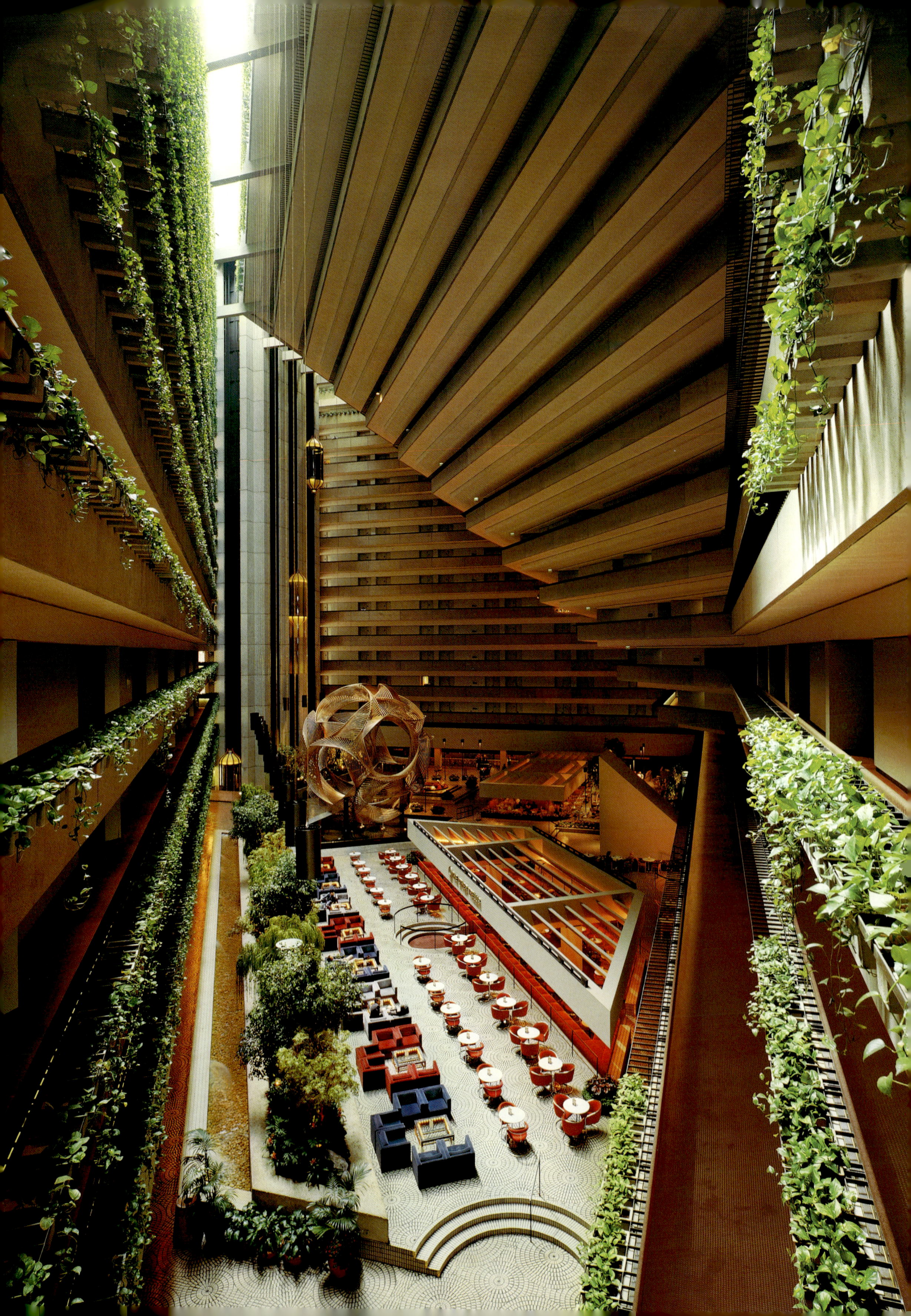

Opposite:
  Atrium of Hyatt Regency Hotel
10 Pedestrian walkway of Hyatt Regency Hotel
11 Lobby staircase detail

10

11

Embarcadero Center 49

12 Pedestrian walkway at Embarcadero Center
13 Interior lobby of west tower
Opposite:
    Main entrance of west tower

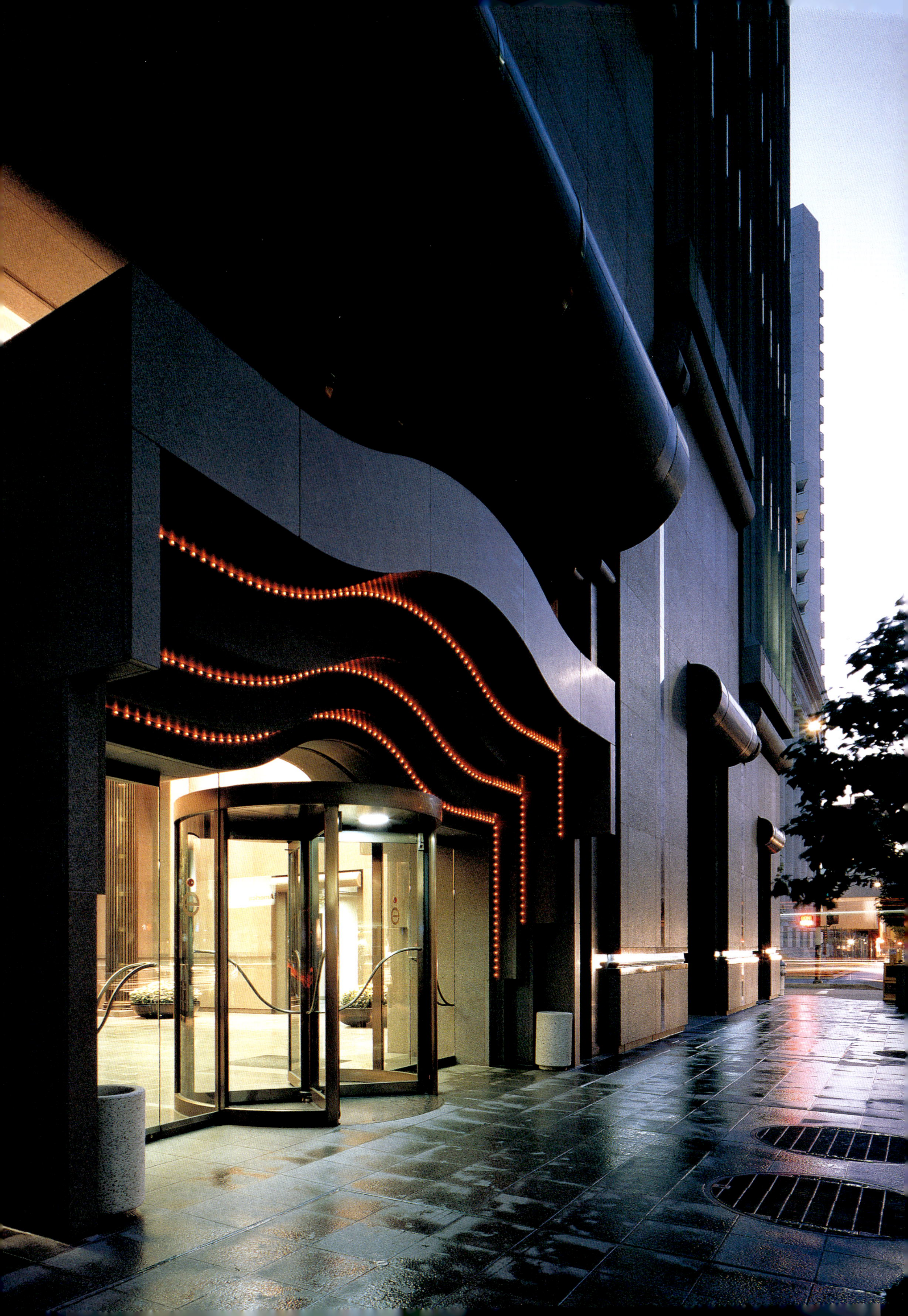

Renaissance Center

Design/Completion 1973 & 1982/1976 & 1988
Detroit, Michigan
Detroit Downtown Development Corporation
1,027,900 square meters
Reinforced concrete, metal paneling, and glass

1 View looking north
2 Site plan
3 Lobby
Opposite:
  Skyward view of hotel tower

Renaissance Center was designed as a multi-phase development that would return life to downtown Detroit after a period in which many businesses had abandoned the inner city. Ford also wanted a significant structure to acknowledge their commitment to the City of Detroit.

The 35-acre site between the Detroit River and a 13-lane freeway was designed to encompass and link commercial, retail, residential, and cultural components via a river walk. The master plan oriented activity toward the river, buffering the freeway noise with a large landscaped berm that housed mechanical and electrical systems for the complex. Pedestrian bridges over the freeway integrate the activity of Renaissance Center with the activity of the rest of the city.

Phase I was a 70-story cylindrical hotel tower and four 39-story office towers rising from a multi-story podium. The private functions of the offices and guestrooms are accommodated in the towers while public activity is contained within the podium and the hotel's revolving rooftop restaurant. The six-level skylit hotel lobby integrates the activity of the retail space with the office lobbies.

Phase II was completed 12 years after Phase I and added two additional 21-story office towers.

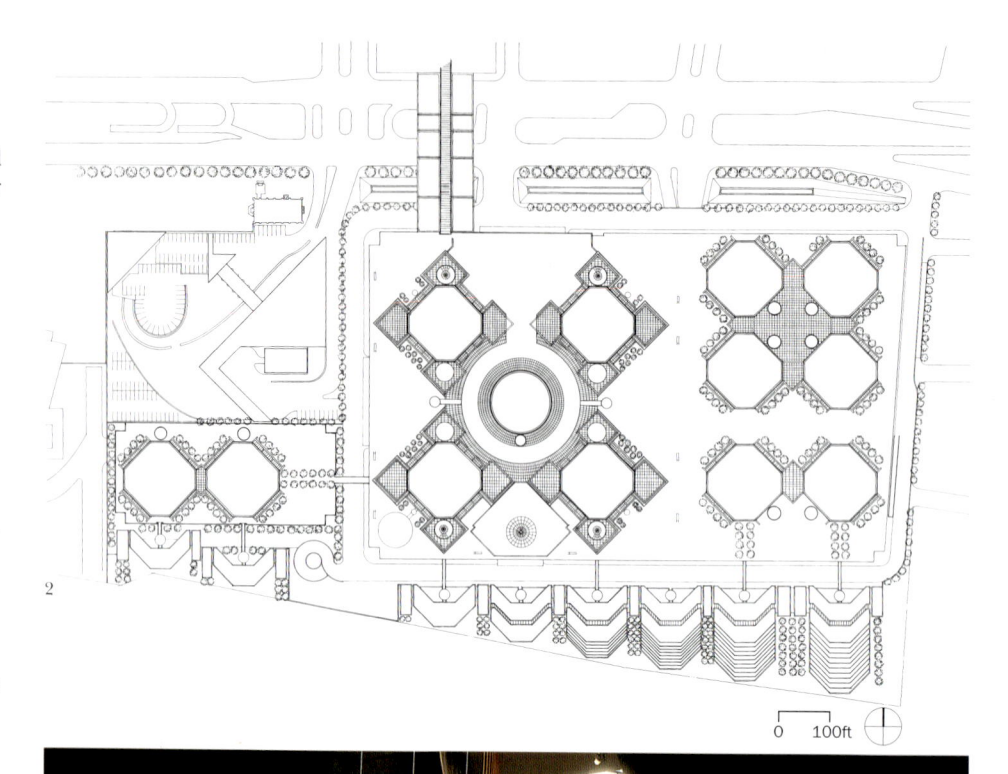

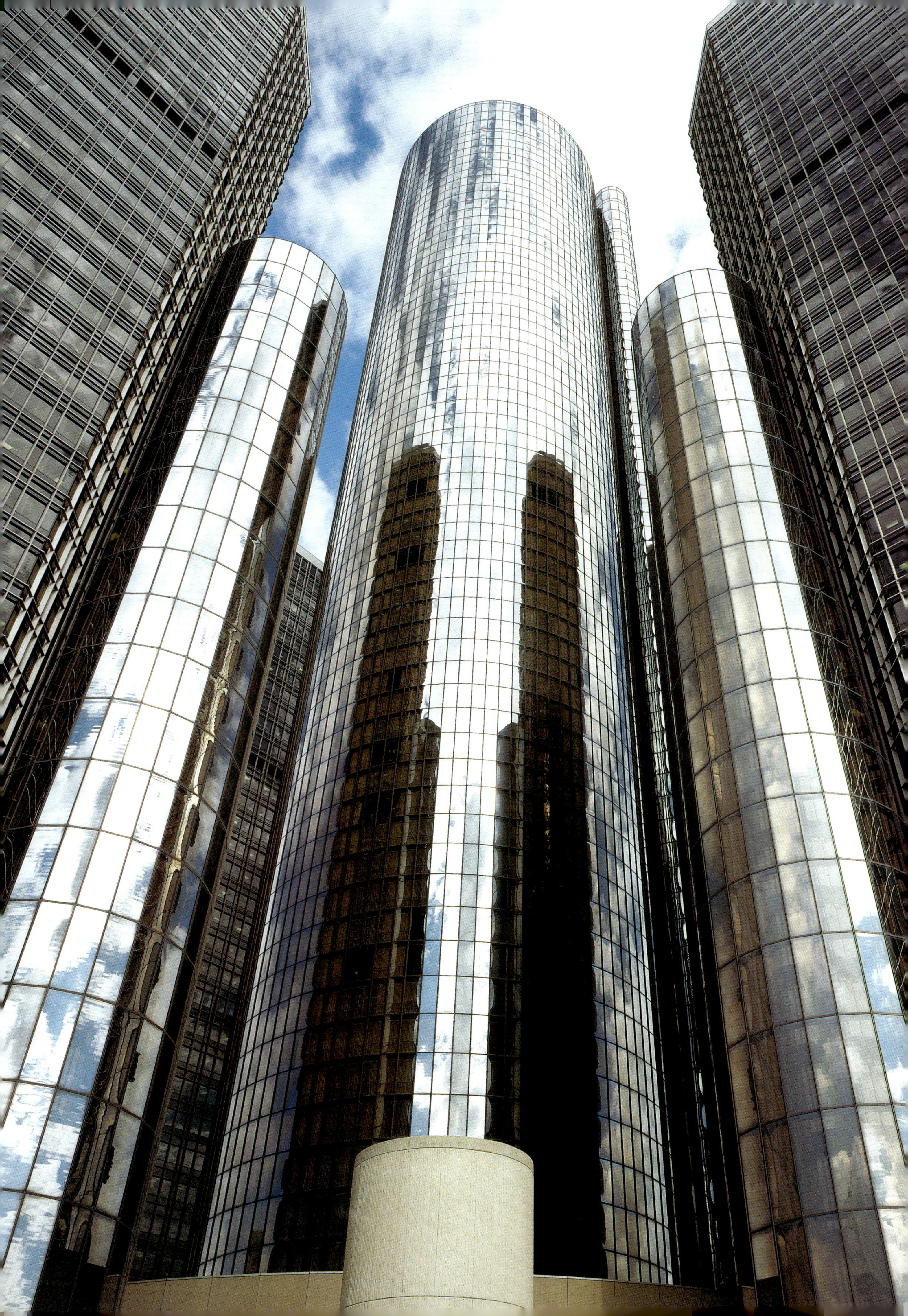

Marina Square

Design/Completion 1984/1987
Singapore
S.P. Tao
371,750 square meters
Concrete, stone, and glass

The three convention hotels and large retail mall that comprise Marina Square were designed to stimulate the economic growth of an undeveloped landfill site on Singapore Harbour by creating a people-oriented destination. The owner originally planned a multi-phase development and solicited competitive proposals on how to proceed. The Portman-Tao team took a unique position and proposed the project as an ambitious single-phase development that focused on creating a new, humanly rewarding environment. The resulting Marina Square became the catalyst that spawned extensive commercial development adjoining the site.

The complexity and massive size of Marina Square was balanced against careful attention to pedestrian scale and a variety of spatial experiences. Singapore's largest retail mall anchors the complex, drawing local residents to the site and enhancing the amenities of the three hotels.

Each of the hotels is built of concrete, and rises above the retail mall with a distinctively different form. An atrium lobby within each hotel opens to shopping, dining and entertainment in the mall. Visitors can enjoy a variety of activities at multiple levels. The mall's landscaped roof includes tennis courts, swimming pools, and extensive sunscreened gardens that offer shade to hotel guests in the tropical climate. To enrich the experience for shoppers and guests, major works of art are prominently incorporated within the hotels, retail mall and their surrounding plazas and gardens, making Marina Square a gathering place for city residents.

1 Aerial view at dusk
2 Aerial view of The Oriental hotel

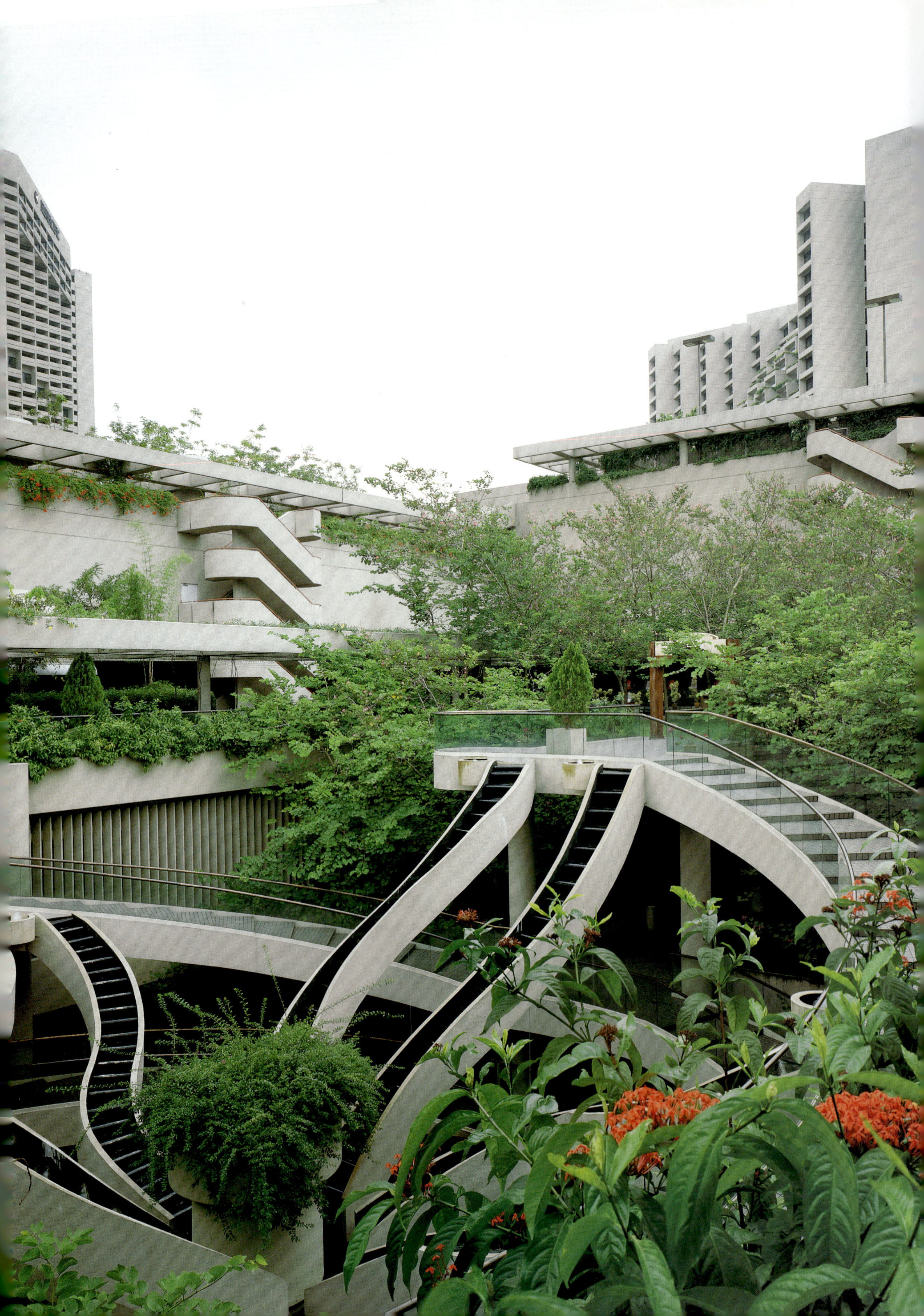

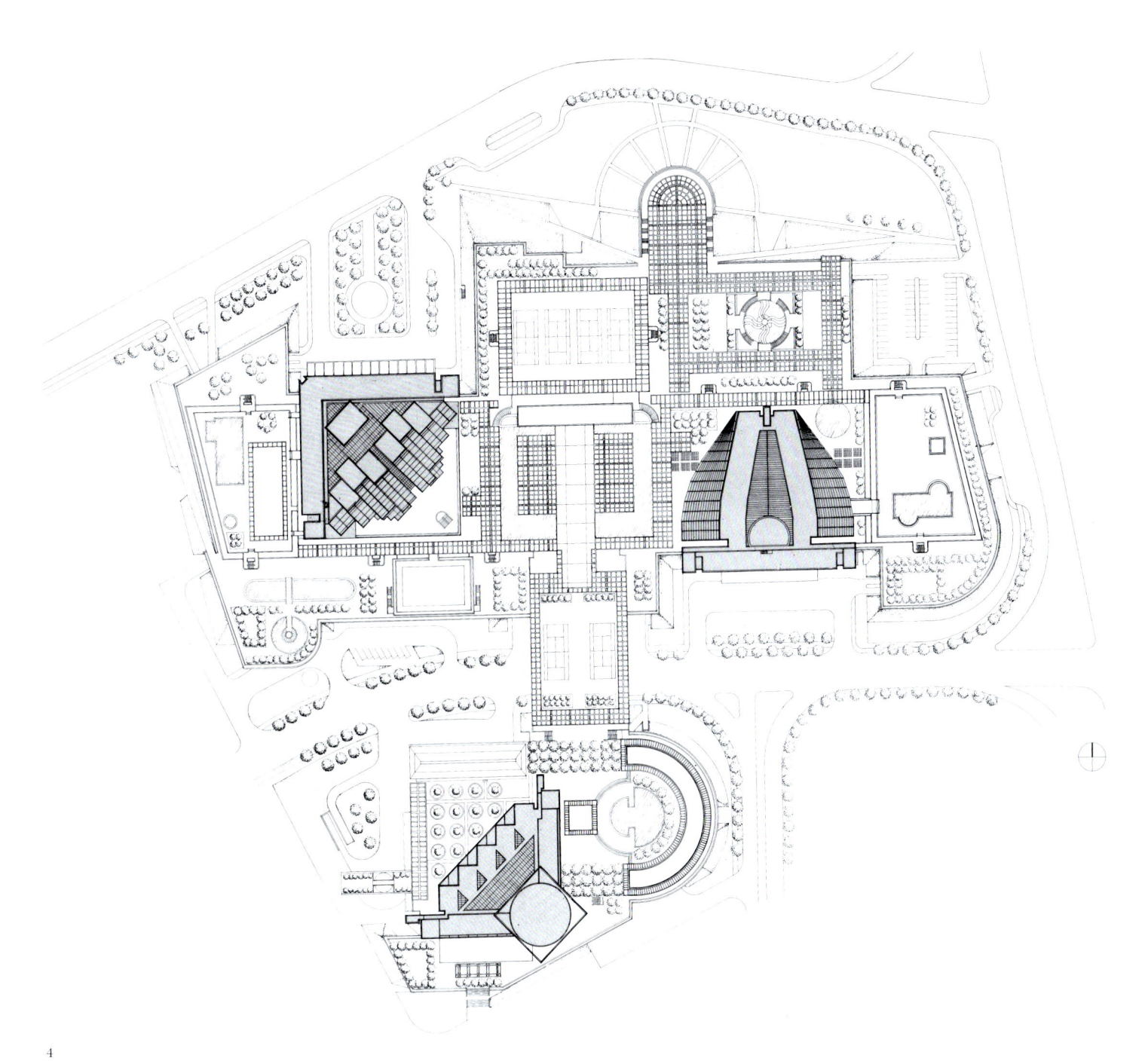

Opposite:
 Roof Garden entry to Retail Mall
4 Site plan
5 Aerial view of trellis

Marina Square 57

6 Interior lobby at The Oriental hotel
7 Plan of roof garden
8 Atrium of Mandarin Hotel

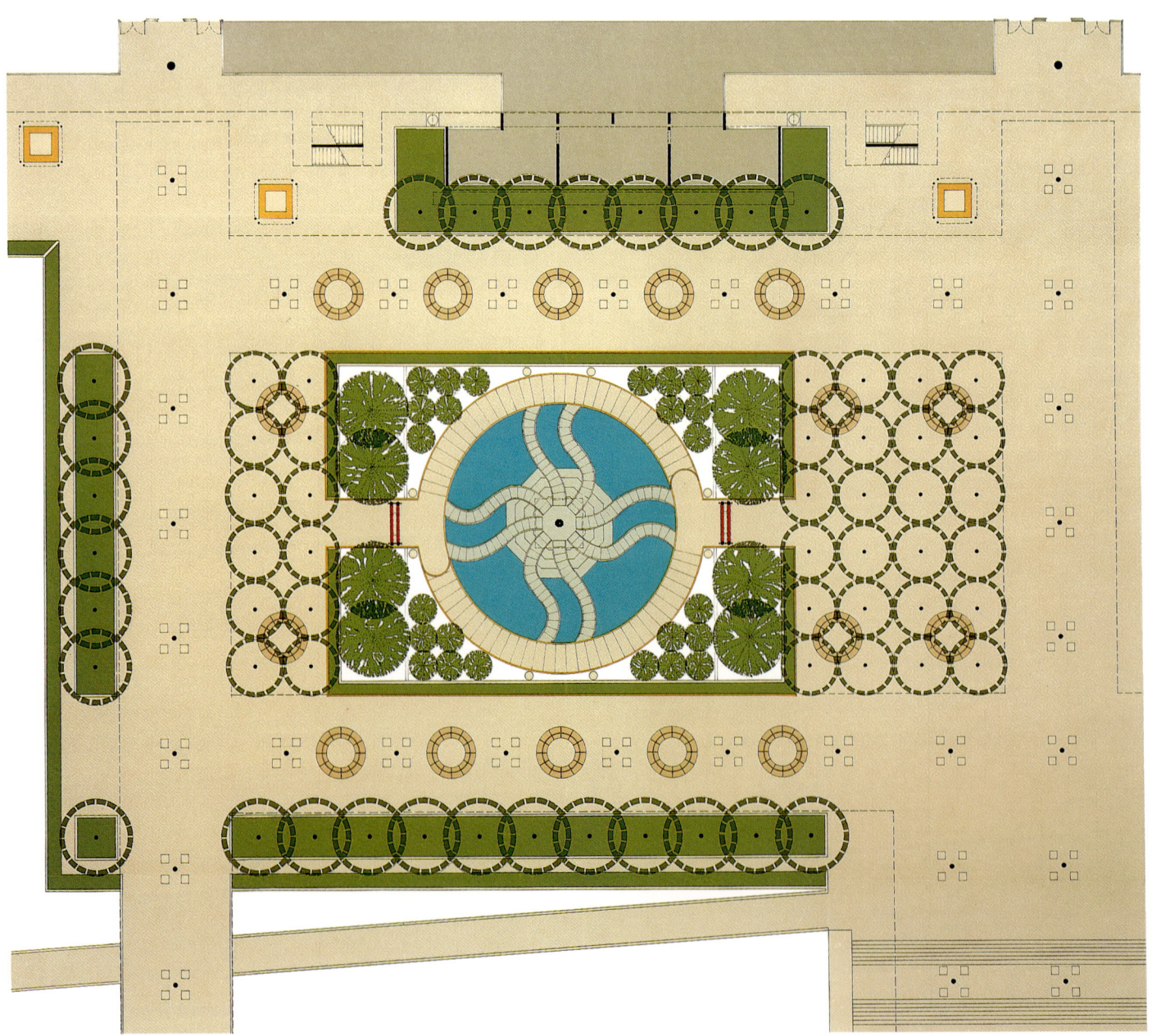

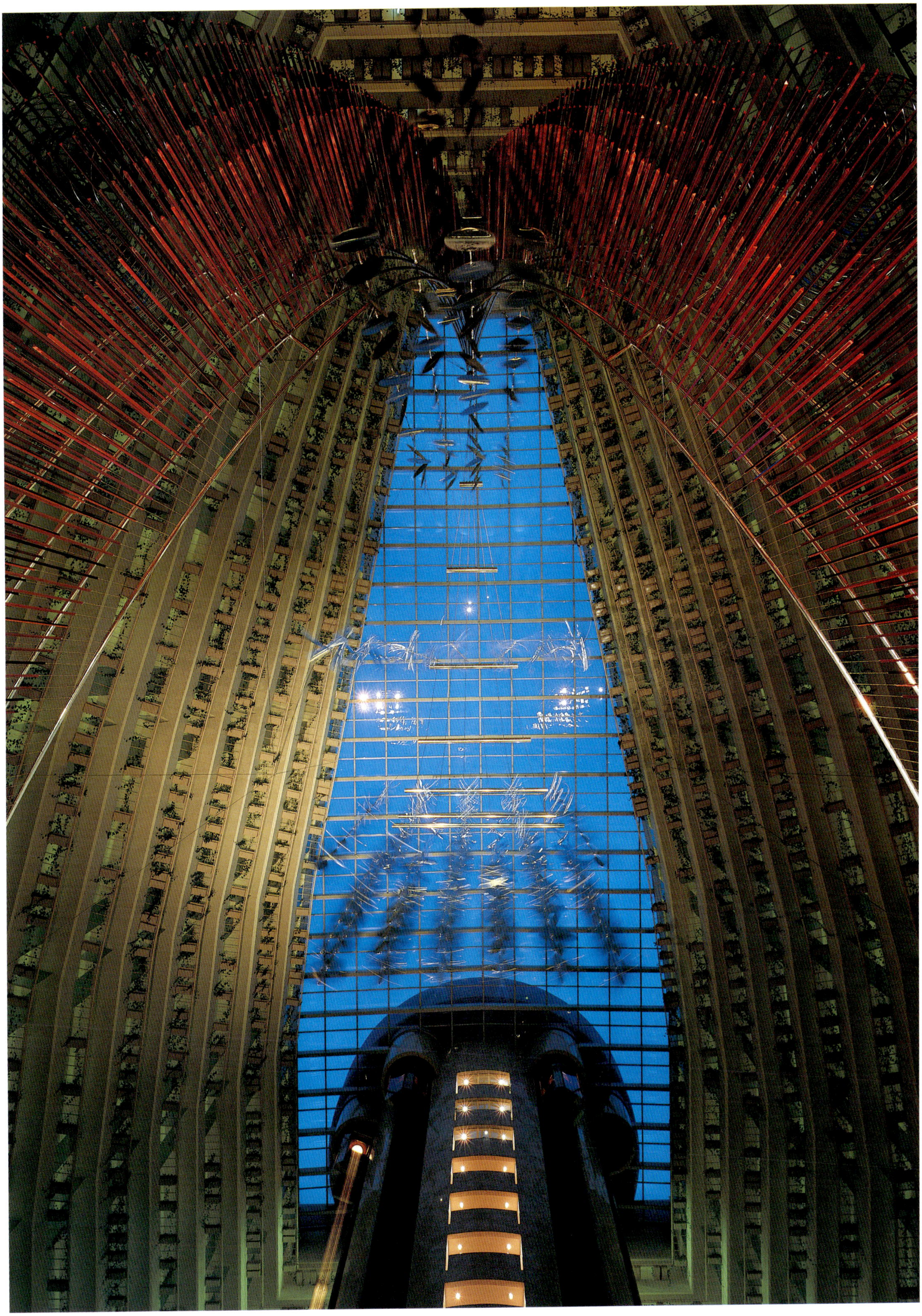

8

Shanghai Centre

Design/Completion 1984/1990
Shanghai, China
Seacliff Ltd.
186,000 square meters
Concrete, stone, and glass

Shanghai Centre is a comprehensive living environment for the international business community. It is comprised of three towers and a podium. The central tower is the 48-story, 700-room Ritz-Carlton Hotel. Two 34-story towers with 500 apartment units flank the hotel. The seven-level podium contains an exhibition hall, a 1,000-seat theater, and office and retail space.

The owners set specific architectural objectives for the project: its functions and style must appeal to expatriates living in Shanghai and it must respect local culture. It was also important that costs be carefully controlled due to the risk associated with this uncharted early venture in China.

The contemporary architecture does not duplicate Chinese forms yet it reflects the essence of Chinese culture. It strives to create an environment that is respectful of its neighboring buildings and inviting to both local and foreign visitors. Space and nature are dominant factors in the design. Grand spaces are created within the entry courtyard and the atrium in the podium above it yet more intimate spaces are carefully woven into the architecture to evoke a variety of responses. The inclusion of nature—trees, water, natural light, and plantings—permeates the complex, changing rooftops into gardens. The use of concrete as the primary building material gave the architects great flexibility in the design while being cost-effective for the owner. High-quality finishes were reserved for areas such as lobbies and restaurants.

1 Site plan
Opposite:
    Aerial view from Nanjing Xi Lu Road

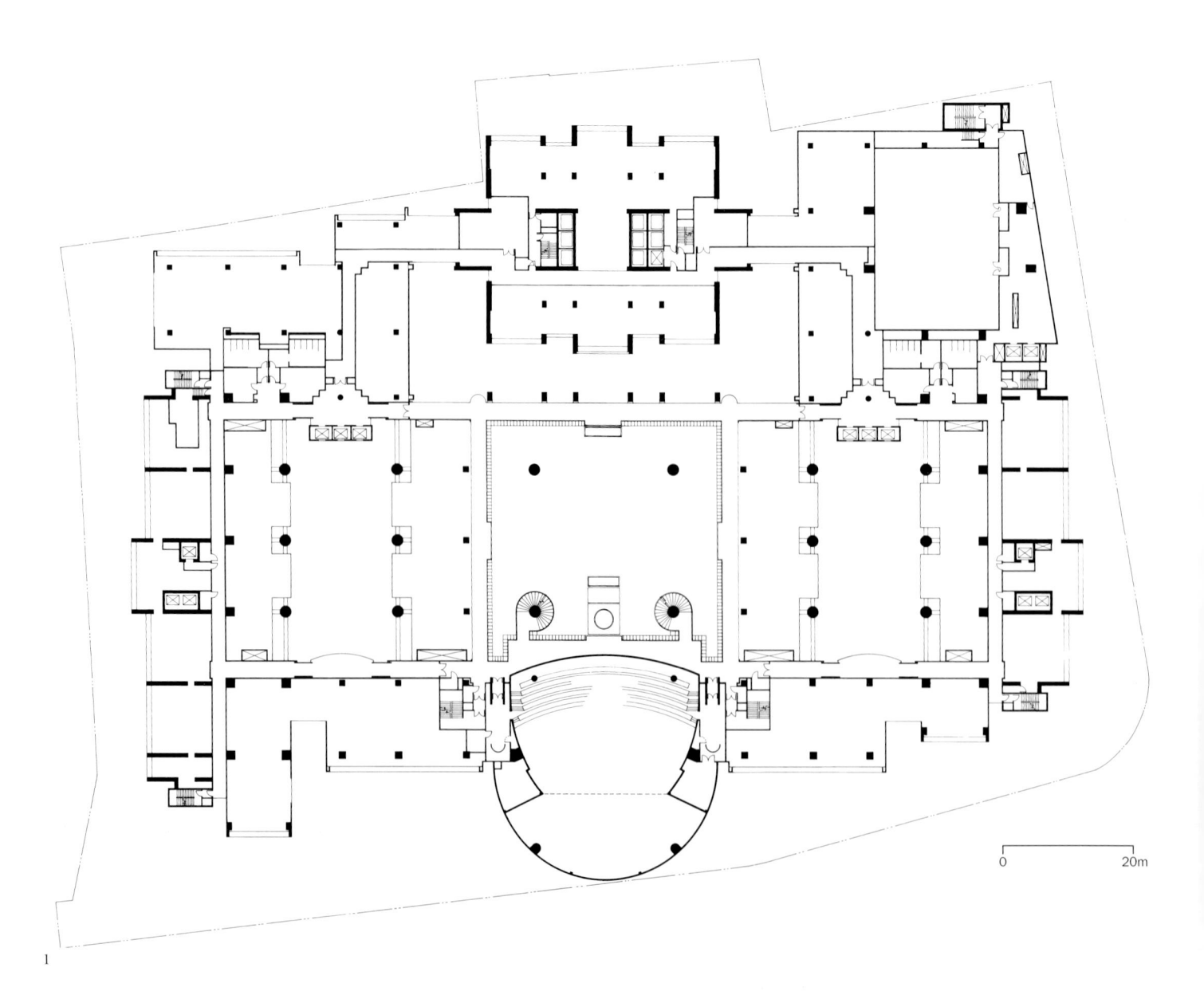

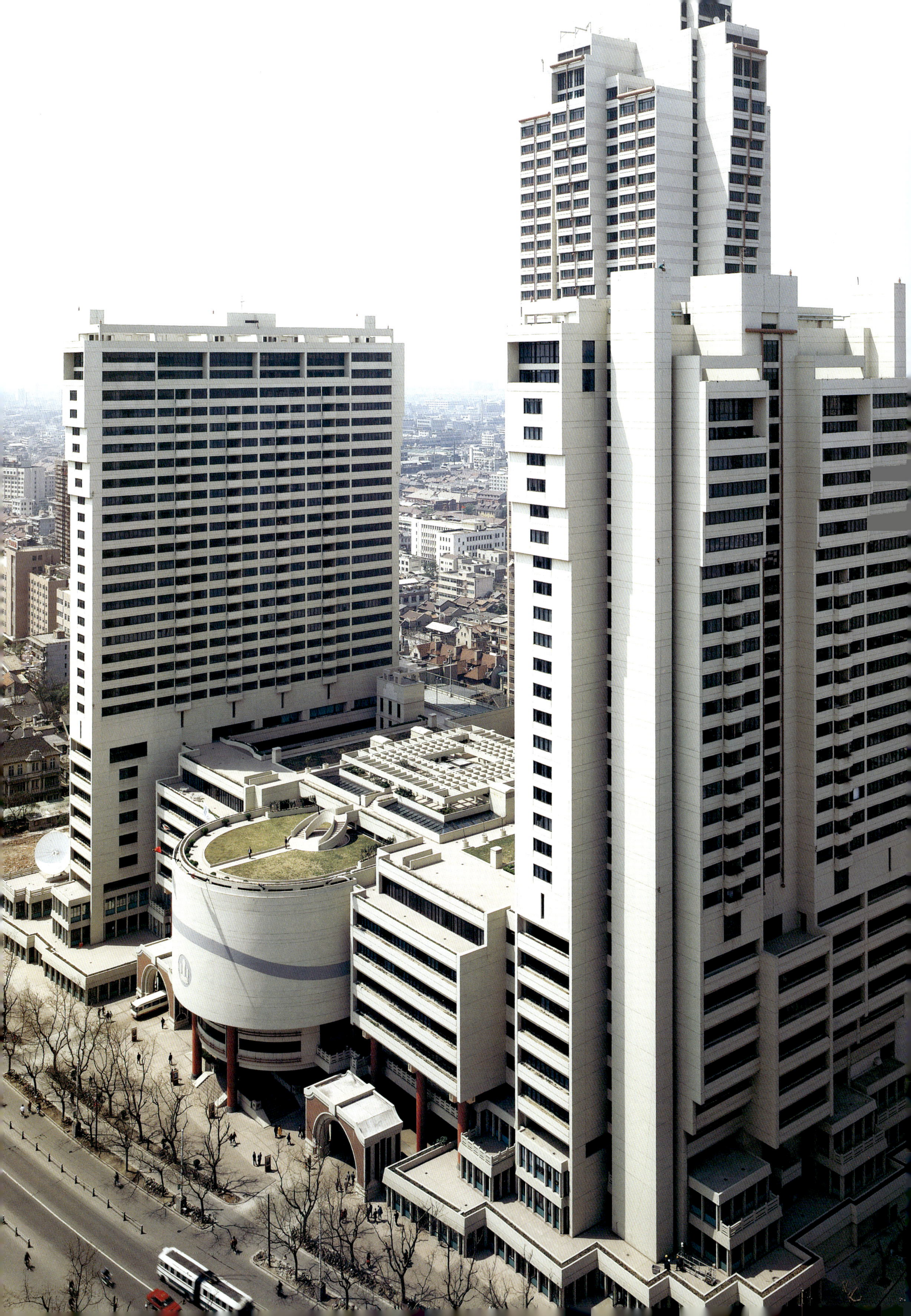

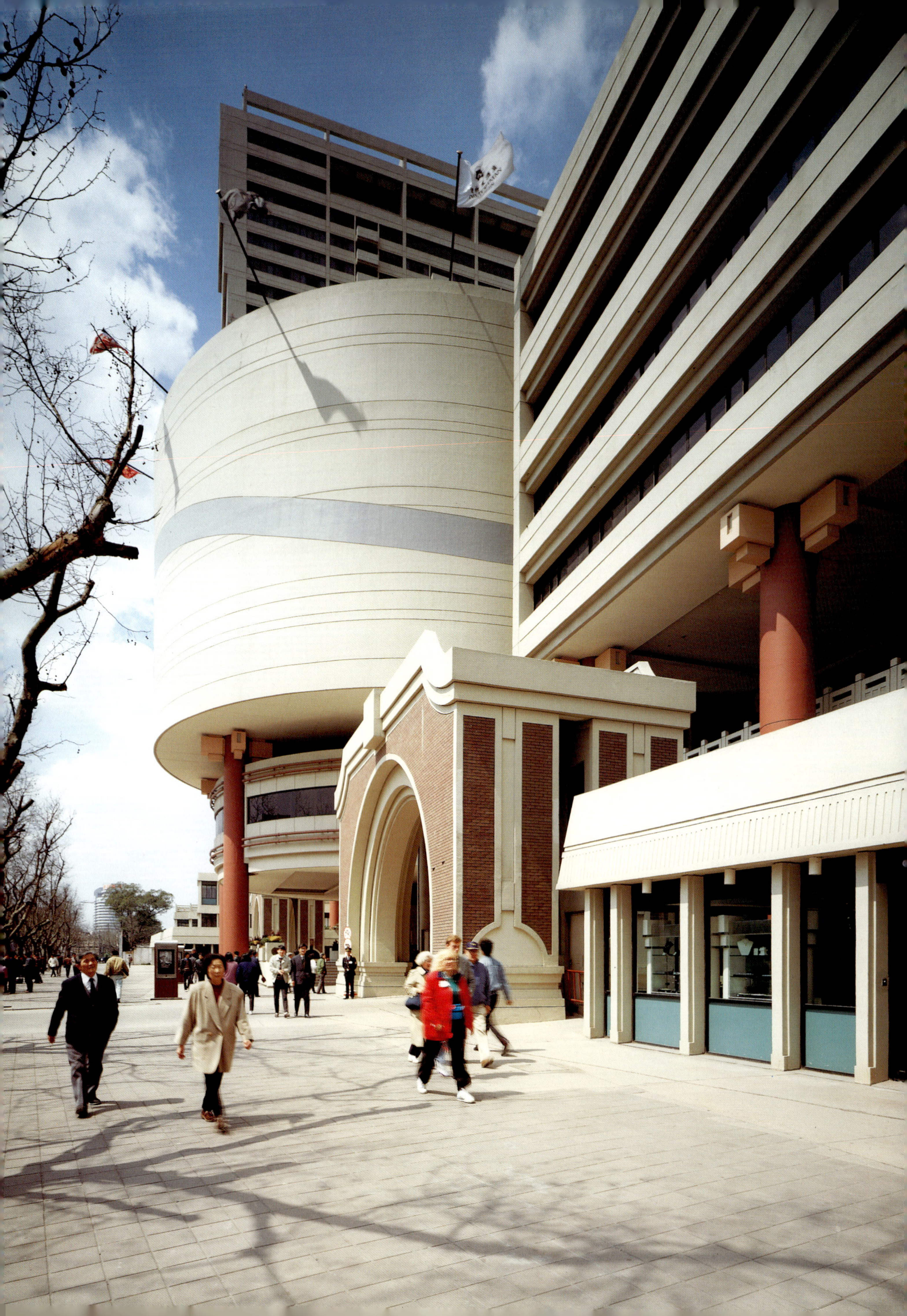

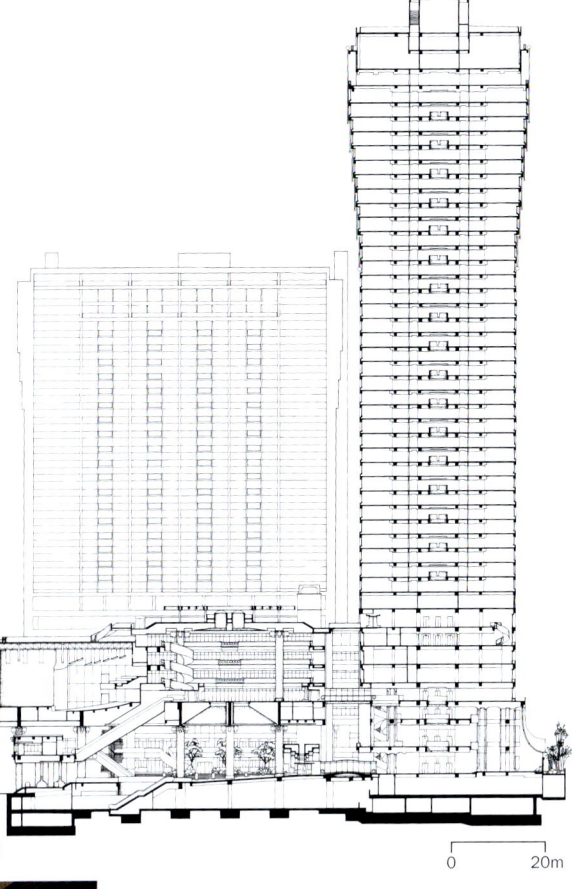

Opposite:
View from Nanjing Xi Lu Road
4 View looking north
5 Section through hotel
6 Lobby staircase

Shanghai Centre 63

7 Hotel atrium stair
8 Office tower entry
9 Exhibition hall

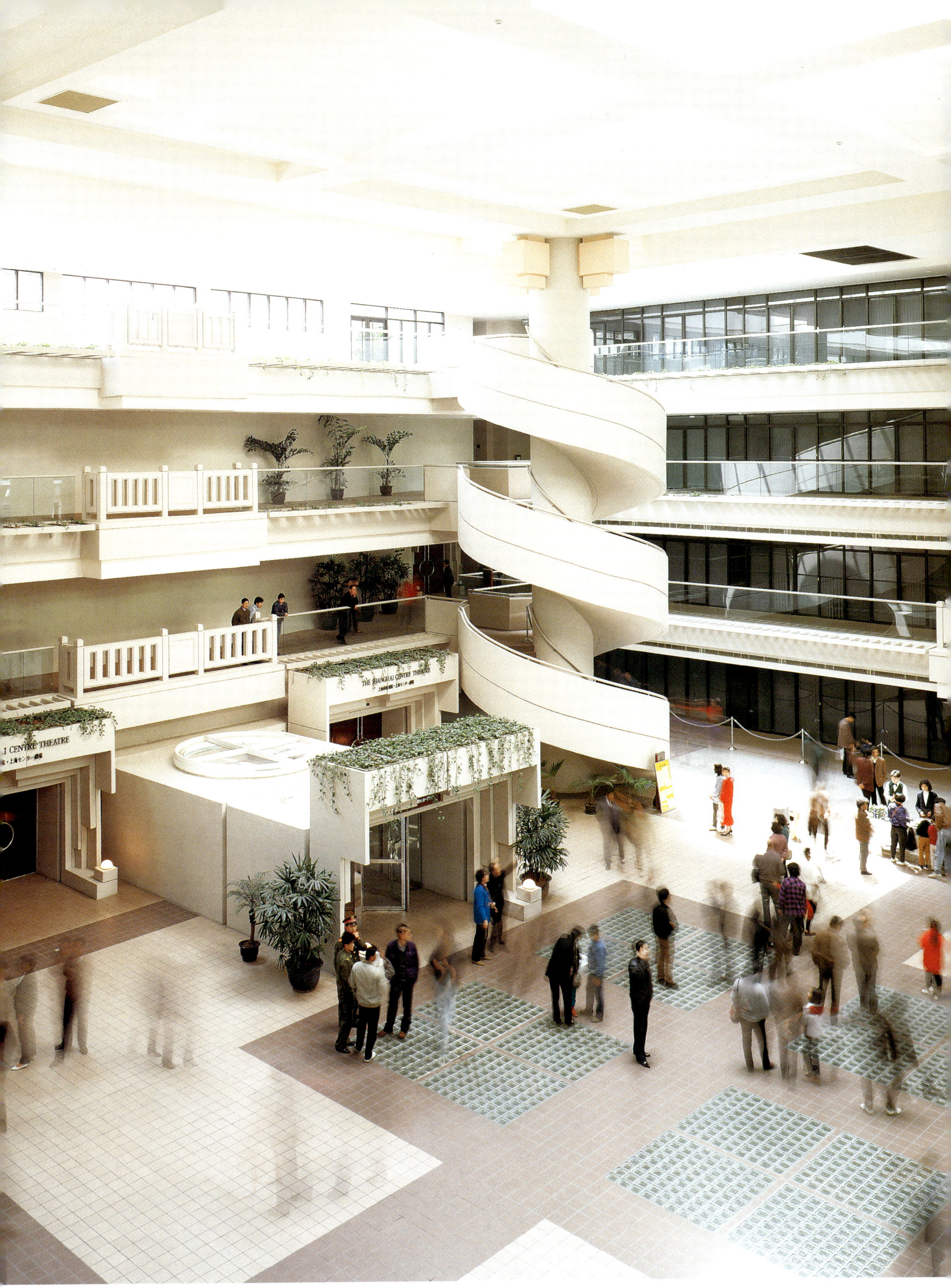
THE SHANGHAI CENTRE THEATRE
CENTRE THEATRE

Capital Square

Design/Completion 1987/1994 (Phase I)
Kuala Lumpur, Malaysia
Capital Square Sdn. Bhd.
346,500 square meters
Concrete, stone, and glass

1 Lobby entry
2 View looking west
3 Reflecting pool fountains
Opposite:
  Skyward view of office tower

Capital Square is poised to become Malaysia's first 'city within a city'. It is a mixed-use development on a 15.2-acre parcel of land and is touted as one of the largest integrated mixed-use developments in Malaysia. Everything an international or Malaysian businessperson might require should they wish to visit or establish an operation in Malaysia will be available within the complex.

The three-phase project includes two 40-story, 65,000-square-meter office towers, a 37,175-square-meter retail shopping center and a five-star, 590-room luxury hotel with conference facilities. Phase I consists of one office tower and the first half of the retail space.

The sculptural form of the glistening white office tower is distinctive on the skyline. A landscaped circular motor entry provides a ceremonial entrance to the grand 15-meter tall lobby. Large total vision glass lobby walls open the interior space to the surrounding landscaped plazas. The reflecting pools and bubbling plaza fountains can be enjoyed from inside or out. Extensive use of imported granite on floors and walls provides a cooling contrast to the tropical climate. The towers' facades incorporate a sunscreen that allows unobstructed views yet minimizes the impact of the Malaysian sun and improves operating cost efficiency and interior comfort.

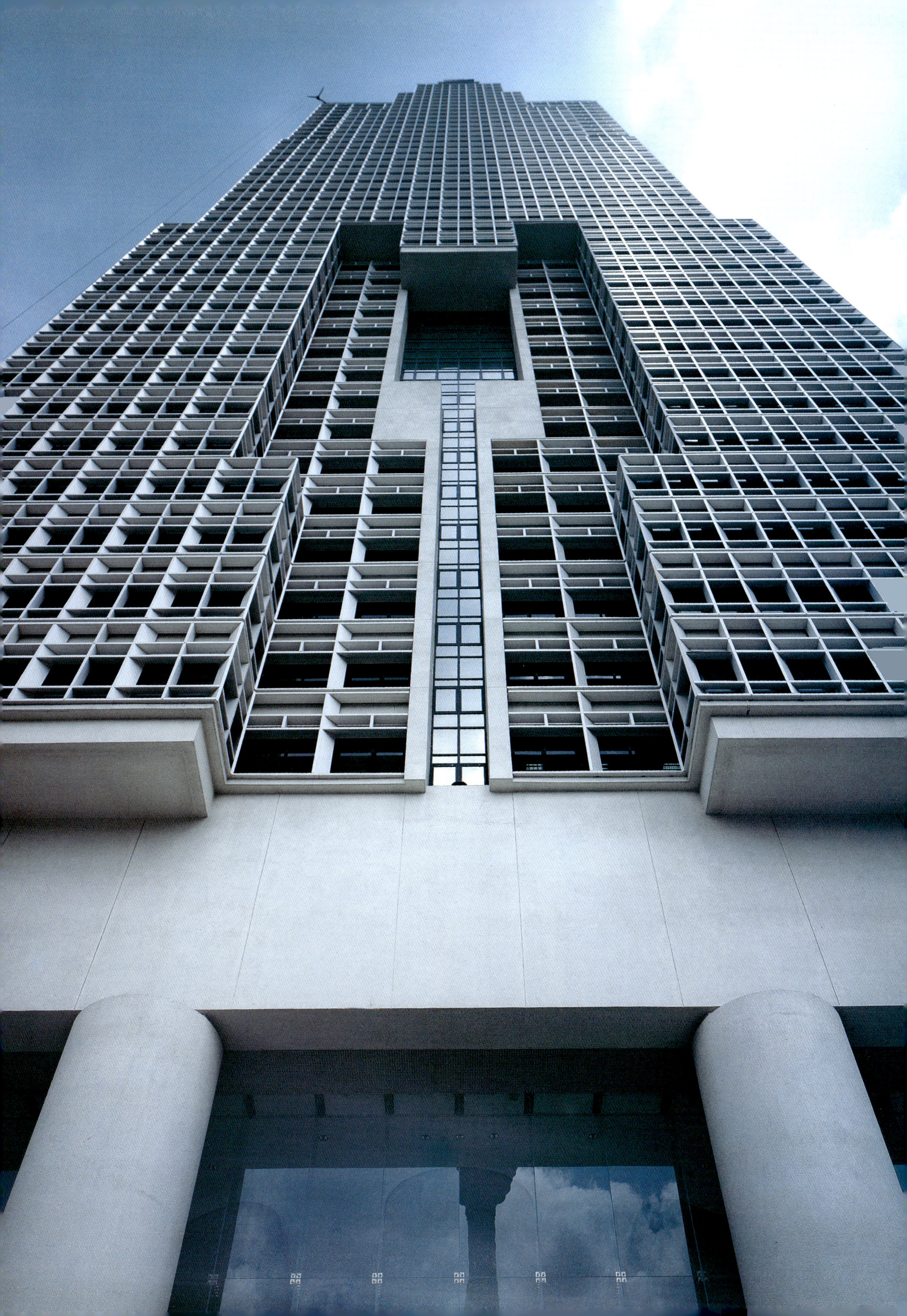

Il Porto Vecchio

Design Proposal 1989
Genoa, Italy
Newport S. P. A.
125,400 square meters
Concrete, stone, and metal paneling

Il Porto Vecchio was a proposed design for a port revitalization to commemorate the 500th anniversary of Columbus sailing from Genoa to the New World. The project aimed to give Genoa a unique architectural focus that would signify the city's past while recognizing its present and projecting its future. It also aimed to become the catalyst for improving the under-used waterfront and linking the area back to the city. The project design added a major new multi-use facility for more people-oriented activities that complemented the historical in apposition.

Il Porto Vecchio is situated on a large prow-like triangular pier built out into the harbor, reached by an arcing drive over the water that separates the new from the old. The project concept contained a marina, hotel, retail shops, restaurants, offices, and a sculpture garden. On shore were pedestrian-linked university classrooms. A major underwater aquarium between the arcing drive and the harbor shore provided a symbolic link between the land, the project and the sea.

The project concept was based on Genoa's relationship to the sea, and was inspired by the harbor's historic sailing ships. The conical form of the 30-story, 275-meter hotel recalls the ships' tall main masts. The project is of the sea and its prow-like podium base with its towering main mast echoes on a large scale the history of the city harbor as it faces the sea.

Genoa's sea focus has limited its large piazzas. Il Porto Vecchio provided for open waterfront promenades and a large central piazza. Shops and arcades would be covered by an open concrete grid sunscreen that enhanced the pedestrian scale and orientation of the project.

1 Rendering

Il Porto Vecchio

2 Model view looking east
3 Rendering
4 Site plan
5 Aerial view of model

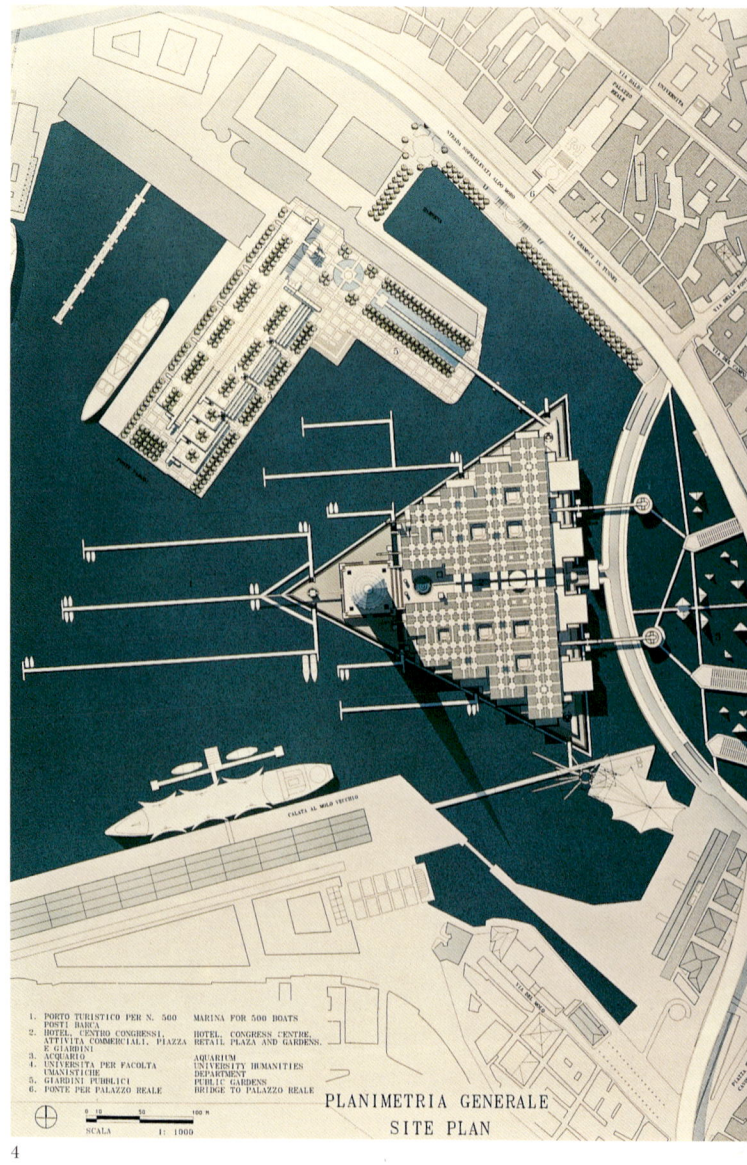

Il Porto Vecchio 71

Shandong Hotel & Conference Center

Design/Completion 1993/2001
Jinan, China
Shandong Building Task Force
65,000 square meters
Concrete, stone, and glass

The Shandong Building provides legislative meeting halls and accommodation for the provincial government, and serves as a conference center for businesses and the community. The primary design objectives were to provide a grand convention facility with supporting halls, meeting rooms and a five-star hotel, and to create harmony within the setting shared with older governmental buildings and gardens.

The People's Hall and the hotel are the dominant components. The 2,500-seat hall is at the end of a grand boulevard and ceremonial public square. The facades are classical Chinese stone and respectful of historic Chinese buildings. A magnificent 22-meter lobby with grand stairs and elevators leading to the balconies is found within. The People's Hall serves not only governmental functions but also business conventions and cultural performances.

The 690-room atrium hotel is at the opposite corner of the site. The semi-circular, 25-story building affords spectacular views. The hotel and People's Hall are linked by a series of prefecture/city level halls and large enterprise level halls with adjacent gardens that enhance the pedestrian experience within the complex. This program element complements the hotel and People's Hall/convention center and is unprecedented in its massing.

1 Rendering
2 View of hotel tower looking north
3 Interior rendering of hotel atrium
4 Aerial view of model

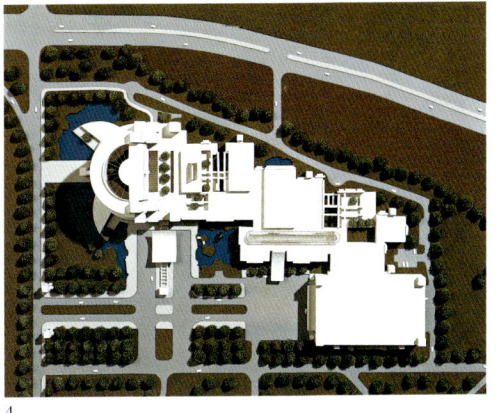

Shandong Hotel & Conference Center

5 View along concourse balcony
6 Lobby atrium at theater
7 View along concourse
8–10 Stone details
11 Site plan

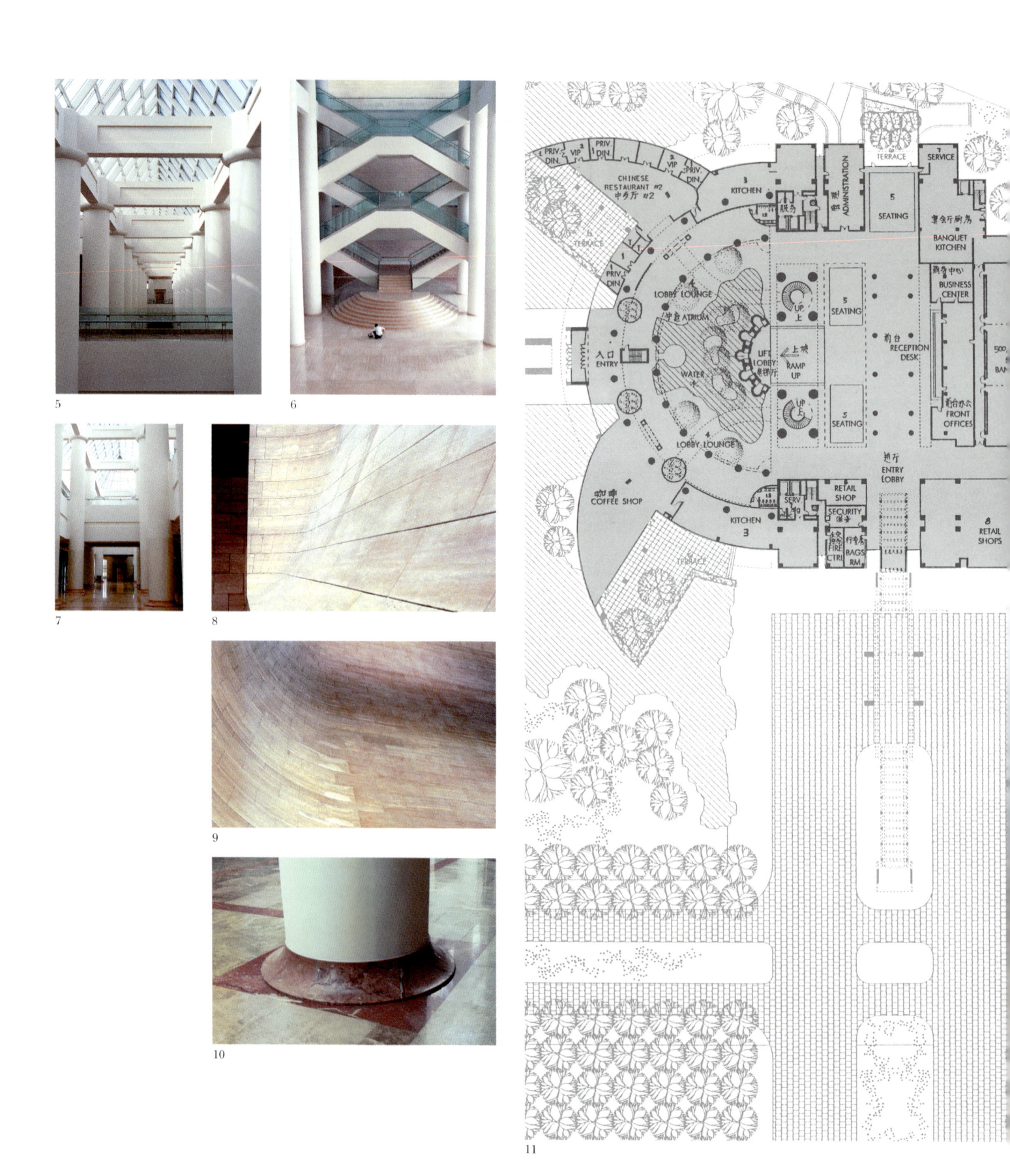

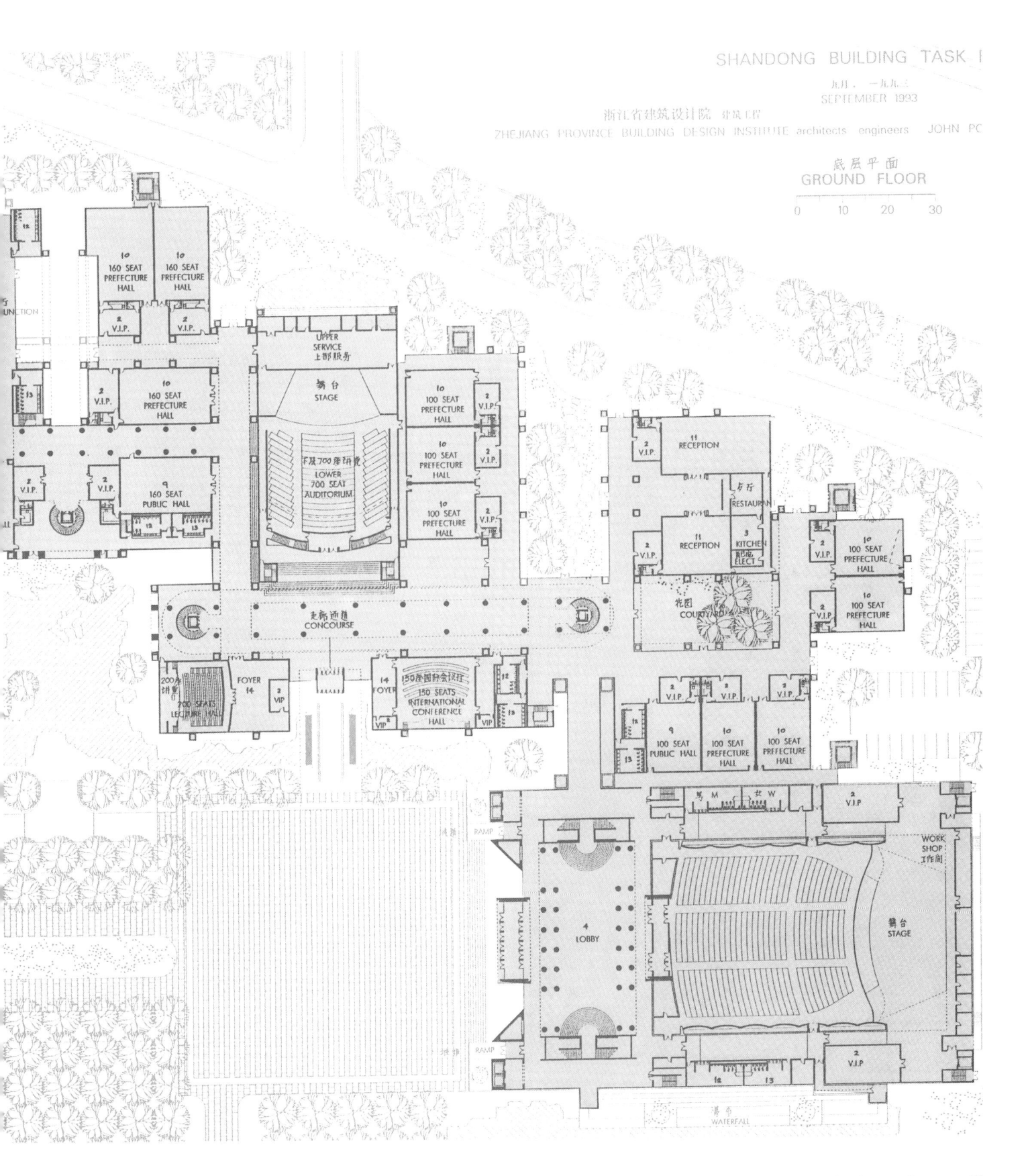

SHANDONG BUILDING TASK I
SEPTEMBER 1993
浙江省建筑设计院 建筑师
ZHEJIANG PROVINCE BUILDING DESIGN INSTITUTE architects engineers JOHN PO

底层平面
GROUND FLOOR
0   10   20   30

Shandong Hotel & Conference Center   75

Tomorrow Square

Design/Completion 1996/2002
Shanghai, China
Shanghai Sunjoy Real Estate General Co.
93,000 square meters
Concrete, stone, granite, metal paneling, and glass

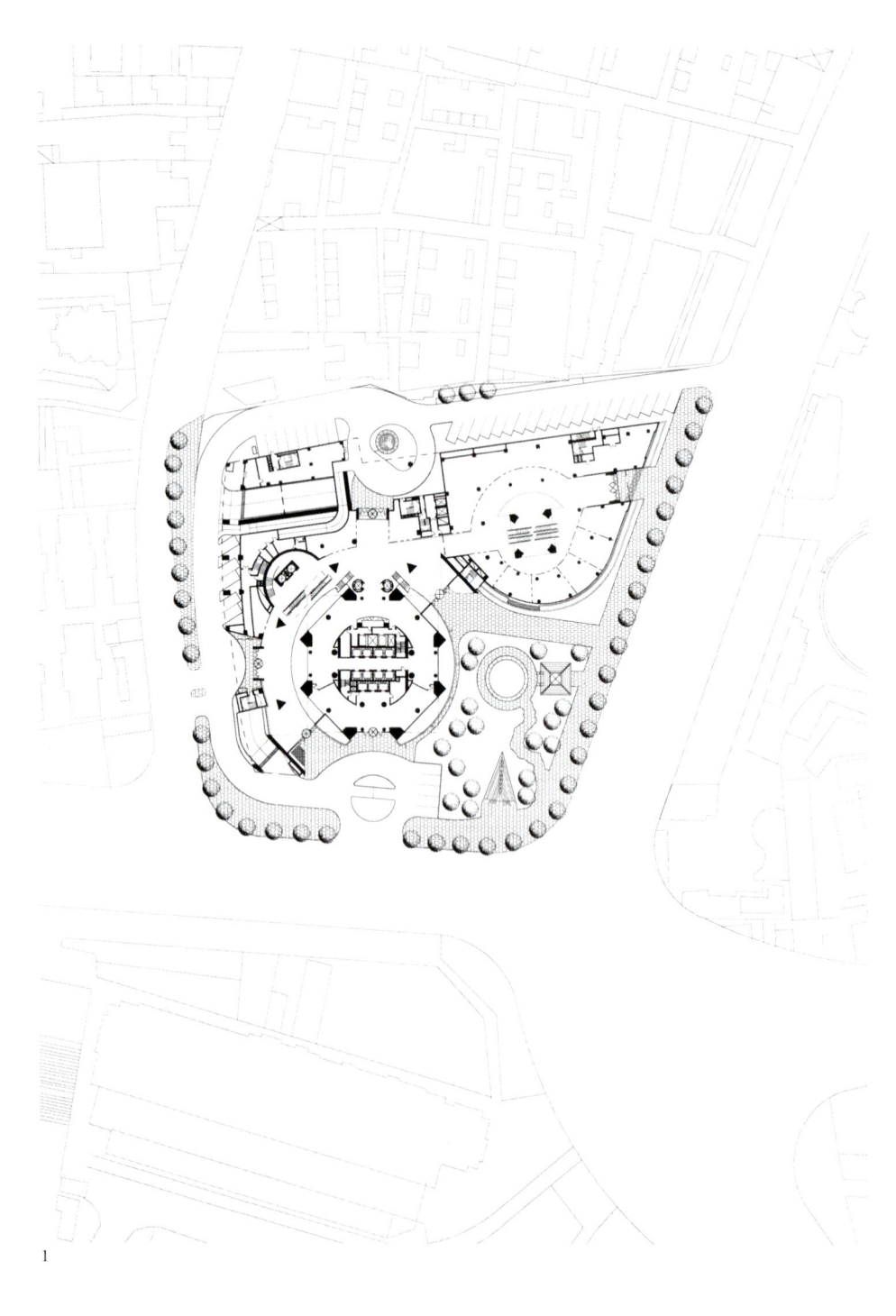

Tomorrow Square is comprised of three major elements on a landscaped plaza. This high-rise tower with hotel and office space is joined to a low-rise podium with a retail galleria and conference center. An atrium links the tower and podium. The client's project goal was to represent the future not the past. Incorporating a comprehensive program of hotel, office and retail functions, Tomorrow Square creates a dramatic new landmark on Shanghai's skyline.

The 55-story tower has aluminum and glass facades that reach upward in a straightforward, geometric progression. The building's basic square plan is rotated 45 degrees at the 37th level to reflect the change of function within. The lower levels are offices and office apartments with the hotel above.

The six-level podium is the retail hub. The granite building extends the width of the site arcing around the tower to maximize the importance of the Nanjing Road entrance. From this main entrance, shoppers descend to a food court, bowling lanes and access to the subway system. Within the skylit atrium, escalators and elevators ascend to shops on the first three levels. Level 4 has restaurants and entertainment venues. Level 5 is the conference center and the health club that is linked to additional facilities on the rooftop including the hotel swimming pool.

1 Site plan
2 Tower detail
3 Looking west

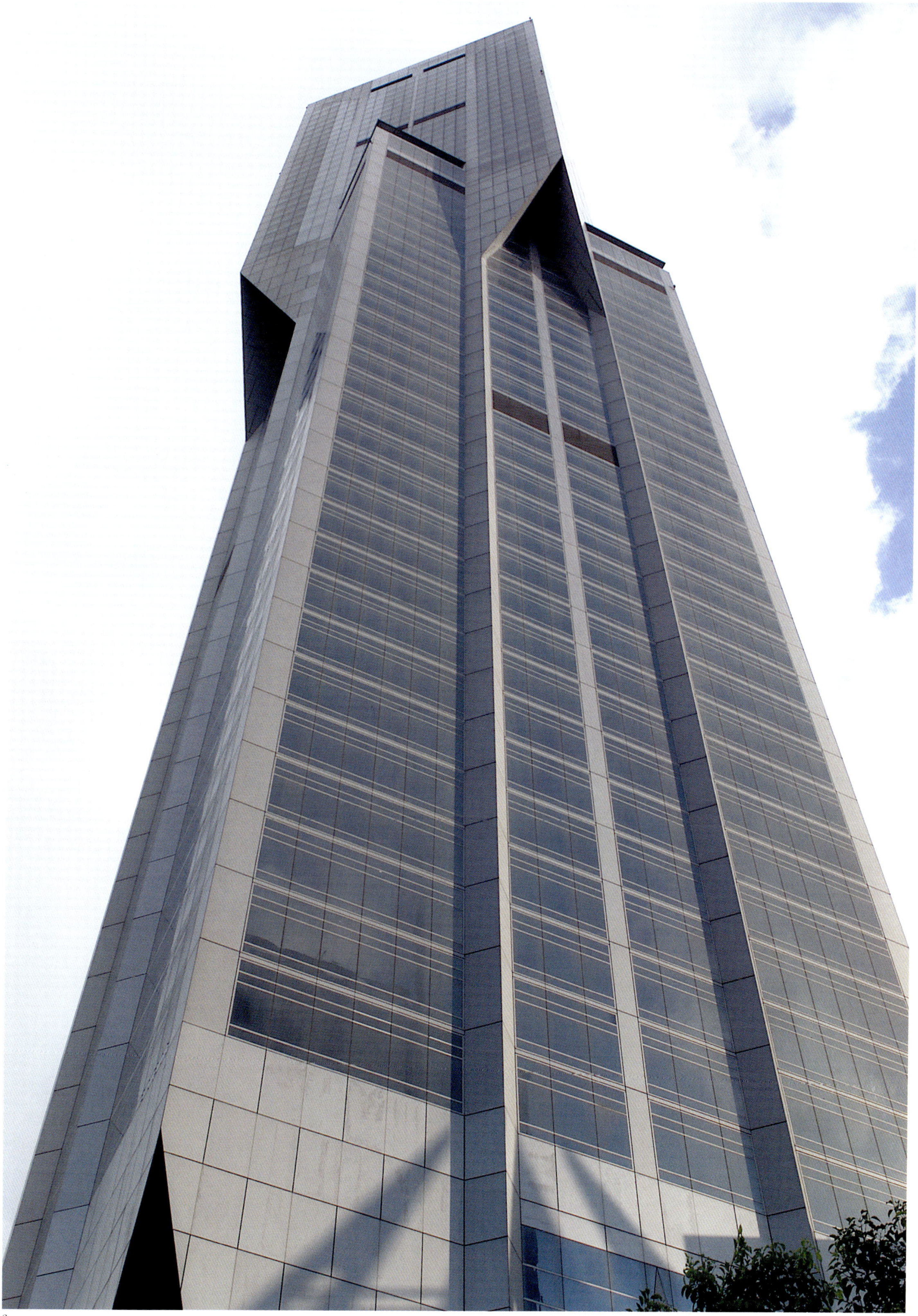

3

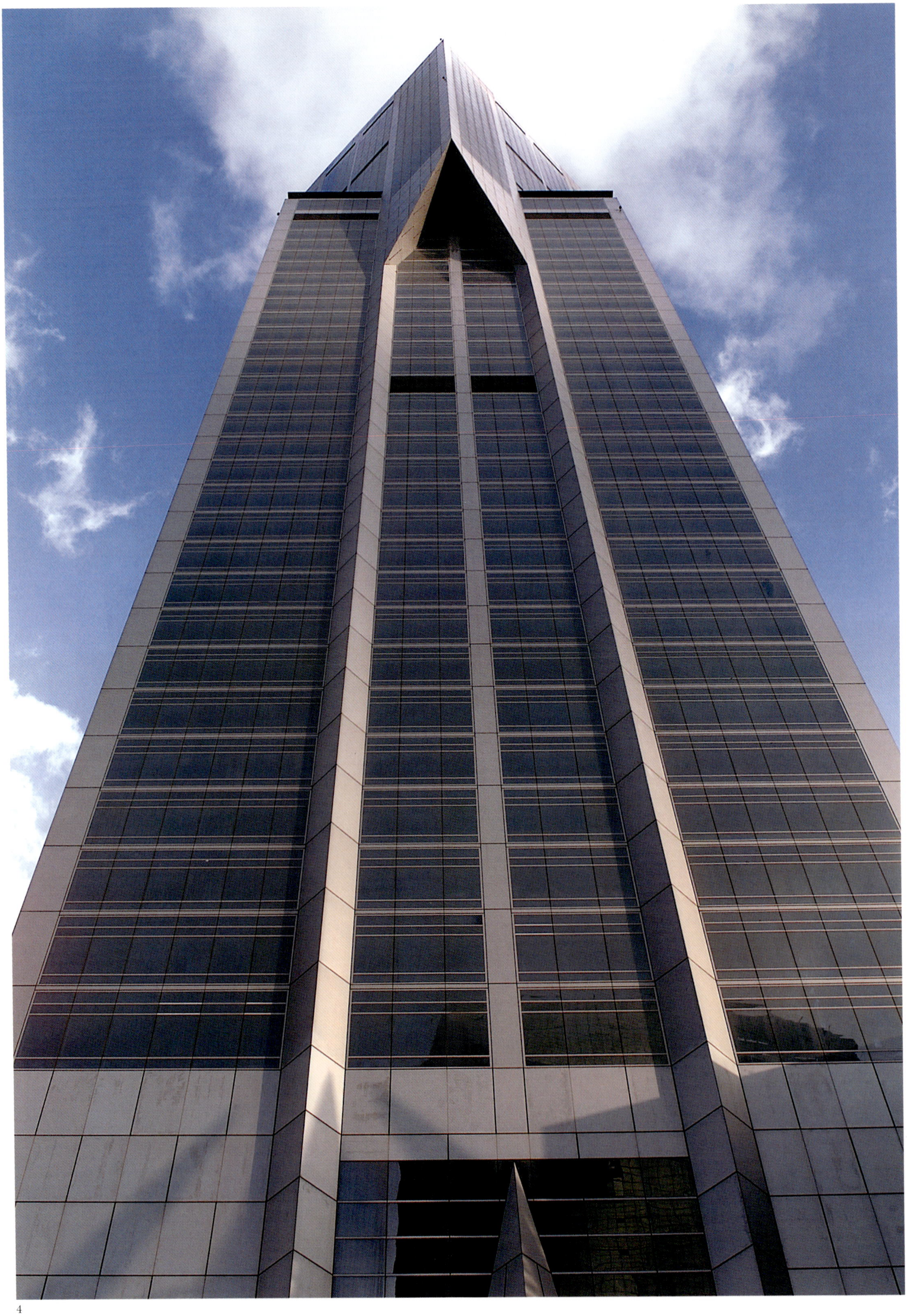

4

5

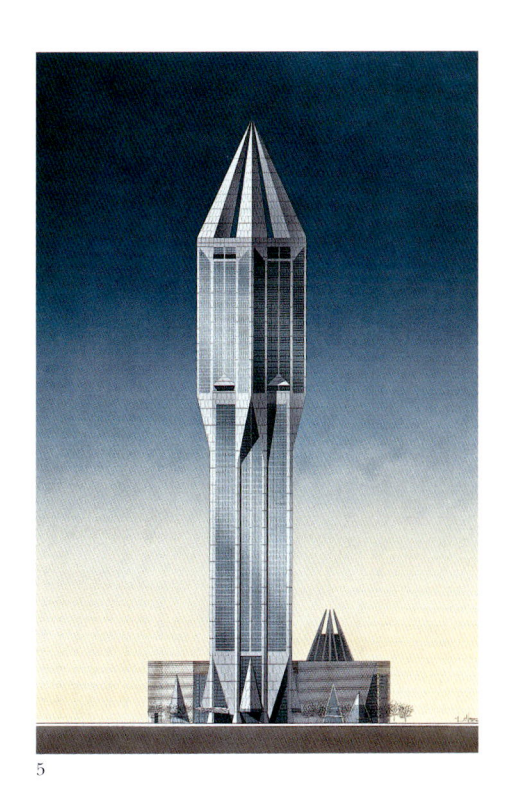

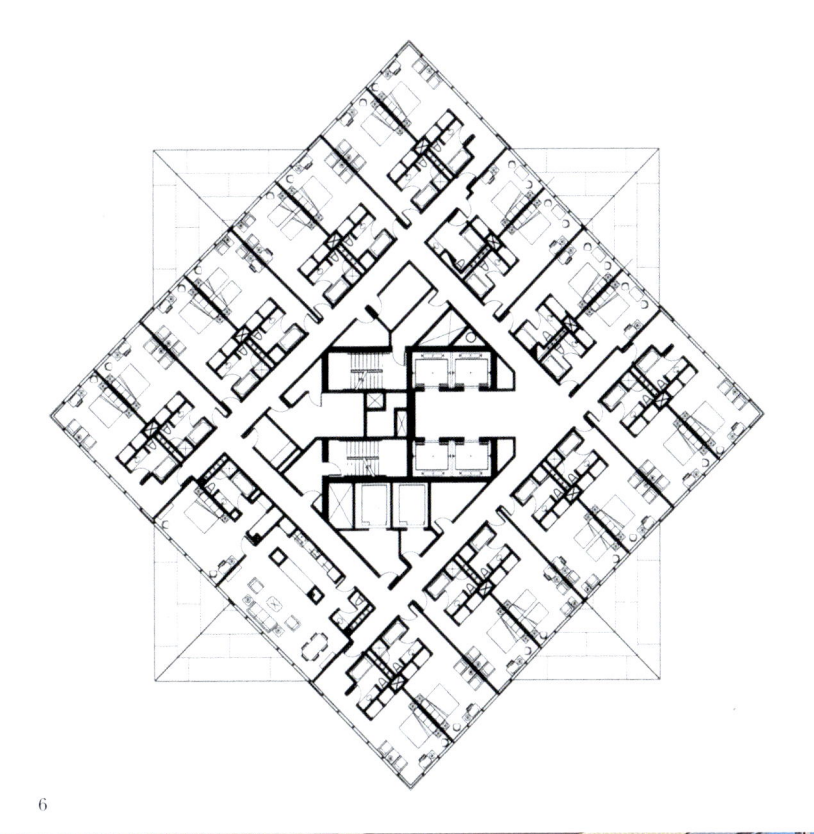

6

7

4&5   Skyward view of tower
6   Typical hotel plan
7   Interior rendering

Tomorrow Square   79

8 Retail plaza rendering
9 Interior rendering
10 Rendering of south elevation

8

9

10

Tomorrow Square 81

11 Rendering of southeast elevation
12 Section
Opposite:
    View from Peoples Park

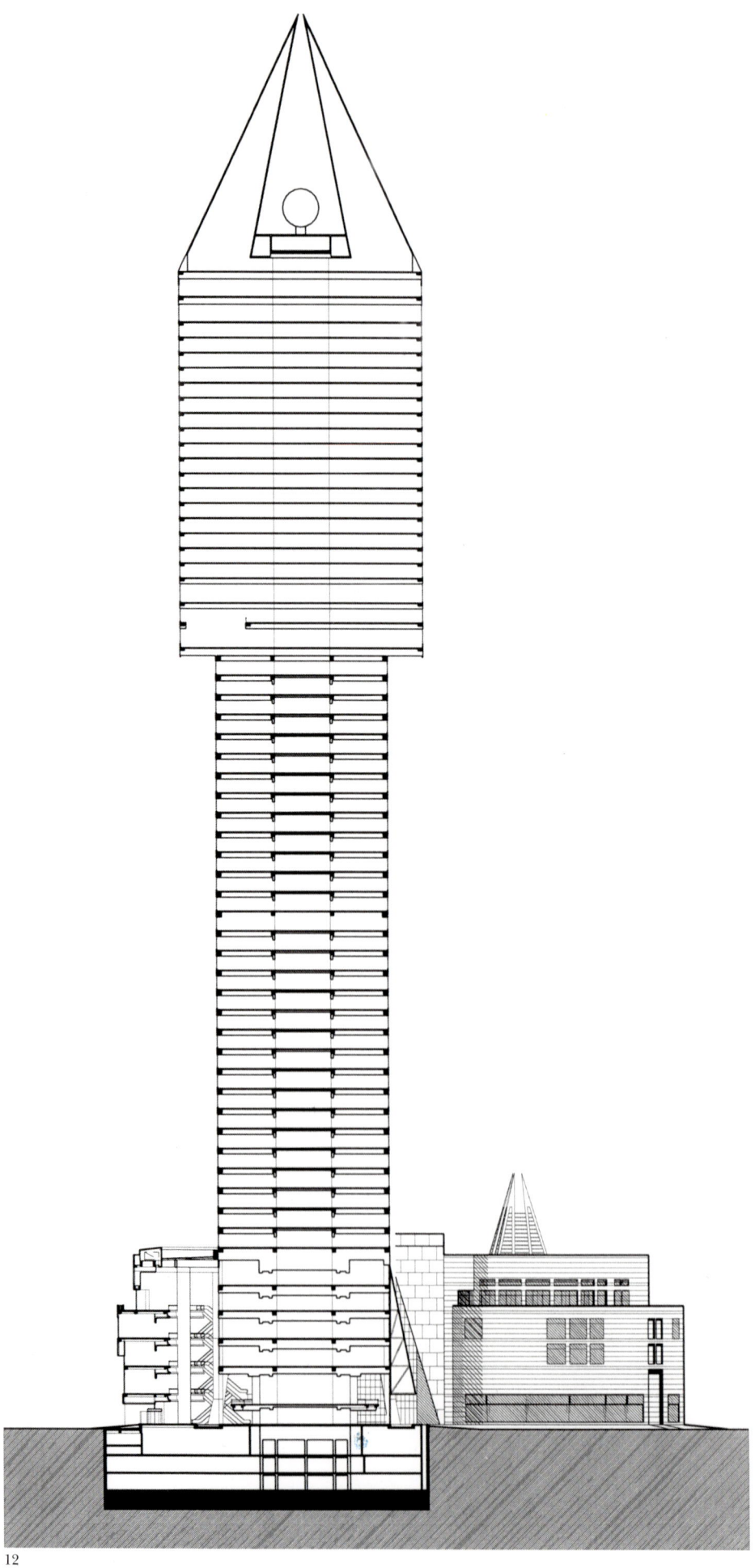

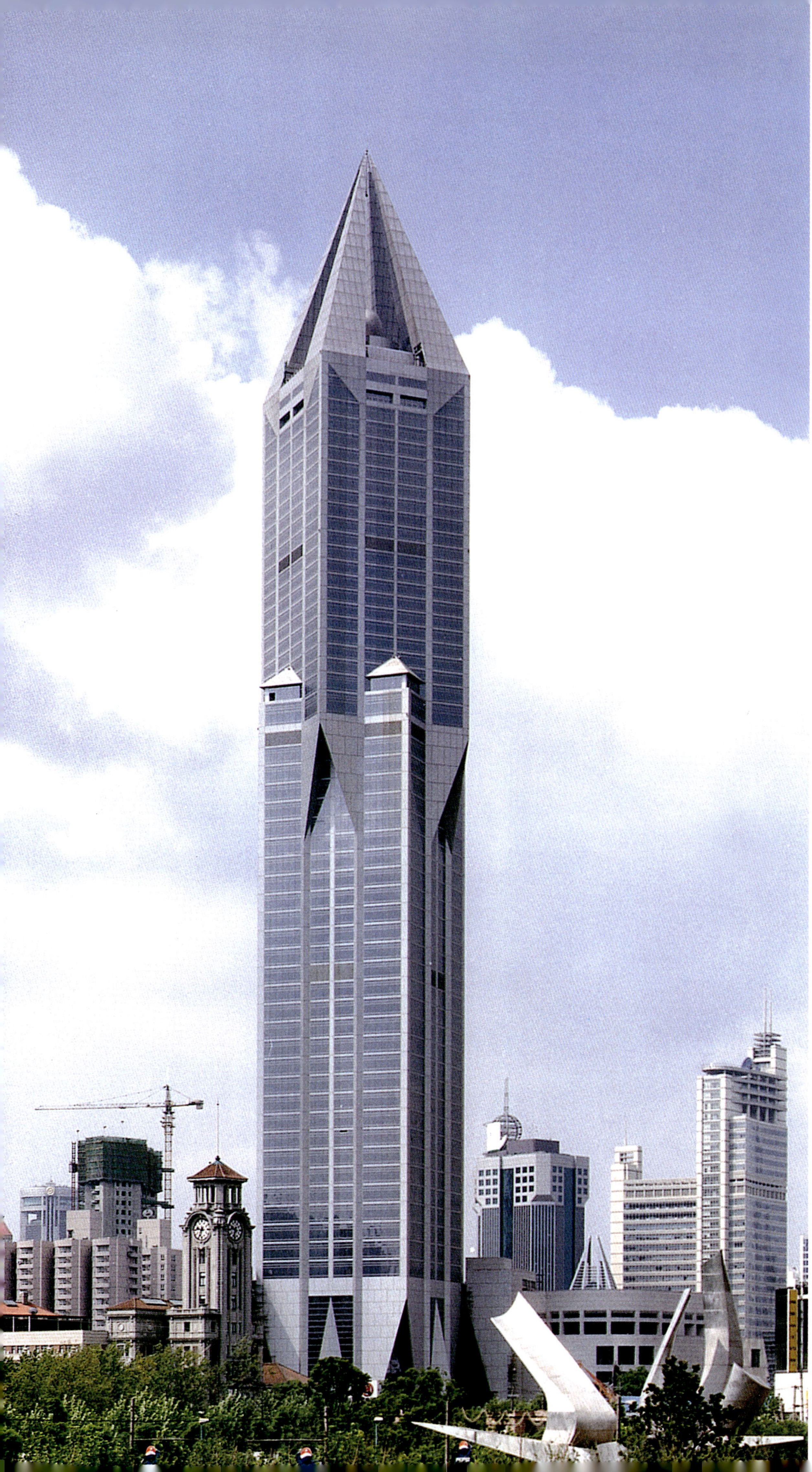

Nile Center

Design Proposal 1978
Cairo, Egypt
Saigol Brothers Ltd.
88,200 square meters
Concrete, stone, and glass

Nile Center is located near the suburb Maadi, which is south of central Cairo. The River Nile is used as a major element for organizing the design of this comprehensive mixed-use development. By creating a canal from the river, water extends from the east bank of the Nile, under the river road, through the hotel atrium, and into the site terminating in a large keyhole-shaped lake.

On the west side of the lake is a semi-pyramidal, 19-story, 884-room luxury hotel facing the ancient pyramids directly across the Nile. On the north and south sides of the lake are two six-story office buildings, each with its own interior courtyard. On the east side of the lake is a terraced nine-story residential structure, conforming to the shape of the lake. At the lake level is a retail village. Behind this is another 16-story crescent shaped residential structure, the ground level of which is a sun sheltered pedestrian environment of shops, walkways, and parking. To the north are recreational facilities including a clubhouse. With diverse activities, care has been taken to carefully separate tourist and international commercial activities from those of the residents.

1 Site plan
2 Regional map
3 Interior rendering
4 Aerial view of model
5 View of model looking north

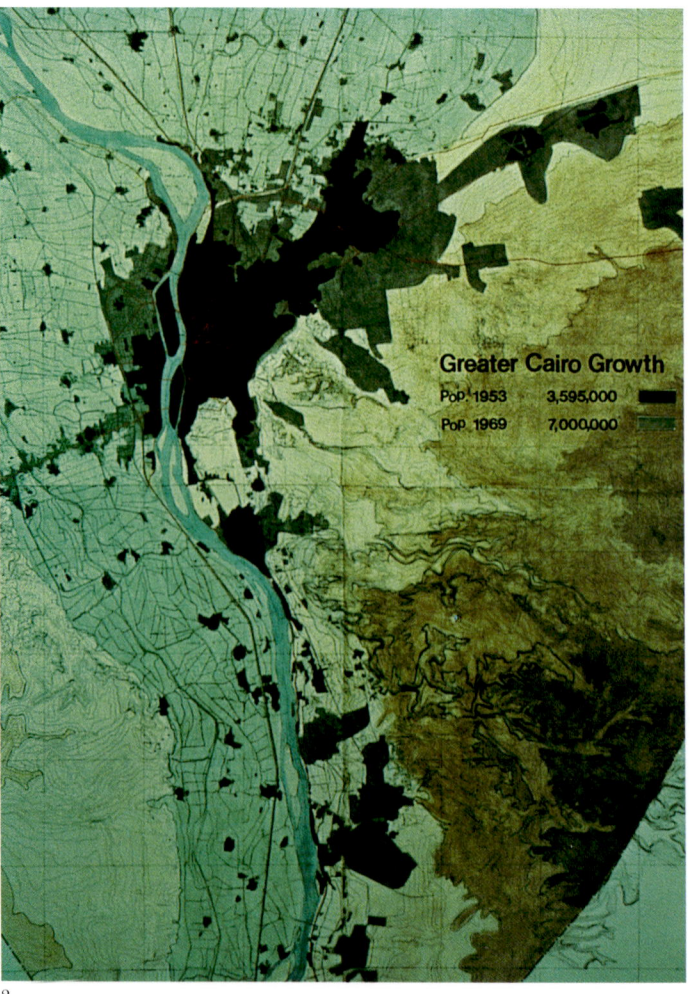

3

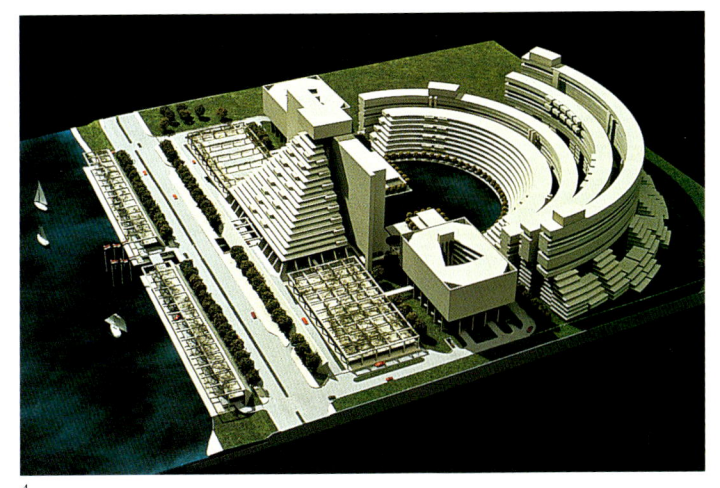

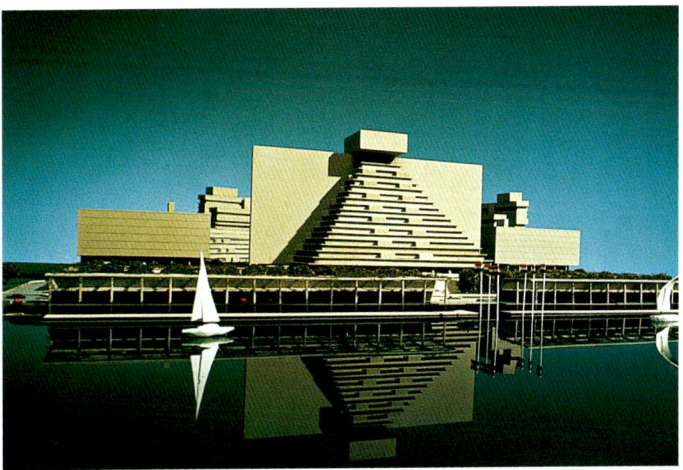

4

5

Nile Center 85

Le Meridien Hotel

Design Proposal 1991
Cairo, Egypt
Le Meridien Hotel Company
11,300 square meters
Concrete, stone, and glass

1   Aerial view of site model
2   Aerial view of model
Opposite:
   Rendering

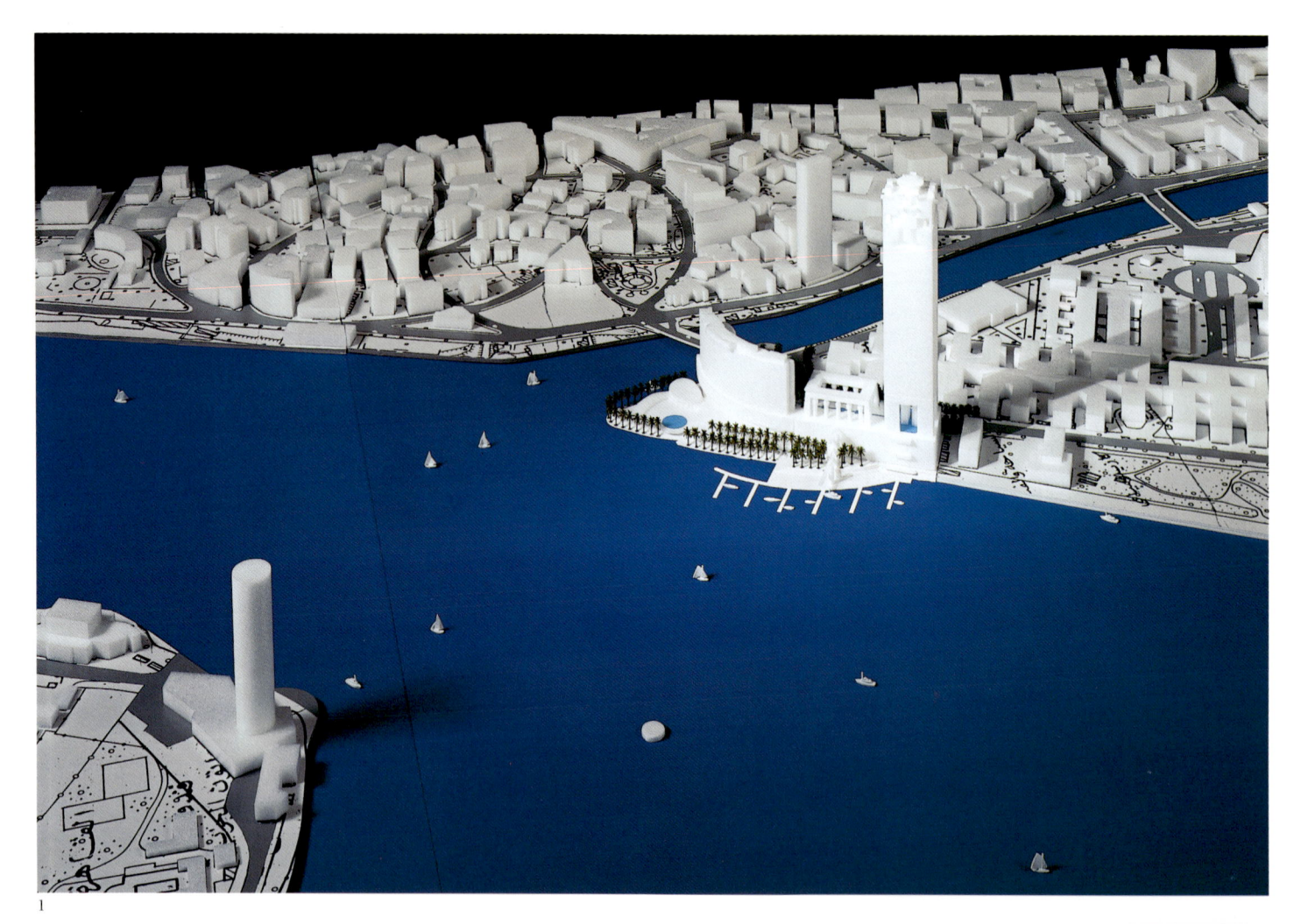

1

Situated on the bank of the Nile River, the existing low-rise Le Meridien Hotel wanted to expand their guestroom capacity and add retail amenities. The challenge was the limited amount of land available for the expansion. The design solution was the erection of a slender high-rise tower, square in plan, at the end of the existing hotel. The 700 guestrooms were accommodated in the 50-story tower with the upper floors used for penthouse suites and a restaurant and lounge with exceptional views of the river. The top of the tower was designed to provide scale to a majestic tower and recall local ancient architecture.

A carefully articulated colonnade with majestic stone columns enhanced the sense of arrival into the motor entrance.

Up-scale retail shops were added along the water's edge overlooking the Nile River and at street level along a pedestrian promenade that linked the older public space of the existing hotel to the new guestroom tower. Between the old building and the new tower, a space surrounded by columns draped with canvas sunshades provided a place for people to gather for various functions supported by magnificent views of the Nile River. The use of indigenous materials such as stone linked the old to the new and the tower's facade incorporated a sunscreen to address the strong Egyptian sun.

2

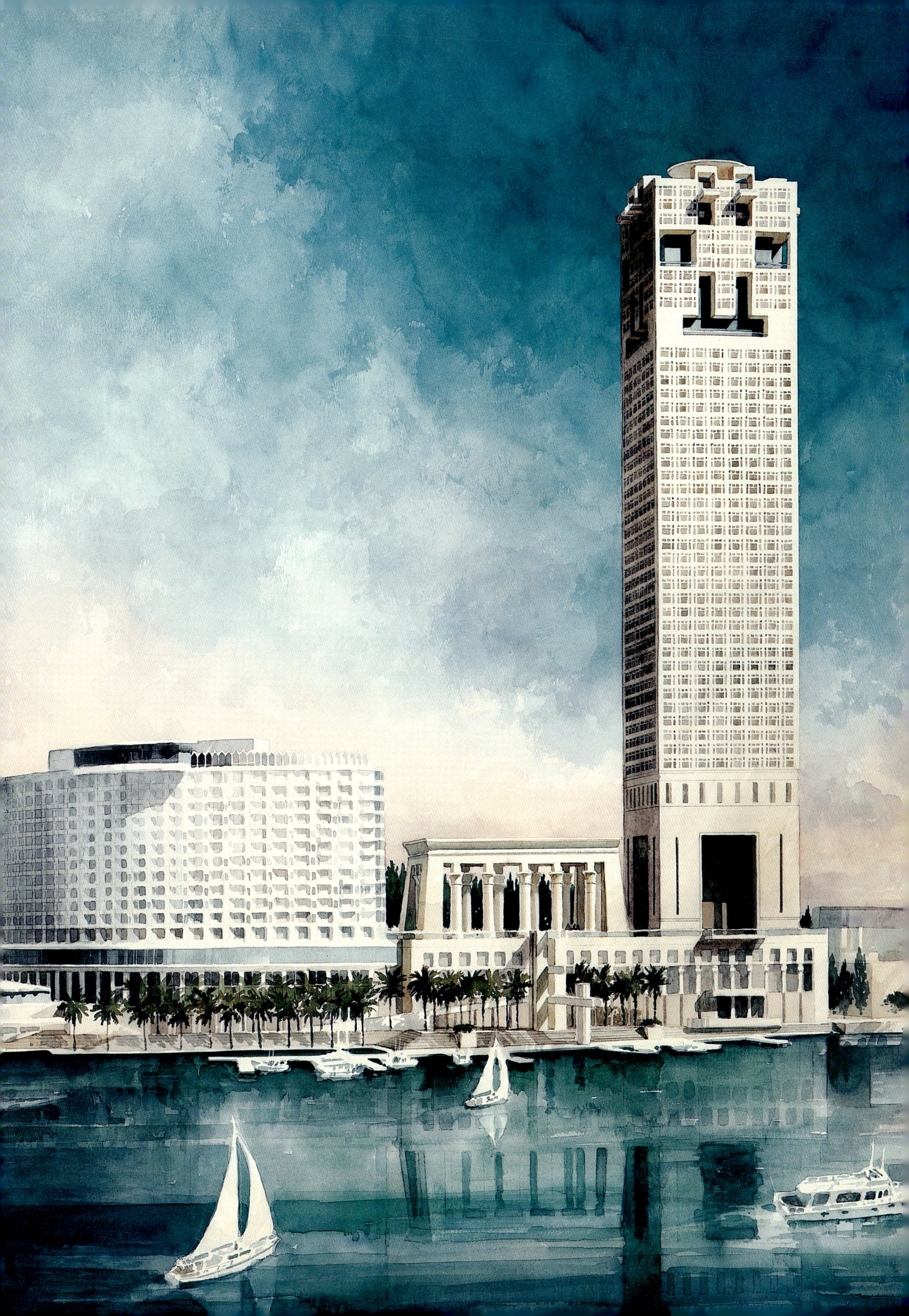

Moscow Centre

Design Proposal 1990
Moscow, Russia
Mossoviet, State Committee for Science & Technology
162,860 square meters
Stone and glass

Moscow Centre marks a change from organizing mixed-use space horizontally to stacking it vertically. It is the architect's first organization of four major functions in a single high-rise tower.

The project is comprised of a multi-use high-rise tower that includes 100 apartment units, 12,550 square meters of office space, a 550-room five-star hotel, and retail space. The site also encompasses a 210-room business hotel with health club and business center, a low-rise office building, and 50 low-rise apartment units. An 11,150-square-meter retail mall provides access to the metro system and surrounding buildings below grade and via covered pedestrian promenades.

Located in the historic Arbat District, the 60-story tower was influenced by and designed to complement the architecture of Moscow's landmark Foreign Ministry Building that is also sited along the ring road.

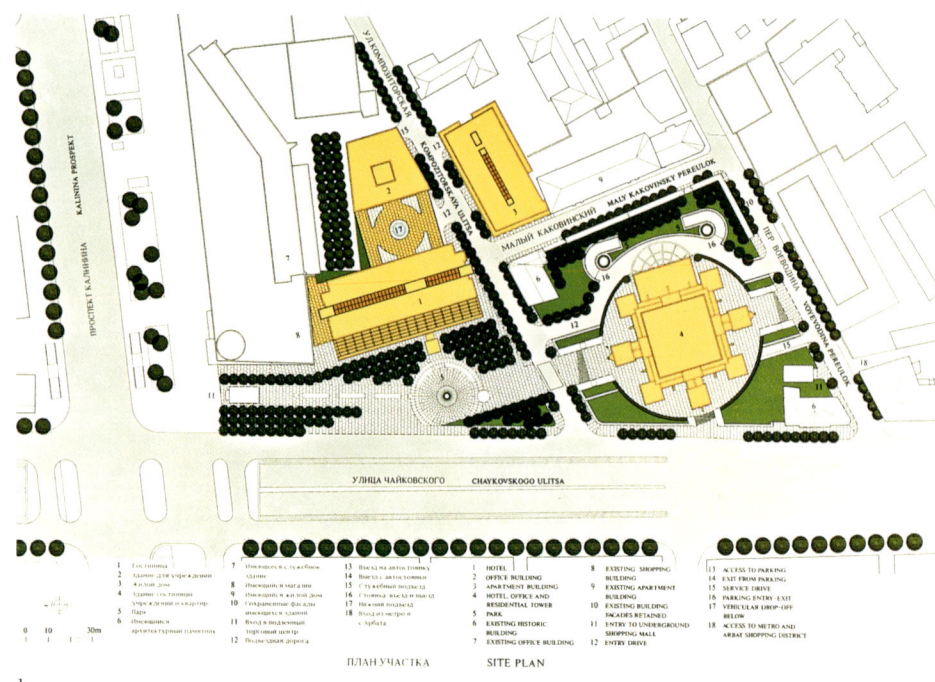

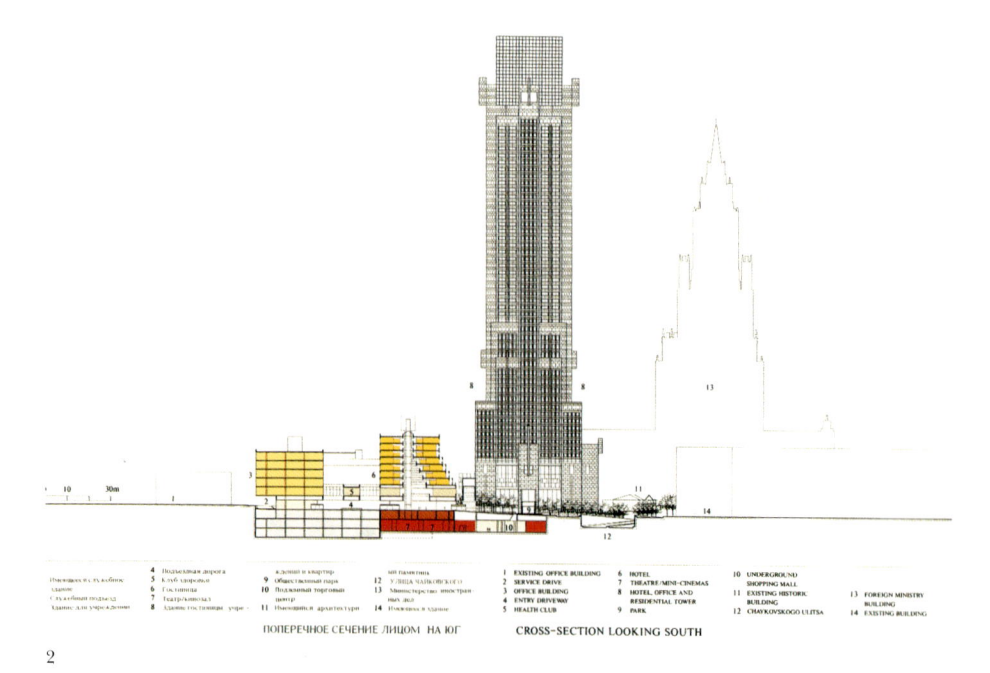

1 Site plan
2 Section looking south
3 Rendering looking south
Opposite:
   Aerial view of model

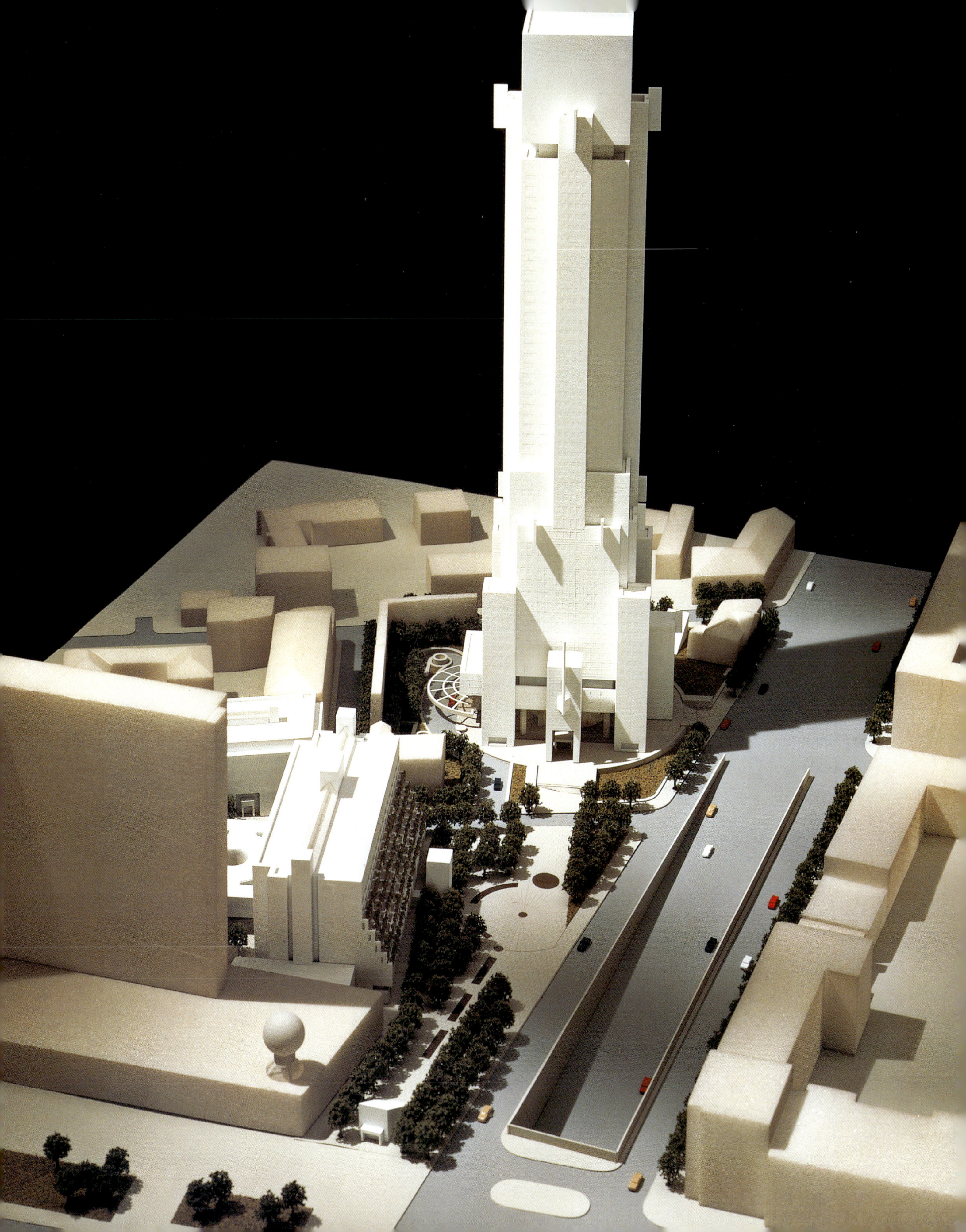

Gateway City

Design Proposal 1994
Yokohama, Japan
Mori Building Development Company
380,000 square meters
Concrete, stone, and glass

Gateway City was designed to maximize the importance of the 11-acre site that connects the train station, the convention center, and park at the water's edge. The program elements include a 50-story tower containing 239,168 square meters of office space, a 510-room hotel, 170 residential units, a three-level shopping mall, and a cultural center.

The soft undulating curves of the office tower with the composition of gateway forms were intended to complement and link the much taller office building at one end with the smaller, curvilinear convention hotel at the other. A simple, bold semi-circular form accommodates hotel guestrooms on the lower levels with the residential suites above. The hotel lobby that is housed in a dramatic glass cone at the intersection of the axis of the pedestrian circulation system linking the convention center with the other components of the project is a focal point. On either side of this axis, which is the main pedestrian component, is a three-level shopping mall comprised of a sequence of open spaces that offer opportunities for special events and public gatherings. Gateway City was designed to support the exchange of information and the enjoyment of festive activities held both day and night.

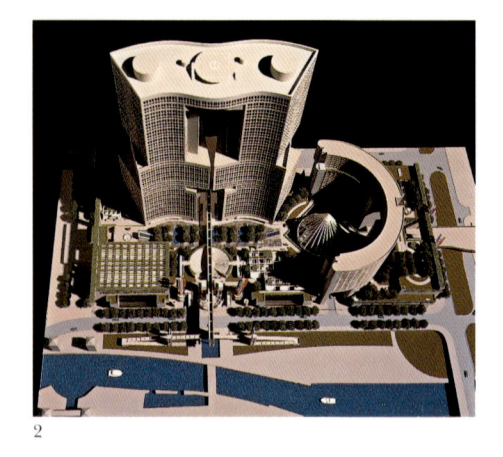

1 Ground floor plan
2 Aerial view of model
Opposite:
   View of model at night

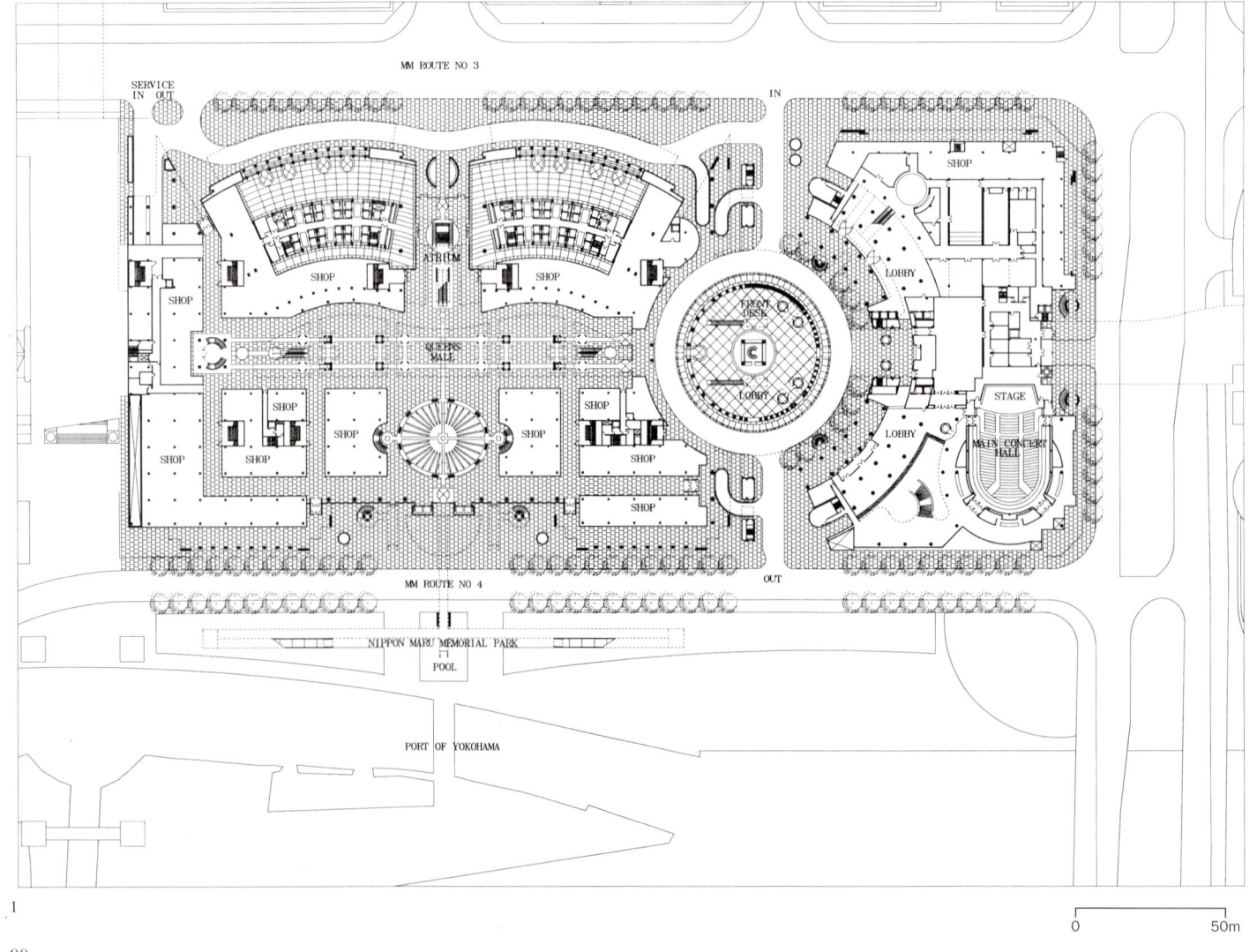

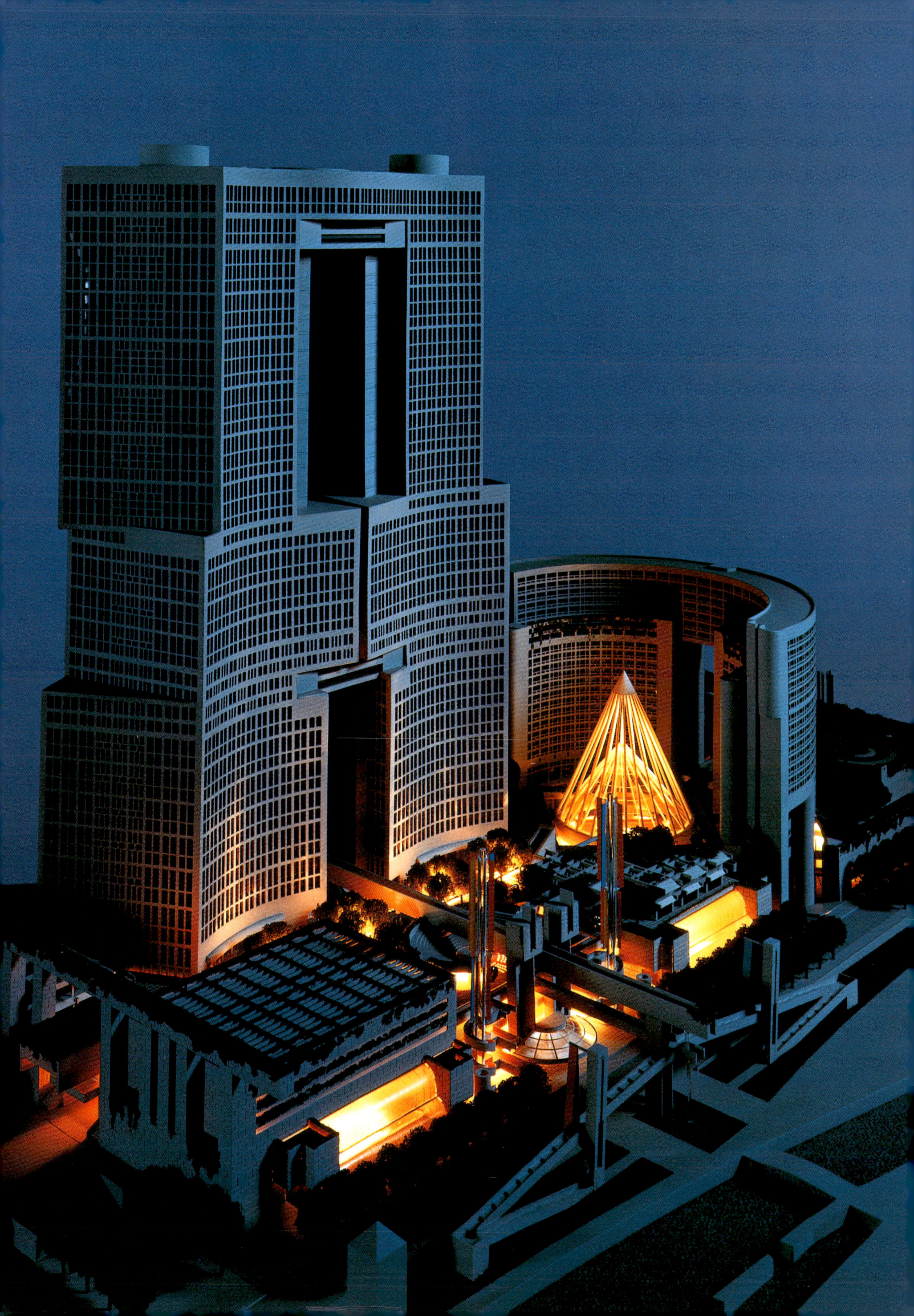

4 Rendering of pedestrian retail entry
5 Site plan
6 Section through shopping mall

4

5

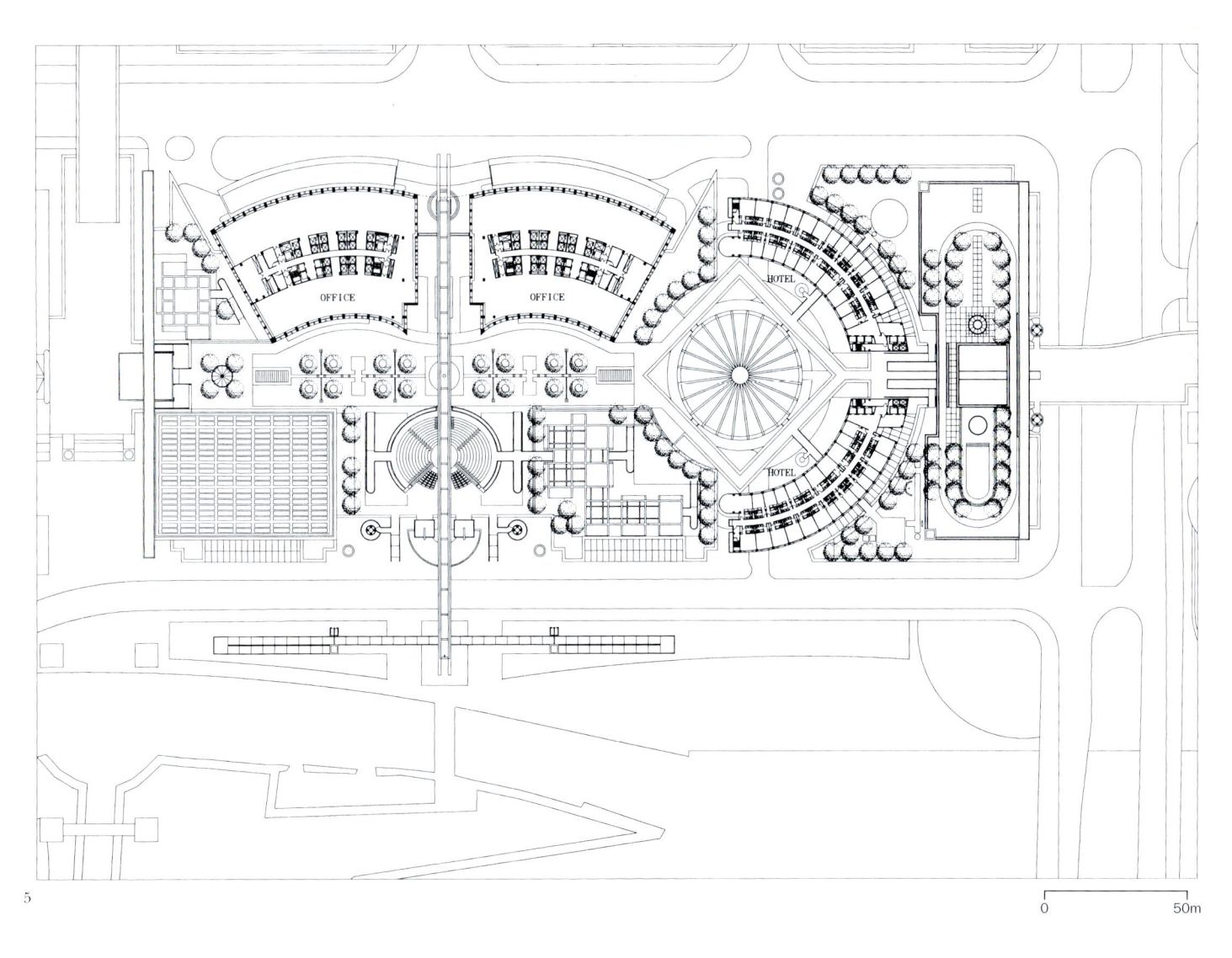

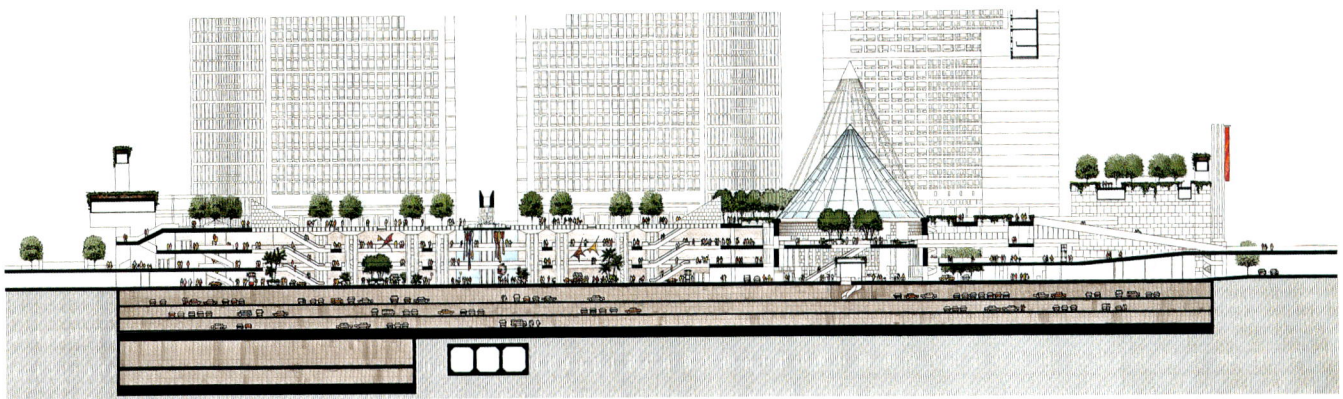

0 50m

6

Gateway City 93

Shanghai Daewoo Business Center

Design Competition 1998
Shanghai, China
Daewoo Corporation
275,500 square meters
Concrete, stone, and glass

Daewoo's proposed presence in Shanghai was to be marked by a distinctive 92-story landmark tower that was designed to symbolize the historic moment in 1992 when China opened its doors to neighboring South Korea.

The business center is comprised of five components: an office/hotel tower, department store, retail galleria, apartment tower, and pedestrian plaza. The 420-meter-tall tower provides offices on the first 61 levels with a public observation level on the 62nd. The hotel is above. The metal and glass facades rise upward in a straightforward progression that marks the functions within. The dramatic tower is square-shaped until it reaches the observation level where the plan is reduced in size and rotated 45 degrees and the corners slope inward to form large glass triangles. The rotation is repeated at the 92nd level where the tower steps in to form the pinnacle where planes of fritted glass form four large diamond shapes that encircle a 41-meter spire.

At the base the nine-story department store embodies large showcase windows that encircle the building at street level, engaging pedestrians and animating the street scene, as does the view through the glass-clad walls of the seven-level retail galleria. The 36-story apartment tower makes the transition in height from the soaring tower to the surrounding buildings. Its cylindrical form complements the square and triangular shapes that dominate the office/hotel tower and department store and echoes the curvilinear form of the retail galleria roof.

1   Section through tower
2   Site plan
Opposite:
    Aerial view of model

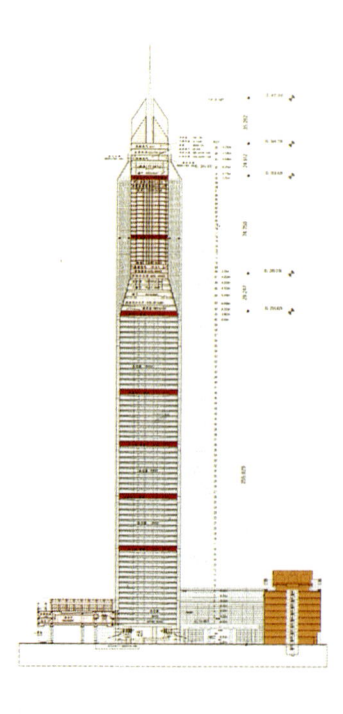

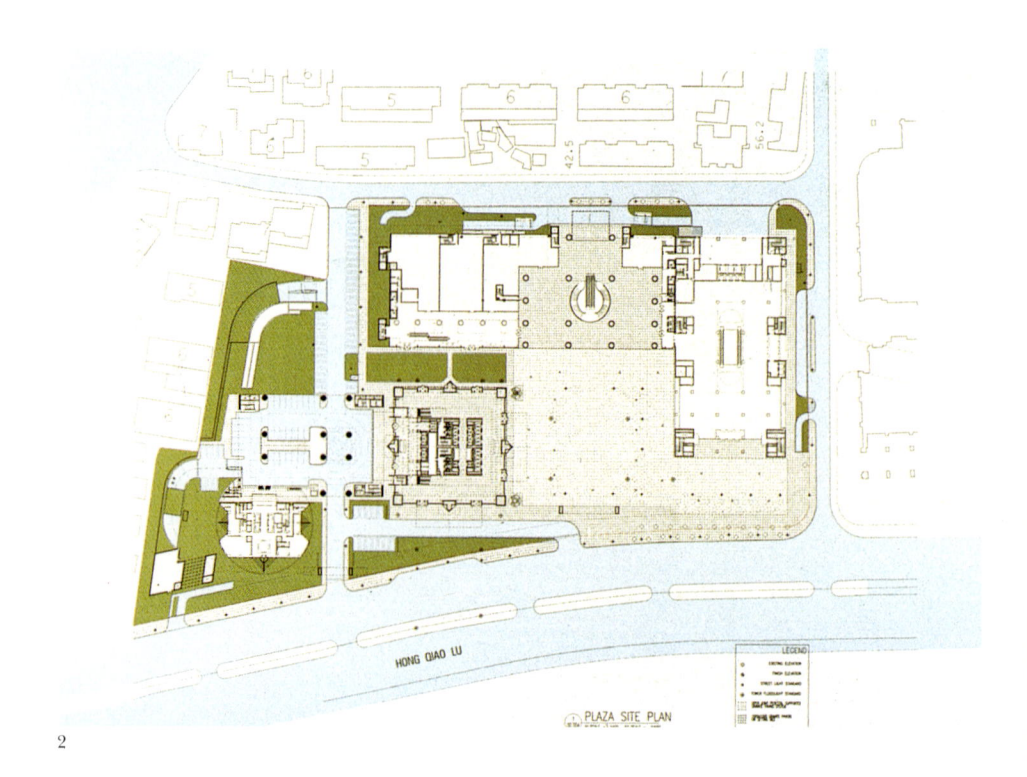

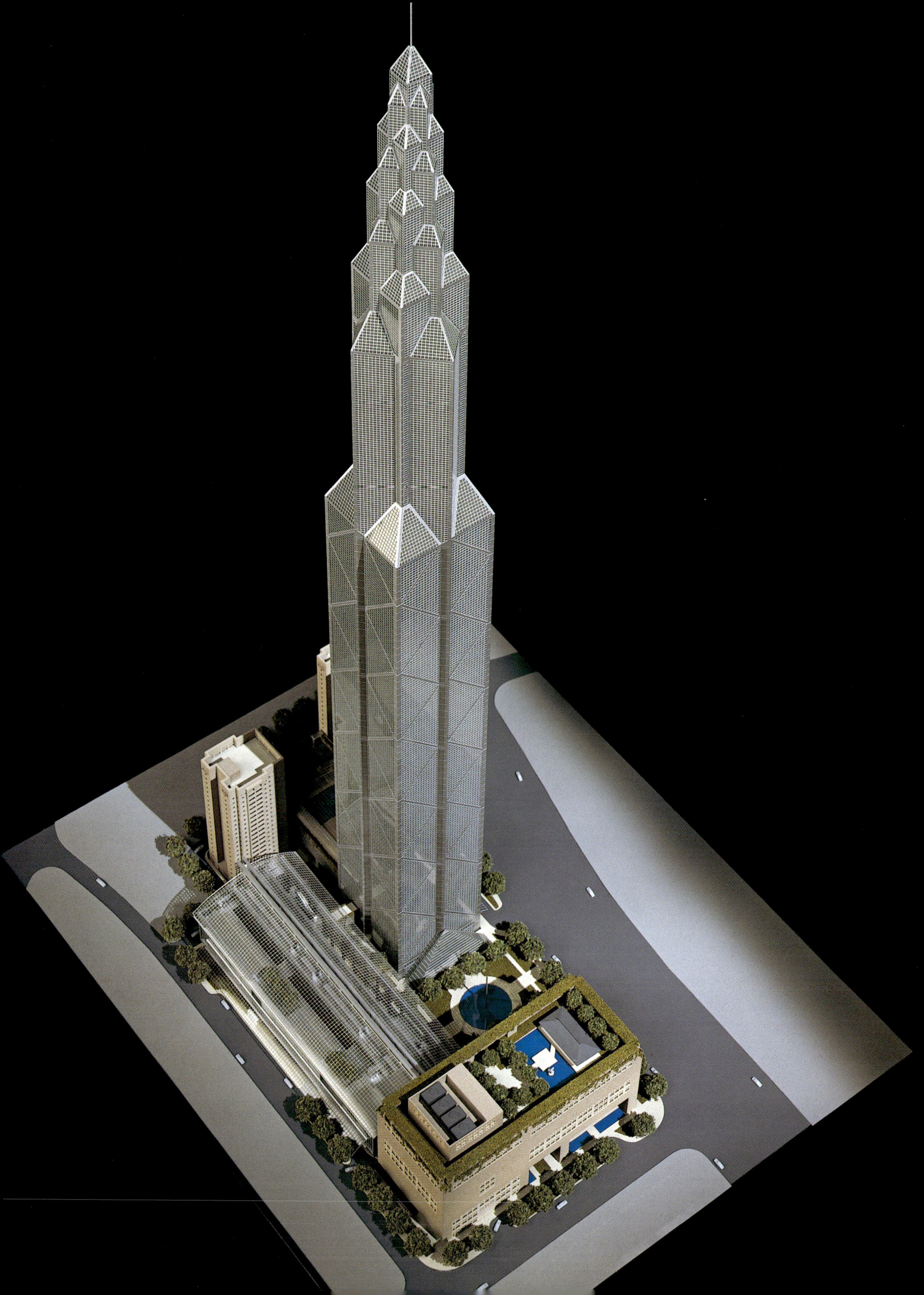

4

4 Rendering of elevation looking north
5 Rendering of plaza

5

Shanghai Daewoo Business Center 97

Chong Qing

Design Proposal 1998
Chong Qing, China
Taihong International Economic and Industrial General Company
252,000 square meters
Concrete, metal paneling, and glass

The strategic location of the 252,000 square-meter site is the North Gate area of Chong Qing Economic and Technology Development Zone. The site is planned for phased development that will begin with the construction of the 100,000-square-meter international convention center. Two hotels will be constructed near the convention center: one will be a 770-room five-star convention-oriented hotel, the other will be a 700-room three-star hotel for more economy minded travelers and/or businesspeople. A significant portion of the site is designated for retail activities, including restaurants and a variety of entertainment for all ages, that will enhance the convention use and support the large residential community on site. The 120,000 square-meters of office space will be presented as a landmark high-rise. The 250,000 square-meters of residential apartments round out the development to provide a comprehensively planned development that will be attractive to the international business community as well as to permanent residents of Chong Qing.

The convention center is comprised of three major components: the Congress Hall, the Exhibition Hall, and the Ballroom Convention Center. The overall program includes several 40-story towers, a five-story hotel, and a five-story retail and low-rise conference center that requires a long-span open area for the main Congress Hall on the top floor.

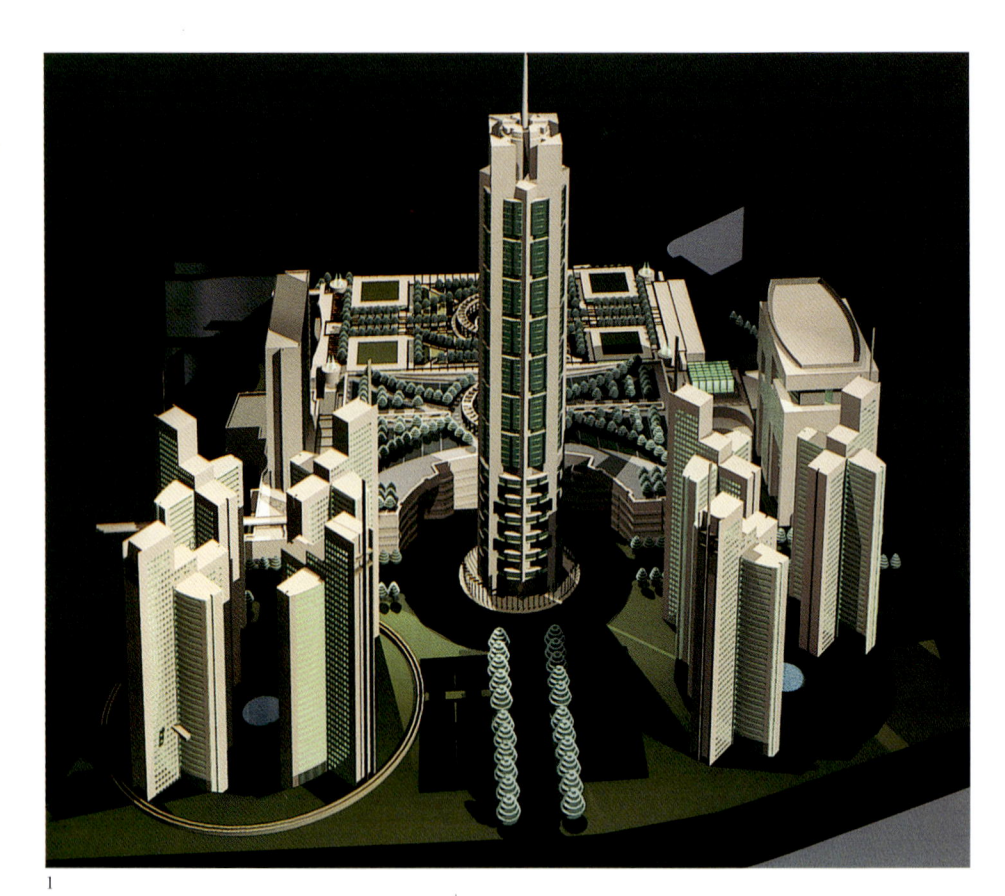

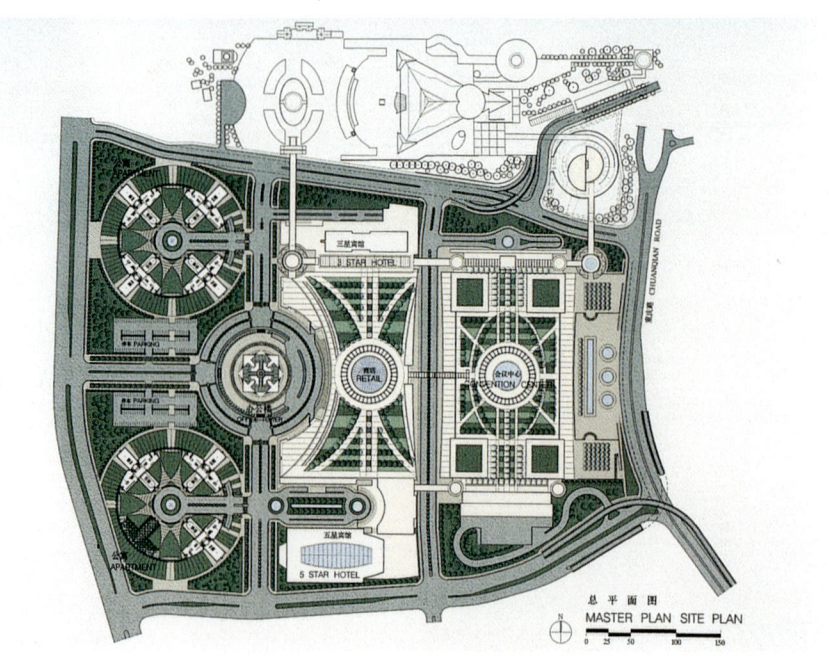

3 East Elevation
4 Building Section East-West

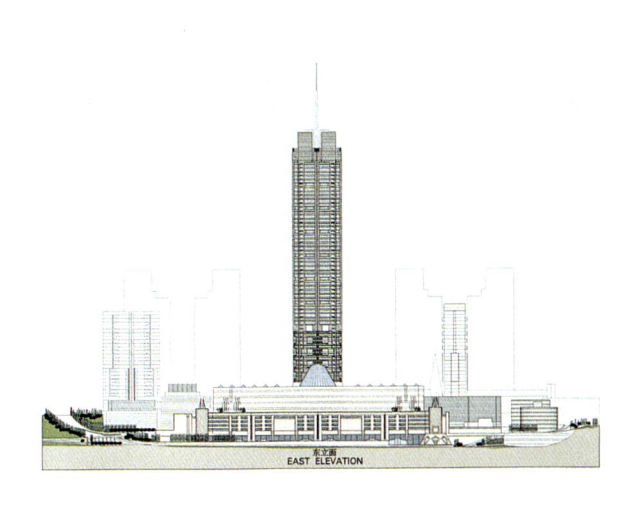

1 Aerial view of model
2 Site plan
3 Elevation
4 Section
5 Aerial view of model

Chong Qing 99

Zhong Xing City

Design Competition 1995
Shanghai, China
Shanghai Zhong Xing (Group) Company
299,500 square meters
Concrete, stone, and glass

Zhong Xing City is a comprehensive mixed-use development comprised of apartments, office, retail, cultural/entertainment, and hotel functions. The project was required to conform to the planning standards of the Ninth Five-Year Plan and to create distinctive architecture that would provide a variety of memorable and dynamic experiences for the nearly 500,000 people it serves.

Each building has unique characteristics that distinguish it from the other structures yet they are all integrated through a coherent circulation system and the use of related building systems and materials. The sense of integration is also achieved at an urban scale through the development of two major civic spaces. The first space is an area for community assembly, recreation, and shopping that is defined by the ring of apartment buildings. The second space is the plaza that is defined by the office tower, cultural center, and shopping mall.

The office tower's distinctive sculpted form maximizes building efficiency. The cultural/entertainment center is organized around a seven-level atrium that contains an occupiable sculpture that is intended to symbolize the vitality, energy, and progressive nature of the development. At ground level the atrium functions as space for exhibitions. The retail mall is organized along a seven-level vertical gallery. The 360-room hotel is comprised of three wings of different heights at the end of the mall. The curvilinear sections are organized around a central atrium that is illuminated by a large glass skylight. Throughout, the space is dynamic and people-oriented.

1

2

3

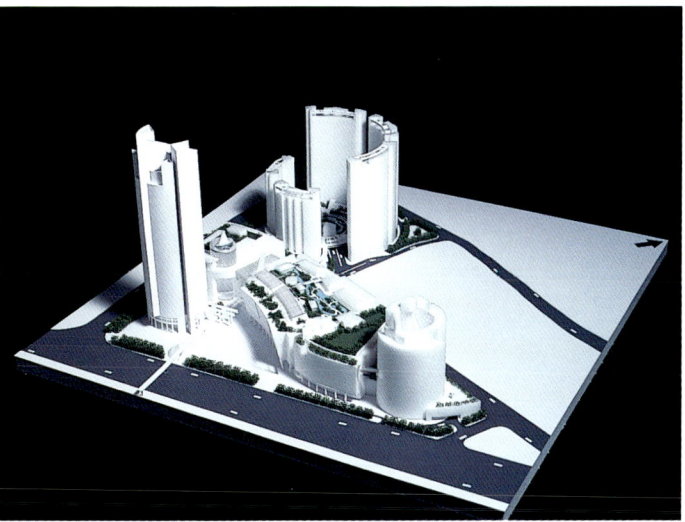

4

1 Rendering of office tower
2 Interior rendering of retail mall
3 Aerial rendering
4 Aerial view of model

Zhong Xing City 101

New Asia Center

Design Proposal 1994
Shanghai, China
Jumbo Link International Ltd.
250,000 square meters
Concrete, stone, and glass

1   Aerial rendering
2   Interior rendering of retail atrium
3   Rendering of pedestrian retail entry
Opposite:
    Aerial view of model

New Asia Center is to be located in the heart of Shanghai's premier shopping and dining district and is designed to be a comprehensive mixed-use development focusing on entertainment and retail activities. The complex is comprised of three towers arising from a podium base. The arrangement of the 39-story office tower, the low-rise retail center, and the 16-story apartment building frames the roof garden plaza level and creates a strong visual axis for the project. The axis becomes the major spine and unifying element for the five-level retail gallery. Located above the street atop the retail center is the garden level that elevates the public life of the project to a level of serene landscaping and reflecting pools.

The detailing of the major elements and vertical expressions that rise from the podium base recall the forms found in the Bund while creating a new modern style and elegance. The use of richly detailed granite panels and large windows provide the framework and character for the towers' facades. New Asia's most recognizable element and the skyline's new landmark is the tower's dome-shaped top. The dome is composed of a network of diagonal open lattice straps that are used to create the spherical form.

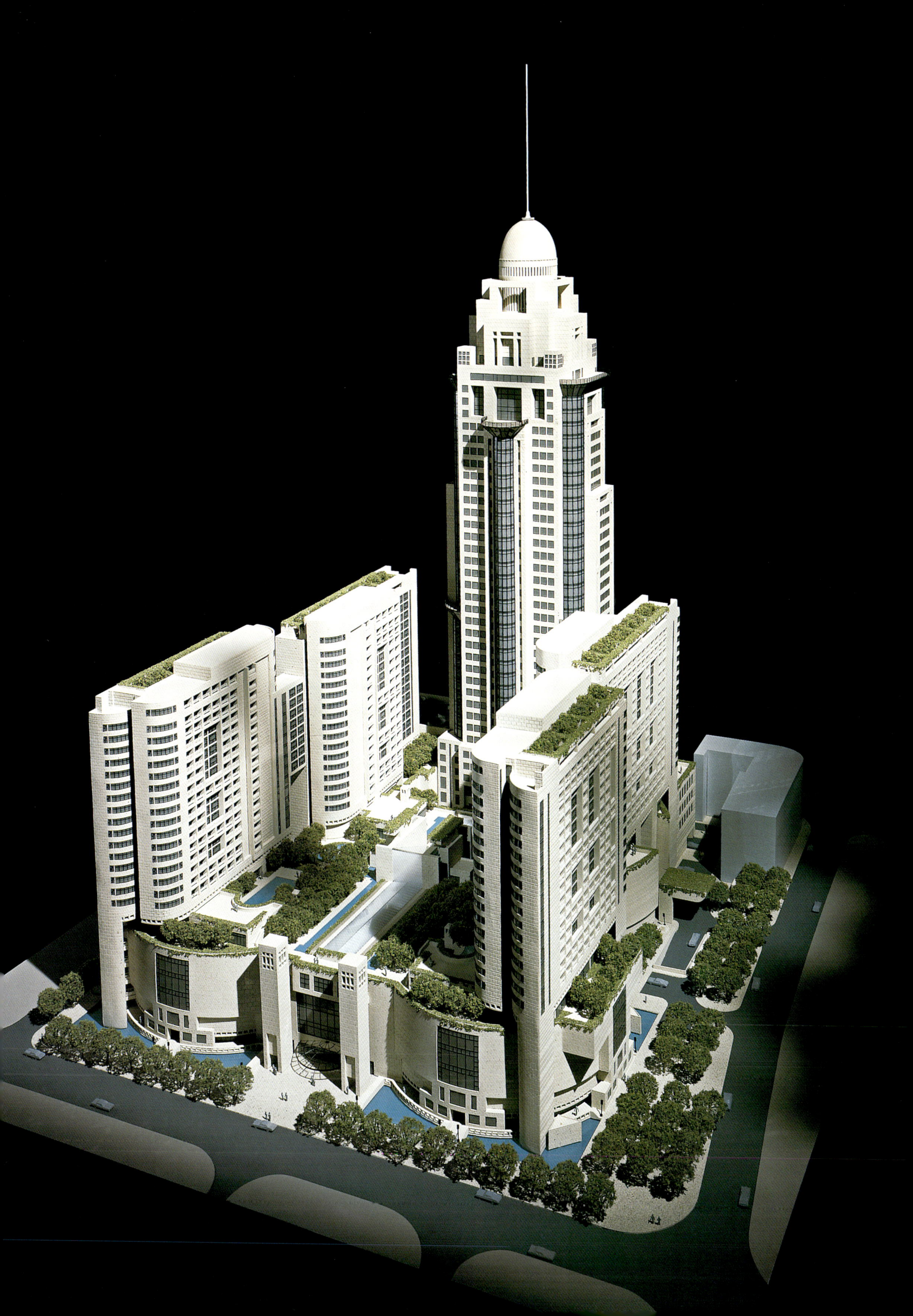

New Ci Hou Plaza

Design Competition 1998
Shanghai, China
Shanghai Real Estate Group Company Ltd.
134,000 square meters
Concrete, stone, metal paneling, and glass

Ci Hou is comprised of three interrelated buildings on a landscaped pedestrian plaza: a seven-story office building, a 42-story residential/retail complex, and a five-story retail podium located beneath a five-story club and office building. The residential/retail tower is the focal point of the complex. The slender tower appears to be suspended above the retail podium. Its curving north facade on Nanjing Road contrasts with the dramatic recessed facade on the south. The sleek glass and metal facade on the north is richly lighted so that the building radiates as a unique flowing backdrop for the sophisticated urban lifestyle along Nanjing Road. The semi-circular form of the office building echoes the curving form of the tower.

Geometric, sculptural form shapes the complex. At the edge of Nanjing Road, a large granite portal marks the entrance to the retail mall and echoes the geometry of the tower glowing behind it. The retail podium adjoins the residential tower, unified beneath the skylight of a spectacular semi-circular atrium. The office and club appear to be majestically suspended above the landscaped rooftop plaza of the retail podium. The curved facade of the building is penetrated above the main entrance to fully reveal the unique glow of the tower beyond.

1 Site plan
Opposite:
   Rendering of west elevation

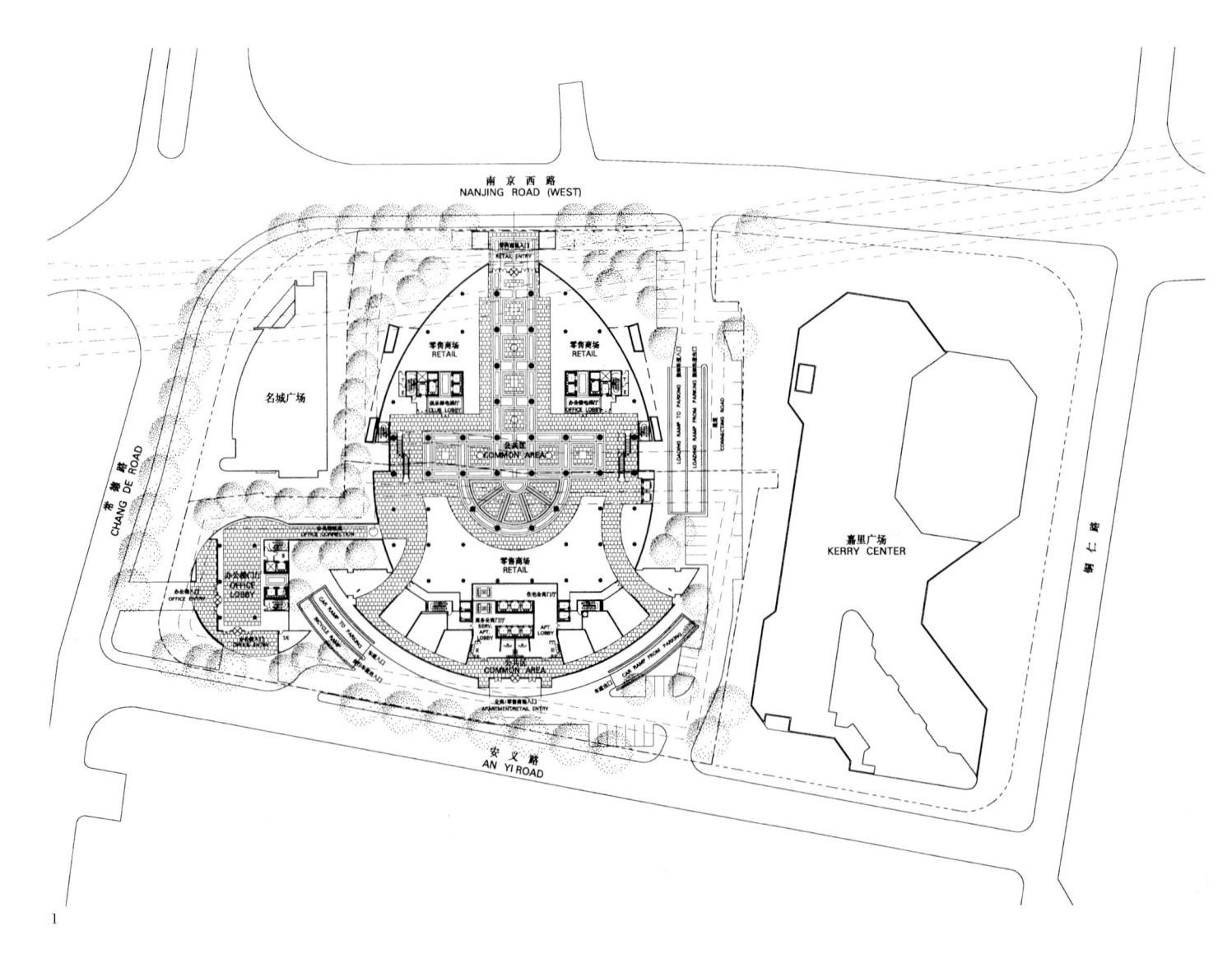

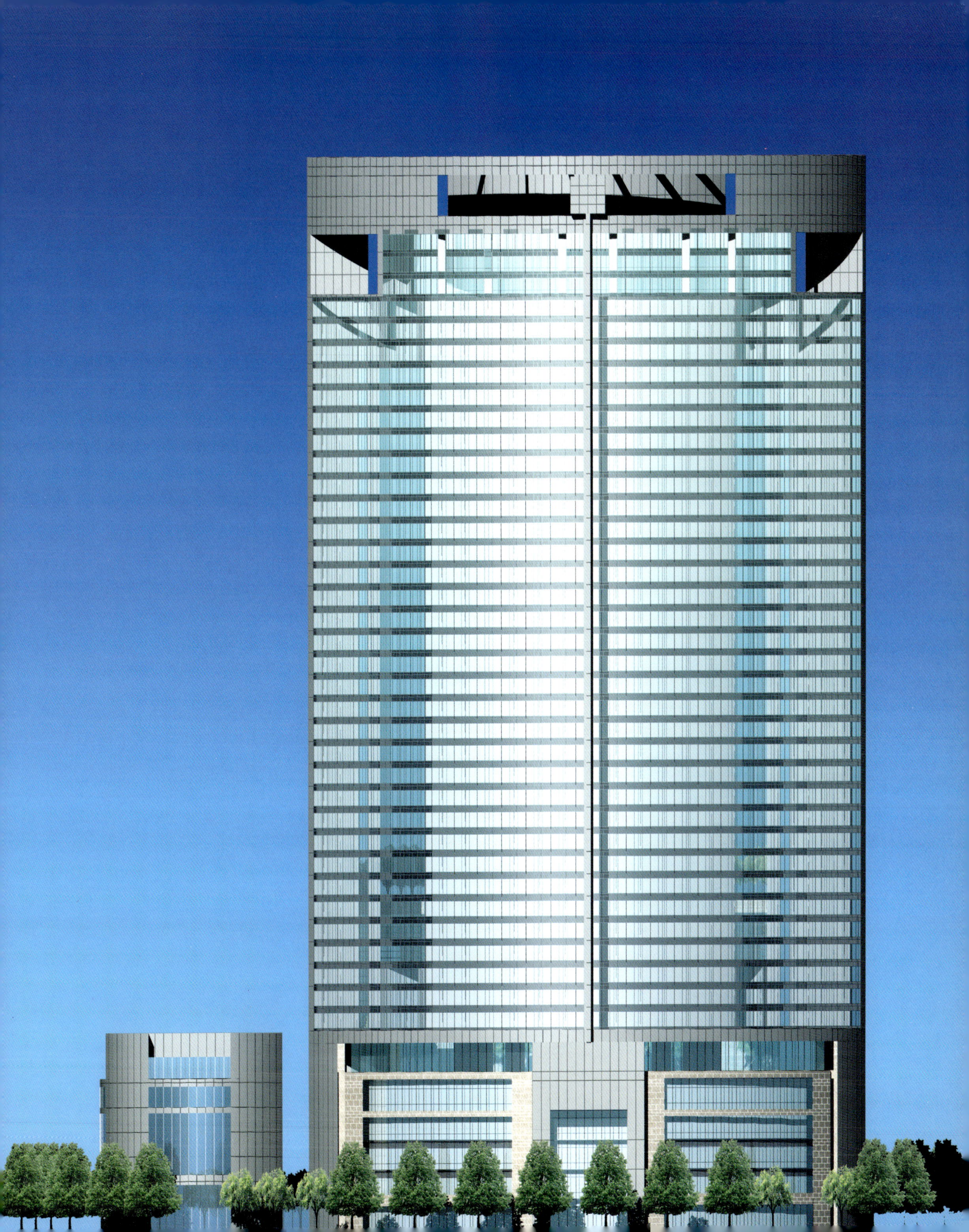

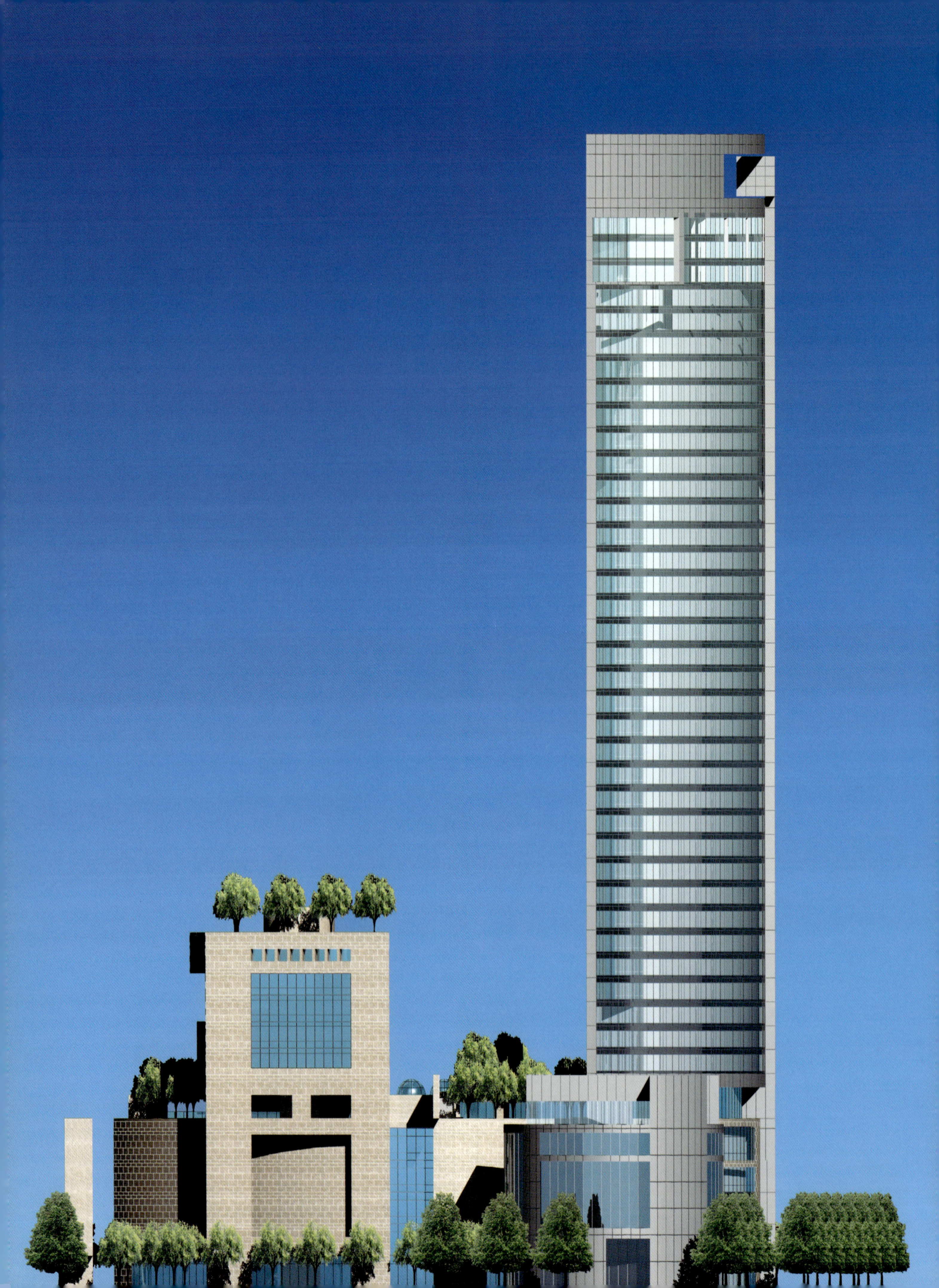

Opposite:
Rendering of south elevation
4   Section
5   Interior rendering of retail atrium
6   Rendering of tower in daytime
7   Rendering of tower at night

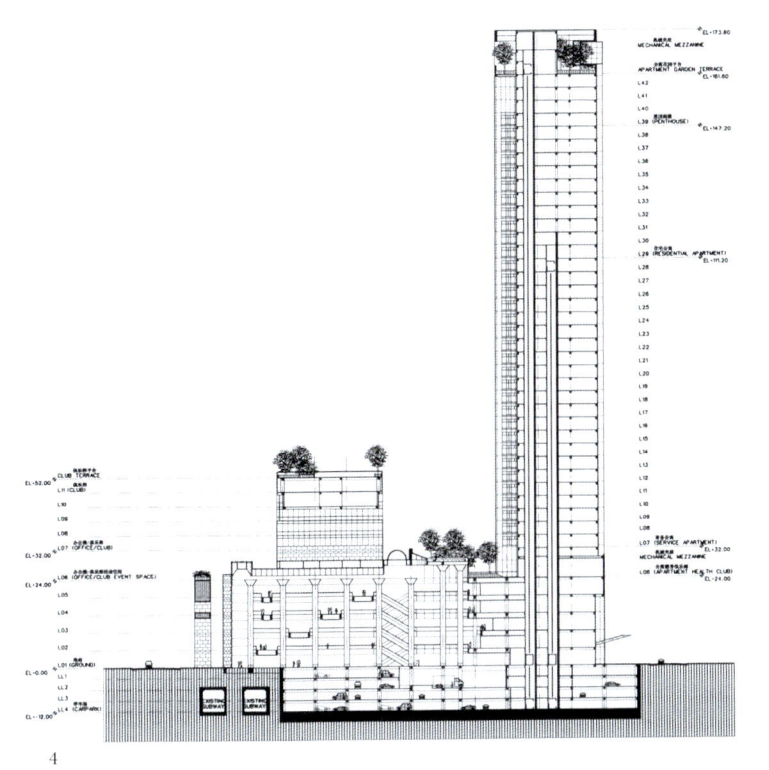

New Ci Hou Plaza   107

Silver Tie World Trade Center

Design/Completion 2001-2002/2005
Beijing, China
China Silver Tie Holdings Ltd.
330,000 square meters
Concrete, stone, and glass

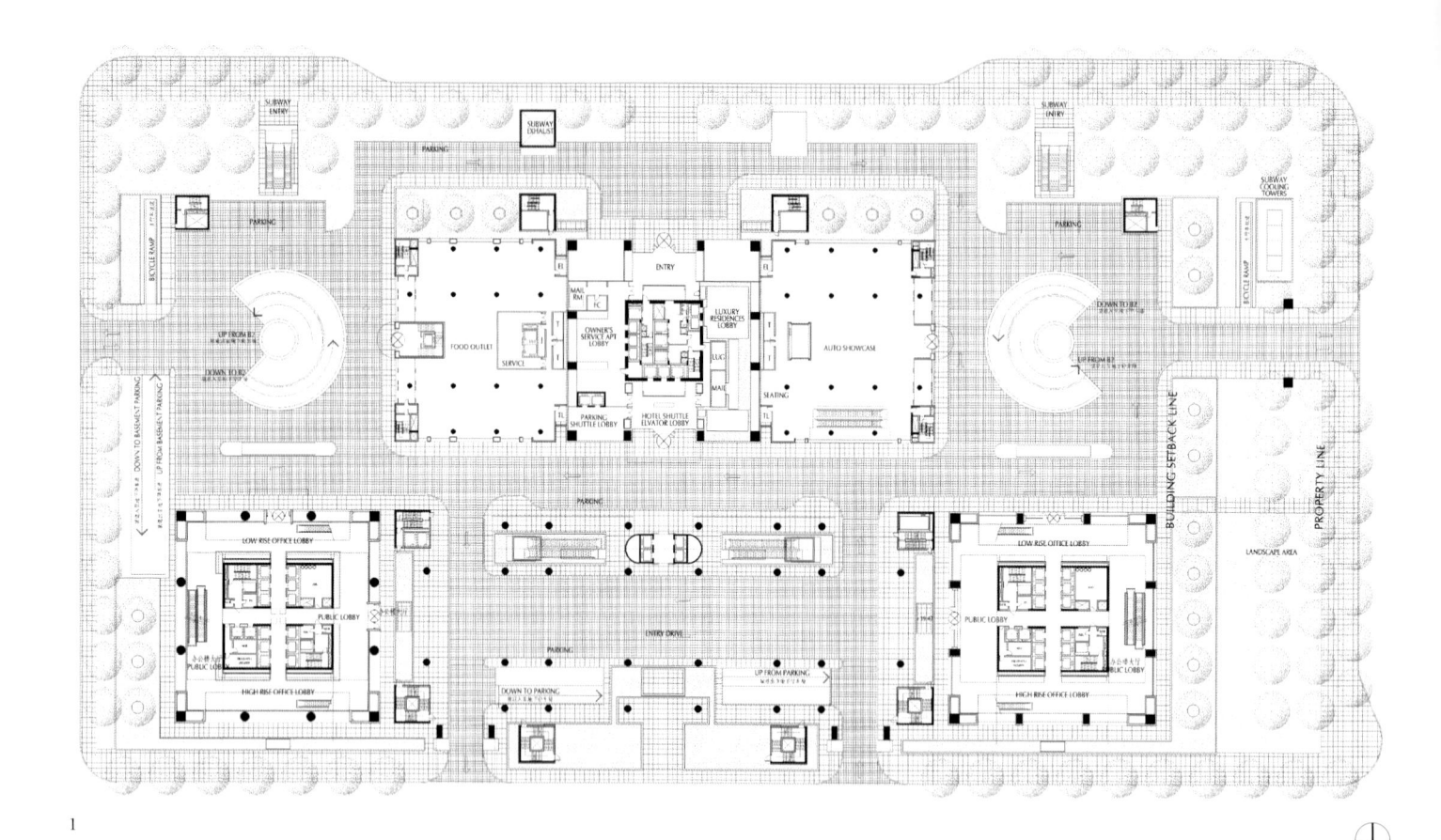

The Silver Tie World Trade Center is a comprehensive mixed-use complex that rises clearly on the Beijing skyline from a water garden park at its base. The three towers are square in form and are studies in simple, straightforward design. The two 45-story twin office towers that flank the 62-story hotel tower echo the hotel's geometry with a variation of their own. Within the hotel tower are 550 guestrooms and 150 luxury serviced apartments. Atop the tower is a large cube that recalls a Chinese lantern. By day the cube acts as a symbol of ancient Chinese architecture, and by night it shines as a beacon marking the site.

At the base a large podium connects the three towers, providing lobbies, meeting facilities, shops, and restaurants. The lushly landscaped roof of the podium expands the gardens at street level to form a multi-level urban park. The extensive use of water features is unique to the site, separating it from the congestion of the surrounding roadways. Motor access to the site is via a large monumental space under the podium that is planned to give each tower its own sense of grand entry. The office towers are each divided into two components that can essentially serve as four separate office buildings, each with its own lobby and sky lobby. The complex's human-scale gardens and water features, and its architectural details that recall ancient Chinese architecture in a contemporary way, enhance the lifestyle of people working and living in Beijing.

1 Site plan
Opposite:
   Aerial rendering

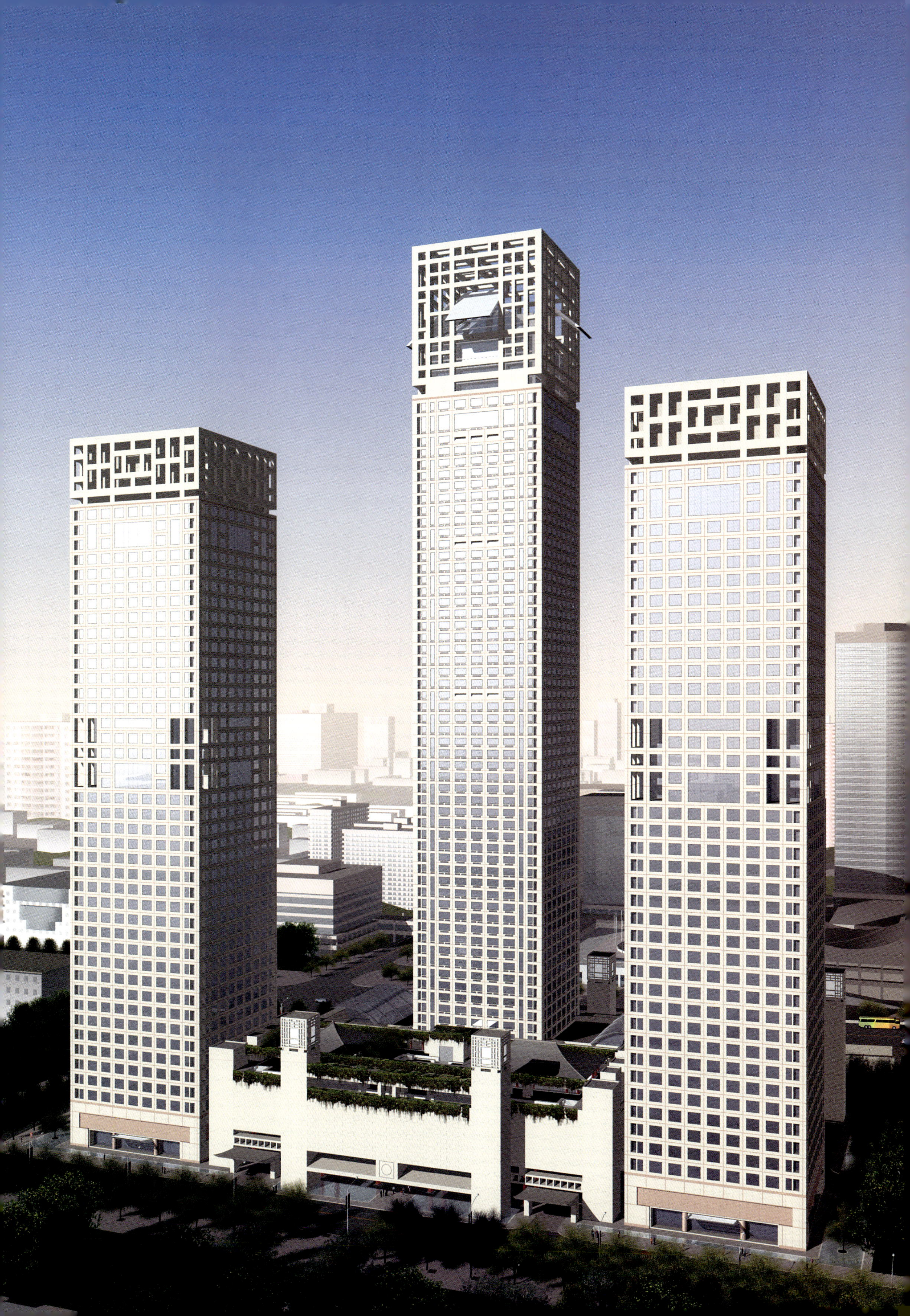

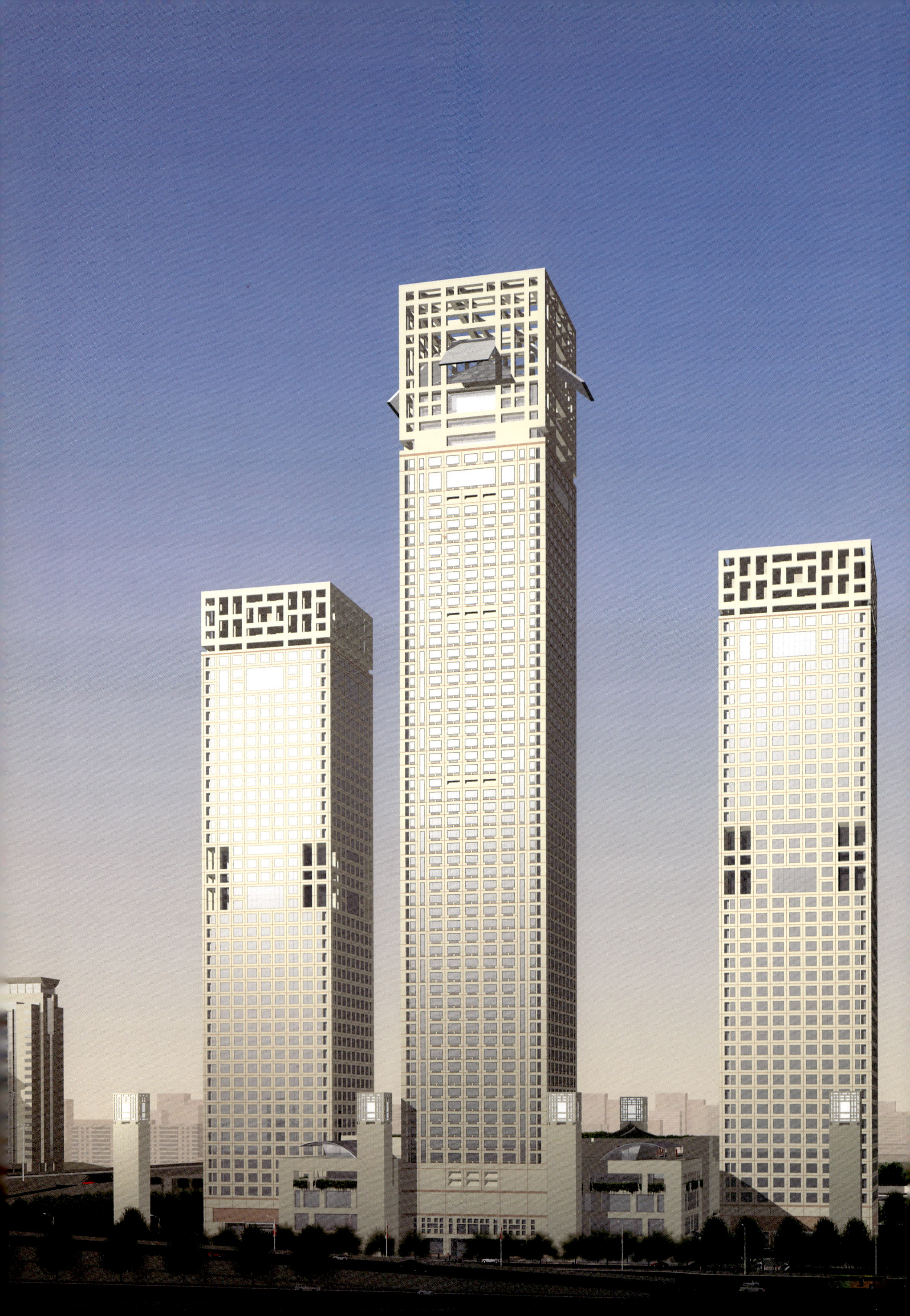

Opposite:
Rendering looking north
4   Rendering looking south
5   Section through office towers

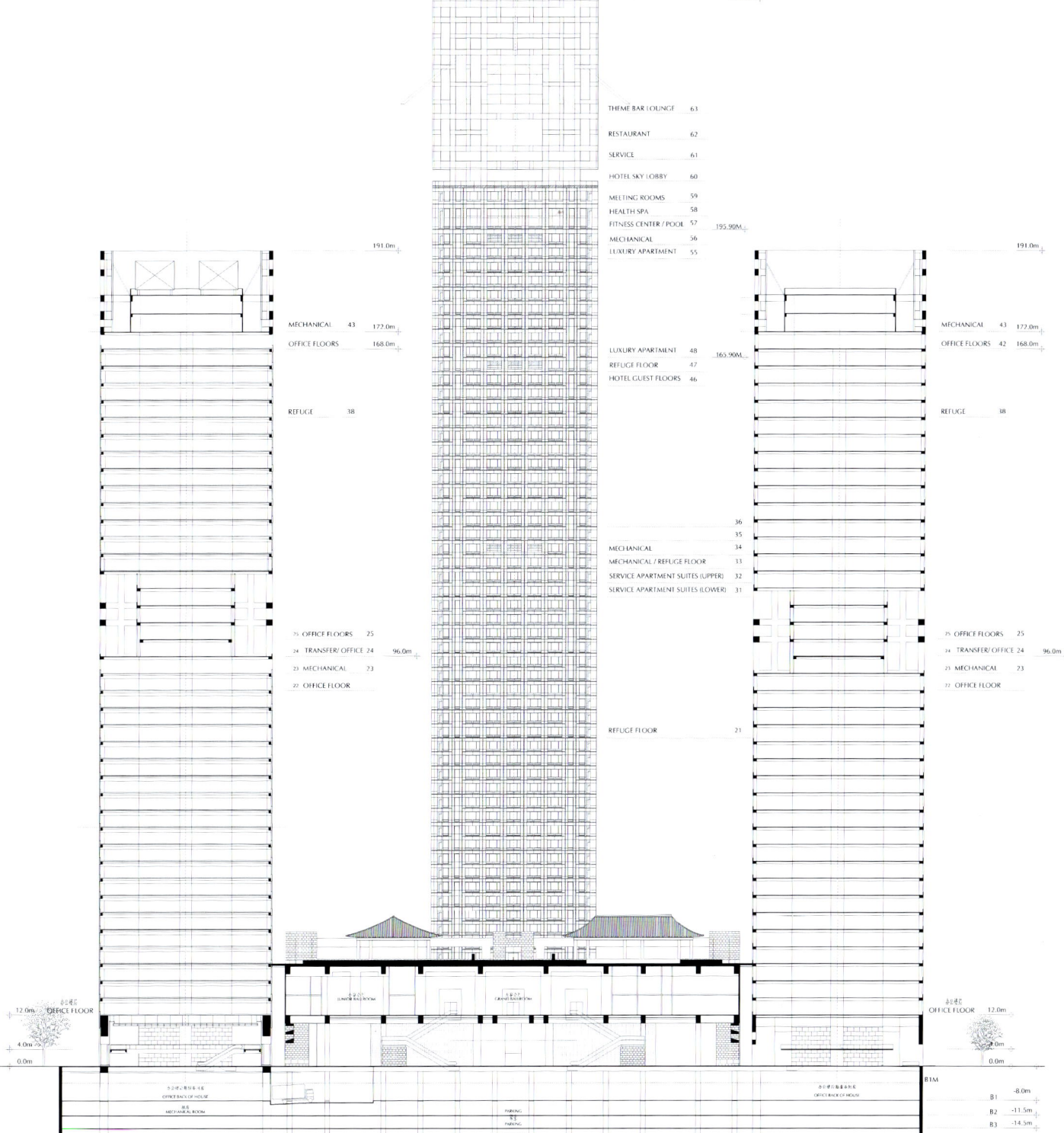

Silver Tie World Trade Center   111

Shanghai Art Center

Design Proposal 2001
Shanghai, China
Shanghai Municipal Government
120,000 square meters
Concrete, stone, and glass

The proposed Shanghai Art Center integrates cultural enrichment with the beauty of nature. The plan for the full-block site composes the building components within a lush urban park. The center provides multiple venues within interconnected structures that enable a wide variety of performances to occur simultaneously without impinging on each other. The four primary building components are: a 3,000-seat theater with flexible seating that can accommodate performances or assemblies, a 2,400-seat classical theater that is acoustically designed for music, a 500-seat experimental theater, and an open-air amphitheater. Below ground is a complex of amenities that includes four cinemas, four restaurants, retail shops, and exhibition space for daily use, not only for the cultural activities at the park level but also for the community at large. In addition, specific areas, such as the exhibition hall, are linked to the theaters above to increase the flexibility of their use for conferences.

The project's central park space is the site for a large glass cone that covers the amphitheater, providing shelter and light by day and glowing like a jewel at night. The theater buildings face and flank the park and cone. Their glass-walled lobbies overlook the garden surrounding the cone, allowing for the opportunity to be seen from outside and for the park to be enjoyed by all.

1 Site plan
2 Section through amphitheater
3 Aerial rendering

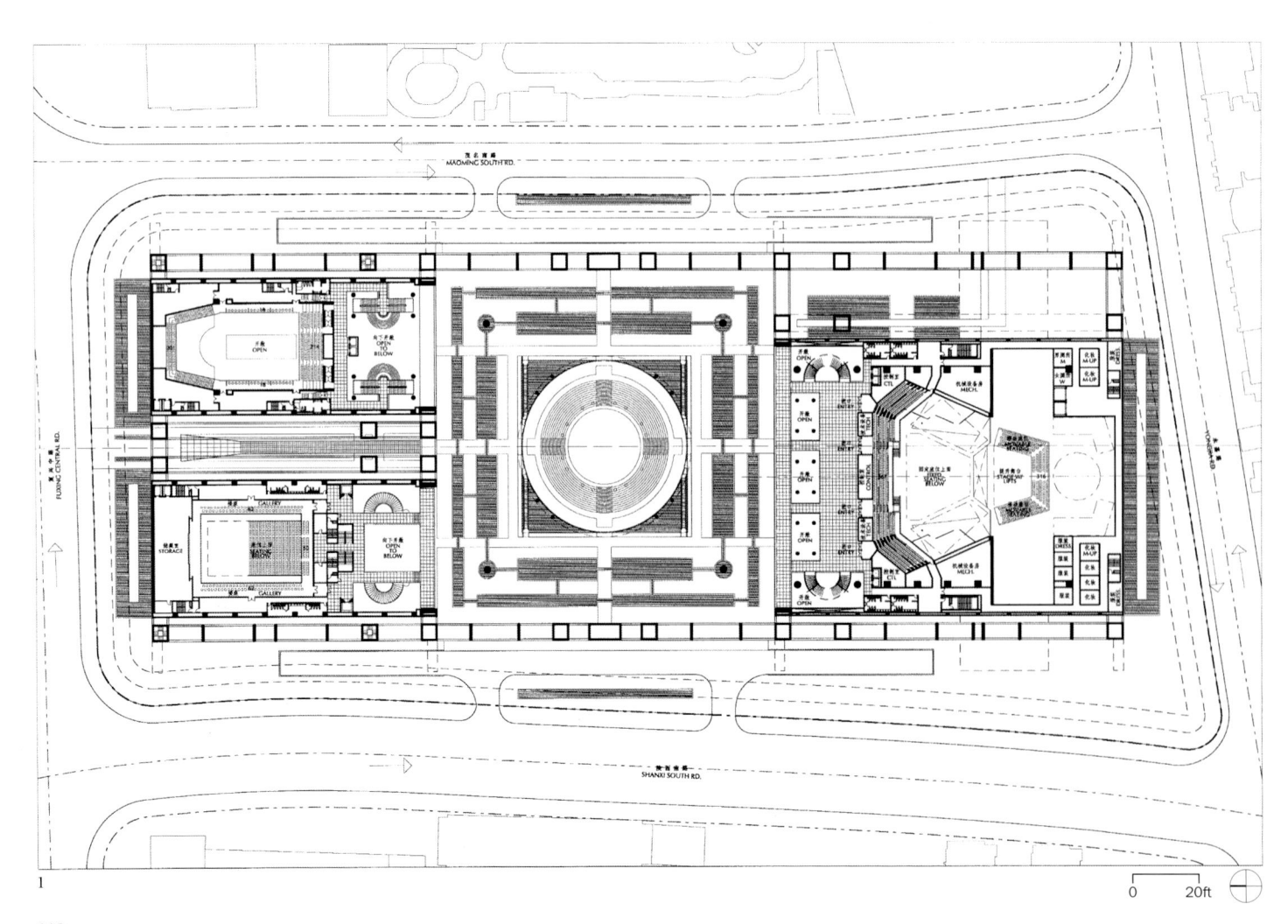

1

Shanghai Art Center 113

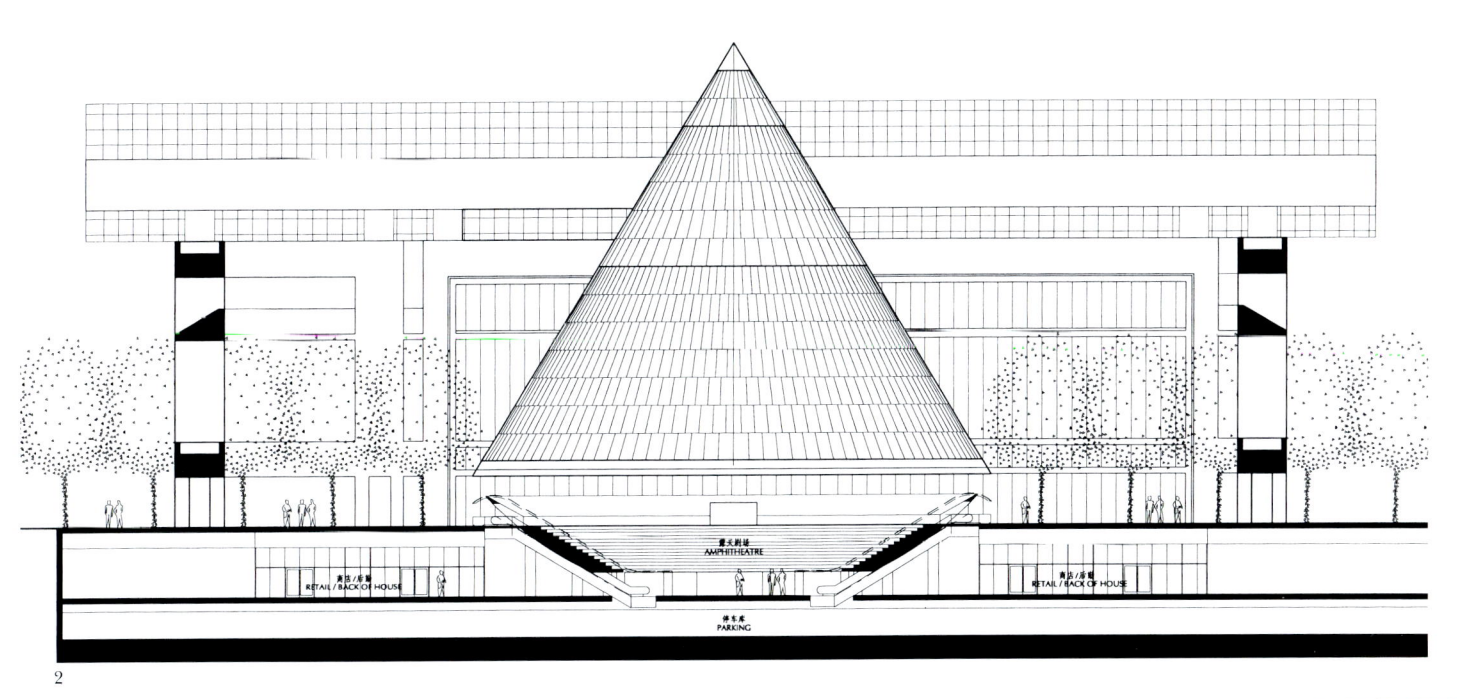

4

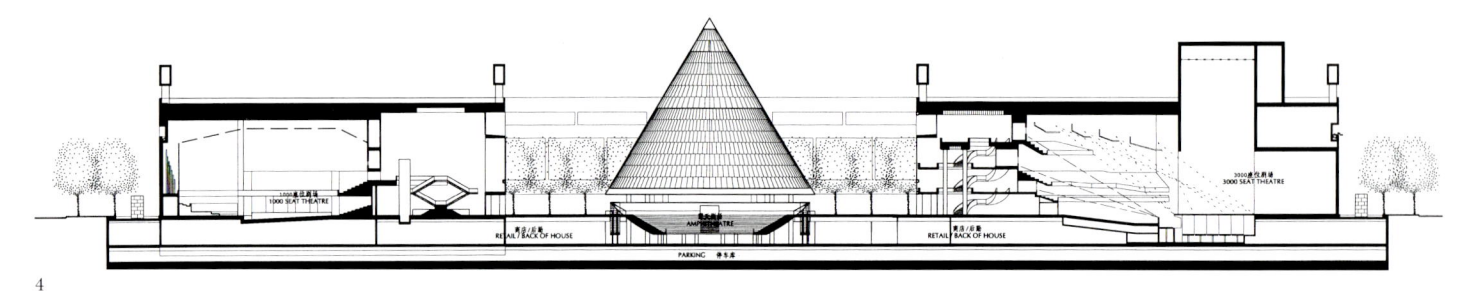

5

6

4   Section through theaters
5   Rendering of east elevation
6   Rendering of amphitheater at night
7   Rendering of north elevation
8   Rendering of amphitheater looking east

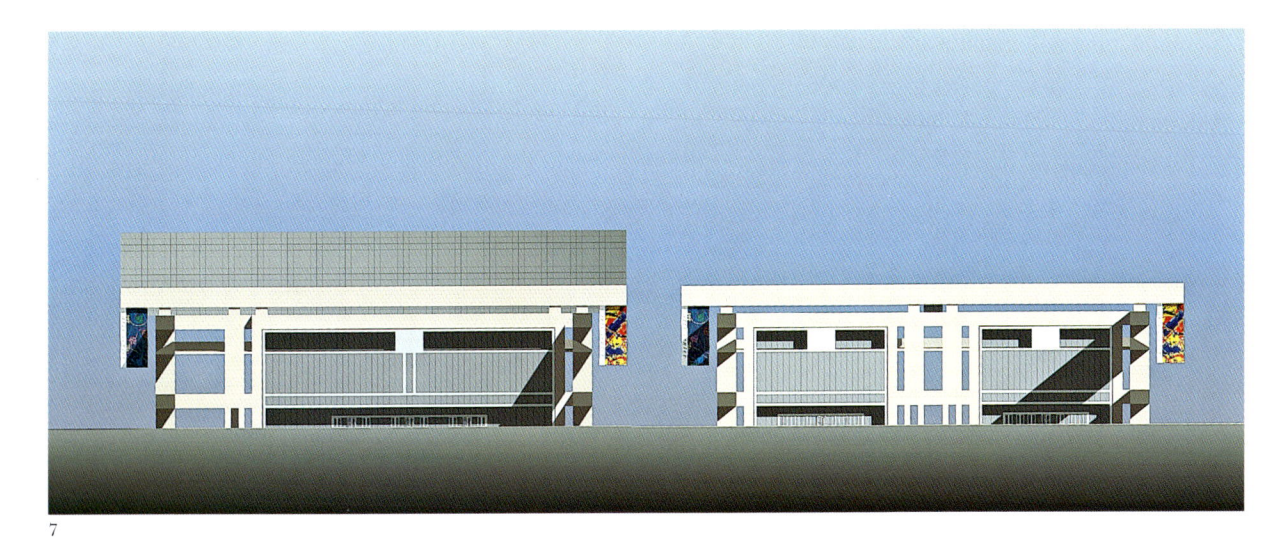

7

8

Shanghai Art Center   115

Facilities for the Airport Terminal Complex—Jing An

Design Proposal 2001
Shanghai, China
Jing An District Government
46,000 square meters
Concrete, stone, metal paneling, and glass

The site of the Jing An Hotel adjoins a variety of low and mid-rise buildings with a limited presence directly at the street's edge, although it makes an important connection with the city's air terminal building that takes passengers to and from the airport. The design challenge was to provide a hotel that would not overpower the neighboring buildings yet had a distinctive presence as it is seen rising from behind some of the neighboring structures.

The building's form is elliptical. The graceful curving facades complement the many angles of the neighboring buildings. To give scale to the mass of the structure and to provide it with a distinctive form, the building steps back at three intervals on the north and south facades, six stories at a time, with two intervening stories between each step back forming large balcony gardens on each side. The lines of the vertical supports for the balconies further reduce the scale. The elliptical shape of the roof crowns the building, opening the space above to skylights for a restaurant at the top of the building. The floors that do not step back provide larger hotel suites for guests conducting business from this prime Shanghai location.

1 Site plan
2 Skyward view of tower
Opposite:
  Aerial rendering looking south

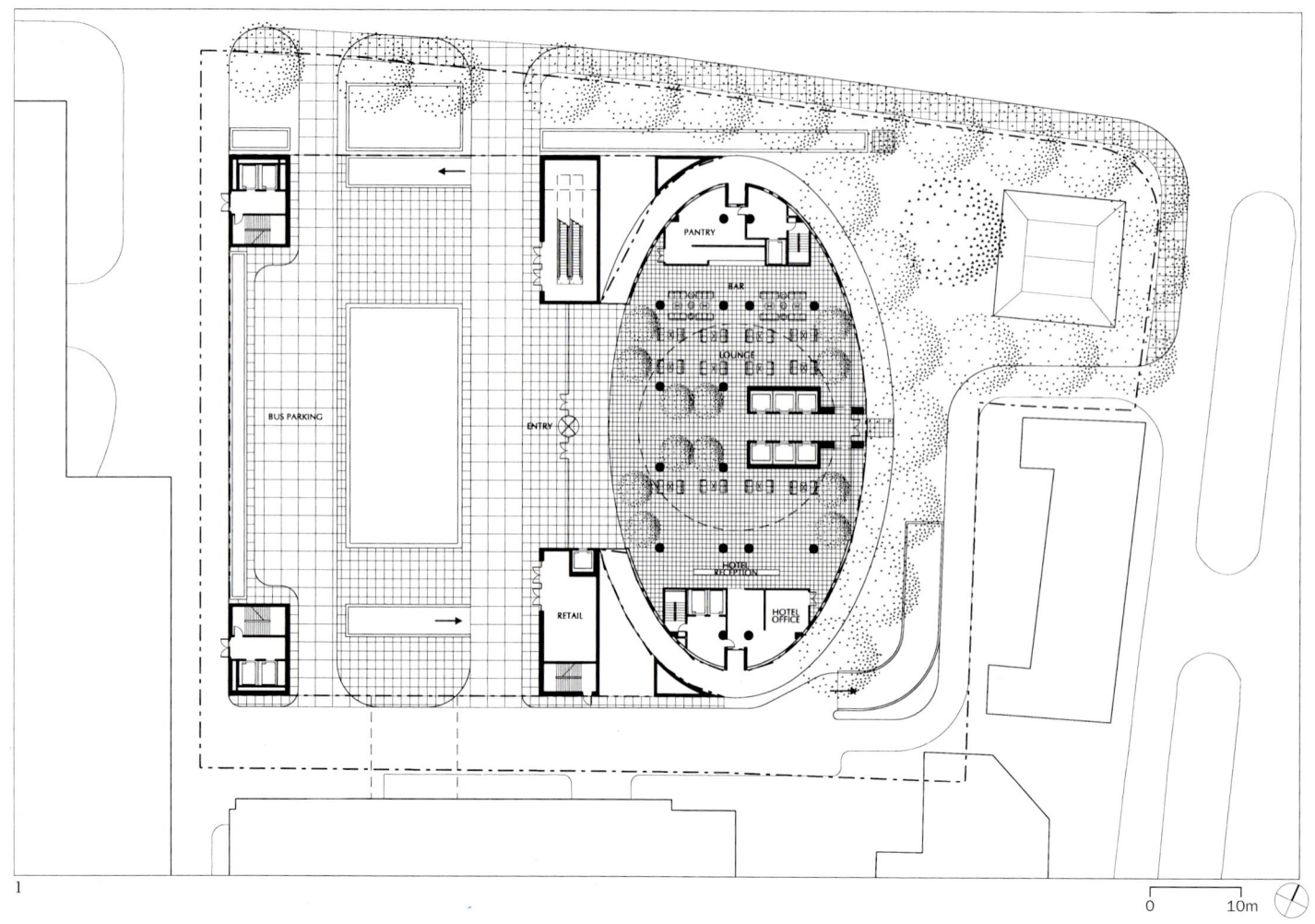

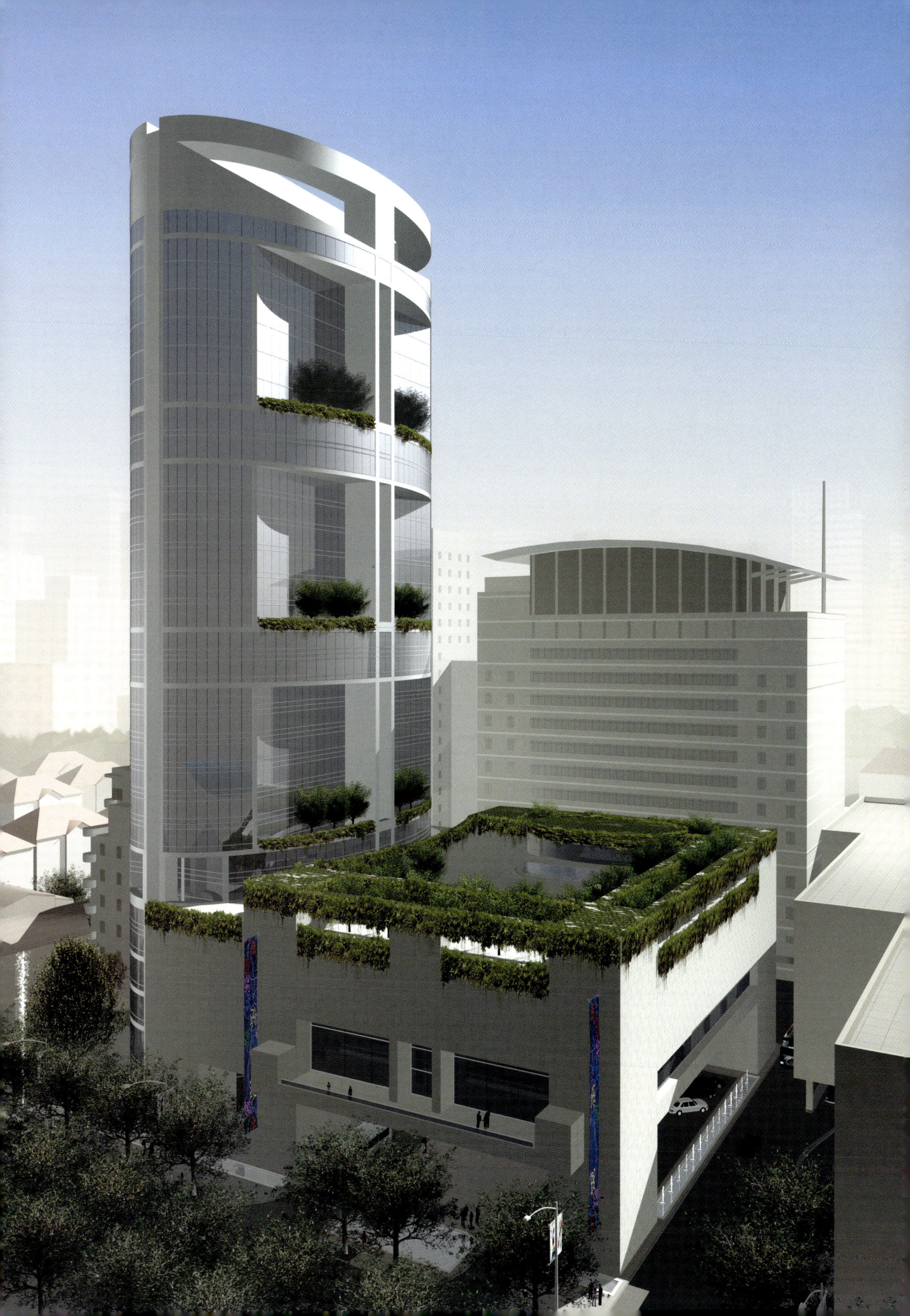

Huading Mansion

Design Proposal 1998
Shanghai, China
Shanghai Multi-Luck Real Estate Development Co. Ltd.
40,000 square meters
Concrete, stone, and glass

1 Site plan
2 Section
Opposite:
  Aerial view of model

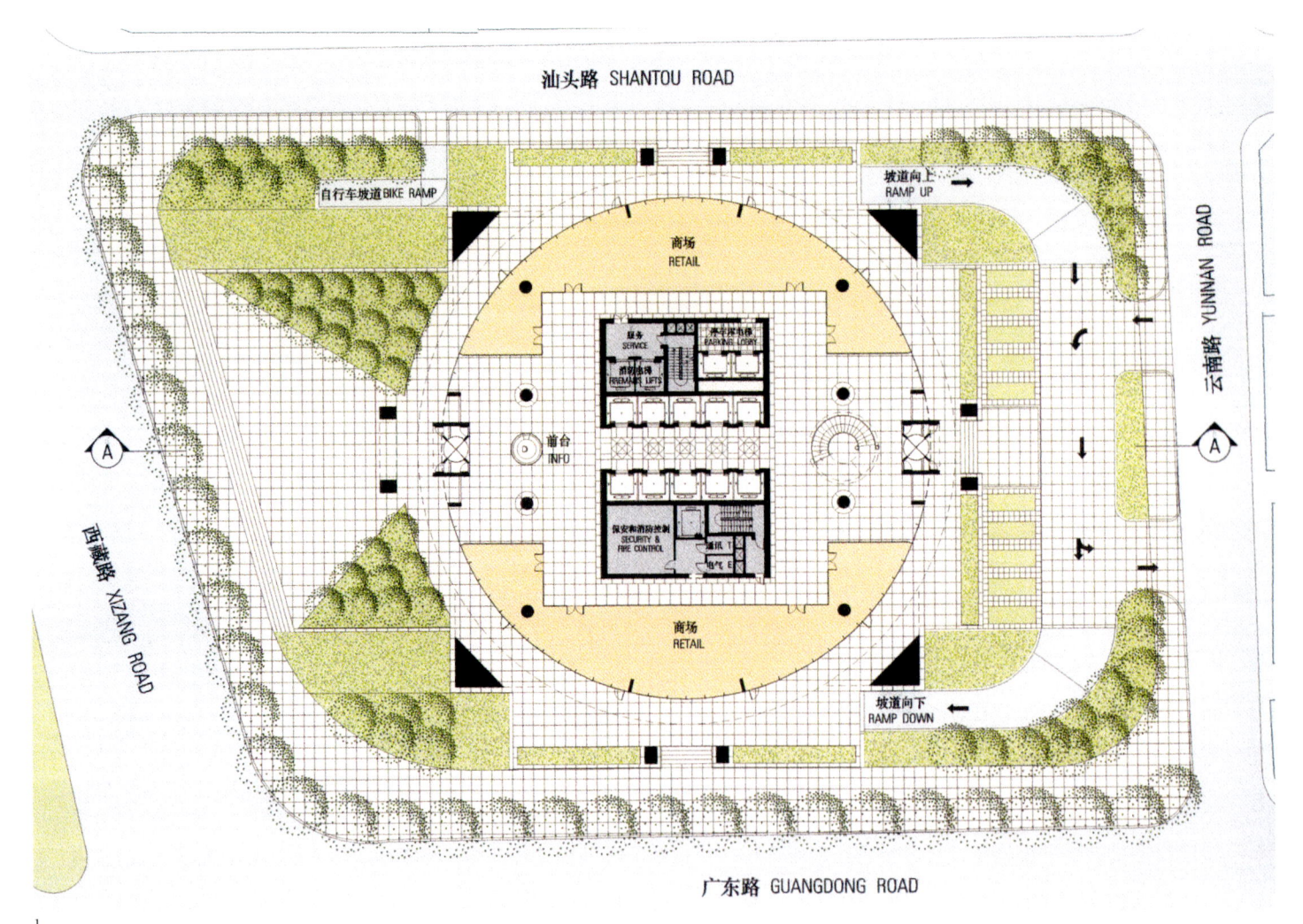

Huading Mansion was designed to meet the needs of a Headquarters Bank with additional rental office space and ancillary amenities including restaurants, retail shops, and entertainment and fitness facilities. The result is a 23-story 100-meter-tall building with 40,000 square meters above ground on a 5,119-square-meter site. There are three levels for bicycle and car parking, and building operations are below grade. The building systems are environmentally sensitive and technically 'intelligent'.

The site is at the eastern side of Peoples' Park in central Shanghai. The design extends the park visually and physically by minimizing the building's site coverage and using extensive landscaping on all sides. The strong geometric shapes expressing different internal functions provide a distinctive form while the stone facades provide a harmonic addition to the surrounding historic and cultural buildings.

The form and scale is further articulated and proportioned to relate to the surroundings by deep setbacks, 25-meter-high freestanding corner columns, and four circular lower floors expanding beyond the square plan. Simple windows, sunscreens on four floors, and landscaped terraces at three tower levels provide additional detail while complementing the forms.

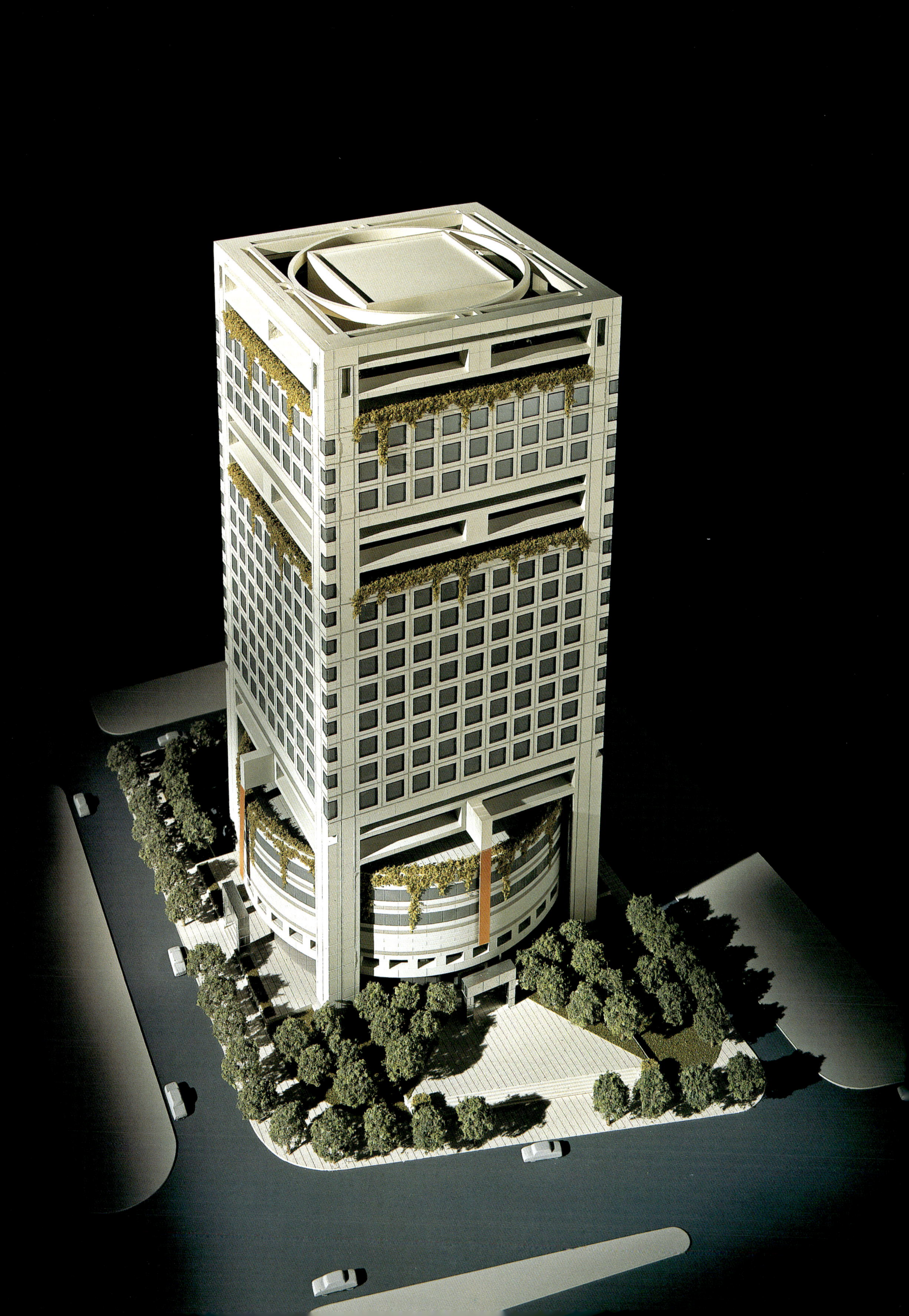

Guangzhou Daily Cultural Center

Design Competition 1998
Guangzhou, China
Gaungzhou Daily Newspaper Group
260,000 square meters
Aluminum, glass, steel, and granite

After carefully analyzing the site to maximize its open space, the program for the Cultural Center is allocated into three primary structures—a high-rise tower, a performing arts/retail center, and a library—that are all configured around a large pedestrian plaza. Below grade, five levels incorporate the conference center and parking. The westernmost portion of the site is reserved for the future development that will include a second high-rise tower for a hotel and apartments and the extension of the performing arts/retail center to provide additional office space with large floorplates.

The performing arts/retail center follows the linear shape of the site along the north portion of the site and is a key component to smooth circulation within the project. The south portion of the site is subdivided for the library on the west and the high-rise mixed-use tower on the east. The pedestrian plaza with the exciting water garden is showcased in the center.

Through the use of classic geometric form the three structures are carefully aligned to give balance and grace to the project. The linear movement of horizontal and vertical lines creates strong architectural form with dramatic results. Squares, circles, rectangles, and triangles are integrated with mathematical precision to create in plan and form a landmark project with dramatic impact that will stand the test of time.

Guangzhou Daily Cultural Plaza is a place to be experienced, a landmark that the world will use to identify Guangzhou as the Cultural Capital of southern China.

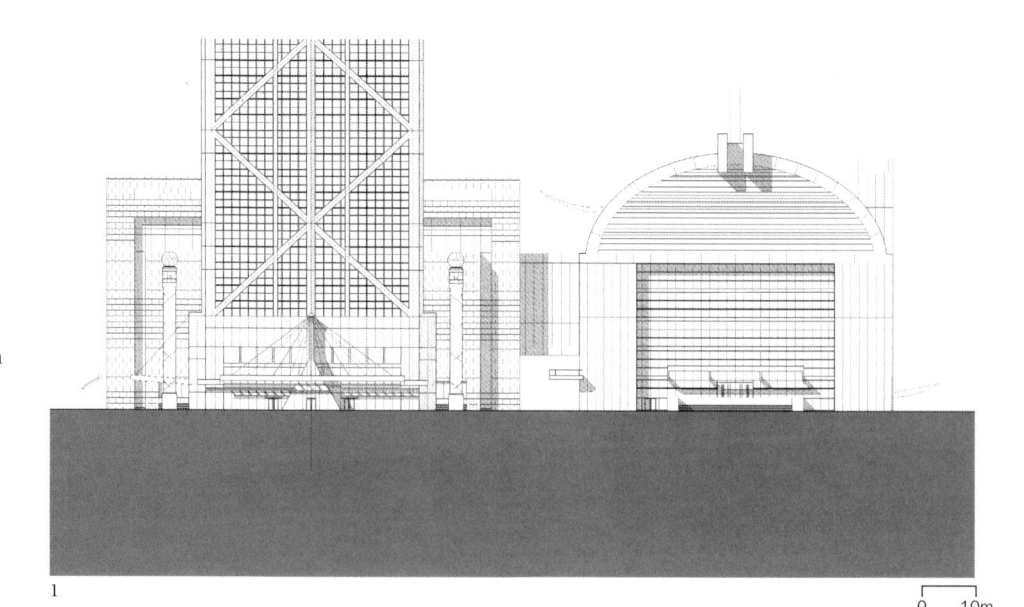

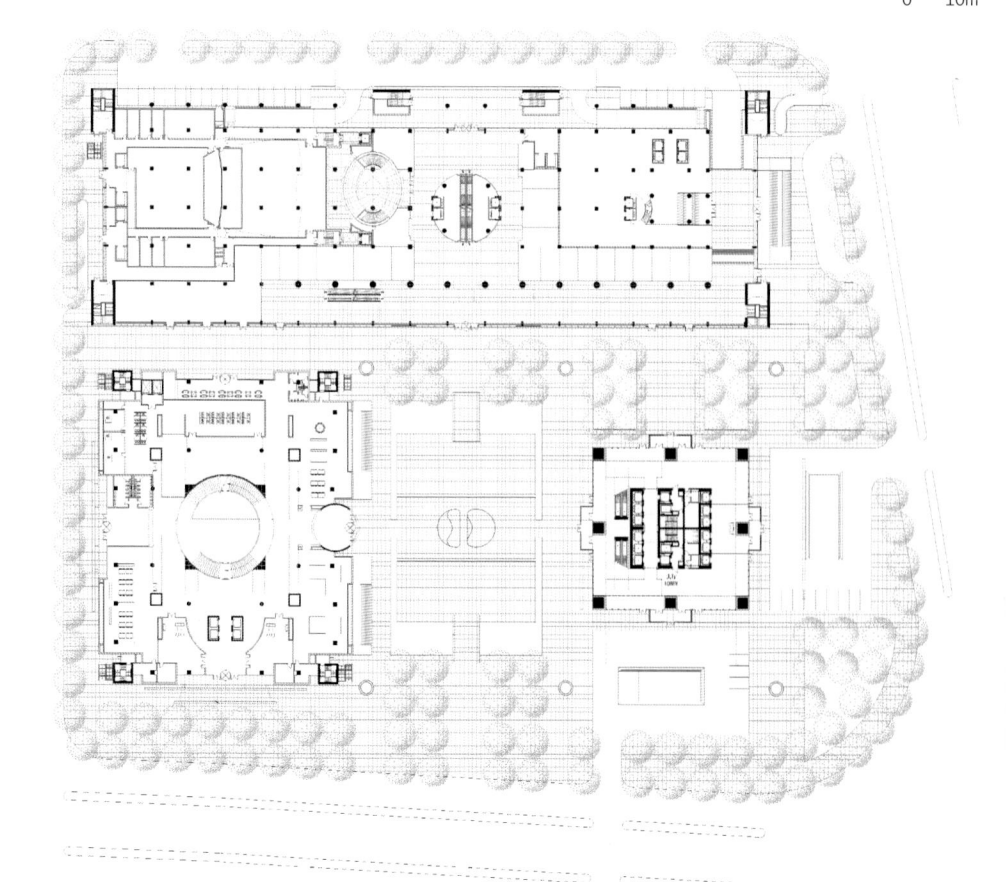

1 Elevations of podium
2 Site plan
3 Aerial view looking north

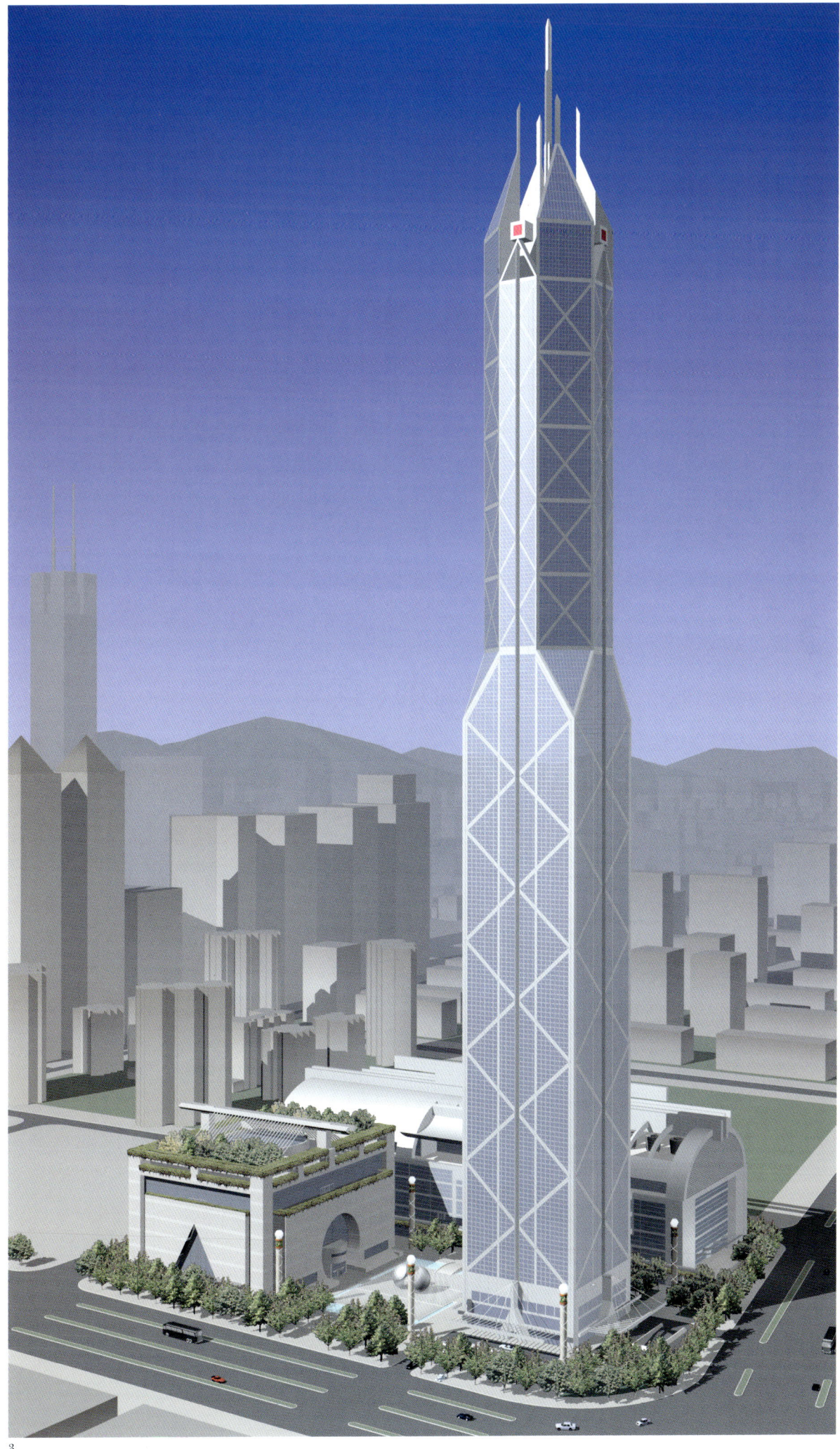

Guangzhou Daily Cultural Center 121

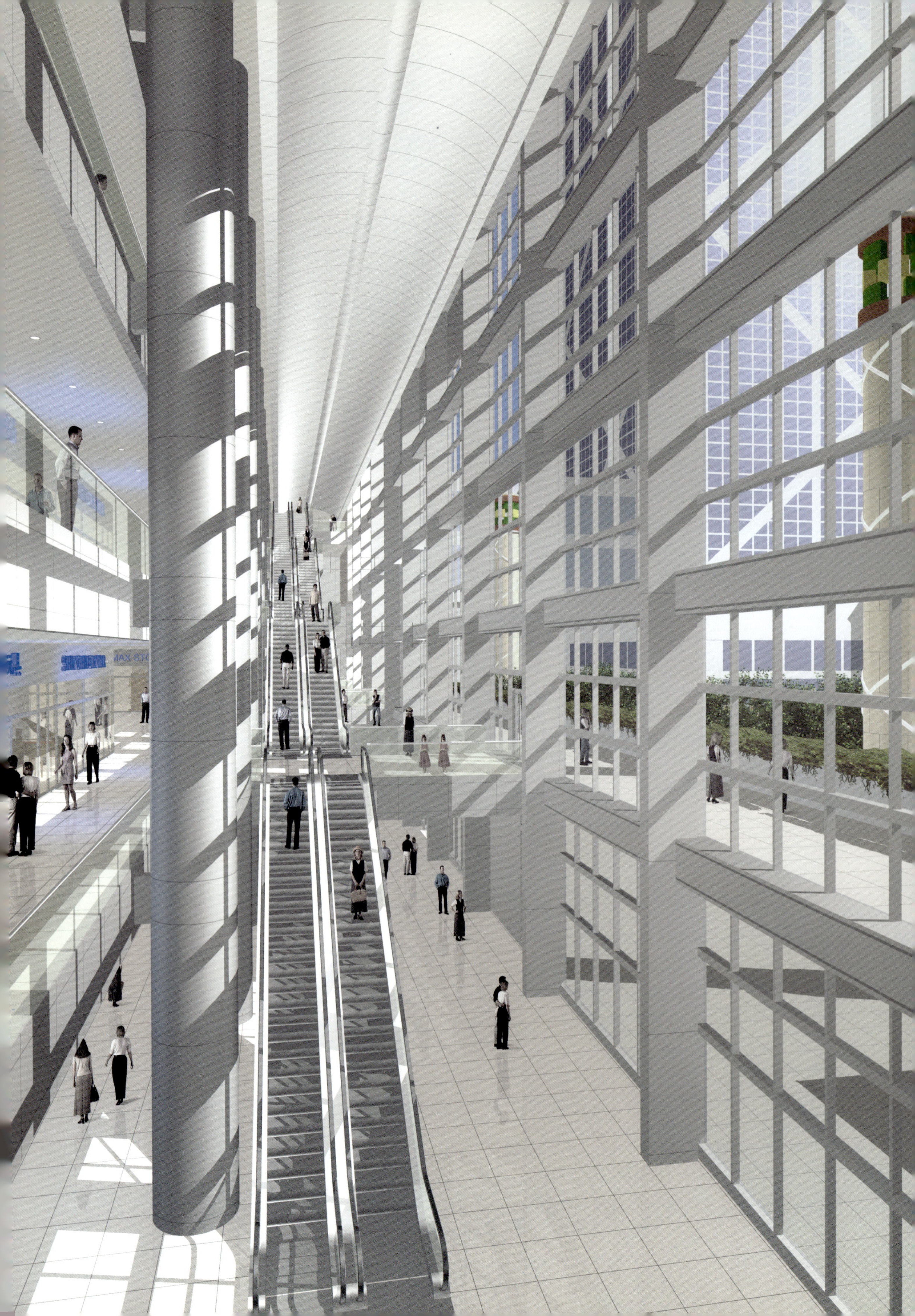

Opposite:
Interior rendering of retail
5   Section of podium

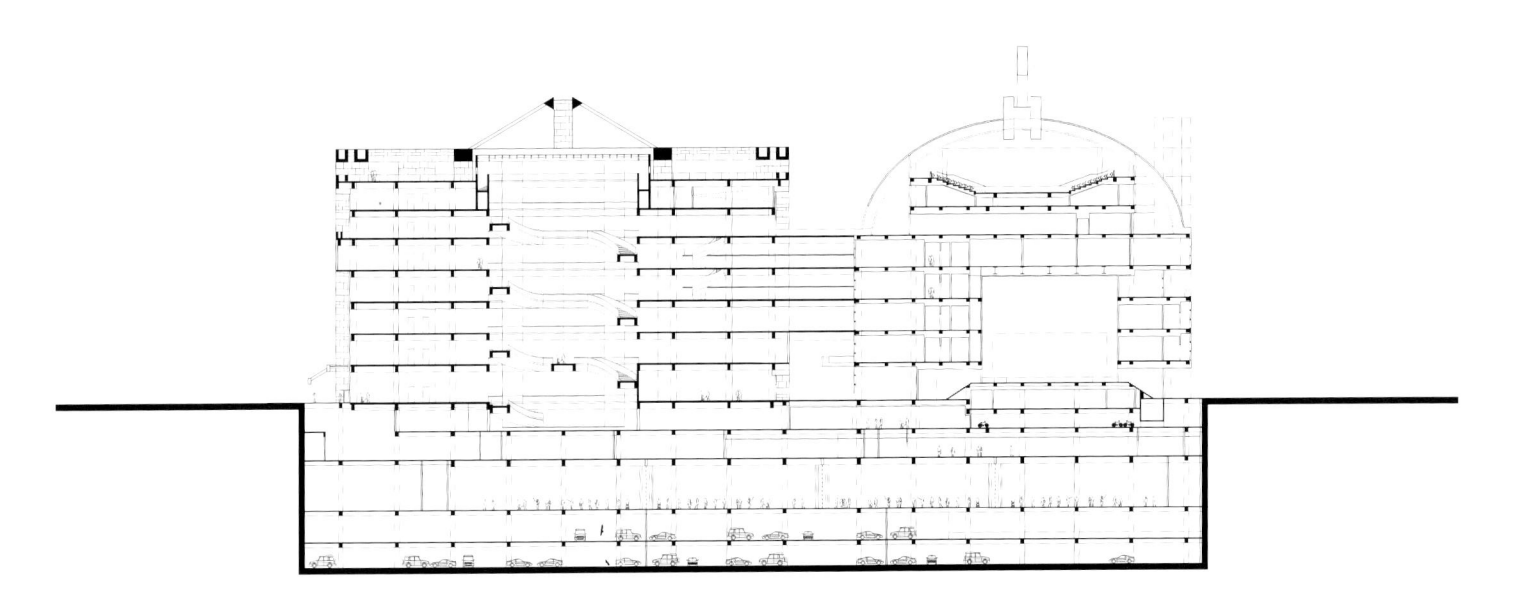

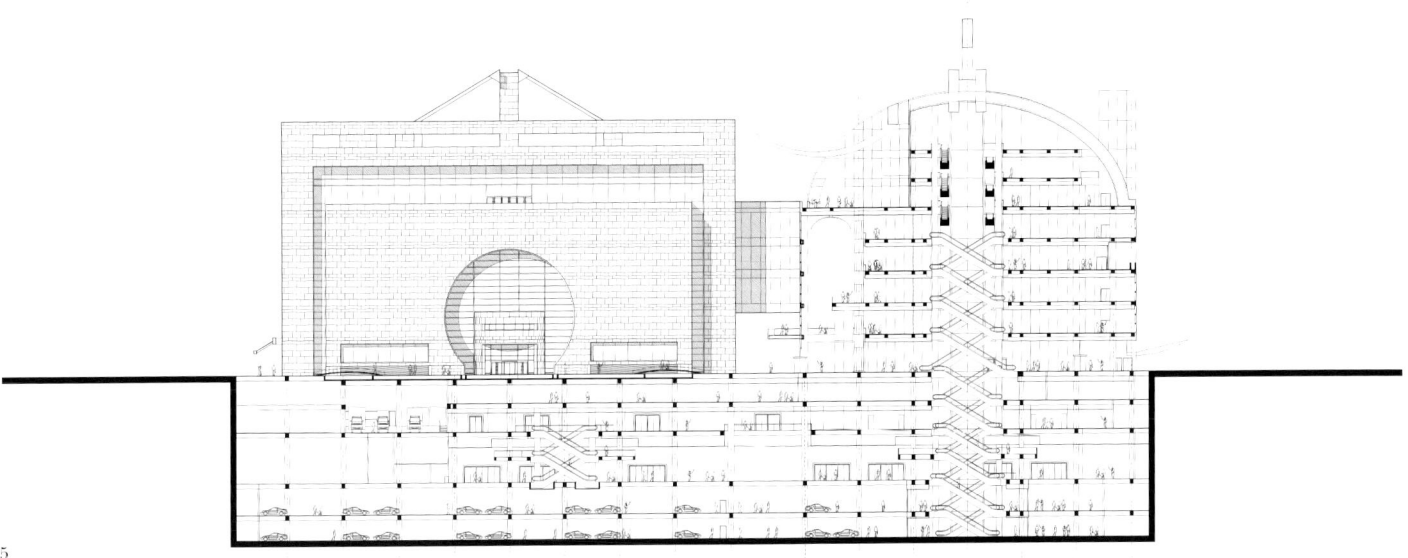

Guangzhou Daily Cultural Center   123

Songdo Daewoo Town

Design Proposal 1999
Songdo, Korea
Shanghai Daewoo Center Development Ltd.
35,343 square meters
Concrete, stone, metal paneling, and glass

Songdo Daewoo Town is an exceptional seaside park community for commercial and cultural activity. To succeed, the master plan needed to be economically viable. Therefore, the clustering of activities, phasing, and efficient use of the site, both above and below grade, were of great importance.

Above grade, activities are clustered in four primary sectors with large areas of the site reserved for a grand central park. Below grade, well-organized retail and parking levels provide year-round activity that connects and energizes the complex. Since construction is phased, each sector is designed to stand on its own, functionally and aesthetically. The full impact will be best appreciated when all components are in place.

Each component is inspired by the park and designed so that nature enhances the built environment. The first and most dominant component is the 102-story office tower and the adjoining 28-story research/office structure, located in the center of the park. The S-shaped hotel/convention center curves gracefully along the north of the park. On the east, the long retail/cultural complex extends along a major boulevard to maximize access to the rapid transit system for visitors to the shops, museum and arts center. To the south are rental offices, condominiums and retail shops, which will be the last components to be constructed.

1

2

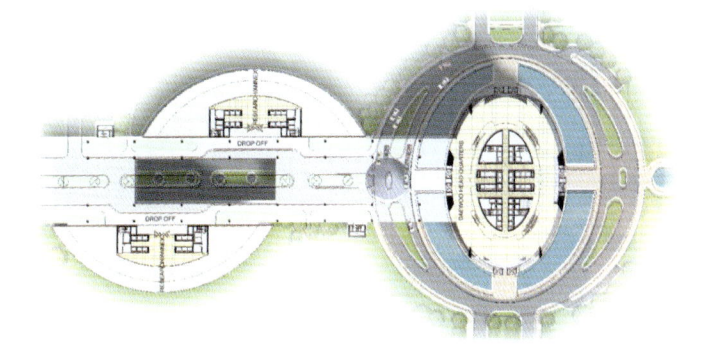

1 Aerial view of model
2 Rendering looking east
3 Plan of office towers

Songdo Daewoo Town

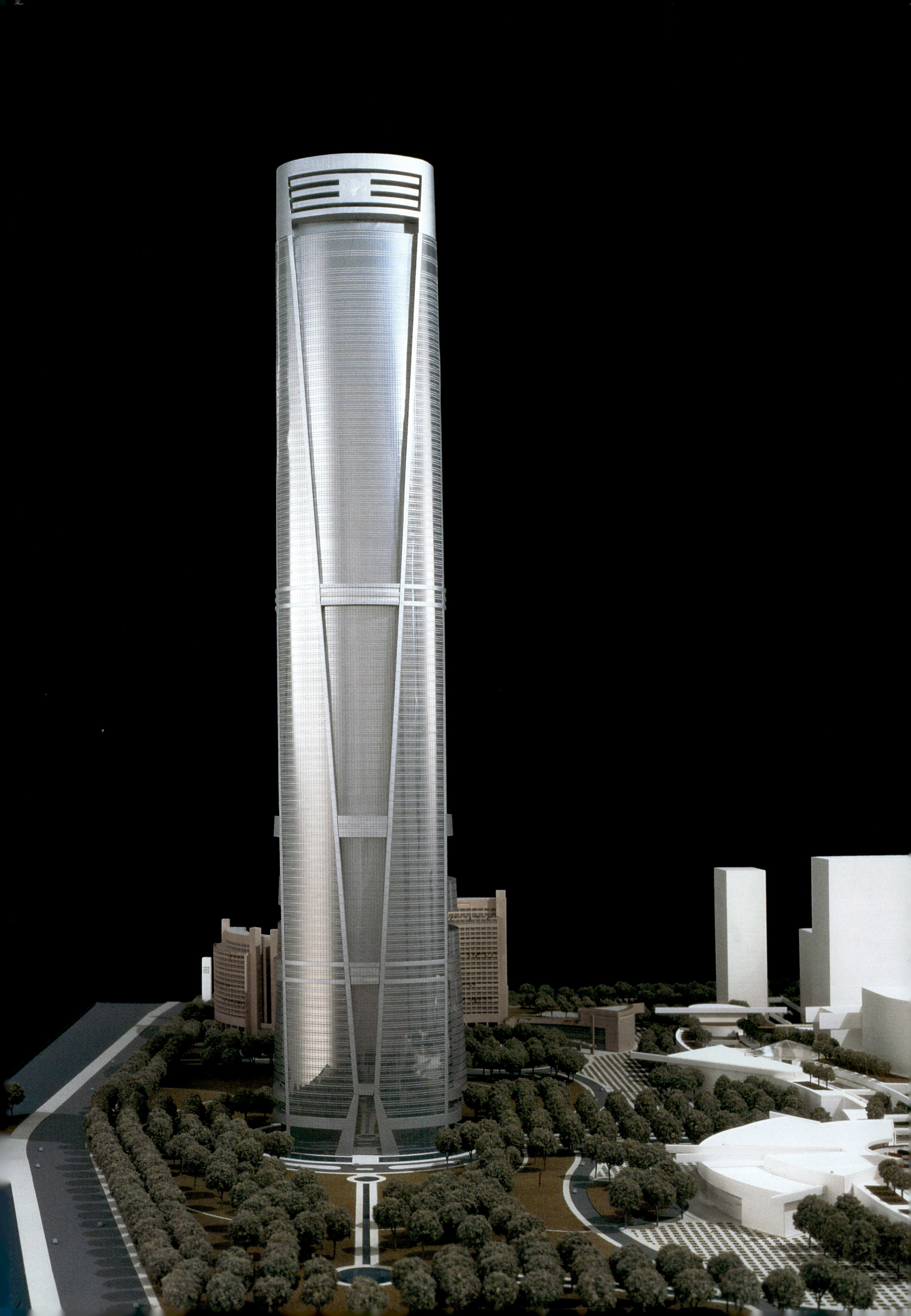

Opposite:
Model view of office tower
5   Ground floor plan of hotel complex
6   Section through office tower
7   Model view looking west

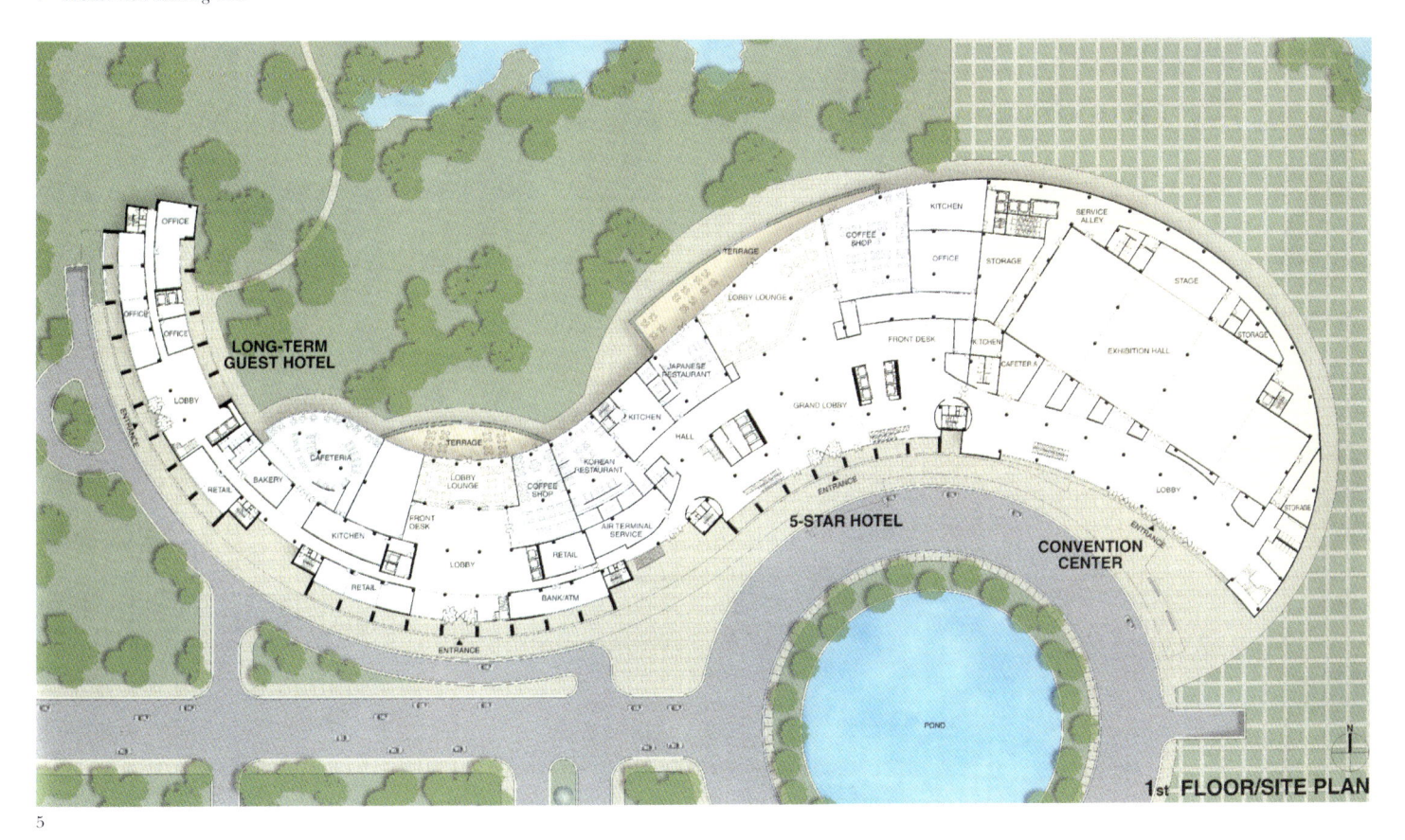

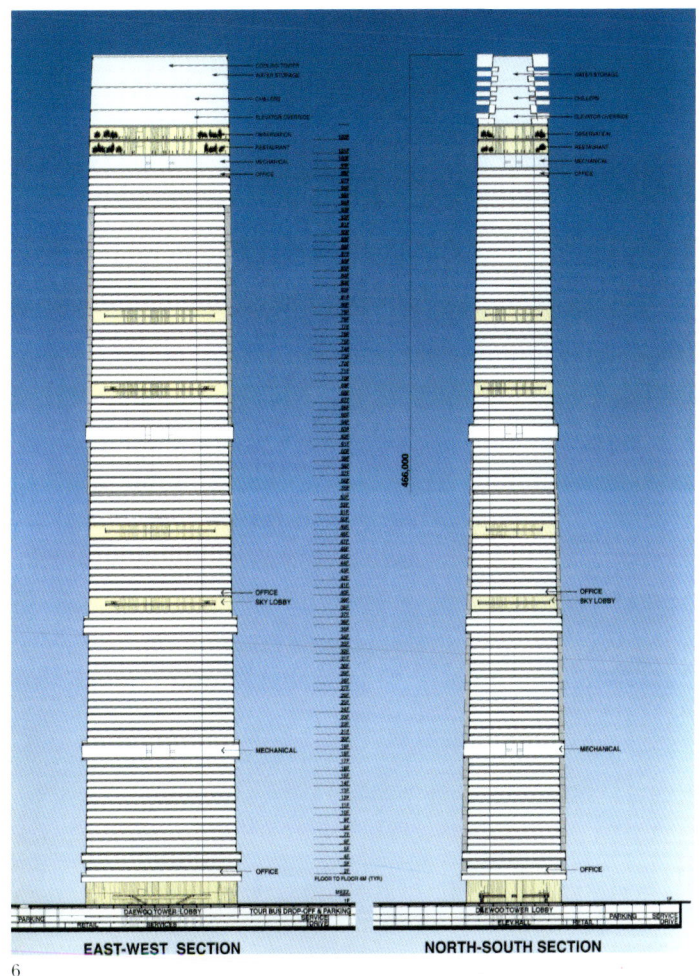

Songdo Daewoo Town   127

8

8 Interior rendering
9 Rendering of office tower at night

9

Songdo Daewoo Town 129

Parcel 8

Design Proposal 1982
Singapore
S.P. Tao & Associates
93,000 square meters
Concrete with metal curtainwall

Parcel 8 is an office tower designed for a site on the edge of historic Singapore. The design aimed to create a high-rise tower that respected rather than obstructing neighboring historic buildings, and provided a respite from the tropical climate. The tower's long slab building supported on large cylinders that open to a public plaza below conforms to the shape of the site. The cylinders provide core elements such as the entry lobbies while the exterior express elevators create a vertical design component. The tower is clad in a metal curtainwall that functions as a sunscreen to diminish the tropical sun and to create a pattern that reduces the large facade to a human scale.

A parking structure at the rear of the site, articulated with landscaping, defines the plaza that extends under the tower and relates to the scale of the historic buildings. The plaza becomes a water garden filled with pools, fountains and landscaping. A quiet, cool public place was proposed to contrast with the heat of the bustling street. This project creates a magnificent place for both its tenants and the public to enjoy exquisite beauty in the heart of the city.

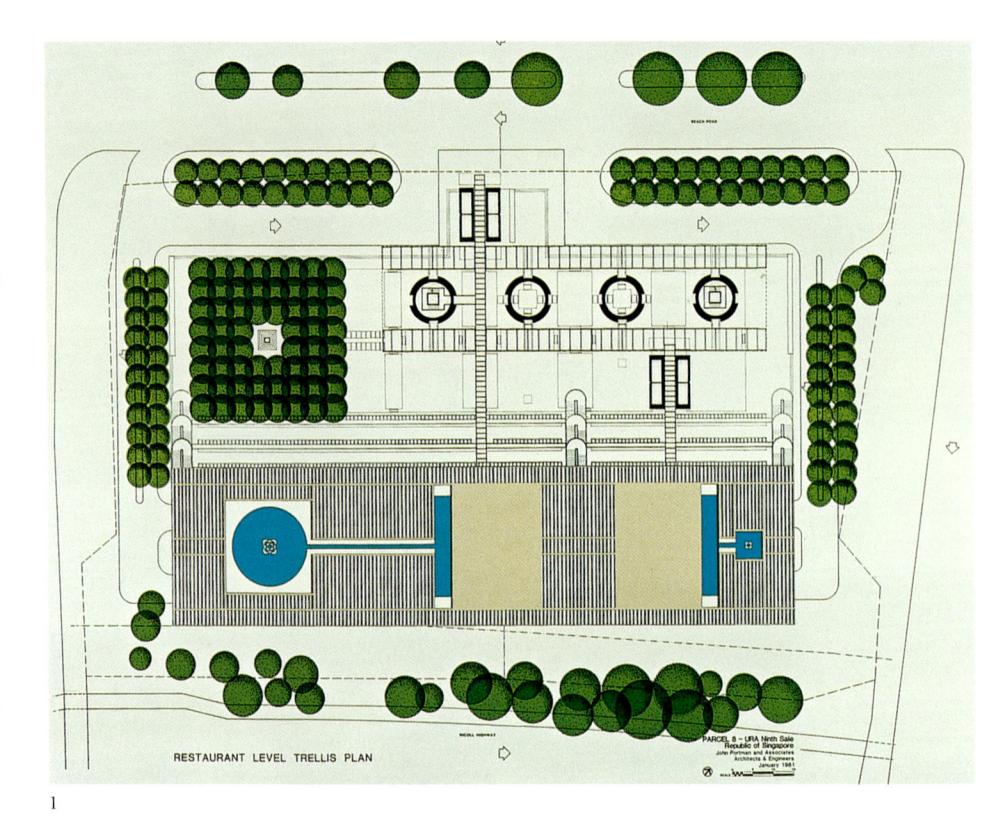

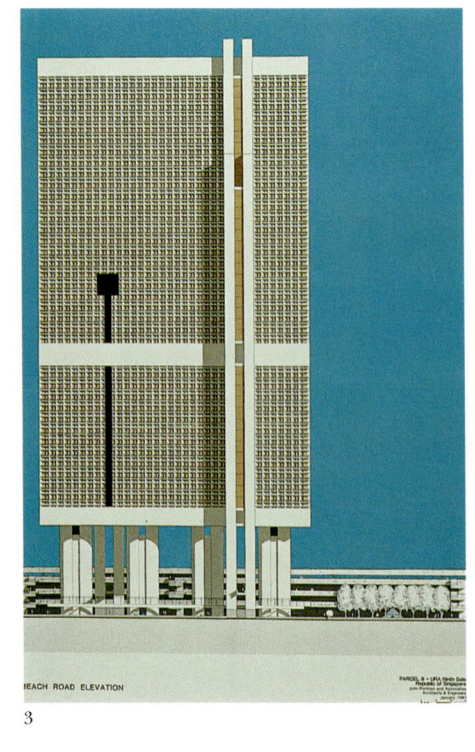

1 Site plan
2 Model view looking east
3 Elevation
4 Rendering at base of tower
5 Elevation
6 Rendering of office tower
7 Aerial view of model

Parcel 8 131

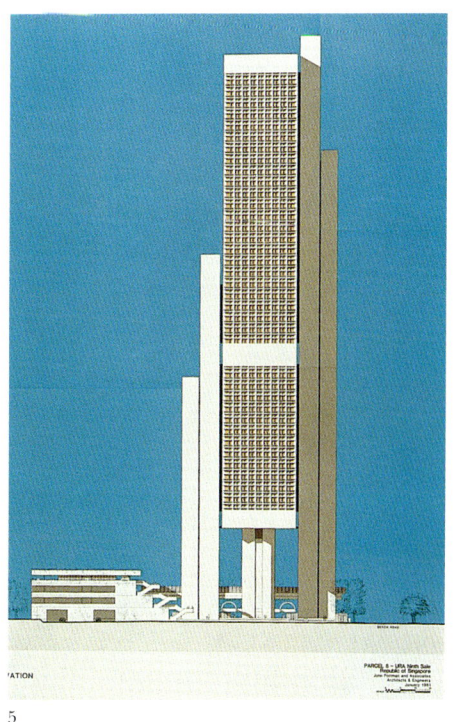

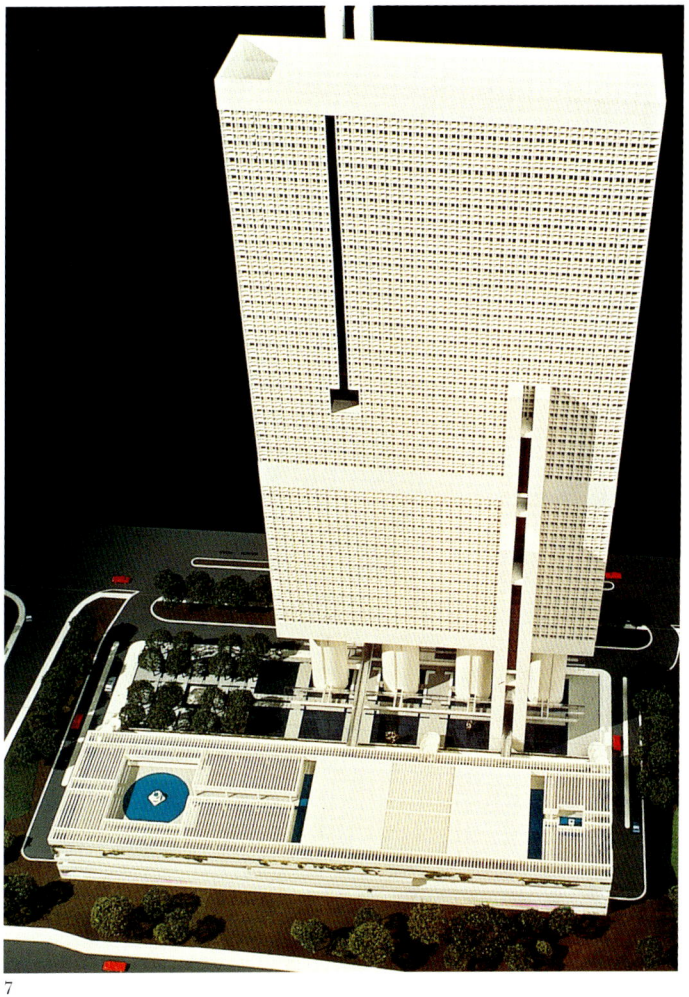

Jin Mao

Design Proposal 1993
Shanghai, China
Shanghai Municipal Government
151,400 square meters
Concrete, stone, metal, and glass

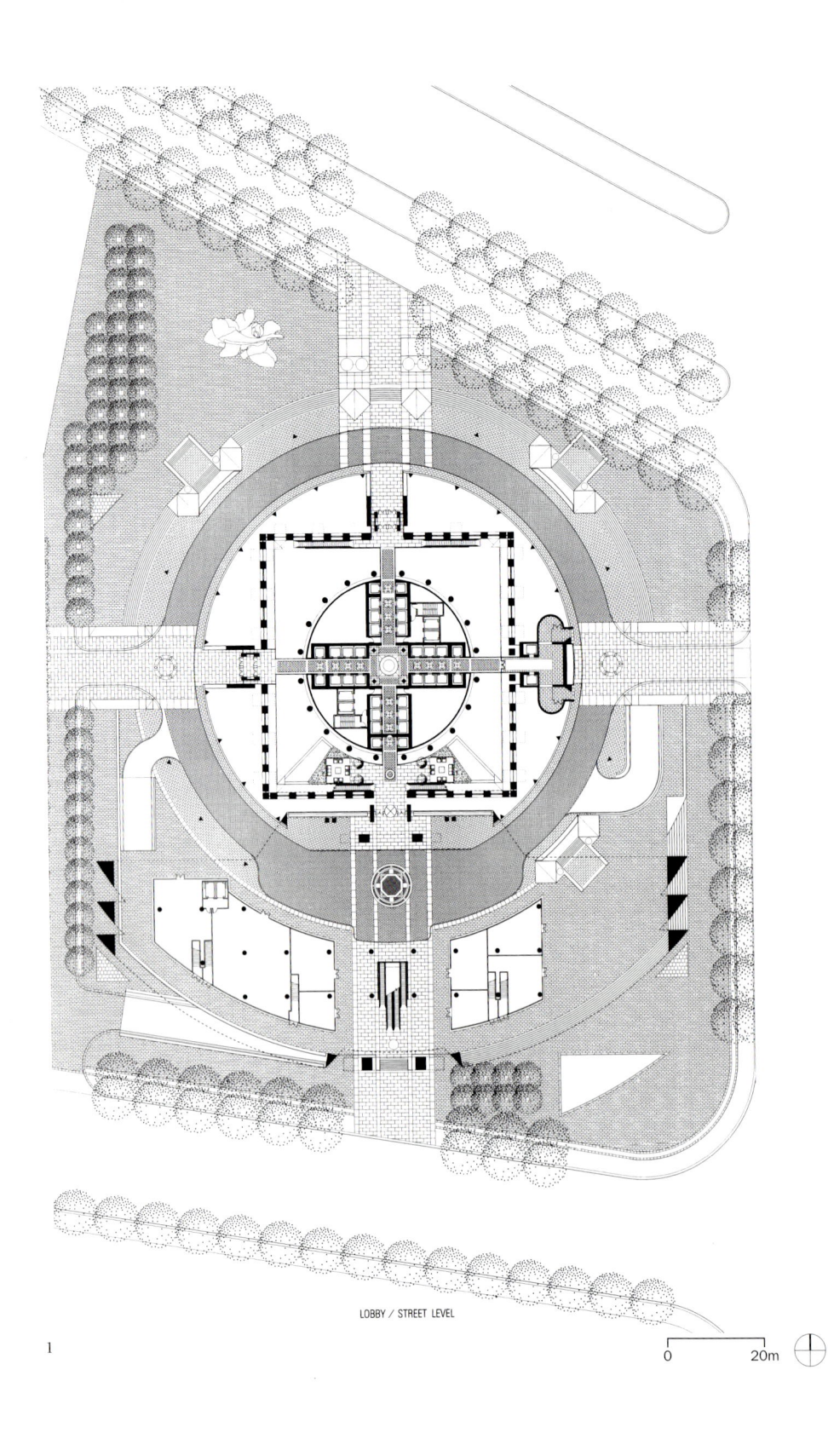

1 Site plan
2 Study model of atrium design
Opposite:
　Model view at base of tower

Jin Mao was designed as a towering symbol of 'The New China'. Located in the Pudong Financial District, its massing and details respect the architecture of the Bund across the river, complementing in a contemporary manner the architecture of the 1920s and 1930s and the architecture of ancient China.

The design of the 88-story tower addresses six separate program elements with a strong focus on human scale. The project integrates six essential components with a functional circulation system that strives for simplicity with maximum efficiency. The components (in addition to parking) are as follows, starting from the top of the building: a private club, an observation level, a 700-room hotel, an office building, a lower retail ring level, and a meeting center. Each of these entities has its own separate public entrance and identity yet is an integral part of the project as a whole. Stacking the functions works effectively because vertical circulation is achieved by a comprehensive double-decked elevator system.

Despite its size, at all points the project is consciously broken down to a human scale. At ground level a canopied ring road and four low-scale entry points reinforce the tower's people-orientation at street level by creating a welcoming ease of access for both vehicles and pedestrians. The project design strives to contribute to the people of Shanghai as well as serving its occupants, thereby merging with the urban environment in a harmonious and changing way.

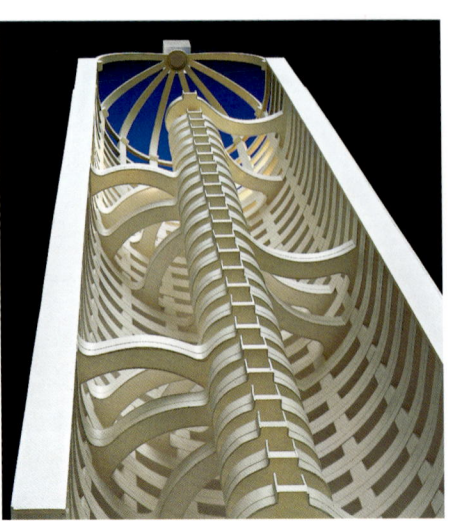

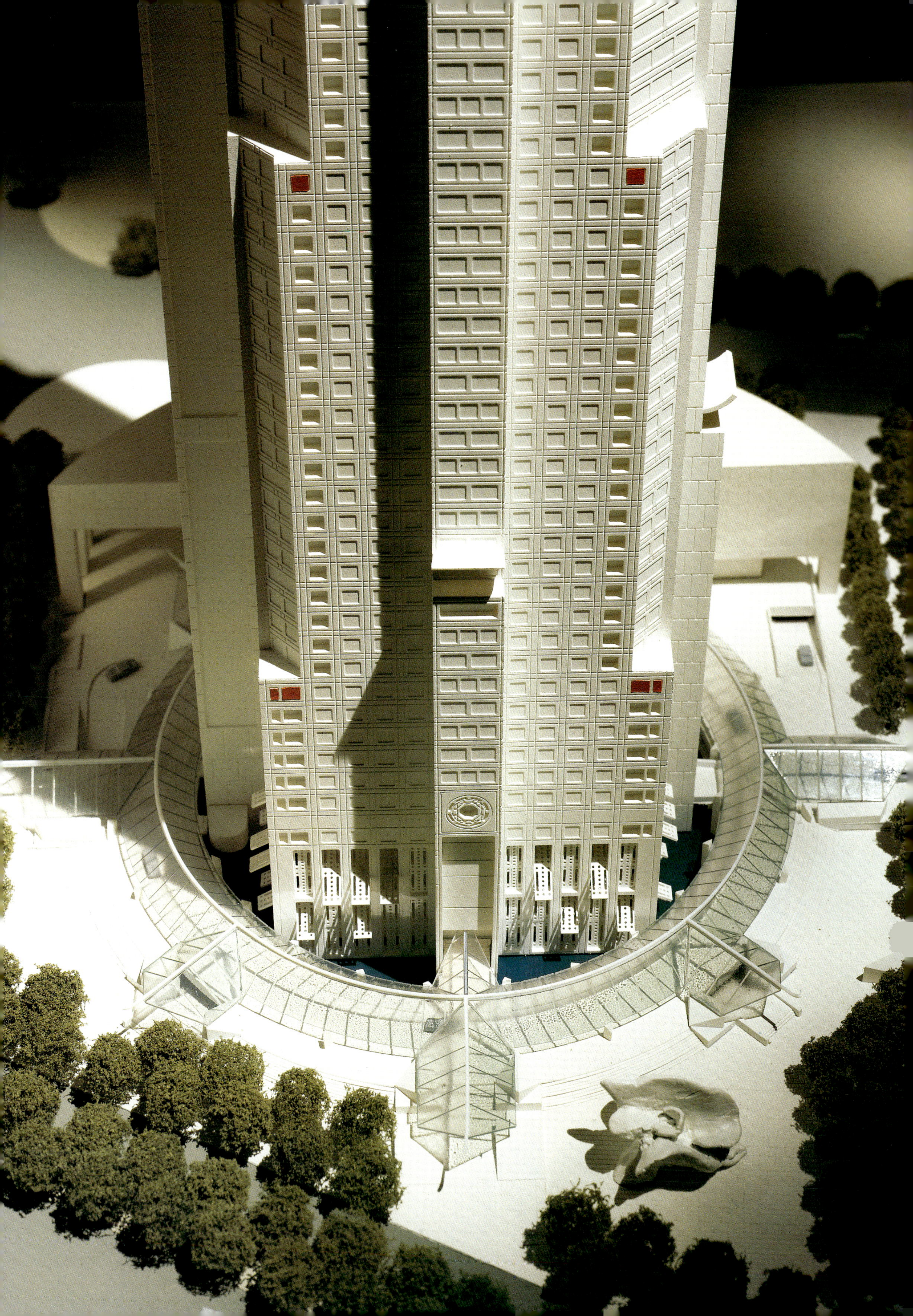

4

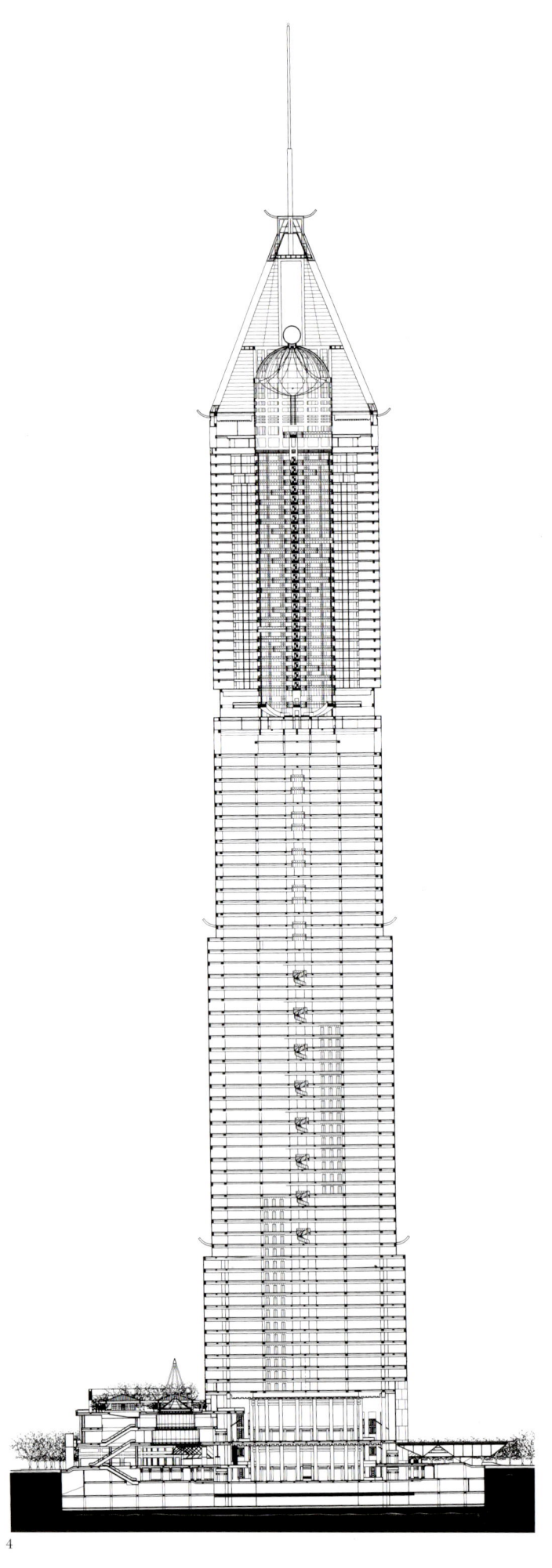

5

134

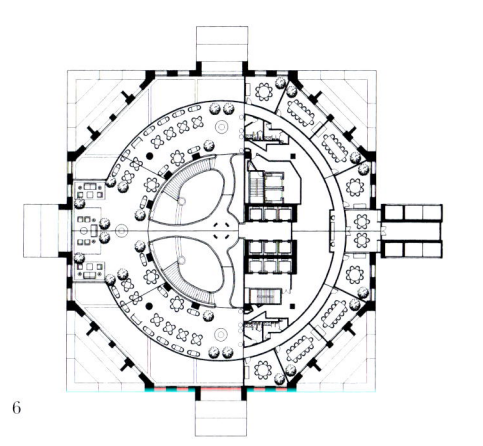

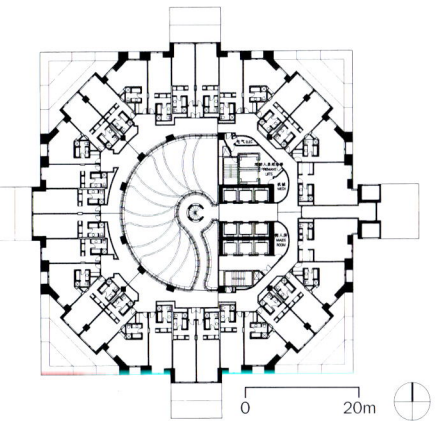

4 Section through tower
5 Rendering of tower at night
6 Plan of tower
7 Rendering of pedestrian ring

Jin Mao 135

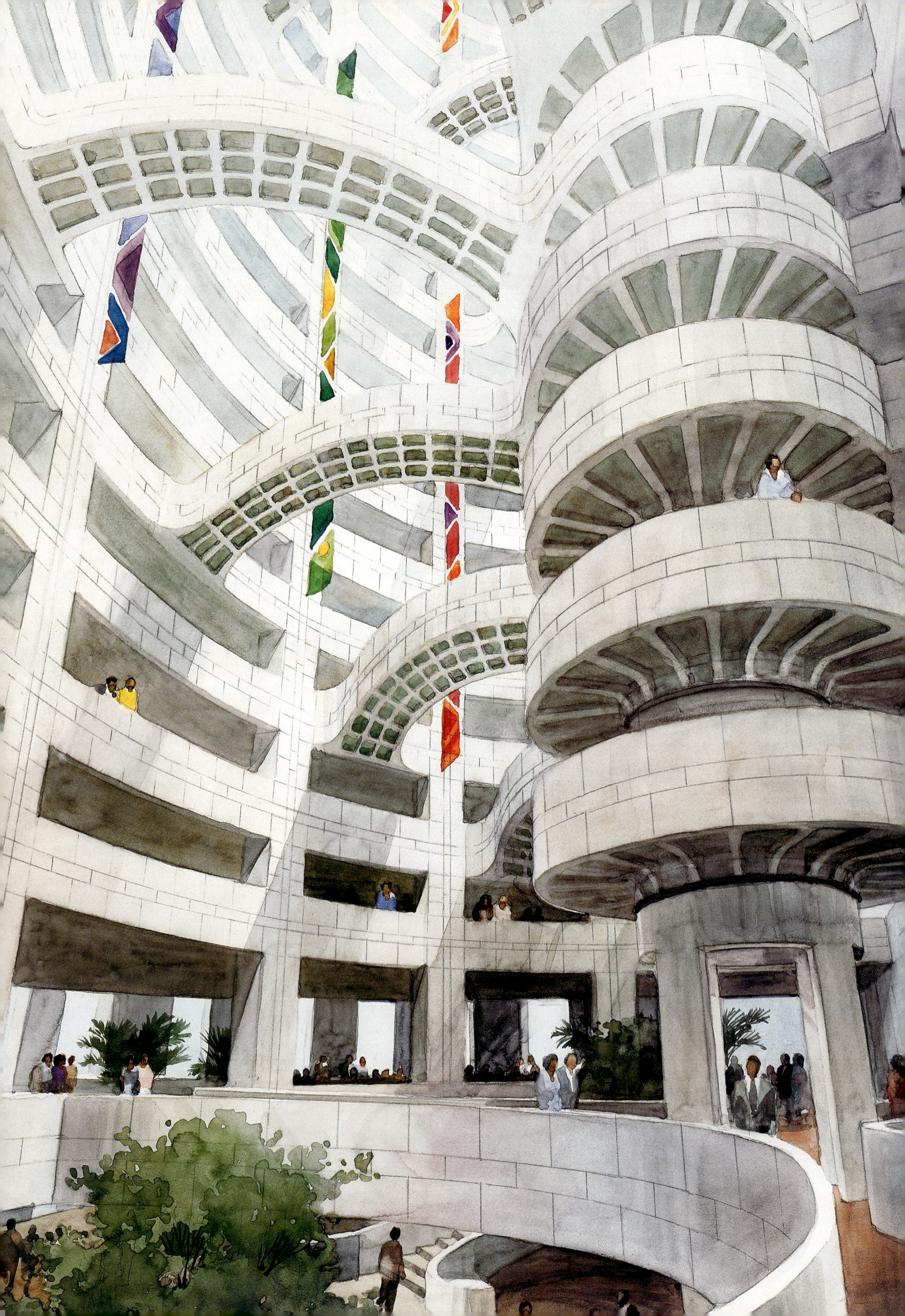

Opposite:
 Rendering of atrium at hotel tower
9 Rendering of pedestrian road
10 Aerial view of model
11 View of model at top of tower

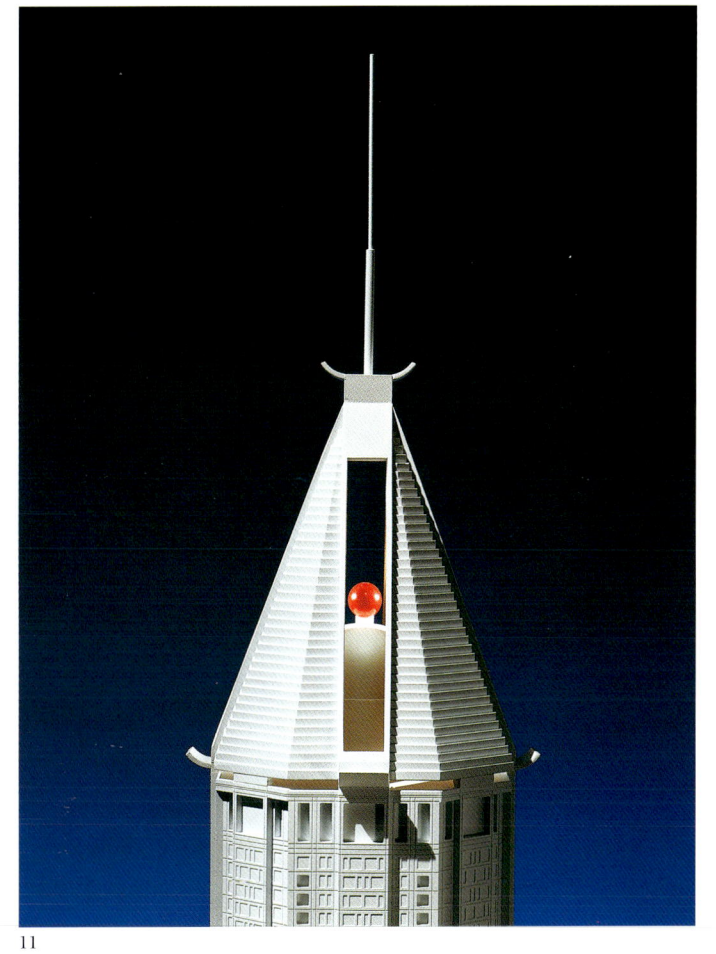

Jin Mao 137

Lot 6

Design Proposal 1997
Jakarta, Indonesia
P.T. Grahama Adisentosa
188,600 square meters
Concrete, stone, and glass

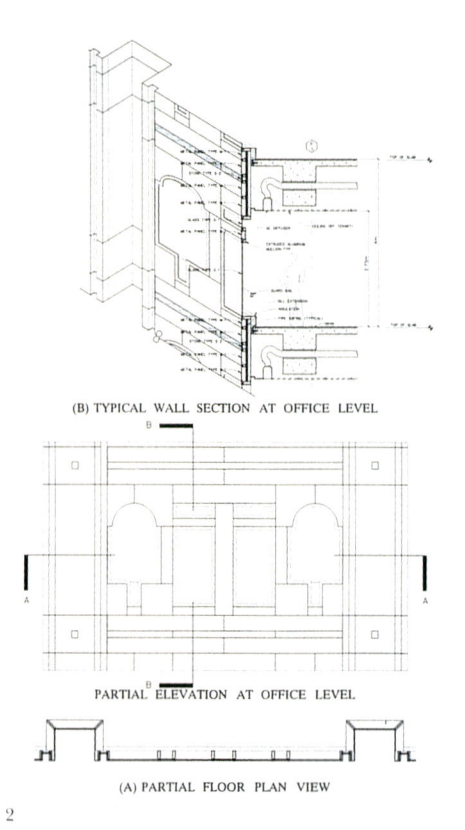

The proposed 75-story building is designed to act as the focal point of the Sudirman Central Business District and to allow three distinct functions to harmoniously co-exist. The tower provides 48 levels of office space and a luxurious 399-room hotel. The podium is a major retail hub that also accommodates the hotel's public functions and strategically links the tower to the other buildings in the business district.

The building's distinctive architectural form symbolizes national pride and introduces a new Indonesian architectural character for the 21st Century. As it rises, the straight lines of the facades extend outward, like the petals of a flower, and express a change in the function of the hotel. The petals give form to 10 curved balconies on each side for the hotel's special suites and lounges. The flower-like form then evolves into other sculptural forms on the rooftop. In the center, five slender, taller forms encircle the rooftop spire and patriotically symbolize the five tenets of Indonesia's state philosophy, the Pancasila.

The architecture employs primary forms to create balance in a time-honored tradition. The scale and proportion of the podium is inspired by the historic architecture of the Borobudur while the emerging form of the tower symbolically reflects the unfolding energy of Indonesia's future. In both, repetitious patterns are strategically broken to create visual interest and to mark functional changes within the structure.

1 Model view of tower
2 Details of curtain wall design
3 Interior rendering
4 Elevation of retail at base of tower
Opposite:
  Aerial view of model looking east

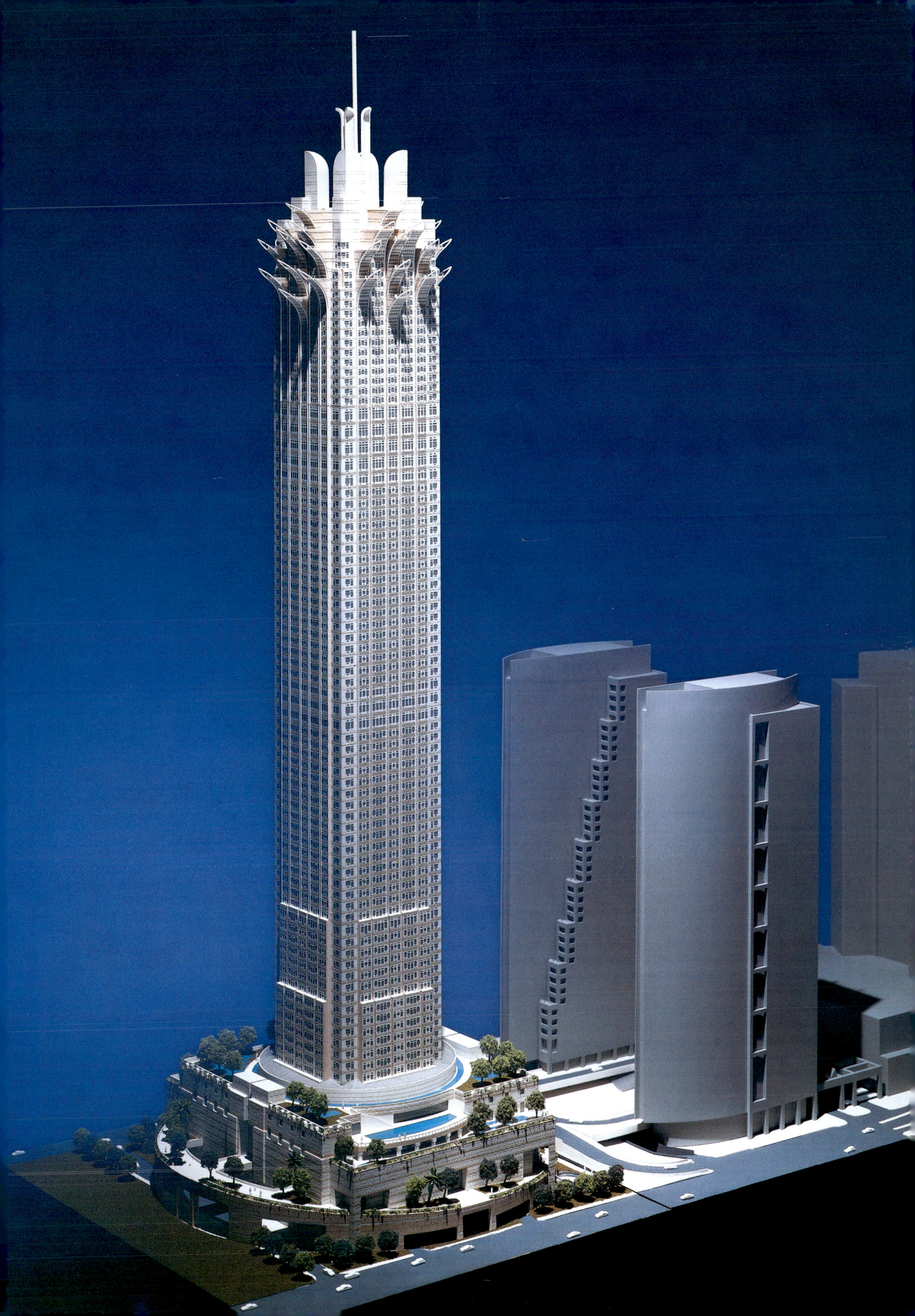

Sampoerna Tower

Conrad International Center
Design Proposal 1996
Jakarta, Indonesia
P.T. Arthayasa Grathatama
66,883 square meters
Unitized aluminum and glass curtainwall with granite panels

1   Rendering of interior lobby
2   Ground floor plan
Opposite:
   Rendering looking south

The twin 38-story office towers are part of a large-scale mixed-use complex, and were designed to flank the 60-story tower that was to be the development's signature building. The design objective for the twin towers was to complement the high-rise tower yet stand on their own as buildings of distinction. The towers were linked to a three-level integrated subterranean retail complex that horizontally unites the entire development. The space above is used as a lushly landscaped plaza for the enjoyment of the people who work and shop there.

The buildings are mirror images. The outer sides are bowed outward eluding a circular form. The sides that face each other are straight, in slab-like form, with the inward slab stepping up progressively at four-story intervals and acknowledging the high-rise signature structure to its north. Each step becomes a balcony for the offices within. Vehicular access is provided to covered drop-off areas with parking and service entries to below-grade functions. Grand lobbies with polished stone provide access to the retail complex below and the offices above. Quality retail and banking facilities are proposed to occupy the leasable space on the ground level.

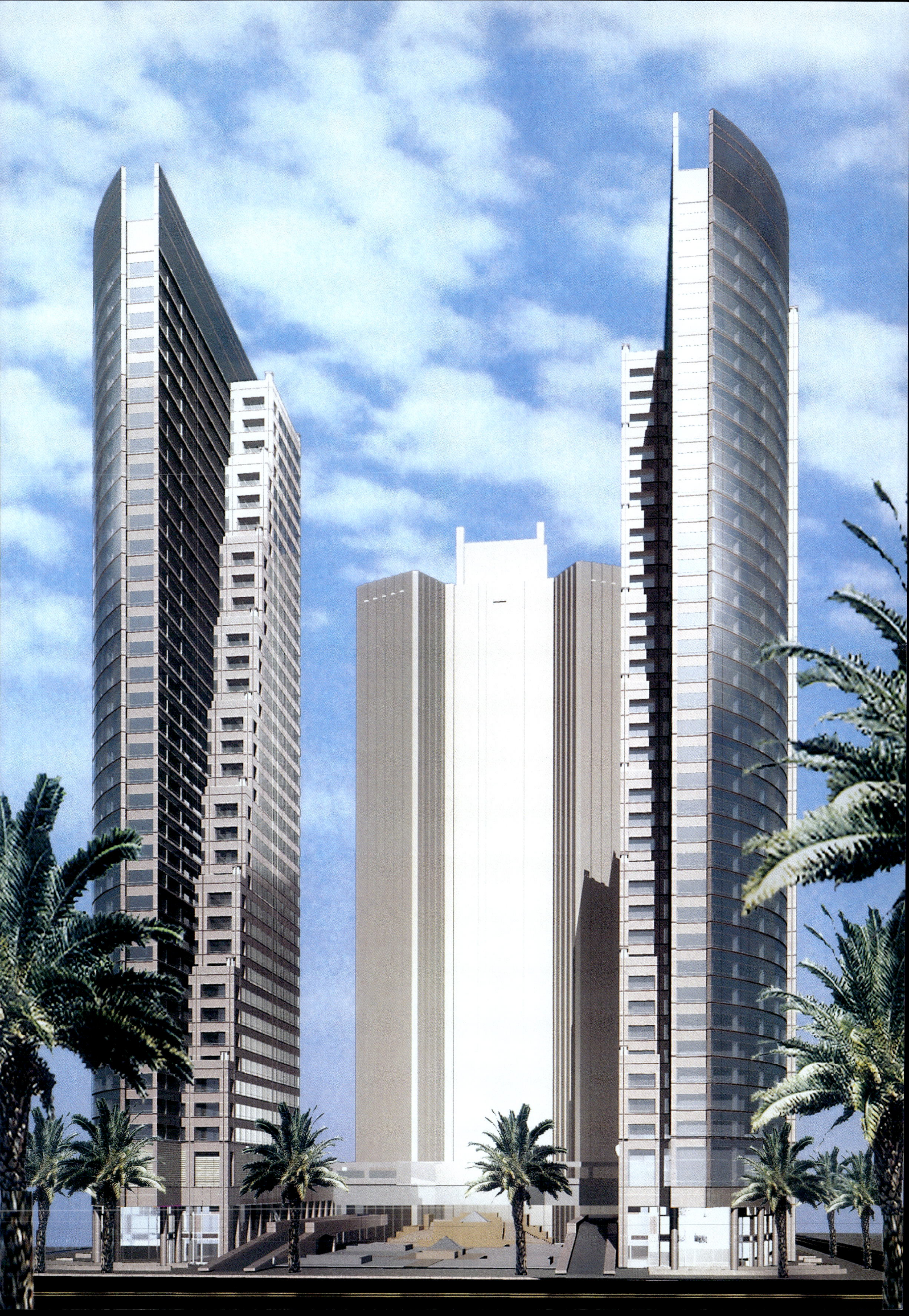

New York Marriott Marquis

Design/Completion 1983/1985
New York, New York
Times Square Hotel Company
167,286 square meters
Concrete, metal paneling, and glass

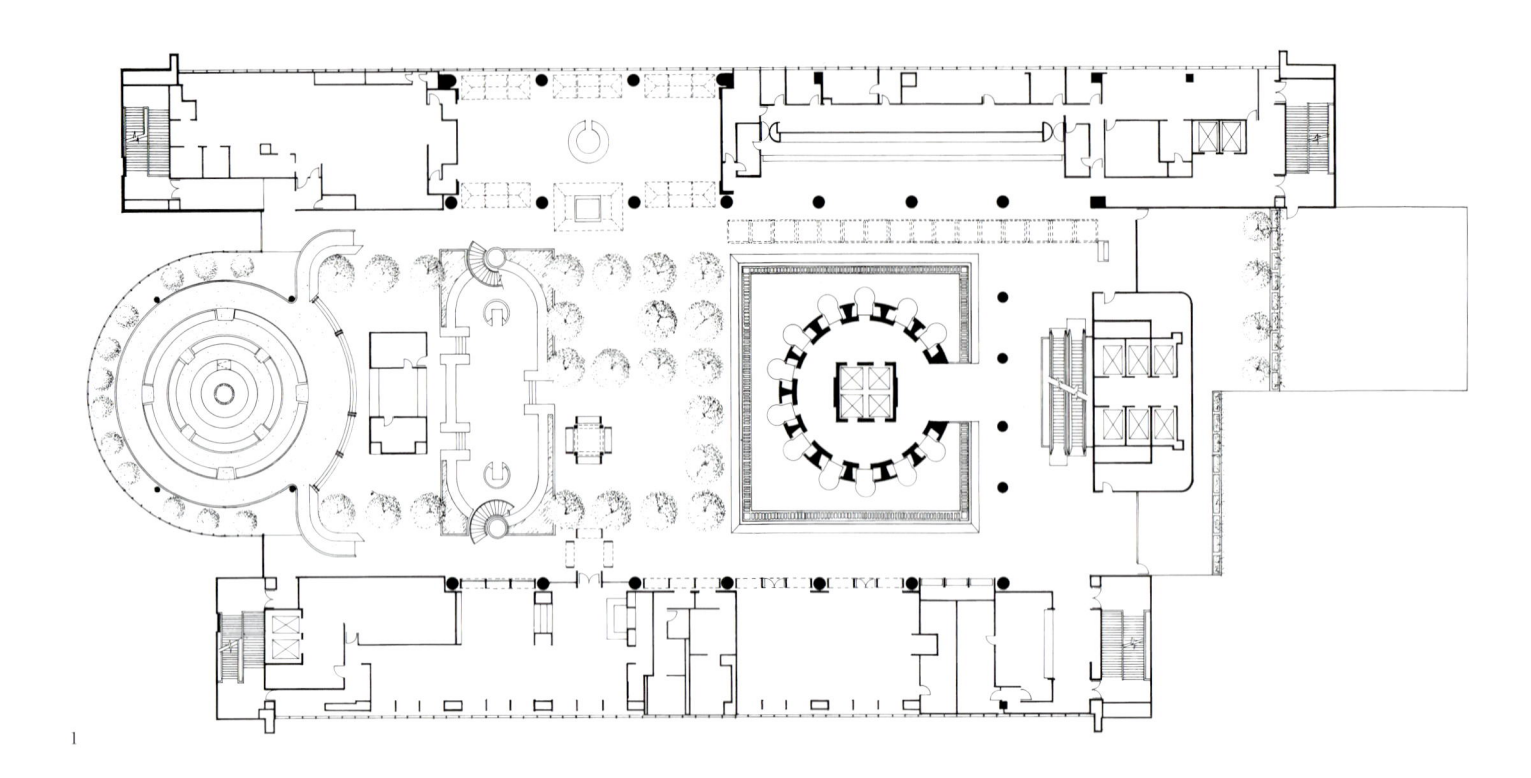

The 1,875-room New York Marriott Marquis played a significant role in the revitalization of the Times Square theater district. It aimed to link some of the nation's finest theaters with a large convention hotel in the heart of New York's theater district. The size, location and drama of the project were conceived to initially be self-sufficient while providing the major catalytic element for the re-development of Times Square and increased growth to the west. The architects worked diligently with the administrations of three city mayors for 13 years to complete the process.

The size and scope of the project were critical to its success. Encompassing a full city block, the hotel is an integral part of the theater district with its electronic billboard reinforcing the excitement of Times Square. The lower levels contain comprehensive facilities for conventions and community events, including the city's largest ballroom and its own 1,600-seat Broadway theater. At the street level is the theater box office and a covered motor entry and motor lobby for the hotel. The main lobby is on Level 8 where the hotel opens to a grand 37-story space that is the antithesis of the congested street outside. Trees and plants fill the lobby, which is encircled by retail shops and restaurants. Glass elevator cabs energize the space as they carry guests to the 35 levels of guestrooms above and to the revolving rooftop restaurant and lounge that has a panoramic view of the city below.

1 Lobby floor plan
2 Skyward view in atrium
Opposite:
  Skyward view from Times Square

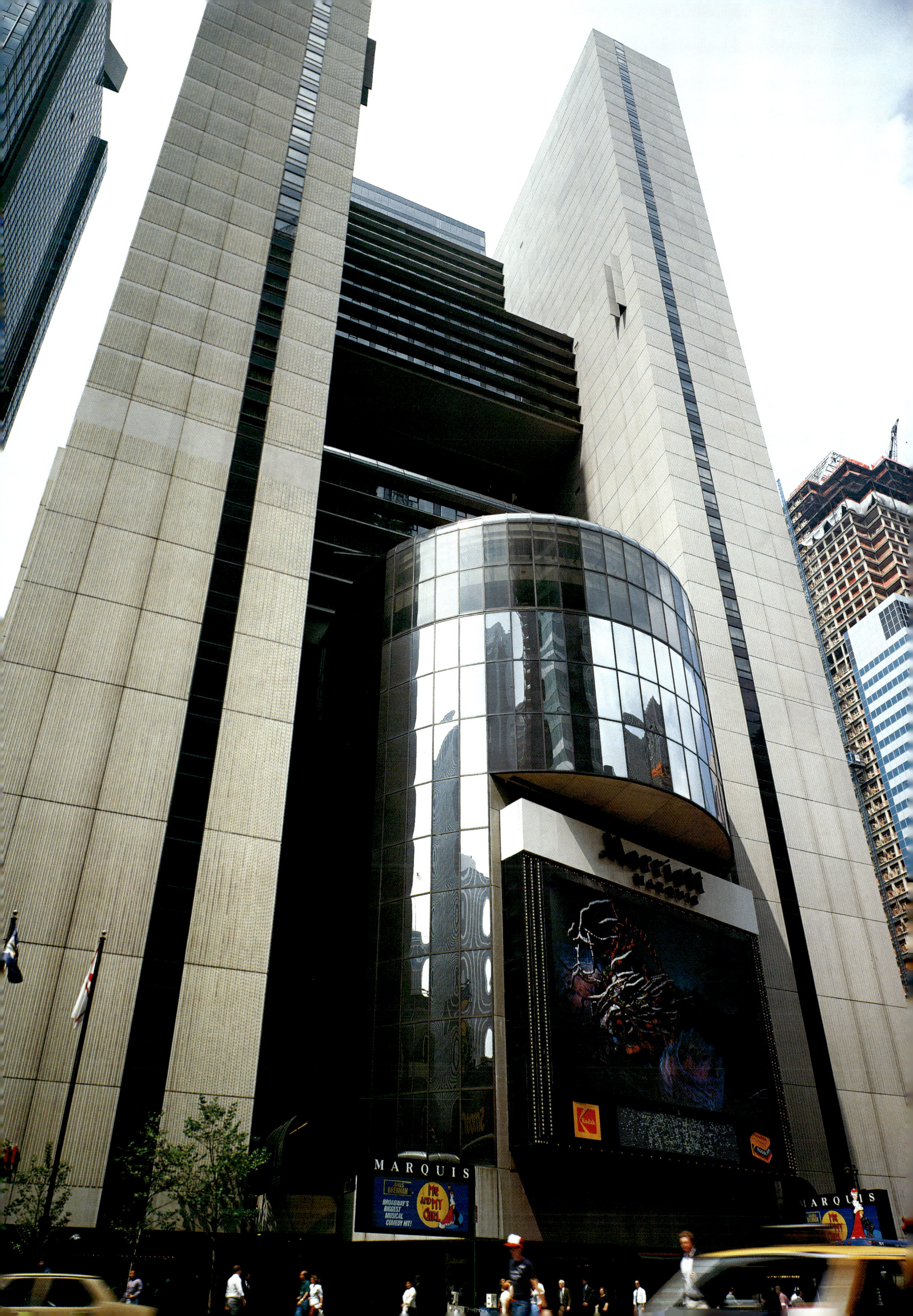

SHELLEY LONG
PIT
RICHARD BENJAMIN Film
Marriott
MARQUIS
HOWARD JOHNSON'S

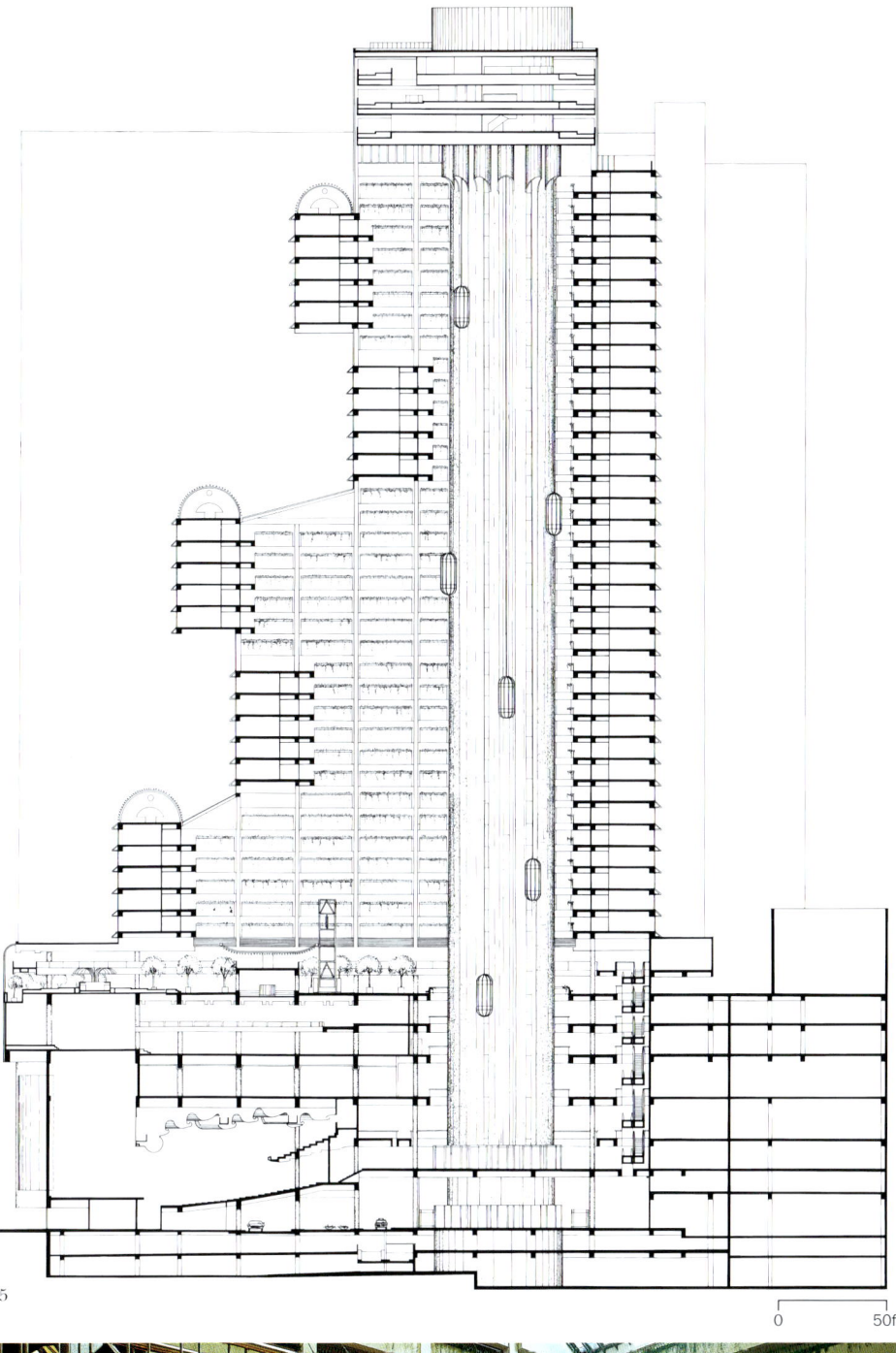

Opposite:
  Aerial view
5 Section
6 Interior view of atrium
7 View from elevator

New York Marriott Marquis 145

The Portman Hotel (now named The Pan Pacific San Francisco)

Design/Completion 1984/1987
San Francisco, California
500 Post Property Ltd. Partnership
37,917 square meters
Brick, stone, and glass

1 Lobby detail
2 Floor plan of lobby
3 Lobby detail
Opposite:
   View looking northwest

This 348-room hotel in the historic Union Square district was designed to complement the traditional architecture of its neighbors and to provide a uniquely luxurious guest experience for business travelers and tourists. The scale and proportion of the 22-story brick building reflect but do not replicate the older buildings adjoining it. Interior and exterior forms are considered to holistically integrate the design of the building unto itself and its surroundings.

The interior is formed around a 17-story atrium lobby with intimate fireplace seating areas. Designed around the Asian concept of valet service, the service functions of the hotel are discretely incorporated to make the guest experience relaxing and hassle-free. The use of luxurious materials such as marble and brass abounds and works of art are used extensively. A small conference center, a luxurious ballroom, and meeting rooms are accessed from the motor lobby entrance. The bar and dining room are on the lobby level. The upper level provides a club lounge and terrace, conference rooms and two penthouse suites. The architect coordinated all aspects of the hotel, from the architecture to the guestroom interiors, artwork, and table settings, to reflect a fully integrated design concept.

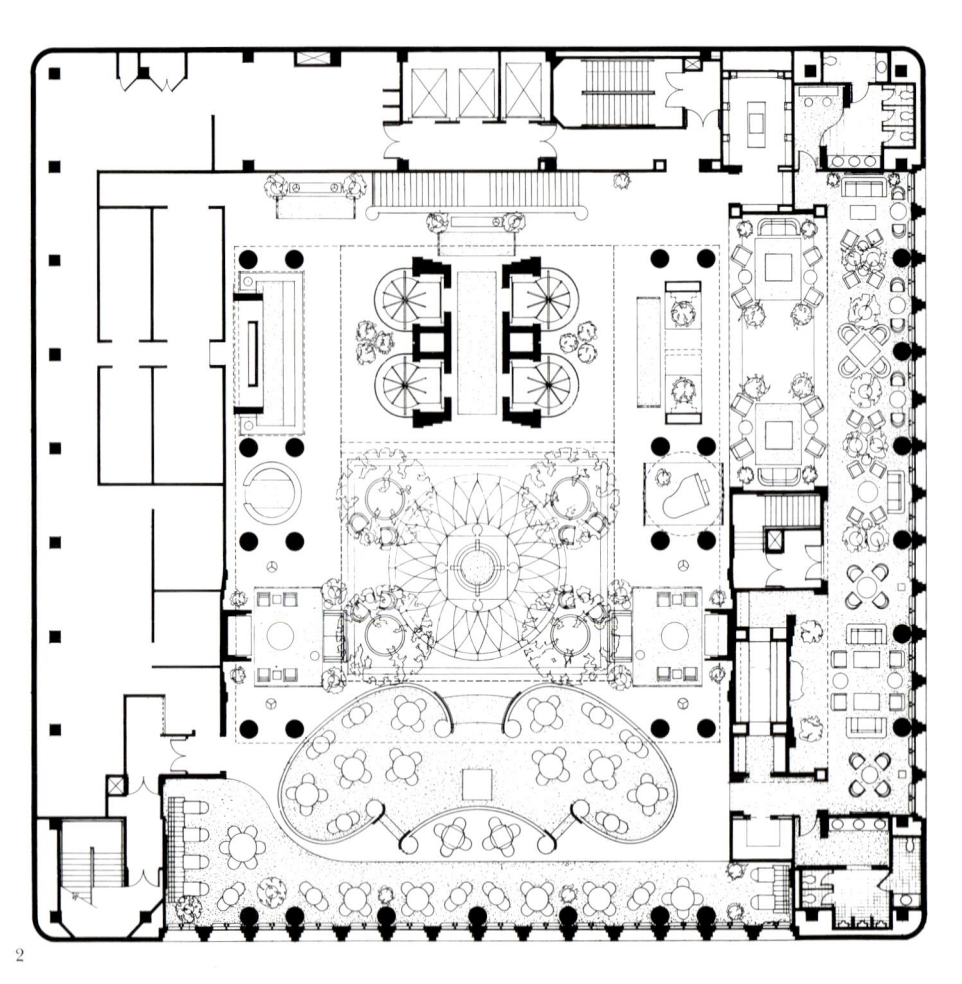

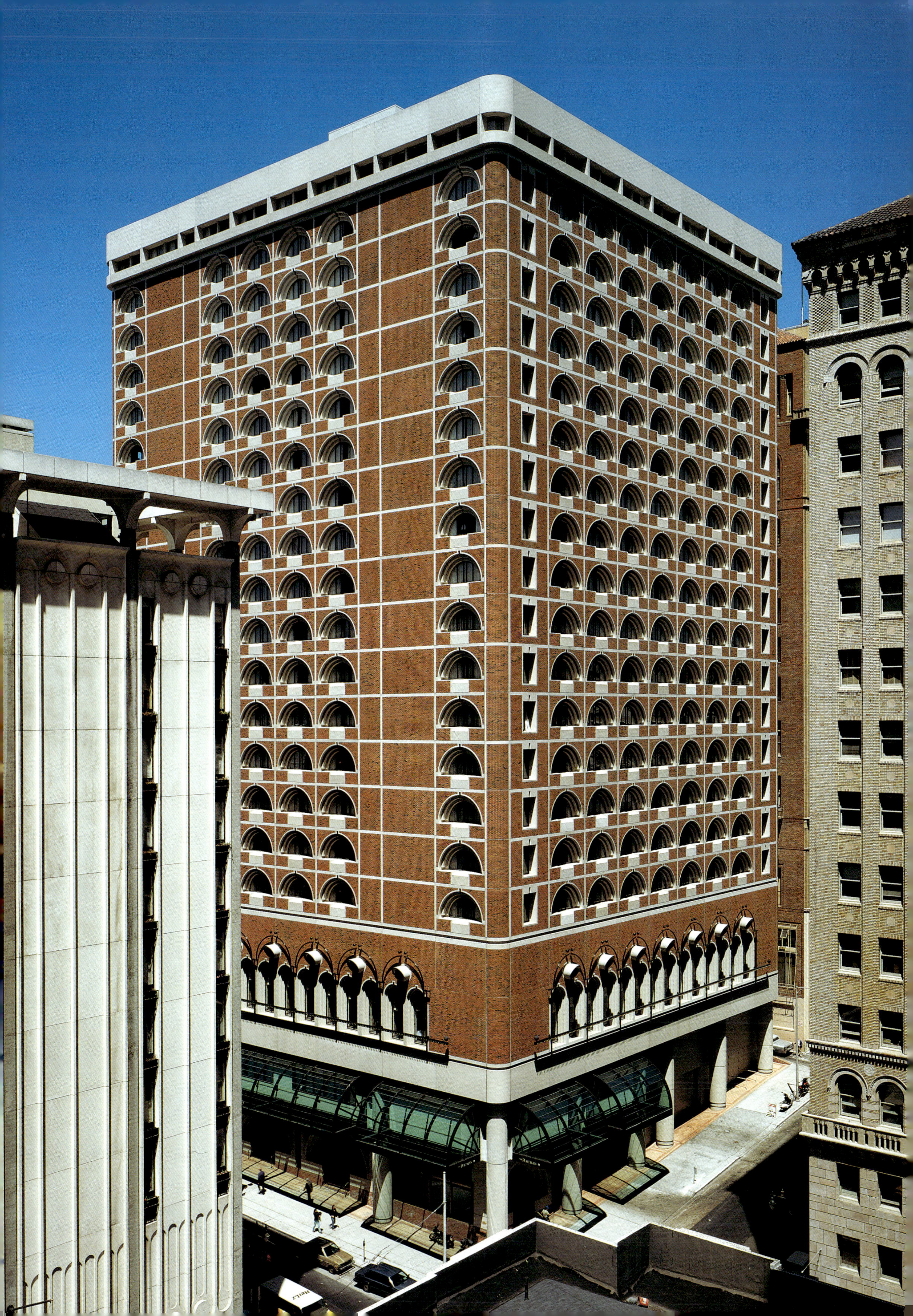

5

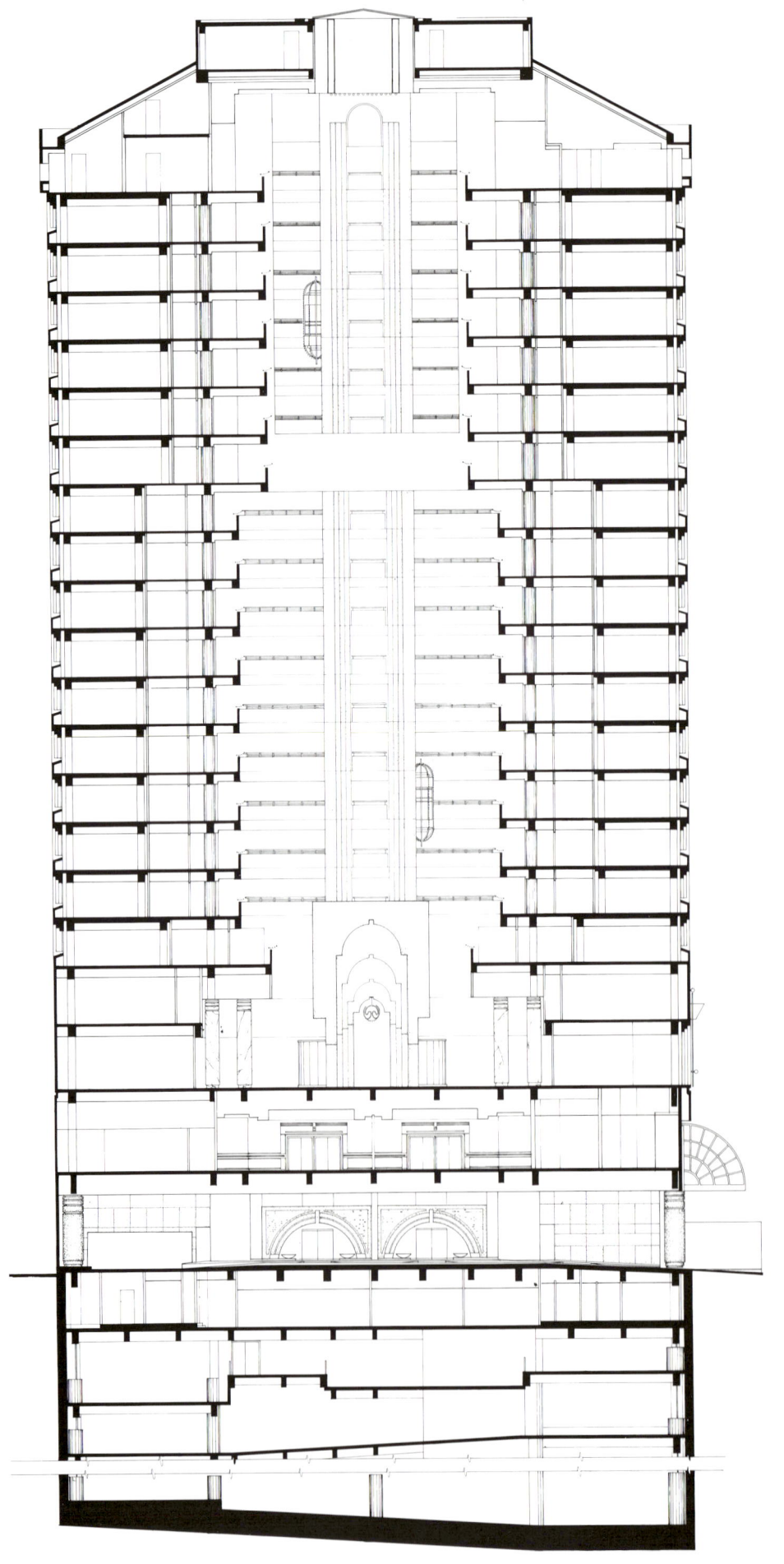

6

148

5   Section
6   Lobby seating area

The Portman Hotel (now named The Pan Pacific San Francisco)   149

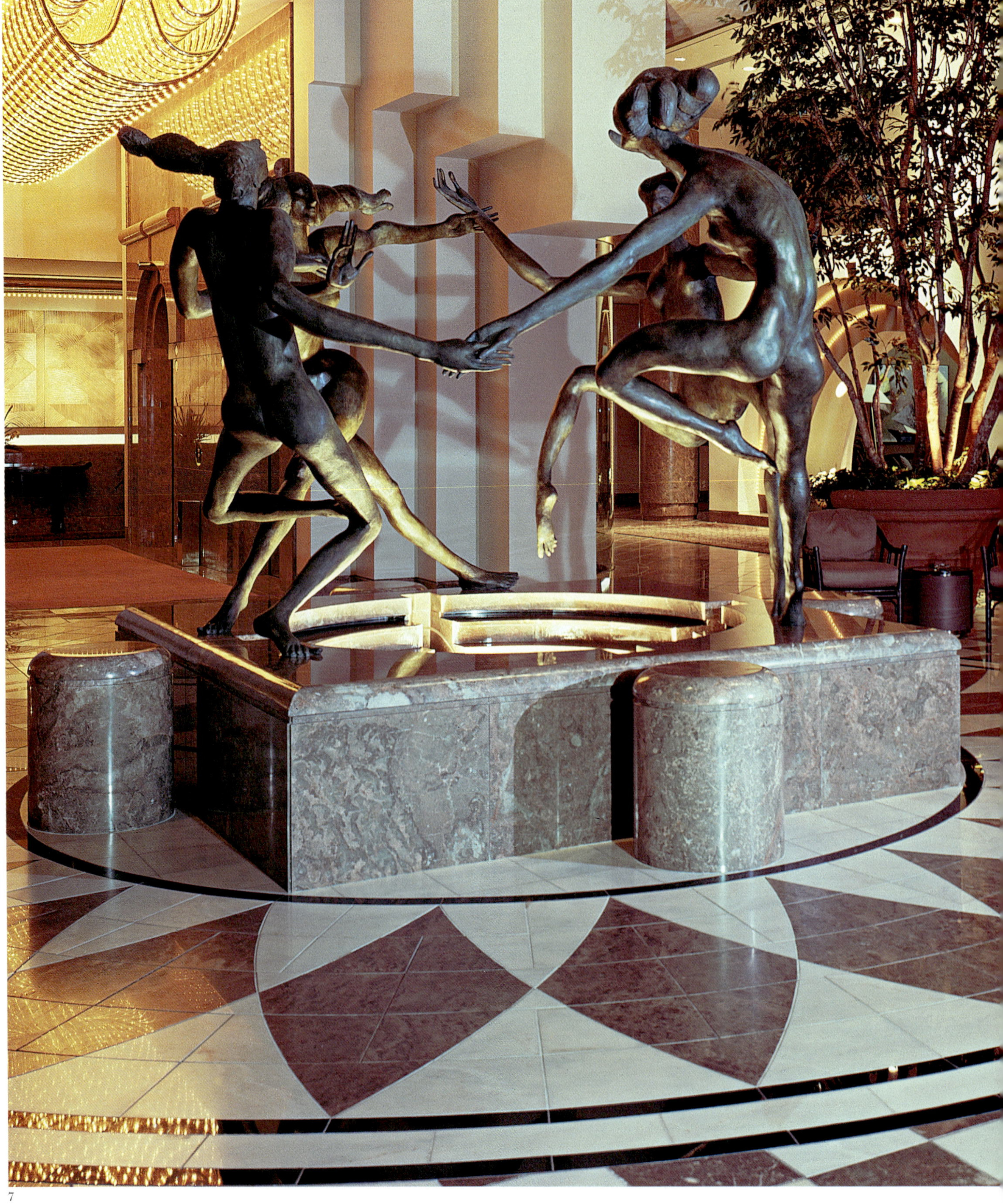

7

7 Atrium lobby with *Joie de Danse* sculpture by Elbert Weinberg
8 View at atrium balcony

The Portman Hotel (now named The Pan Pacific San Francisco) 151

The Regent Singapore

Design/Completion 1980/1982
Singapore
Pontiac Land (PTE) Ltd.
37,000 square meters
Concrete, stone, and glass

1   Ground floor plan
2   View of atrium
Opposite:
    View looking northwest

The design of the 504-room hotel had to be not only successful for selection by Singapore's Urban Redevelopment Authority but it also had to be a unique architectural structure to cater to the highly competitive luxury hotel market.

The site—a long, narrow parcel—dictated a basically rectangular structure. With no other constraints dictated by the site, a major architectural concept was to capitalize on Singapore's lush, green tropical environment. This was achieved on the exterior by designing planter boxes into the structure at each guestroom level as the levels step back on the east and west sides.

An atrium design evolved to bring this tropical quality into the hotel. The atrium is formed by two slab-like guestroom wings on the north and south sides that are separated by two east–west guestroom-floor elements. These east–west elements step in at each guest level from the base toward the top, permitting a skylight sufficient to allow natural light into the interior with minimal heat gain. Lush interior landscaping and water features recreate the tropical environment in the comfort of climate-controlled space. Shops, restaurants, and lounges surround the lobby to energize the space. Illuminated glass elevator cabs become kinetic sculptures, emphasizing other artworks especially commissioned for the hotel. Of note is 'Singapore Shower', an airy kinetic sculpture by Michio Lhara.

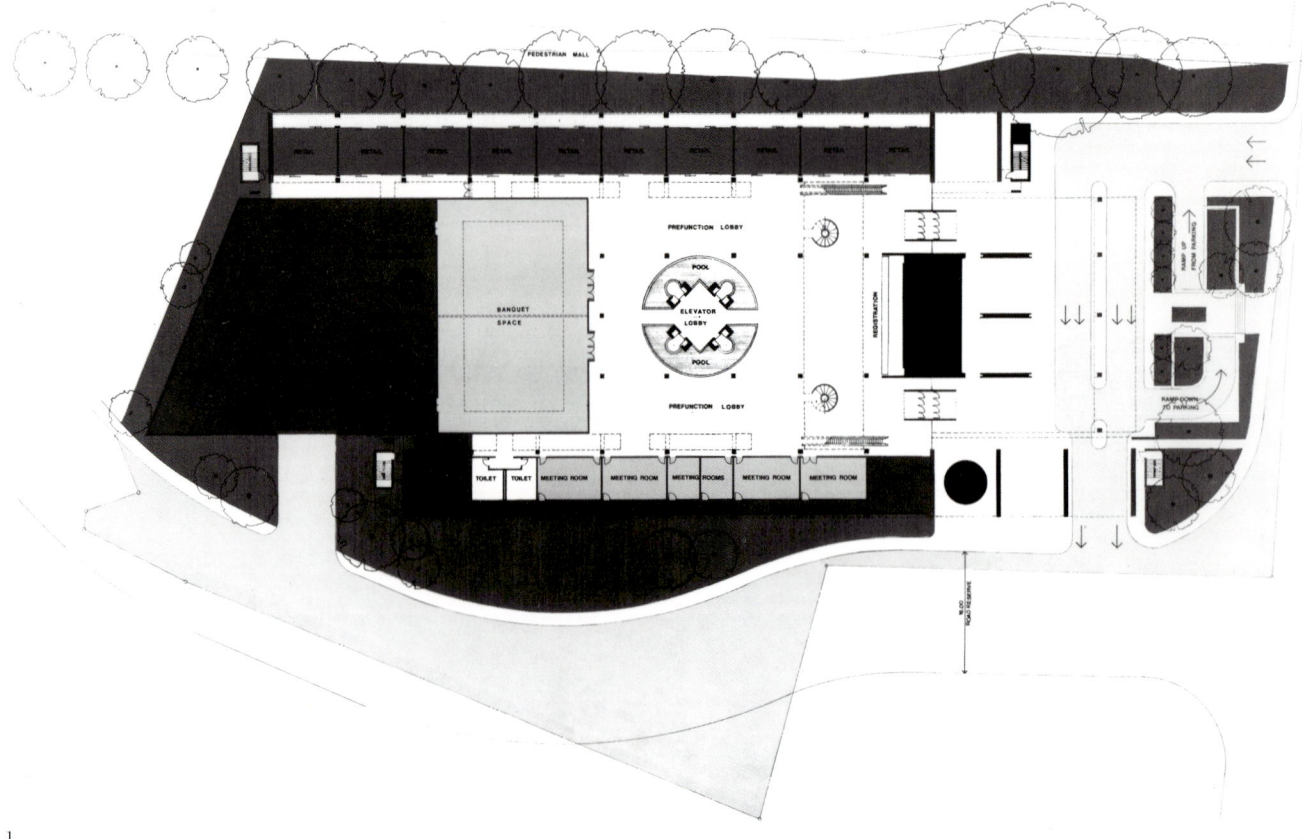

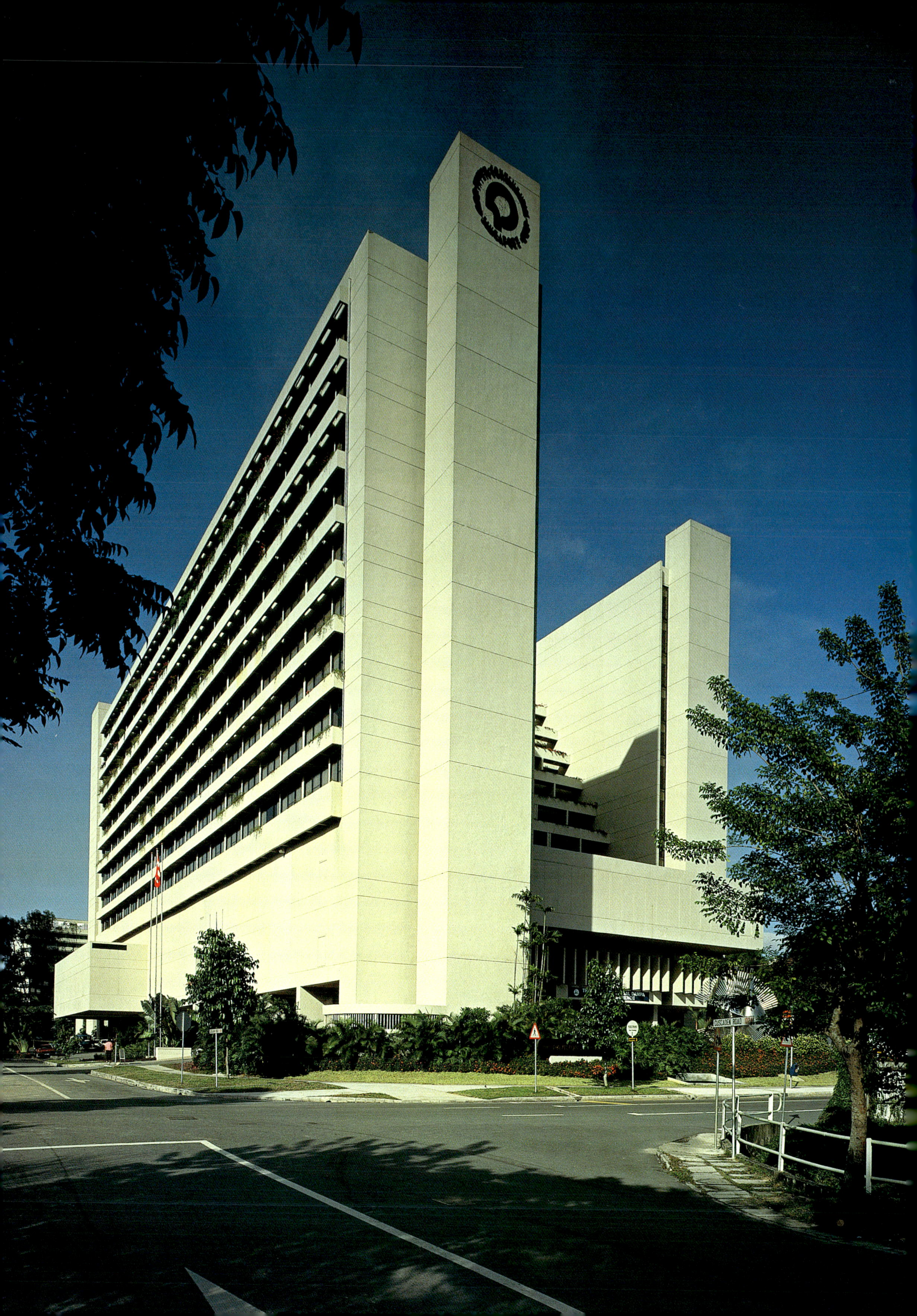

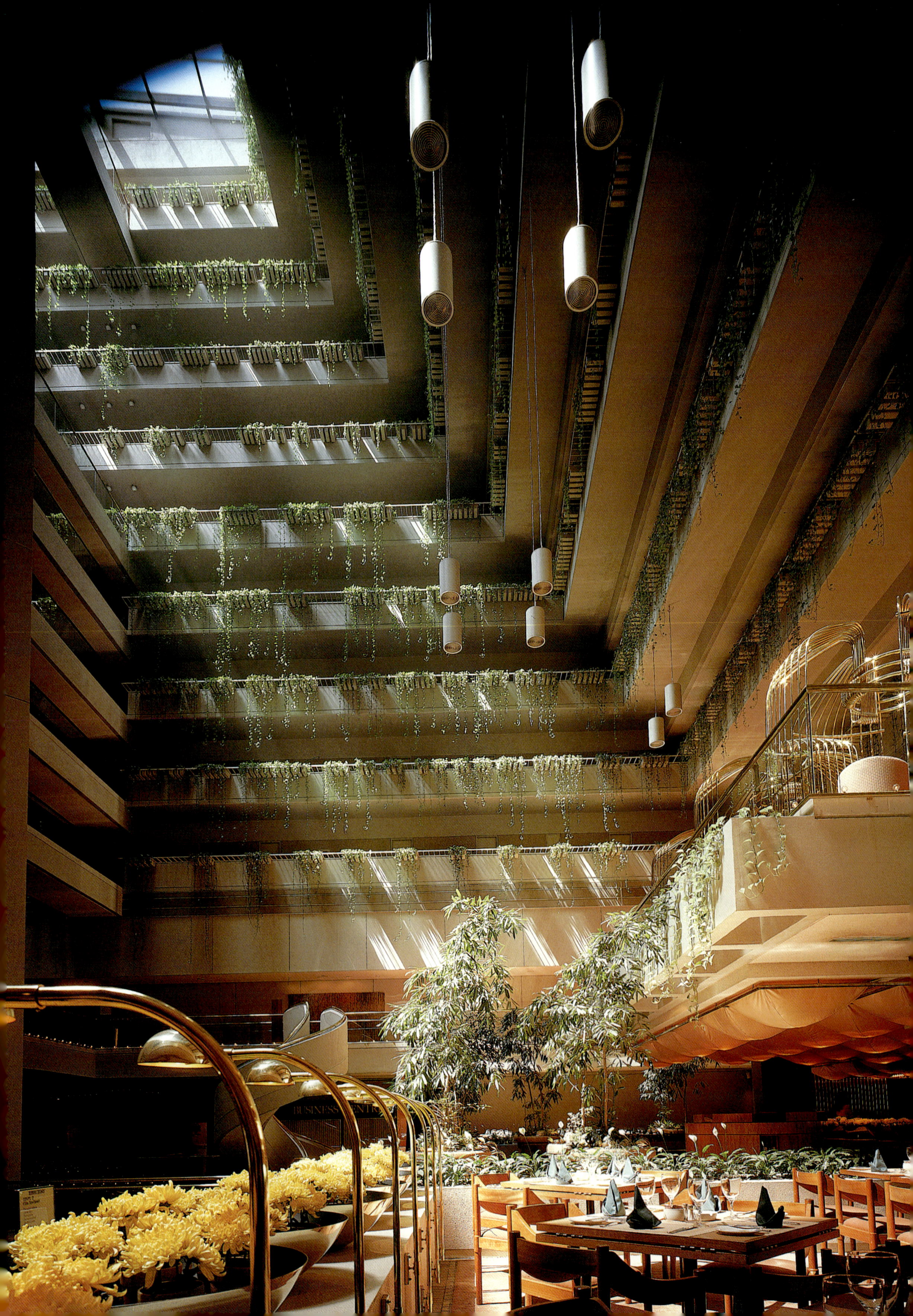
BUSINESS

Opposite:
   View of atrium lobby
5 View of atrium lobby elevators

Westlake International Hotel

Design Proposal 1996
Hangzhou, China
Rui Ming Investment Company Ltd.
21,400 square meters
Concrete, stone, metal paneling, and glass

The enchanting beauty and rich heritage of Westlake make this one of China's most popular tourist destinations. The design, therefore, needed to pay homage to the beauty of the lake and the magnificent culture of the City of Hangzhou.

The project is comprised of three major components: the 379-room hotel, 266 apartment units, and a retail complex. The hotel is the centerpiece of the complex. Its crescent-shaped plan embraces the lake with open arms and maximizes the magnificent view for the hotel guests. Beyond the hotel, the apartments span the length of the site nearest the city itself and are linked to the hotel by a multi-level retail complex that provides shopping and food service. The building height is limited to respect views of the lake from the city beyond.

The traditions of the region are planned to be an integral part of the luxurious hotel. Elements of nature such as water features and landscaping are carefully integrated into the project to reinforce the psychological link between the built environment and the natural beauty of the site. The stone facades of the buildings reflect the enduring quality that is vested in this project and speak to the timeless quality of the contribution it strives to make to the community.

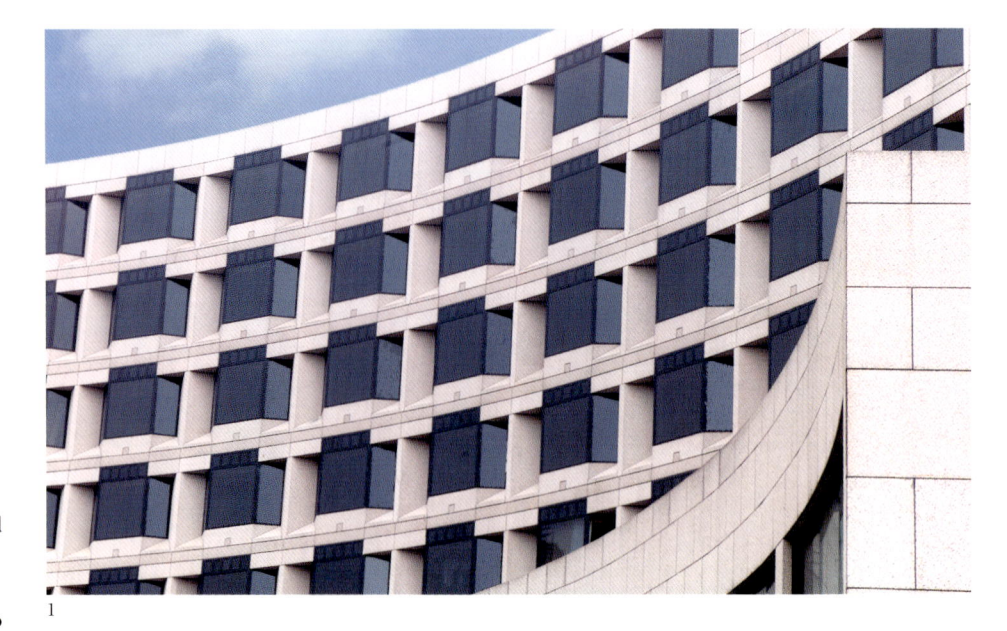

1 Exterior detail of hotel windows
2 Rendering looking across Westlake
3 Detail of sunscreen

Westlake International Hotel 157

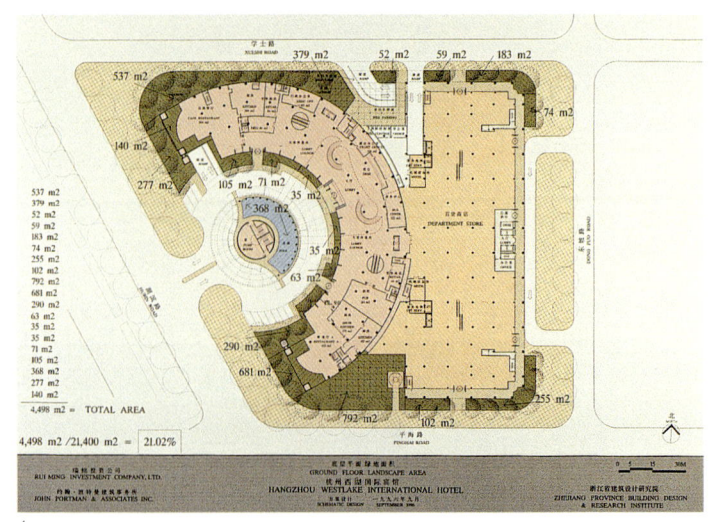

4 Ground floor plan
5 Detail of sunscreen
6 Skyward view of hotel

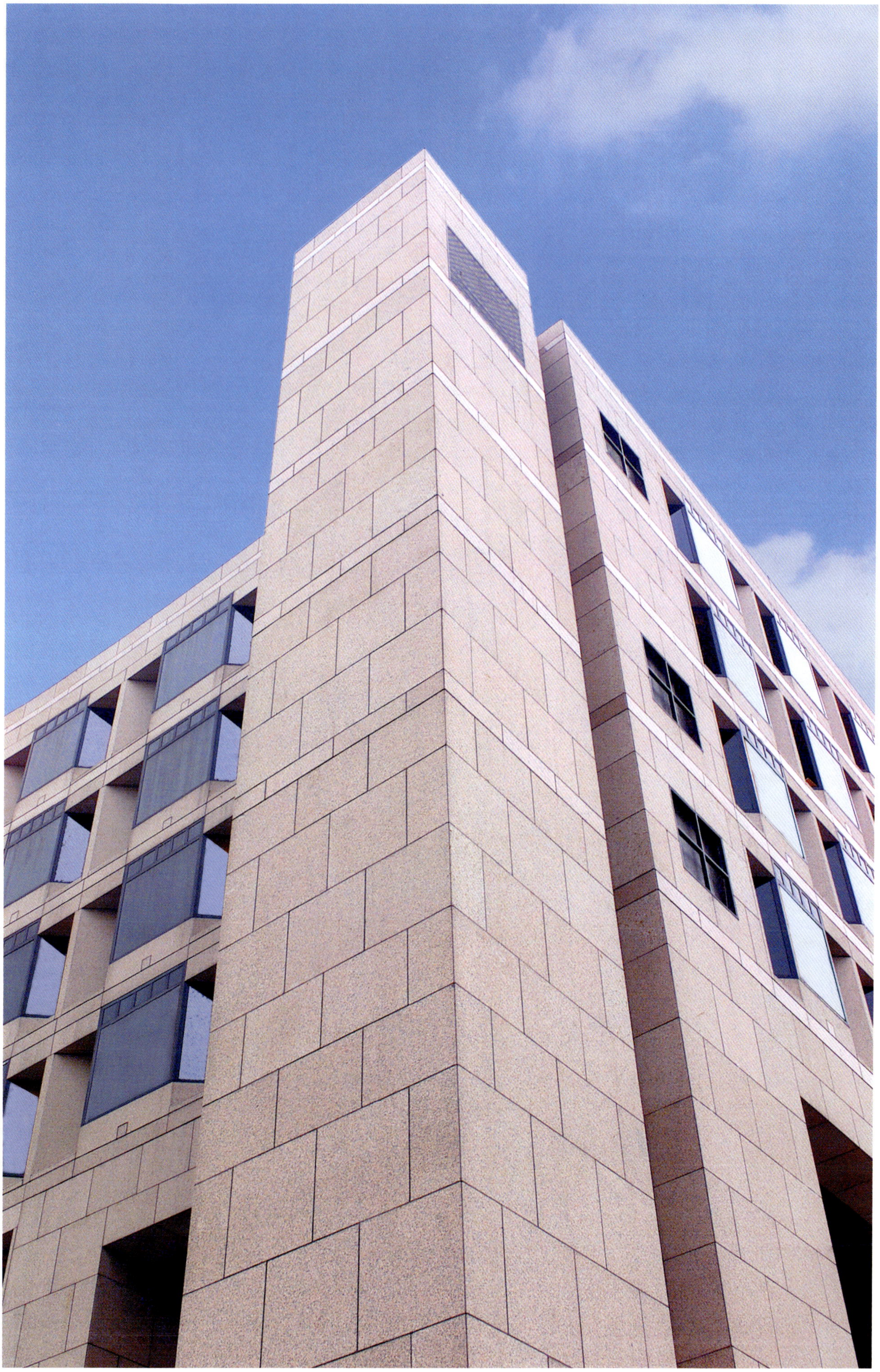

6

Hotelero Business Monterrey

Design Proposal 1994
Monterrey, Mexico
Grupo Las Aguilas
67,000 square meters
Concrete, stone, metal, and glass

1   Section
2   Rendering looking west

This 500-room luxury hotel was designed as the largest in the city. The hotel's strategic location, across from Cintermex (Mexico's large trade center), meets the demand for hotel rooms created by the activities in the trade center and the nearby amphitheater and park.

Monterrey is located in a valley surrounded by mountains. The unique shape of the mountain terrain was a primary influence on the design of the hotel. The tower's shape works in concert with these profiles in nature. The hotel was also meant to create a strong presence on the streetscape with the large ballroom spanning over the hotel's passenger drop-off. This strong triangular form, which is accented by artwork indigenous to the region, was to act as the focal point on the street.

Other amenities include 14 meeting rooms, three restaurants, two lounges, a business club, a fitness center/pool, and retail shops. In addition there is parking below grade for 700 cars and a rooftop helipad.

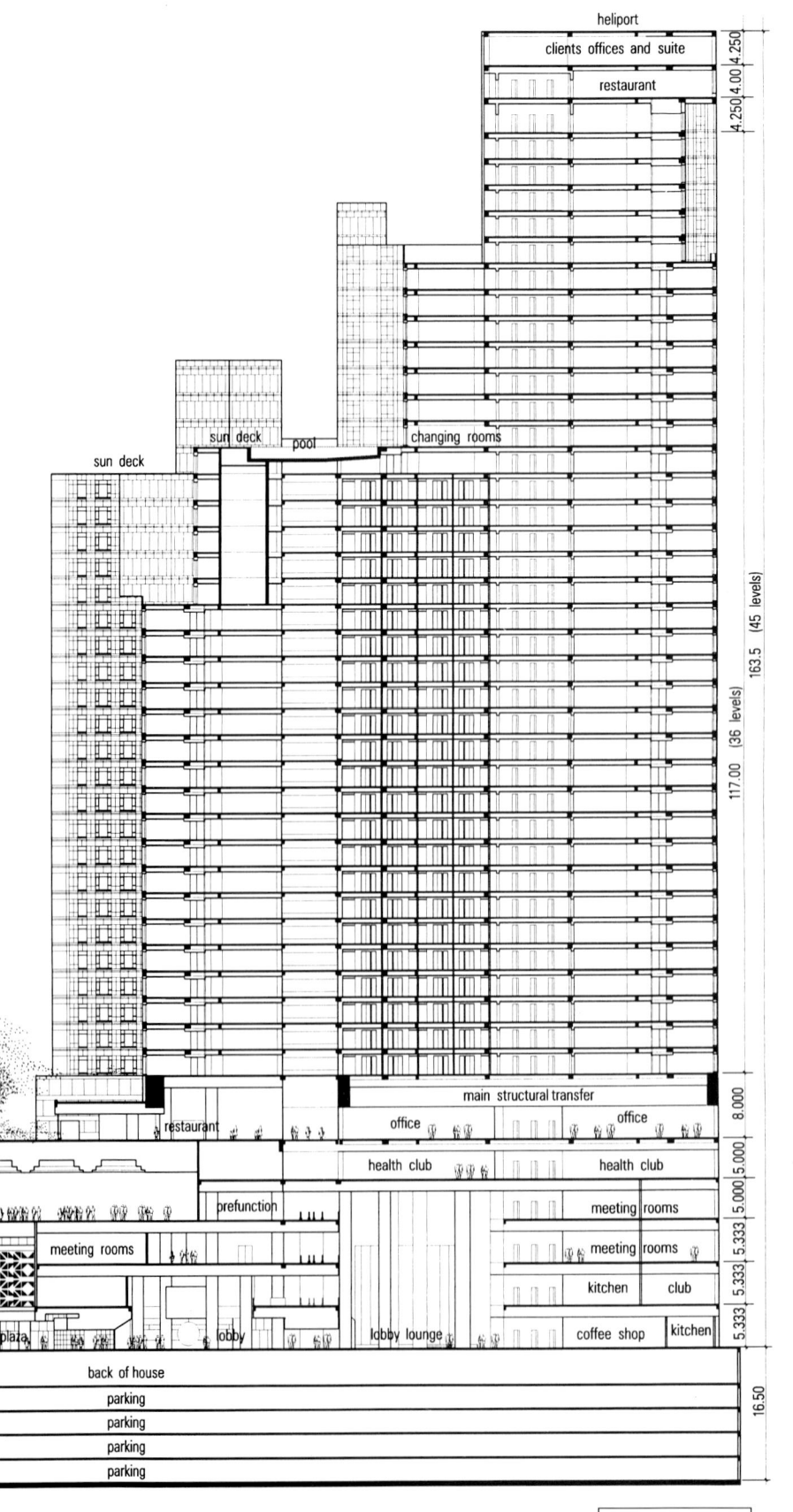

1

Hotelero Business Monterrey 161

'W' Hotel and Residences

Design/Completion 2000/2001
Philadelphia, Pennsylvania
Philadelphia Hotel Partners LLC
26,500 square meters
Brick with limestone accents, Exterior Insulation Finish System (EIFS)

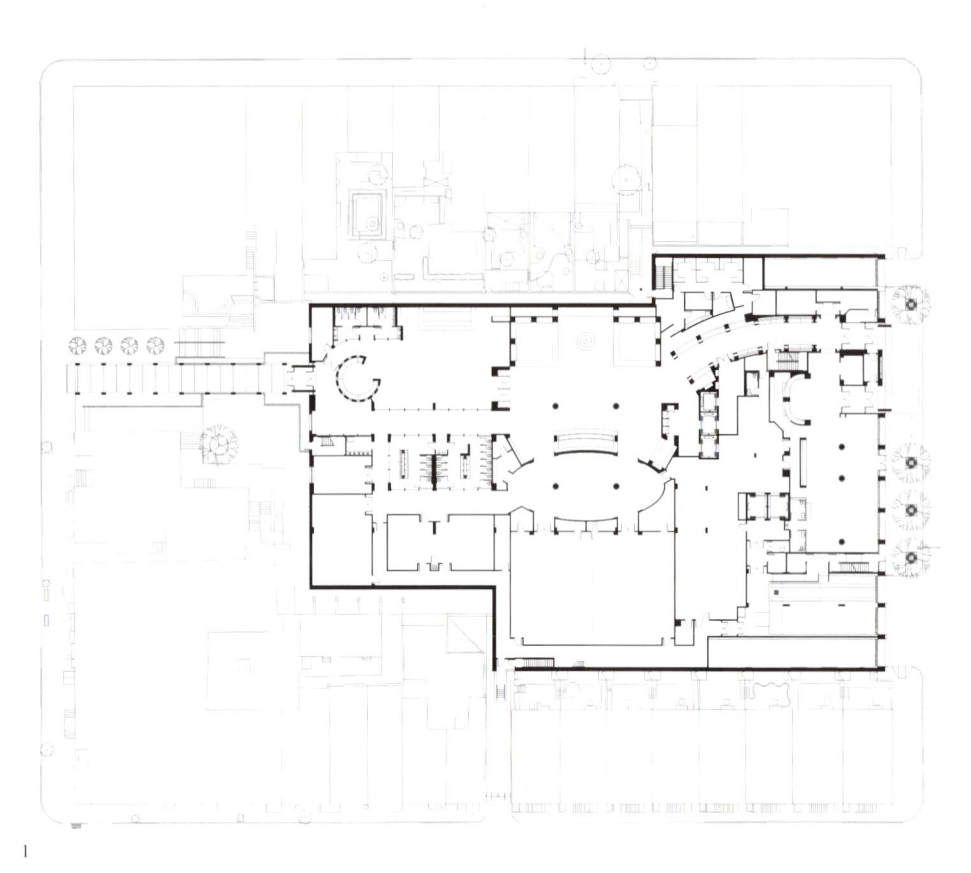

The Philadelphia 'W' Hotel and Residences is located in the historic Society Hill residential area of the city and is surrounded by housing. The design was required to take its cues from the historic elements of the surrounding brick architecture to create a modern yet sensitive response. The building is planned in a 'T' shape configuration. The top of the 'T', which faces the Delaware River, is taller than the remaining mass. The intent was to maximize the views of the river and the City of Philadelphia.

The project program consists of a 200-room boutique 'W' Hotel and 26 luxury condominium units. The hotel amenities include a ballroom, meeting facilities, the 'W' Café, a health club, a retail spa, a special restaurant and a bar/cocktail lounge that acts as the hotel's signature 'living room' as well as providing a popular local attraction. The hotel facilities and guestrooms occupy levels 1 through 6, while the 26 condominium units occupy levels 7 through 10. There are two levels of below-grade parking with approximately 170 parking spaces, both self-parking and valet.

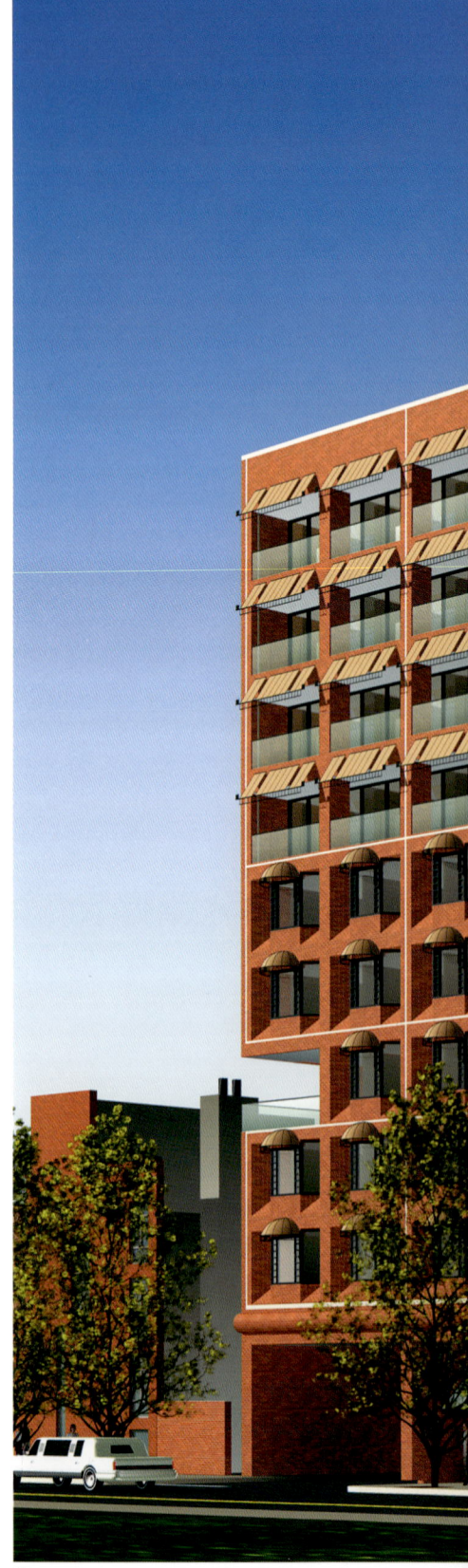

1   Ground floor plan
2&3 Rendering from Front Street

'W' Hotel and Residences 163

Westin Hotel Charlotte

Design/Completion 1998/2002
Charlotte, North Carolina
Starwood Hotels and Resorts Worldwide Inc.
50,200 square meters
Concrete, metal paneling, and glass

One of the primary design goals, in addition to meeting the basic program objectives, was to create a complex that would integrate with the surrounding fabric and encourage infill development from the city center south along a major urban corridor.

The hotel complex consists of three major components, which are integrated through a podium structure to be read as one: a 700-room hotel tower, a conference center, and a mid-rise office building. In addition, the project incorporates the city's trolley system, linking the city center to the historic district to the south. A 1,650-space parking structure accommodates the hotel complex and provides additional parking for the convention center. The parking structure is primarily located beneath ground level to minimize its impact on the overall project.

The podium includes the hotel lobby and other major public spaces such as the restaurant, lobby lounge and pre-function space. Through the use of expansive glass walls, various water features and extensive landscaping, the public spaces extend the hotel into the surrounding streetscape. The separation of the tower and the podium is clearly expressed through the articulation of massing and the use of materials. The materials at the street level recall the scale and texture of the surrounding building fabric while above the podium, aluminum panels and glass curtainwall express its presence on a developing skyline.

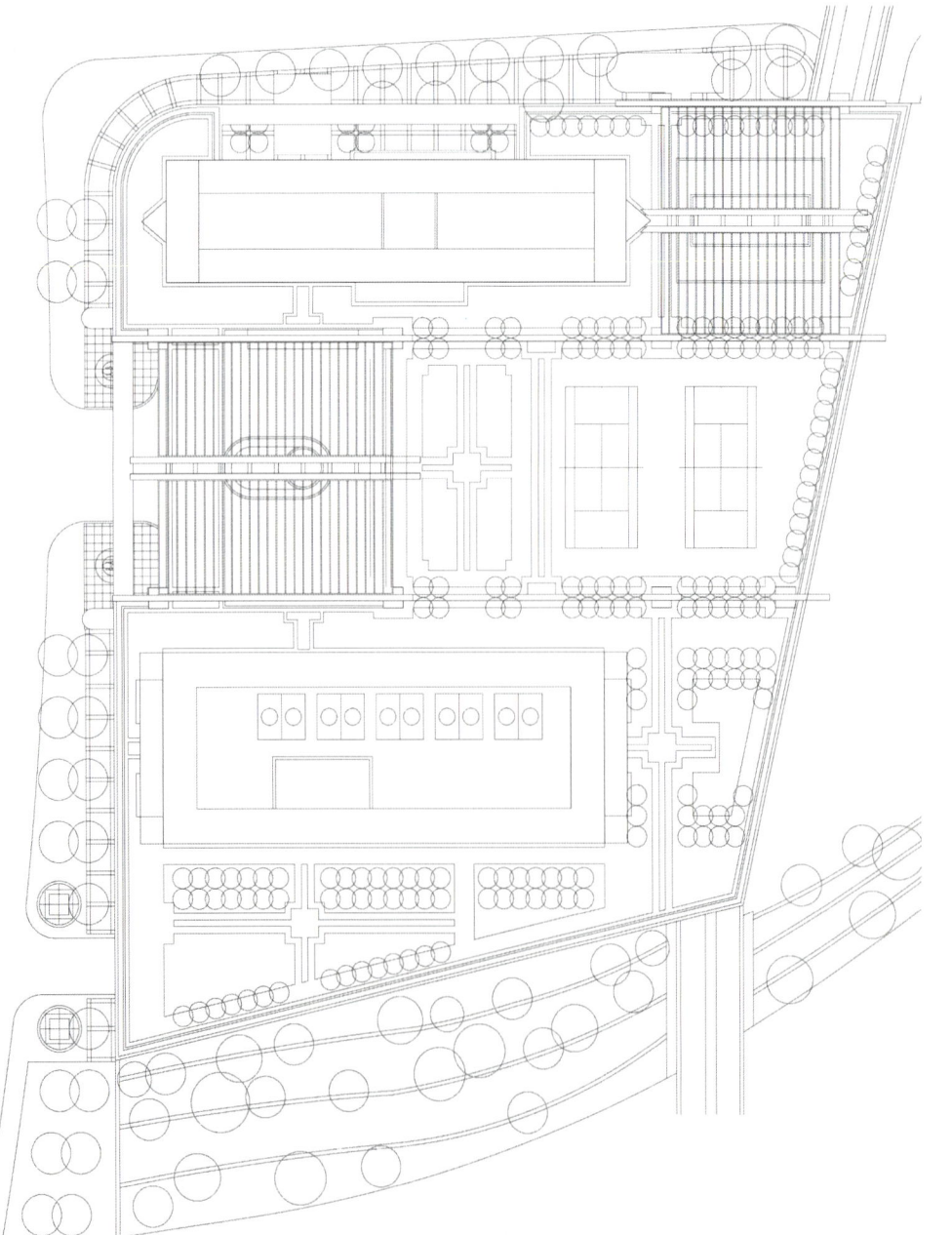

1 Site plan
2 Rendering of view looking southeast
3 Rendering of view looking east
4 Rendering of view looking west
5 Section through hotel and office

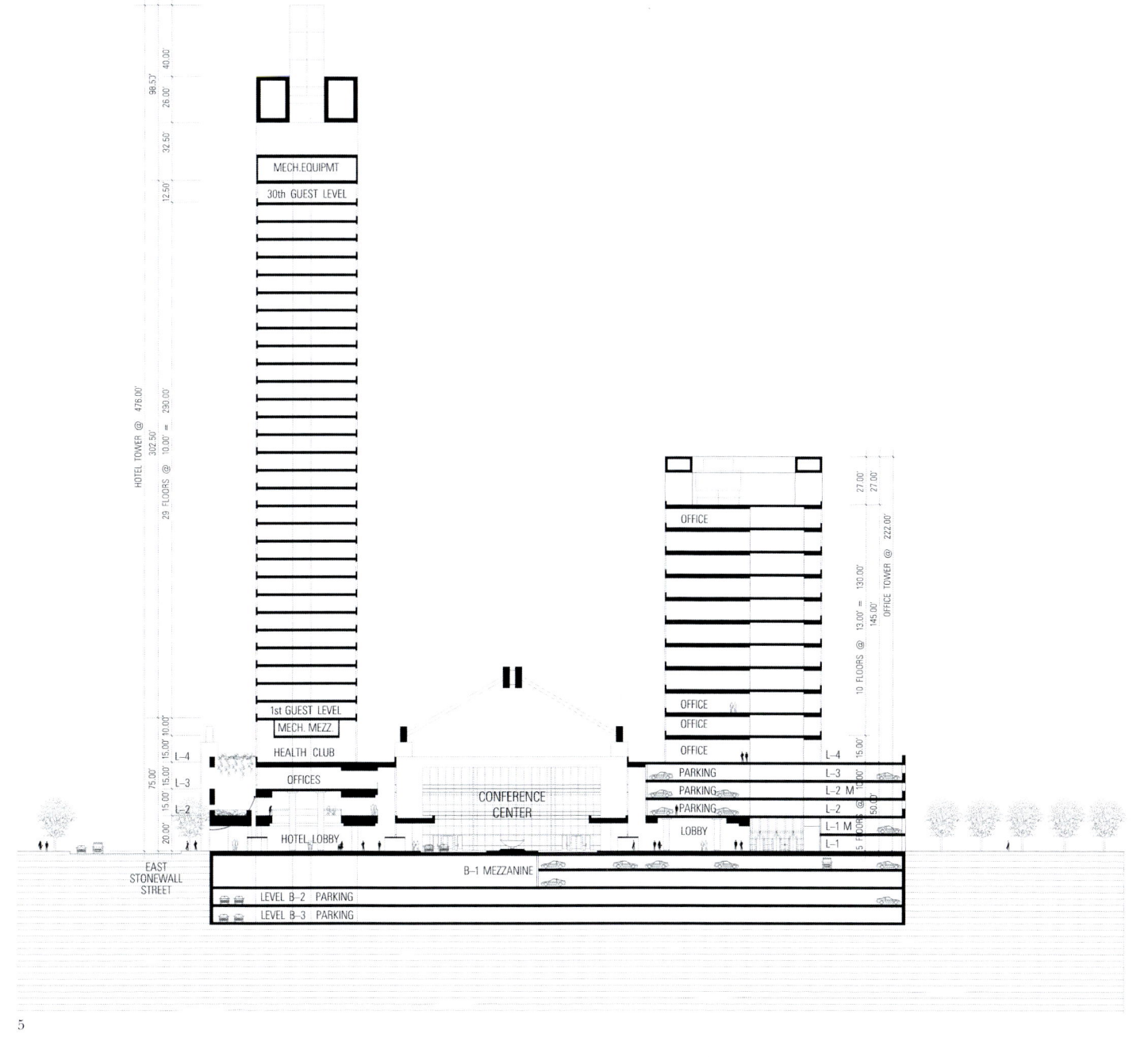

Westin Hotel Charlotte   165

Village of Schaumburg Convention Center, Performing Arts Theater, and Convention Headquarters Hotel

Design/Completion: 2002/2005
Schaumburg, Illinois

The Schaumburg project is a response to the need for world-class exhibition and meeting facilities and three-and-a-half to four-star hotel properties in Chicago's Northwest Suburbs. The inclusion of a 2,400-seat performing arts theater into the project serves to augment the amenities available to convention and meeting planners, and provides an exceptional entertainment venue for hotel guests, the community of Schaumburg, and residents of the greater metropolitan area.

Located on a prominent and previously undeveloped site along the Northwest Tollway (I-90) and Meacham Road, the project will form a visual 'entryway' into the Village of Schaumburg. Featuring highly flexible assembly spaces and highly functional shared support facilities, the project's components will be linked via enclosed connections and will be located around a new and lushly landscaped water feature. The complex's quality of architecture and high standard of functionality, as well as the site's high visibility and proximity to an expansive and highly successful corporate and retail business district, will make the facility the destination of choice for high-profile local and regional conference and meeting functions.

The complex will play an integral role in the continued economic growth of the Village of Schaumburg and will serve as an architectural icon for the Village. The image and quality of the project will position Schaumburg as the leader of Chicago's Northwest Suburbs and will enhance the commercial and general quality of life for this dynamic community.

1 Ground level plan
2 Atrium level plan
3 Section through hotel
4 Aerial view of model looking northeast
5 Aerial view of model
6 Model view of hotel and theater
7 Model view of hotel

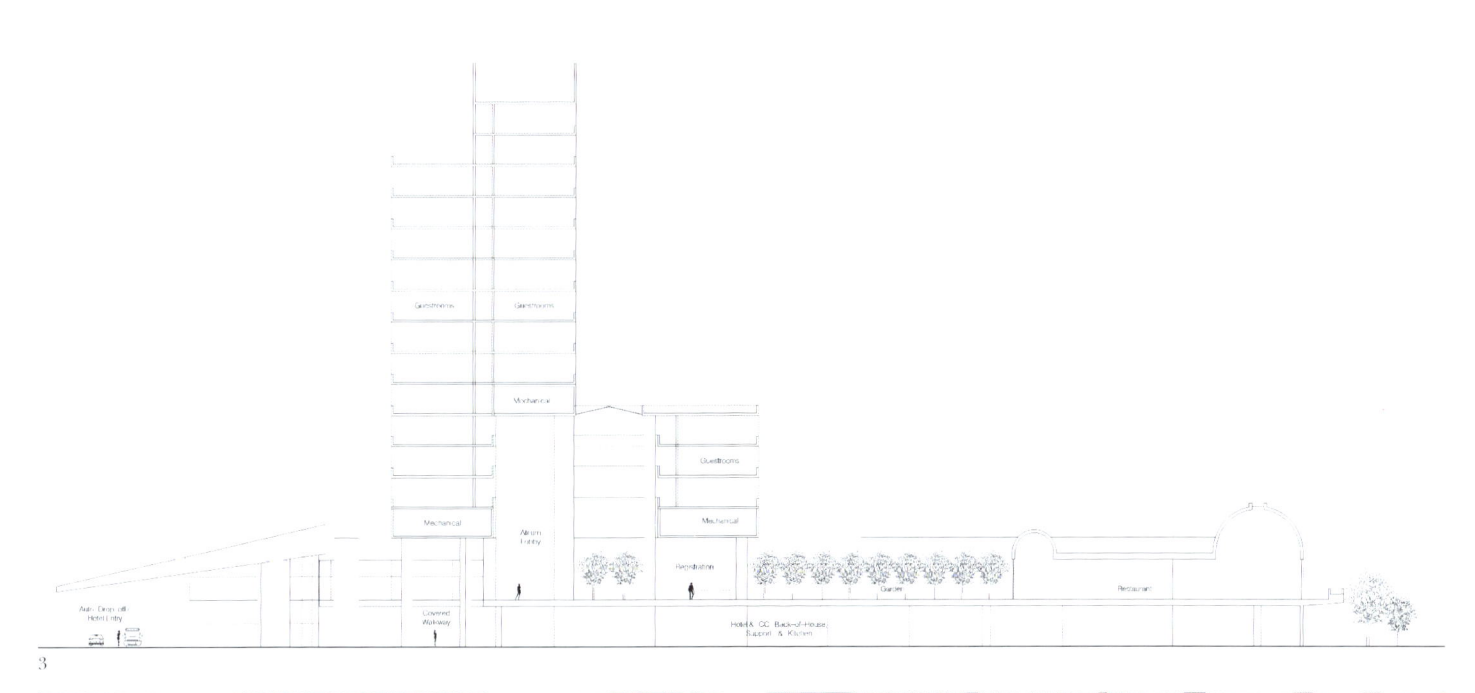

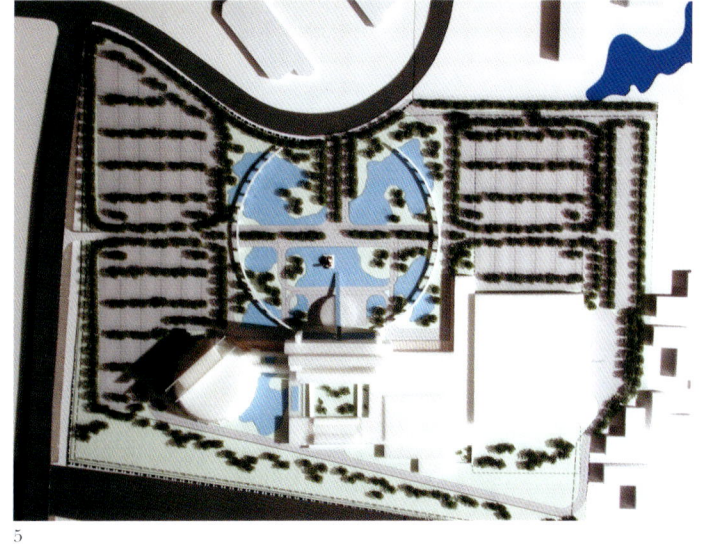

Village of Schaumburg Convention Center 167

Westin Hotel

Design/Completion 1998/2003
Warsaw, Poland
Hotel Atrium Sp. z o.o.
24,000 square meters
Concrete, stone, and glass

1 Typical hotel plan
2 Rendering from Jana Pawla looking south
Opposite:
    Rendering of glass atrium looking skyward

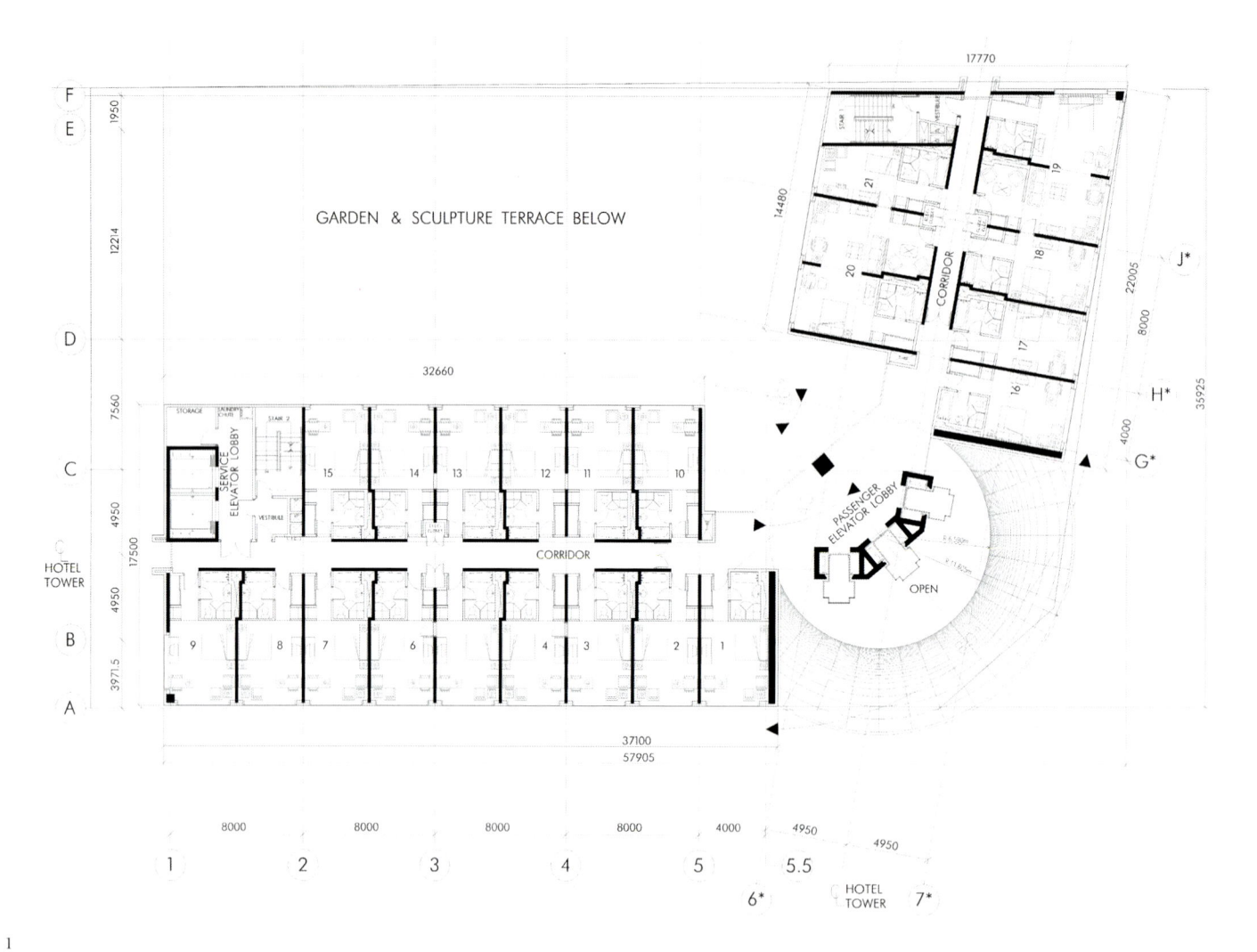

1

The Westin Hotel is redefining Warsaw's central business district in order to create one of Poland's most dynamic hotel developments. Situated in the existing Atrium North and South development, developed by Skanska International and Portman Holdings, the hotel will serve as the center point of the complex. The 366-room Westin Hotel is supported by a 530-square-meter ballroom with 450 square meters of meeting rooms and boardrooms that incorporate the latest in electronic technology. The importance of the hotel's location at the corner of Grzybowska and Jana Pawla II generated the design of a glazed vertical tube that will act as a beacon for Warsaw's Wola District.

The hotel tower's L-shape utilizes an efficient double-loaded corridor design. At the corner between the two legs will be a glass atrium, which will serve as the focal point of the building. It is also the point where the tower's vertical circulation is located. Dynamic illuminated glass observation elevator cabs provide an exciting experience for guests and a kinetic sculpture for the citizens of Warsaw.

2

Westin Hotel

East Seaport Apartment and High Rise Hotel Addition

Design Proposal 2001
Ningbo East Seaport Hotel Company Ltd.
Ningbo, China
76,650 square meters
Precast concrete, brick, and glass

The design of the East Seaport Apartment and High Rise Hotel Addition strives to capture the spirit of Ningbo's rich historic culture in the architectural forms, detail, gardens, and colors. The complex is a mixed-use project that includes the existing 14-story 50-meter-tall hotel guestroom tower, and the new 34-story 100-meter-tall high-rise residential, hotel, and office tower.

The site is located in the scenic coastal port city of Ningbo, in Zhejiang province. The total site area, including the existing Ningbo East Seaport Hotel, is 17,865 square meters. The project will integrate the functions of the high-rise five-star residential apartments, hotel guestrooms, and public functions in an internally complementary manner that also complements the existing hotel tower to enhance the use of the site.

The site arrangement acknowledges the historic Chinese symmetrical organization of space. The complex is entered through open gateways, much like the ancient palaces of China. Great effort has been made to give each room a sense of the surrounding city, with ample views of the city from each room. The design marks an evolution in the city's architecture and will make a significant contribution to Ningbo's urban architectural heritage in the new millennium.

1 Rendering of interior atrium
2 Site plan
3 Rendering looking north
4 Elevation

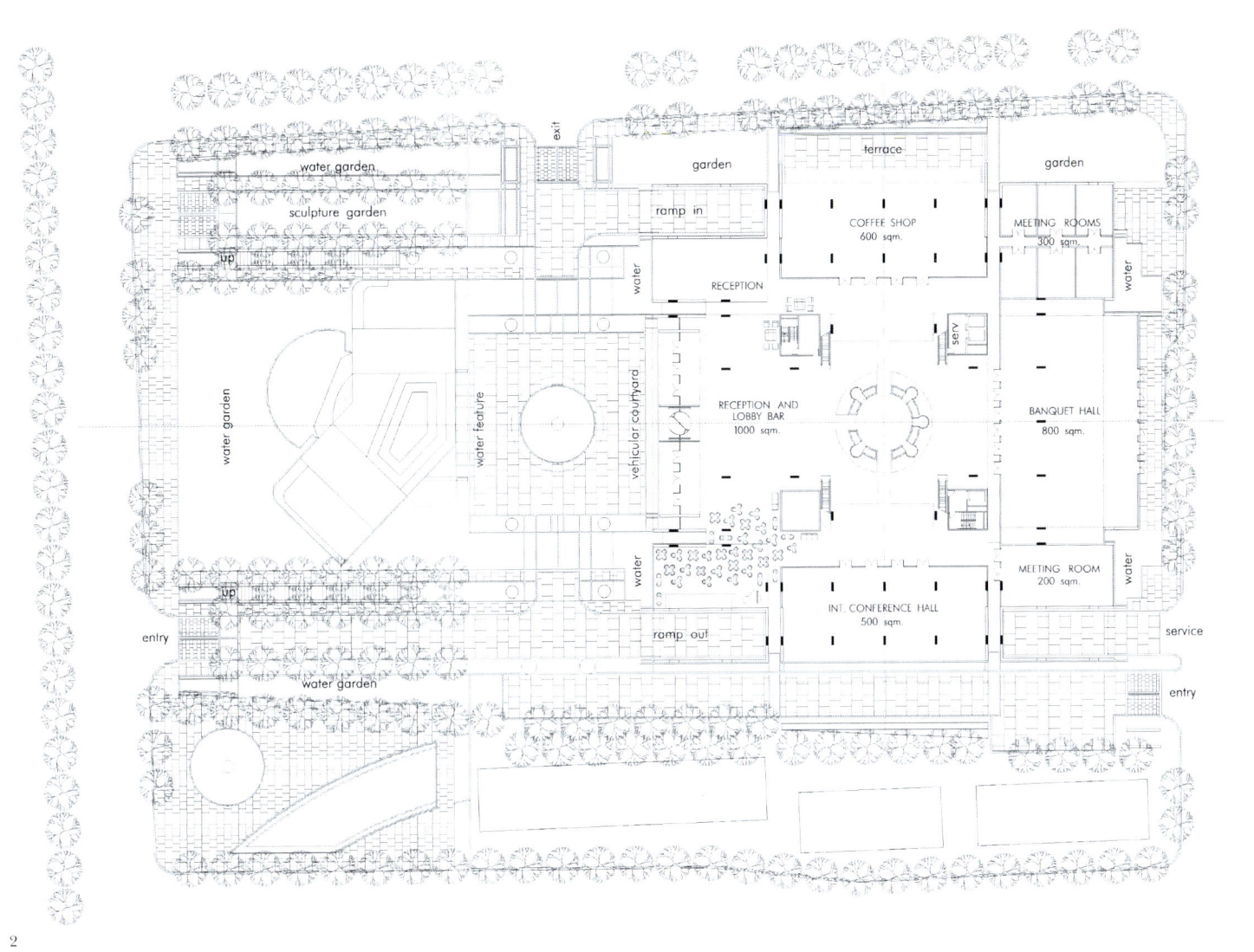

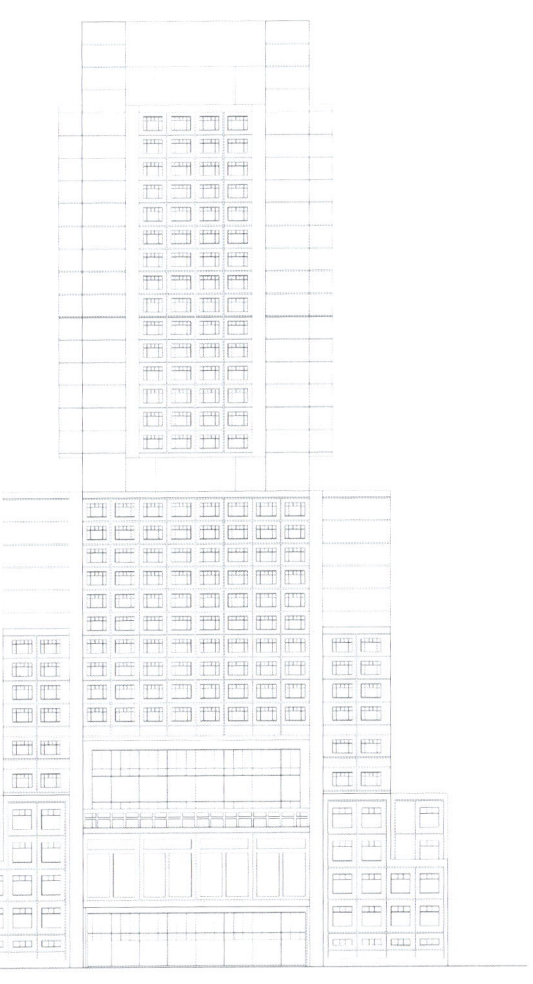

East Seaport Apartment and High Rise Hotel Addition   171

Bank of China

Design/Completion 1993/1995
Hangzhou, China
Bank of China
55,000 square meters
Concrete, stone, and glass

The Bank of China wanted a building with a strong and distinctive presence in the central business district of Hangzhou. The tower provides offices for the bank and other tenants and a grand banking hall for its commercial operations. The tower steps back from the large podium base that accommodates the more public functions of the building. A large rectangular portal, flanked by two smaller towers, counterbalances the tower beyond and creates a ceremonial entry to the banking halls.

Local Chinese character is preserved through the use of native stone and attention to scale and proportion to echo the architecture of ancient China. As the tower rises there are three changes in the form of the facade. The roof above the podium and the tower is used as landscaped gardens for the tenants.

1 Aerial view of model
2 Aerial view of model
3 View of model looking west
4 Rendering looking west

Bank of China

Bank of Communications

Design/Completion 1997/2000
Shanghai, China
Shanghai Shen Tong Real Estate Company
29,000 square meters
Concrete, granite, and brick

The award-winning Bank of Communications is a dual-function building. The 17-story structure provides 20,000 square meters of space for the bank's operational functions and 9,000 square meters of prime rental office space.

In addition to the program requirements, the design challenge was to maximize the site's location, access and scale while blending with the surrounding historic areas to create a signature building. Particular attention was paid to the detail and selection of quality materials and building systems, while addressing present and future space requirements with maximum flexibility.

The architecture is distinctive yet in harmony with the quality and context of neighboring buildings in the Bund. The plan of the granite-clad building relates to the parallelogram-shaped site to maximize coverage of the site. The two functions within the building are separated at the 7th level with the bank below and the rental office space above. Each separate function has its own entrance and mechanical system.

1 Rendering
2 Ground floor plan
Opposite:
   Skyward view of atrium roof detail

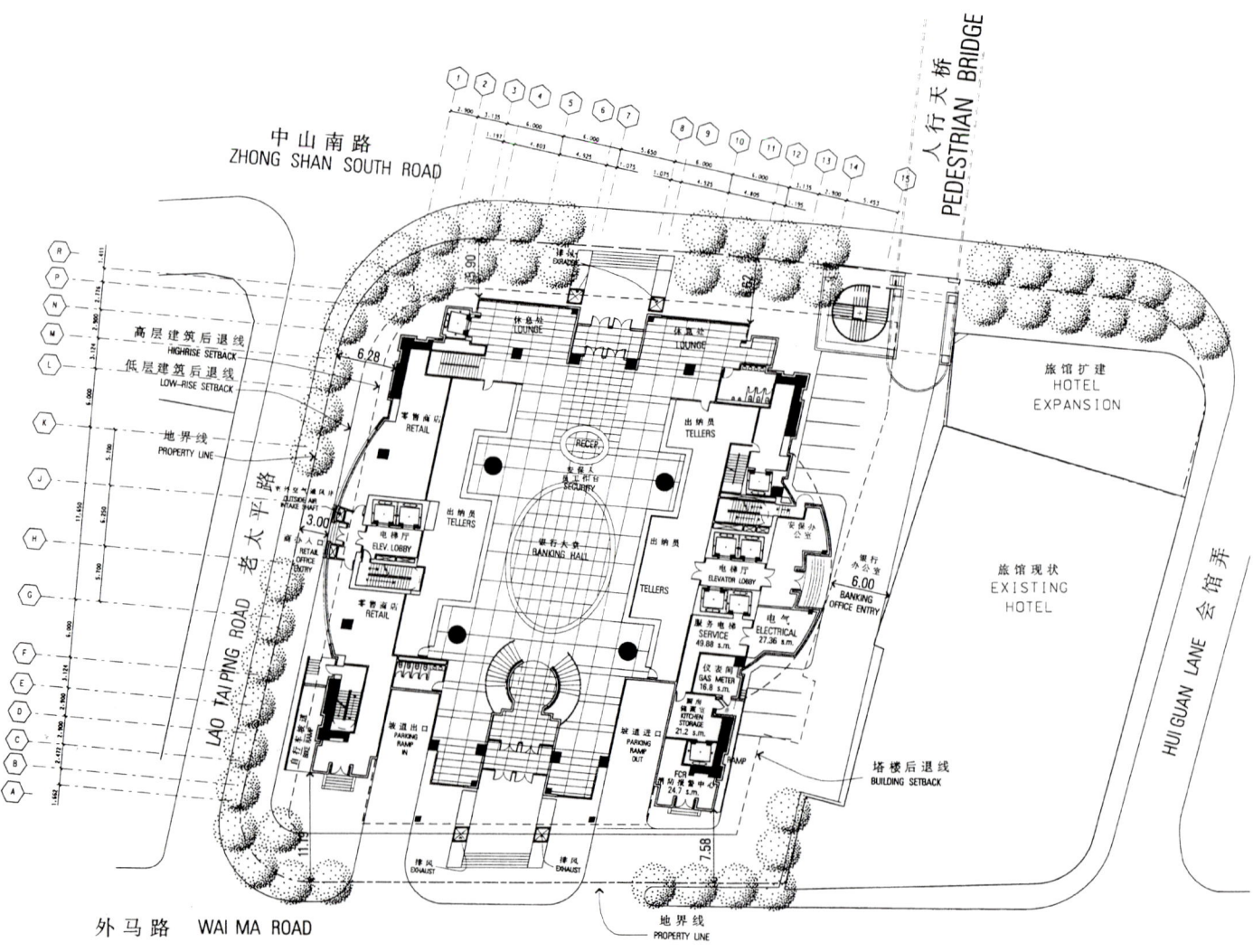

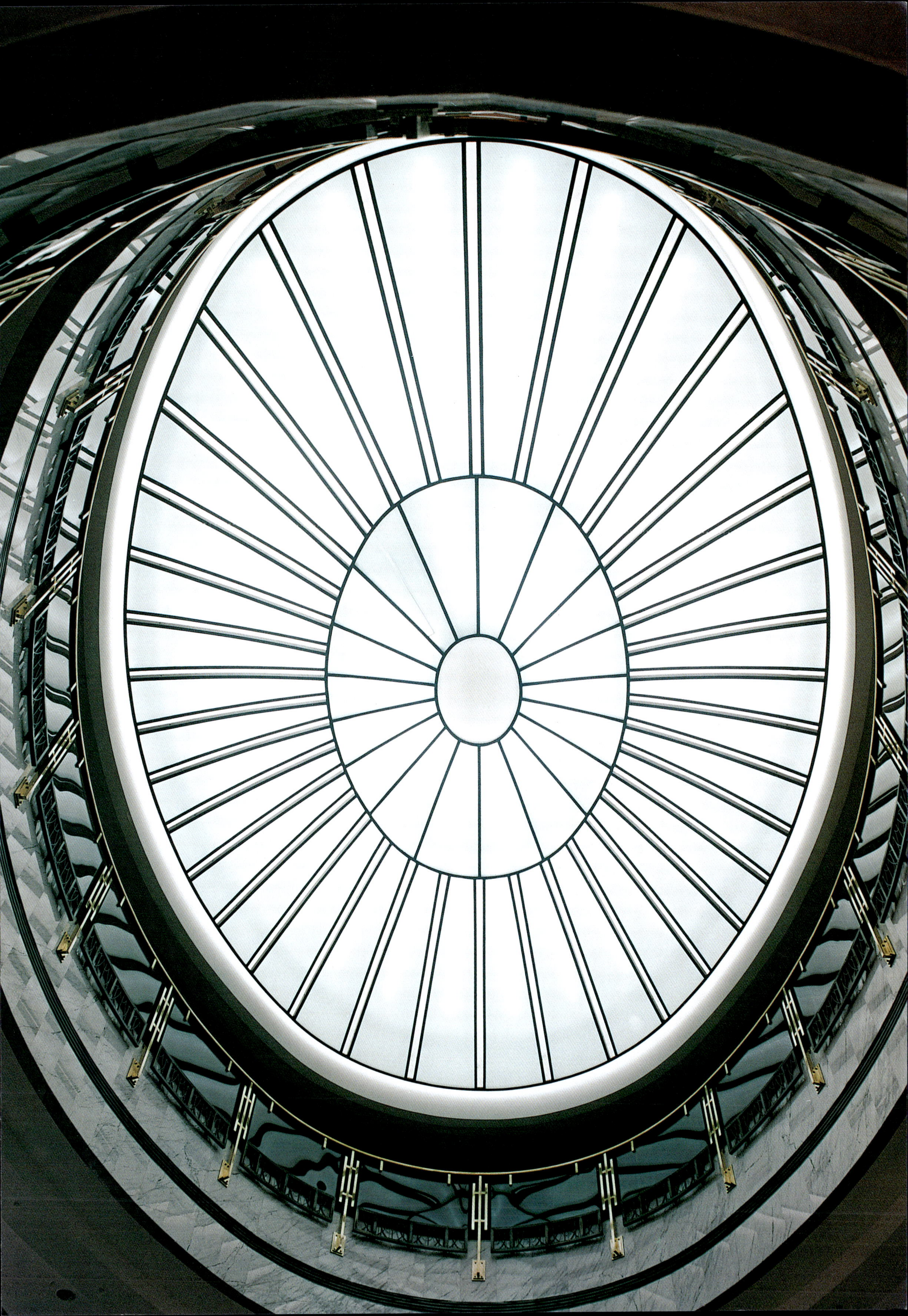

4 Interior rendering of atrium
5 Skyward view
6 Building section

屋顶
ROOF LEVEL

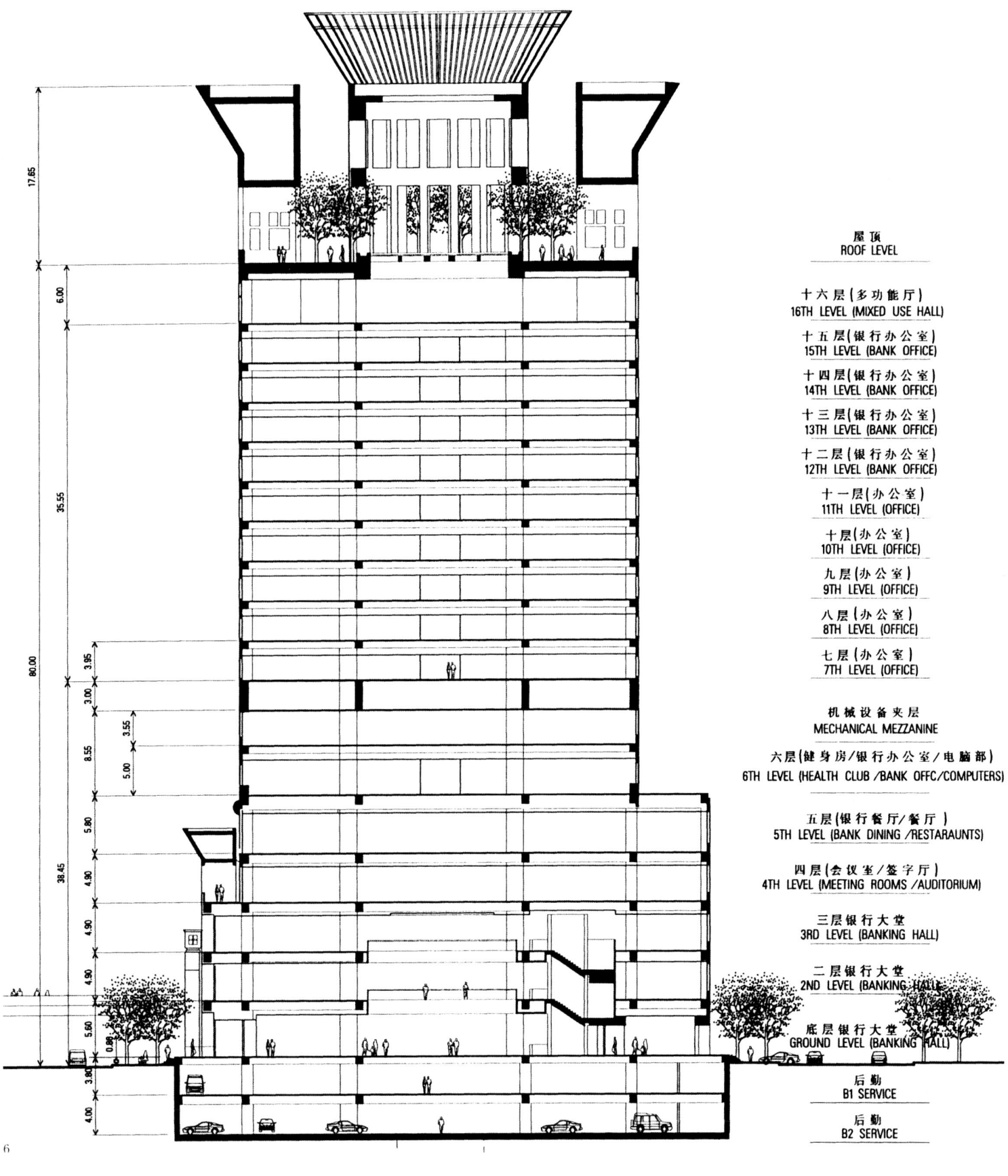

十六层（多功能厅）
16TH LEVEL (MIXED USE HALL)

十五层（银行办公室）
15TH LEVEL (BANK OFFICE)

十四层（银行办公室）
14TH LEVEL (BANK OFFICE)

十三层（银行办公室）
13TH LEVEL (BANK OFFICE)

十二层（银行办公室）
12TH LEVEL (BANK OFFICE)

十一层（办公室）
11TH LEVEL (OFFICE)

十层（办公室）
10TH LEVEL (OFFICE)

九层（办公室）
9TH LEVEL (OFFICE)

八层（办公室）
8TH LEVEL (OFFICE)

七层（办公室）
7TH LEVEL (OFFICE)

机械设备夹层
MECHANICAL MEZZANINE

六层（健身房/银行办公室/电脑部）
6TH LEVEL (HEALTH CLUB /BANK OFFC/COMPUTERS)

五层（银行餐厅/餐厅）
5TH LEVEL (BANK DINING /RESTARAUNTS)

四层（会议室/签字厅）
4TH LEVEL (MEETING ROOMS /AUDITORIUM)

三层银行大堂
3RD LEVEL (BANKING HALL)

二层银行大堂
2ND LEVEL (BANKING HALL)

底层银行大堂
GROUND LEVEL (BANKING HALL)

后勤
B1 SERVICE

后勤
B2 SERVICE

Bank of Communications 177

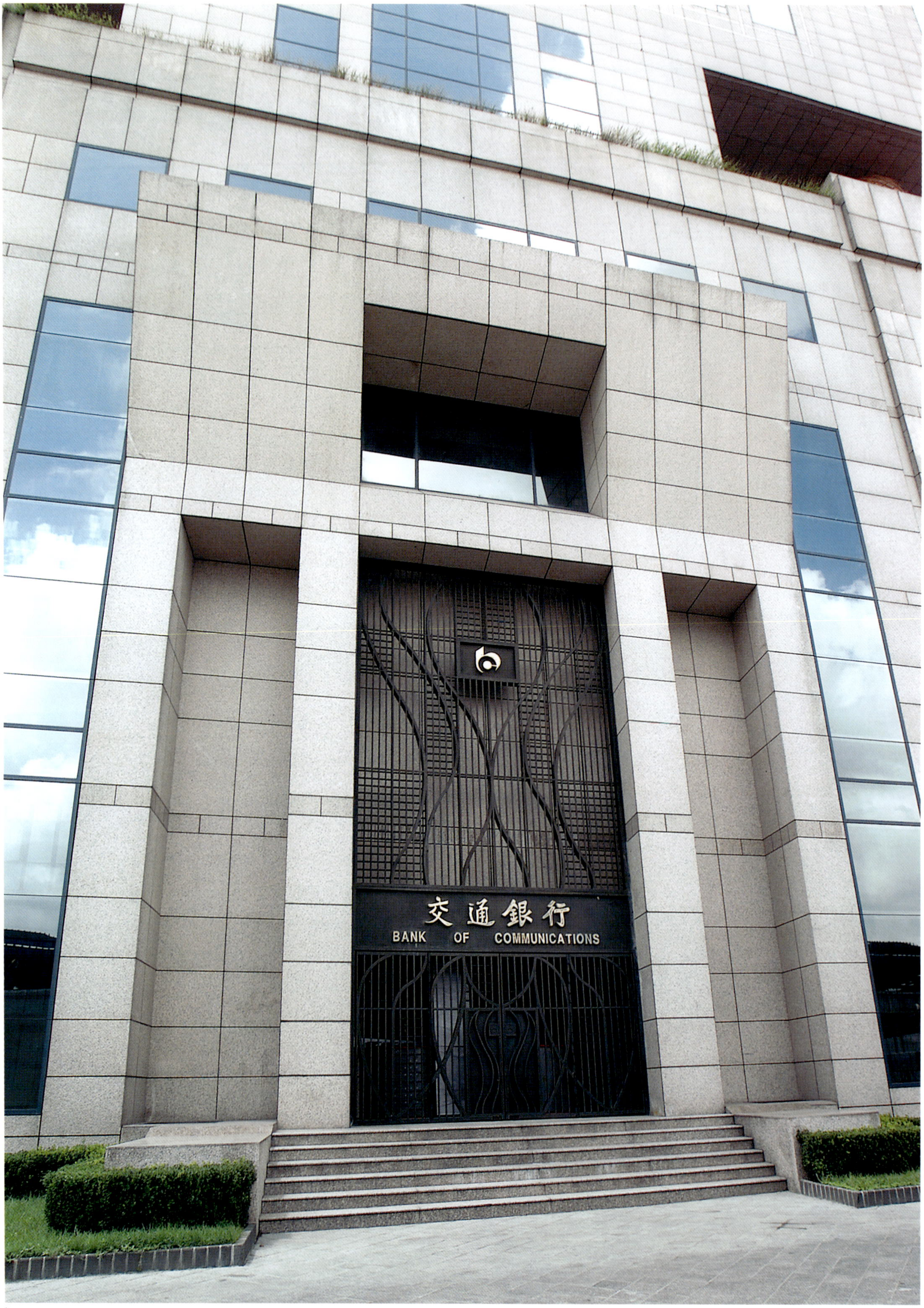

7

7 Detail of bronze gates at front entrance
8 View of atrium
9 Entrance detail

Bank of Communications 179

Great Park

Design Proposal 1979
Atlanta, Georgia
Land Use Consultants Inc.
219 acres
Master plan

In response to a proposed freeway expansion by the Atlanta Regional Commission, a master plan was developed that grouped issues into three categories: 1) transportation; 2) cultural, recreational, historic, and educational activities; and 3) housing. The site links the eastern edge of the downtown business district with a historic suburban residential community. Part of the site adjoins the city's rapid transit system.

The plan proposed constructing much of the freeway as a tunnel to make large areas of land available for park development. Two major land areas are within the Great Park. The central site was to be an International Cultural Village featuring foreign nation art pavilions (similar to the Venice Biennale) and various community festivals. Another magnet was a performing arts amphitheater, an aquarium, and historic and cultural museums. Winding through the site from downtown and extending into the four legs of the park was a network of bicycle, jogging, and walking trails that interconnect the many passive recreation uses and terminate at the proposed site of the Carter Presidential Library.

Housing was an integral component of the plan, making a logical transition between the older established neighborhoods and the newly constructed freeway and park. Both single family and duplex housing were proposed to meet the city's growing need for good-quality, close-in housing. The plan was not implemented due to the failure of various political jurisdictions to reach agreement. The Carter Presidential Library was the only part implemented, not in the planned location, but in the heart of the site.

1 Master plan
2 Park rendering
3 Rendering of water park
4 Rendering of pedestrian trail
5 Landscape plan

2 Water Park Within Festival Area

3 Pedestrian Trail Through Sculpture Garden

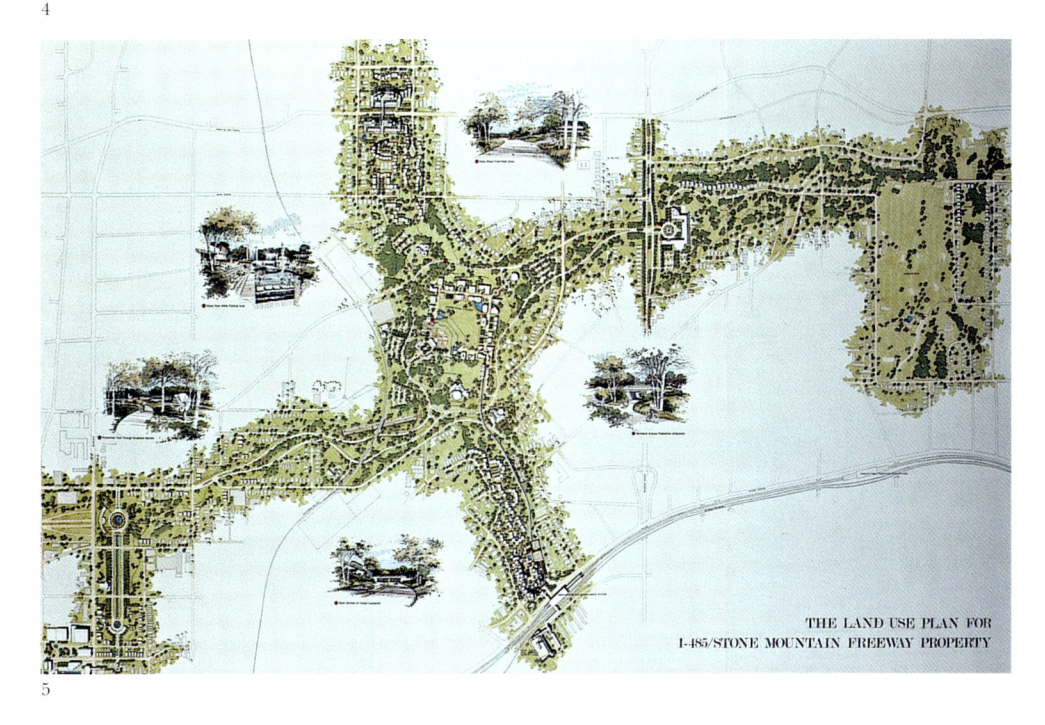

THE LAND USE PLAN FOR
I-485/STONE MOUNTAIN FREEWAY PROPERTY

Great Park 181

BSD New Town

Design Proposal 1995
Near Jakarta, Indonesia
PT Bumi Serpong Dumai Development
4.6 million square meters
Master plan

To counter the exponential growth and high density of Jakarta, the client wanted to plan a new town 30 kilometers east of the city in which the master plan would provide for a significant improvement in the function of the community and the lifestyle of its residents. The issues to be addressed included: transportation (regional, internal, light rail, pedestrian, and bicycle); program and zoning; open space; block development; development phasing; drainage; sewage; and water and power supply.

A river valley that intersects the site became a key component in the planning. The business district was divided into two, with one side focusing on governmental activity, and the other focusing on commercial activity. A ring road encircles the two. A secondary spine runs the length of the two districts and is the collector for light rail, pedestrian, and bicycle traffic. A strongly defined 'wall' of buildings is programmed for both sides of the river with distinct breaks in the wall at major cross-axial malls on each side. These open malls establish the identity of each district with the commercial square on the east and the government center on the west.

The river is left as an open natural park with a series of low-scale island developments along its course. The most visible features of the park are the natural lakes and the four bridges that cross the river. The master plan strives to fully integrate nature with the built environment and to evolve a town that is physically and emotionally uplifting.

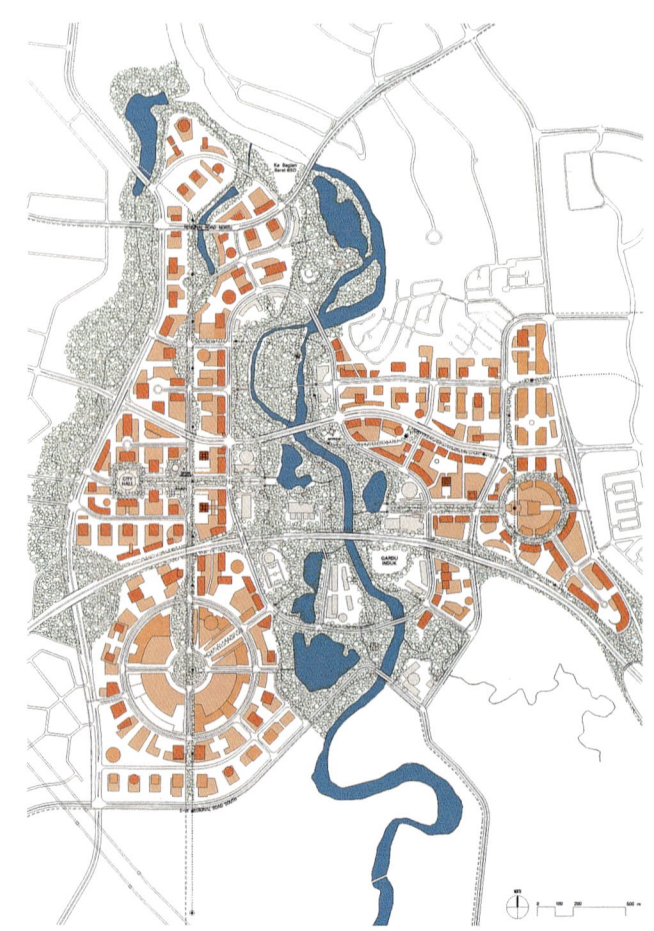

1 Rendering along river
2 Rendering at lake
3 Master plan
4 Aerial view rendering of town
5 Rendering along Ring Road

4

5

BSD New Town 183

Hsinchu Regional Master Plan

Design Proposal 2001
Taipei, Taiwan
Taiwan High Speed Rail Corporation
Master plan

Hsinchu is a major center of global information technology and semi-conductor production. It is vitally important in Hsinchu to comprehend the regional urbanization process within an international complex. To that end, Taiwan High Speed Rail Corporation sought to establish a comprehensive real estate development plan along its rail line.

The objective of the 2001 Hsinchu Regional Master Plan is two-fold. Firstly, that the quality of life for the communities that will be created and the definition of their new urban identity in the context of local traditions are addressed. (The planning focuses on the open space network, pedestrian network, and regional committees.) Secondly, that the planning is integrated with the traditional neighborhoods on the periphery of the rail line.

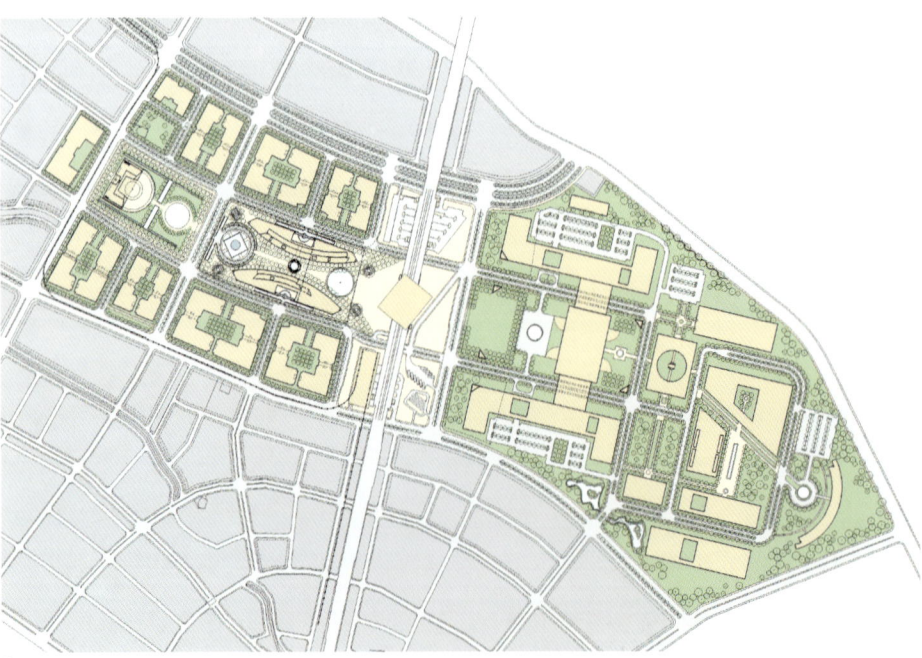

1 Rendering of amphitheater
2 Site plan
3 Rendering of office tower

Hsinchu Regional Master Plan 185

Dream Lake Mountain Villas

Design Proposal 1996
Near Hangzhou, China
Hong Kong Golden Horse International Joint Corporation
472,000 square meters
Master plan

The Zhejiang Province Tourism Development Zone, near scenic West Lake, afforded an opportunity to plan a resort community that enjoys the atmosphere of a modern city within the tranquility of the beautiful countryside. The topography of the site was a driving factor. Gentle slopes encircle two valleys. The central area of the eastern valley is a large pond comprised of terraced fields with steep slopes on both sides. Importance is placed on the complementing landscape elements of mountains and water and how they enhance the resort experience.

The design intent was to create a resort with an international flavor unique to Southeast Asia, while reflecting Chinese culture and philosophy. The resort is comprised of residences, an assembly center, and open space. The majority of the site is residential, utilizing villa cluster communities. One hundred and twenty units are zoned for cluster housing with 445 residences allocated to detached villas. The assembly center functions as a mixed-use town center with a hotel, restaurants, shops, a conference center, and recreational facilities. The remainder of the site is dedicated to open space with parks, waterways, and lakes linked by a road system of winding paths with scenic views.

1   Master plan
2   Rendering of Assembly Center Garden
3   View of Assembly Center from across the lake
4   Aerial view rendering

3

4

Dream Lake Mountain Villas 187

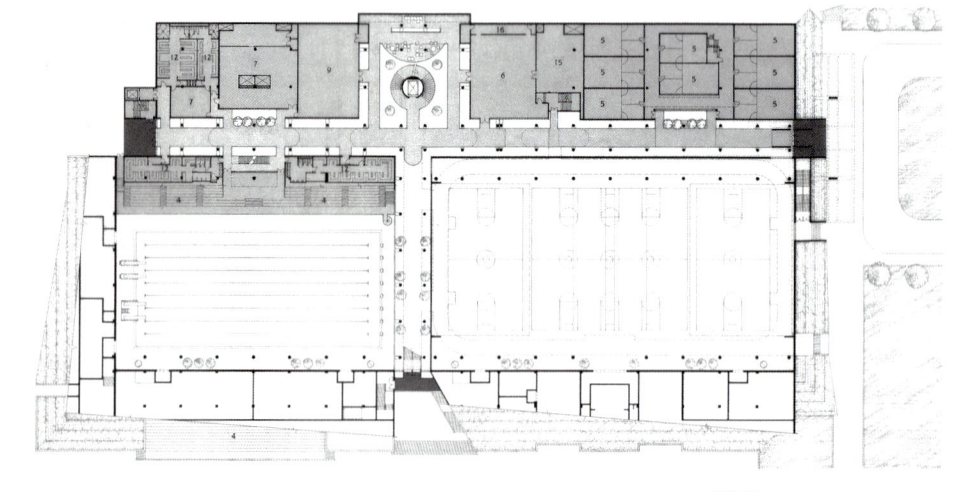

George W. Woodruff Physical Education Center

Design/Completion 1980/1983
Atlanta, Georgia
Emory University
17,379 square meters
Concrete, stone, and glass

1   View from field
2   Longitudinal sections
3   Ground floor plan
4   Site plan
Opposite:
   Interior view of playing courts

Emory University wanted to implement a building program to enhance the quality of campus life for its students and faculty. At the time, their ambitious program requirements included two buildings that met budget and schedule requirements. The first of the two buildings, which face each other across one of the main campus streets, is the Physical Education Center. It comprises intramural sports program facilities, including a biomedical research center, a basketball court, squash courts, a wrestling space, an indoor running track, an Olympic size swimming pool, a dance studio, and tennis courts on the roof.

The building is located on the site of an existing student pedestrian path between the campus educational buildings and nearby residential-scaled fraternity houses. The goal was to preserve the circulation route without intruding on the scale of the low-rise fraternity houses. To do so, the three-story building was designed with a multi-level spine penetrating the length of the building. Passing students can observe the building's activities through interior glass walls, thereby creating a desire to participate.

In order to diminish the large size of the building, which is adjacent to the intramural athletic fields, one side is slid into the existing hillside. Landscaped berms and bleacher seating are incorporated into the opposite side overlooking the exterior track and main athletic fields. The elongated rectilinear plan with a flat roof was designed as a garden, incorporating tennis courts that create a great park-like space in the middle of the campus linking the fraternity houses.

188

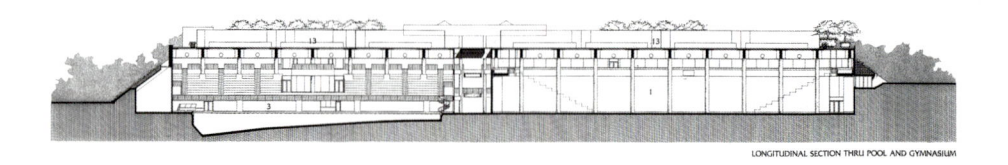

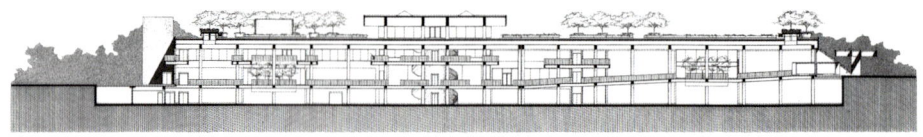

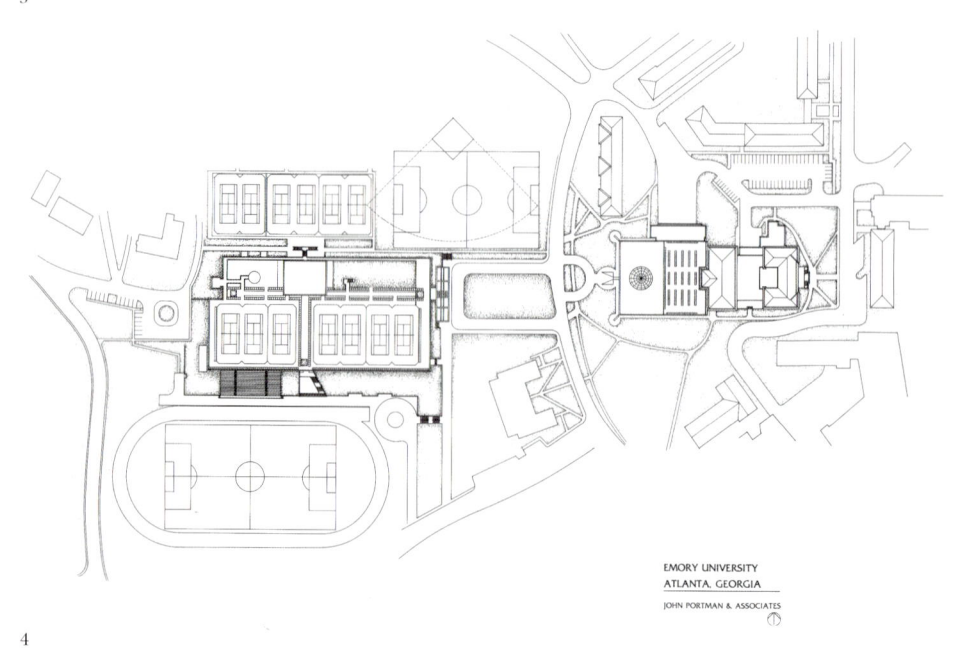

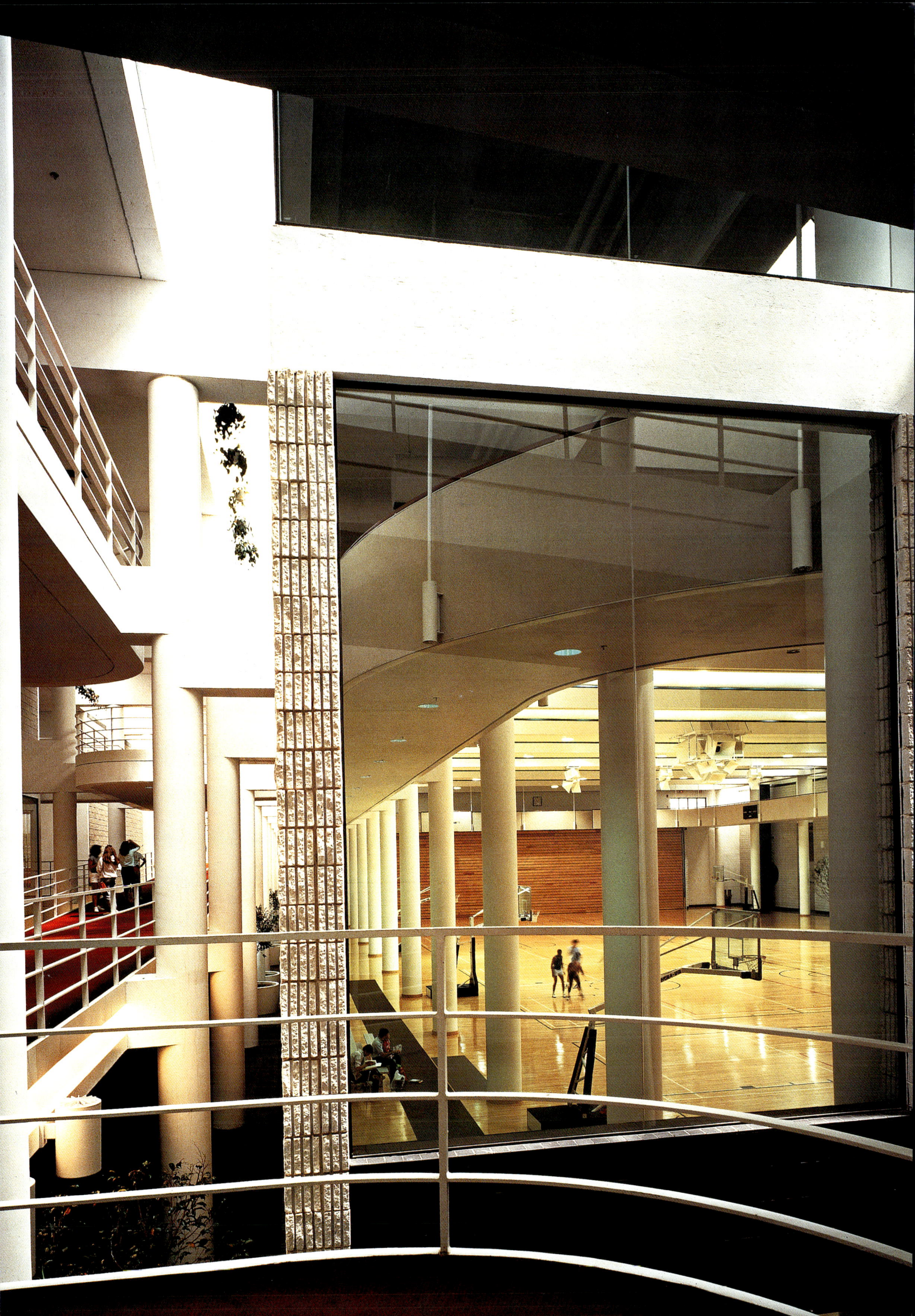

R. Howard Dobbs University Center

Design/Completion 1984/1986
Atlanta, Georgia
Emory University
8,495 square meters
Concrete, stone, and glass

The University Center contributes to the university's plan to enhance campus life for the students and faculty. The project involved renovating the existing historic student union building and expanding its services with a major addition that included space for food preparation, dining, a ballroom/banquet room, a post office, a bookstore, a lounge and service areas. The renovated building includes two theaters, administrative offices, and student activities.

The new building literally embraced and was wrapped around the older building, preserving the existing historic building while relating to the new Physical Education Center directly across a campus street. This multi-level shared space has become the campus 'living room'. The historic facade is preserved while a grand interior theater-like space is created. The old and new spaces are joined in a manner inspired by Teatro Olimpico in Vicenza, Italy, and take the form of a tiered amphitheater. Within this grand interior piazza, students hold concerts, dine, study and socialize.

The white marble exterior replicates the building materials of the older campus buildings. The exterior of the University Center addition also relates strongly to the Physical Education Center across the street. The central axis of that building continues through the rotunda of the University Center. The entry facade with its deep overhang provides a large contemporary porch in the tradition of the gracious Southern porches of old, welcoming everyone to this campus gathering place.

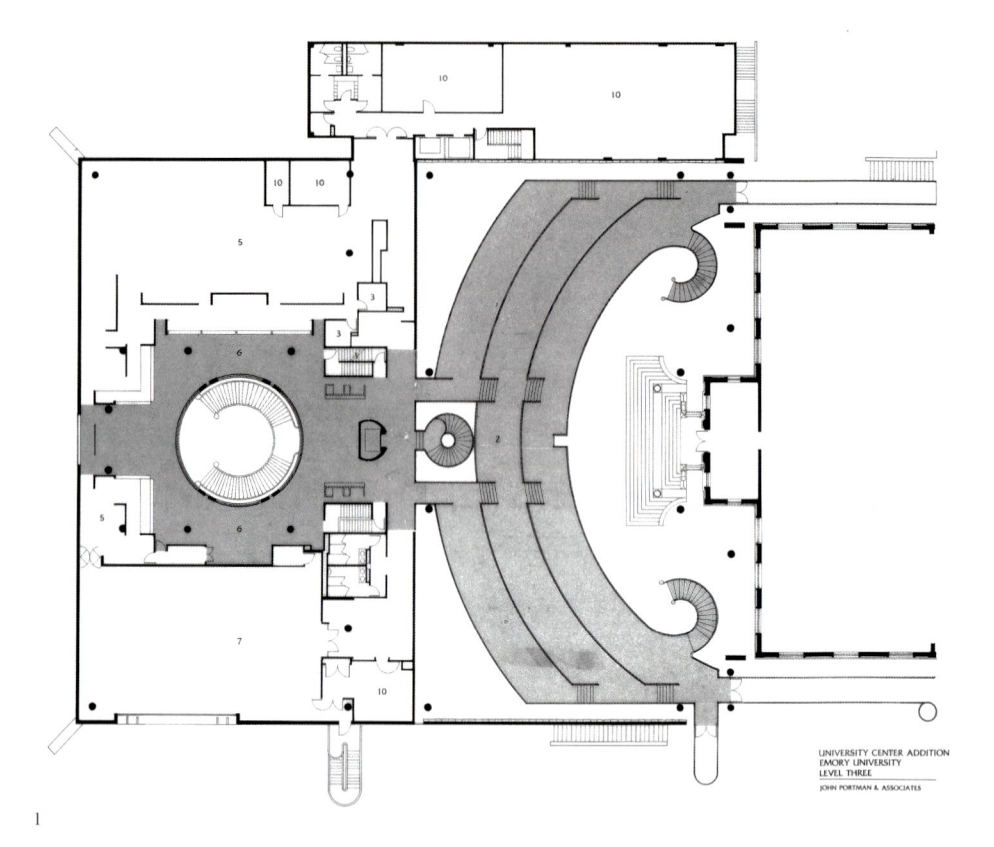

1 Balcony level plan
2 View at side entry
Opposite:
   Skyward view in atrium

R. Howard Dobbs University Center

4 Main entrance at night
5 Section through atrium and balconies
6 View from balcony
7 View at entrance courtyard

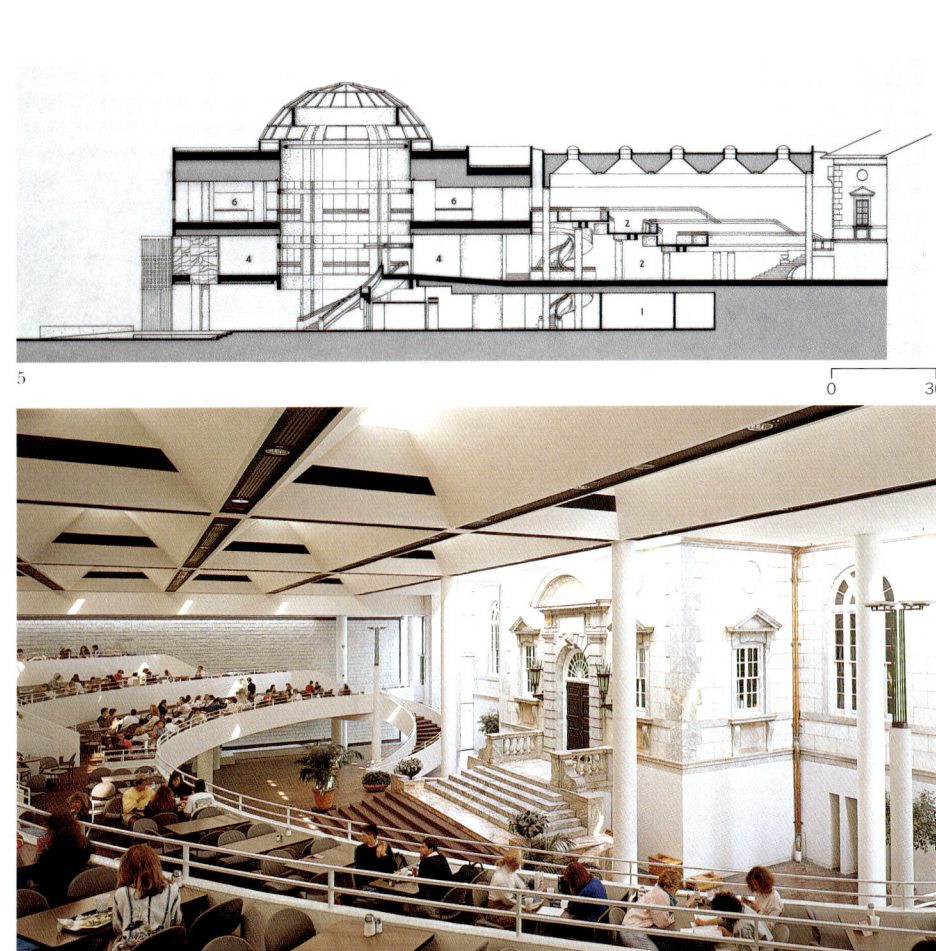

R. Howard Dobbs University Center 193

University/Olympic Apartments

Georgia Institute of Technology
Design/Completion 1994/1996
Atlanta, Georgia
Board of Regents of the University System of Georgia
Brick veneer with C.M.U. back up on concrete structural frame system

The 350 apartments were part of a housing program that aimed to provide lodging for athletes of the 1996 Summer Olympic Games and to expand on-campus housing for university students. The master plan required a brick exterior to complement the campus architecture. The interior needed to be competitive with off-campus apartments in order to attract student residents.

The two brick buildings are rectilinear, parallel and off-set to form a courtyard and to create a common activity room linking the apartments. Architecturally, the repetitive program of identical apartments is expressed in the circular bays that enrich the interior living space as well as the exterior form. The rhythm of the circular towers is contrasted with the rectangular entrance portals that house the student lounge areas on each of the floors.

The apartments are comprised of four-bedroom suites that share a common living/dining/kitchen area. Each suite has commercial cable/CATV access and two-port communications outlets that link the apartments with the campus computer system.

1 Rendering
2 View looking north
3 Site plan
4 View from Center Street

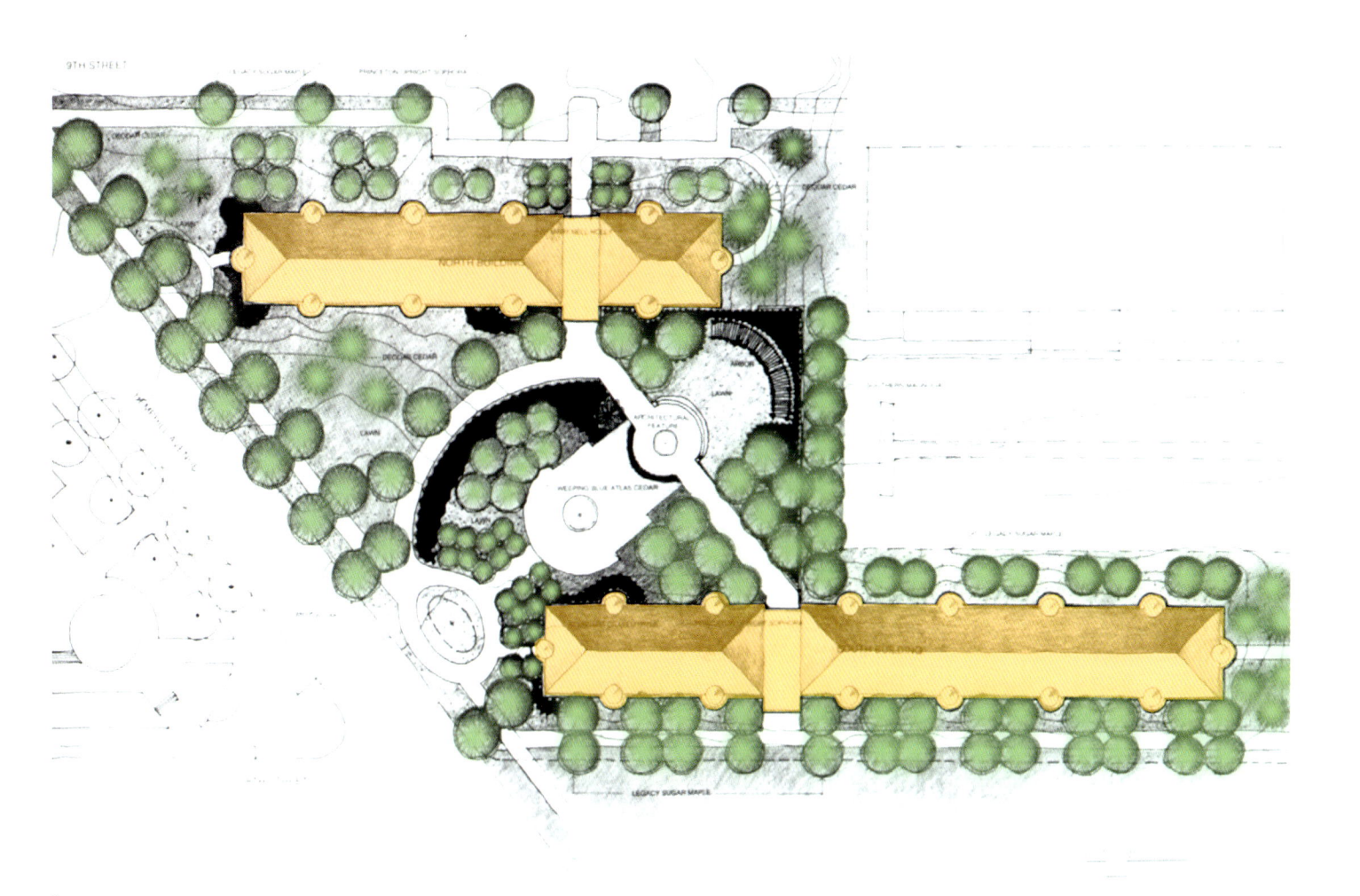

University/Olympic Apartments 195

Nursing, Health Science and Outreach Complex

Macon State University
Design/Completion 2000/2002
Macon, Georgia
Board of Regents of the University System of Georgia
7,435 square meters
Brick, metal, and glass

1 Section through entry
2 Ground floor plan
3 Rendering of south elevation
4 Rendering looking north

The Nursing, Health Science and Outreach Complex was designed as a three-phase project to meet the client's growth and budget objectives. The first phase provides classrooms, laboratories, offices of various sizes, and a 72-seat auditorium. Brick was selected to harmonize with the other campus buildings and to conform to their scale. The three-story structure has a long rectilinear plan that is partially cut into a hillside to minimize its mass. The arc of its barrel vaulted roof is split by the flat plane of the atrium skylight, breaking the strong linear form of the building and emphasizing its main entrance.

A canopy extends from the rectangular entry portal. The main entrance is into the skylit atrium that is the common space for students and faculty to gather between classes. From the atrium, space is divided unequally with one third to the right and two thirds to the left. The auditorium is one level below the entry level and is equipped with the latest technology for distance learning capabilities. By locating the science labs on the upper level, their ventilation system was incorporated into the roof design as distinctive architectural elements. Phases II and III will offer the addition of a conference center and information technology building with the atrium entrance serving all three complex components.

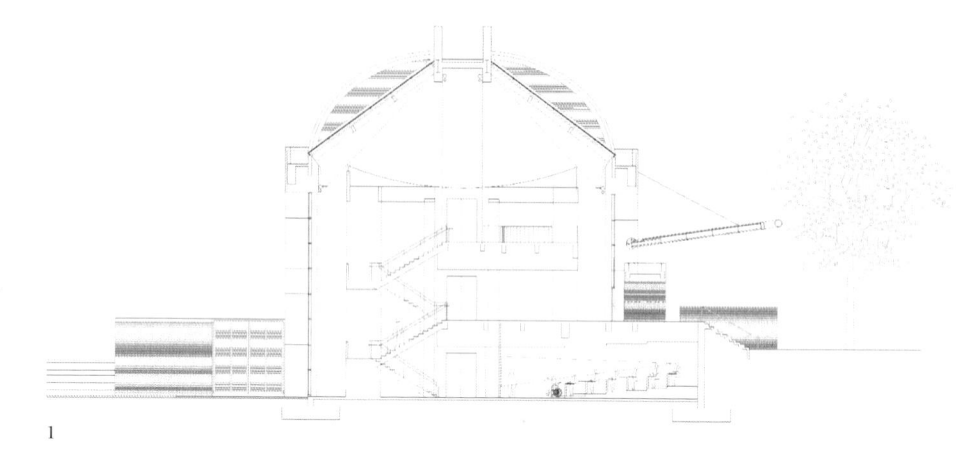

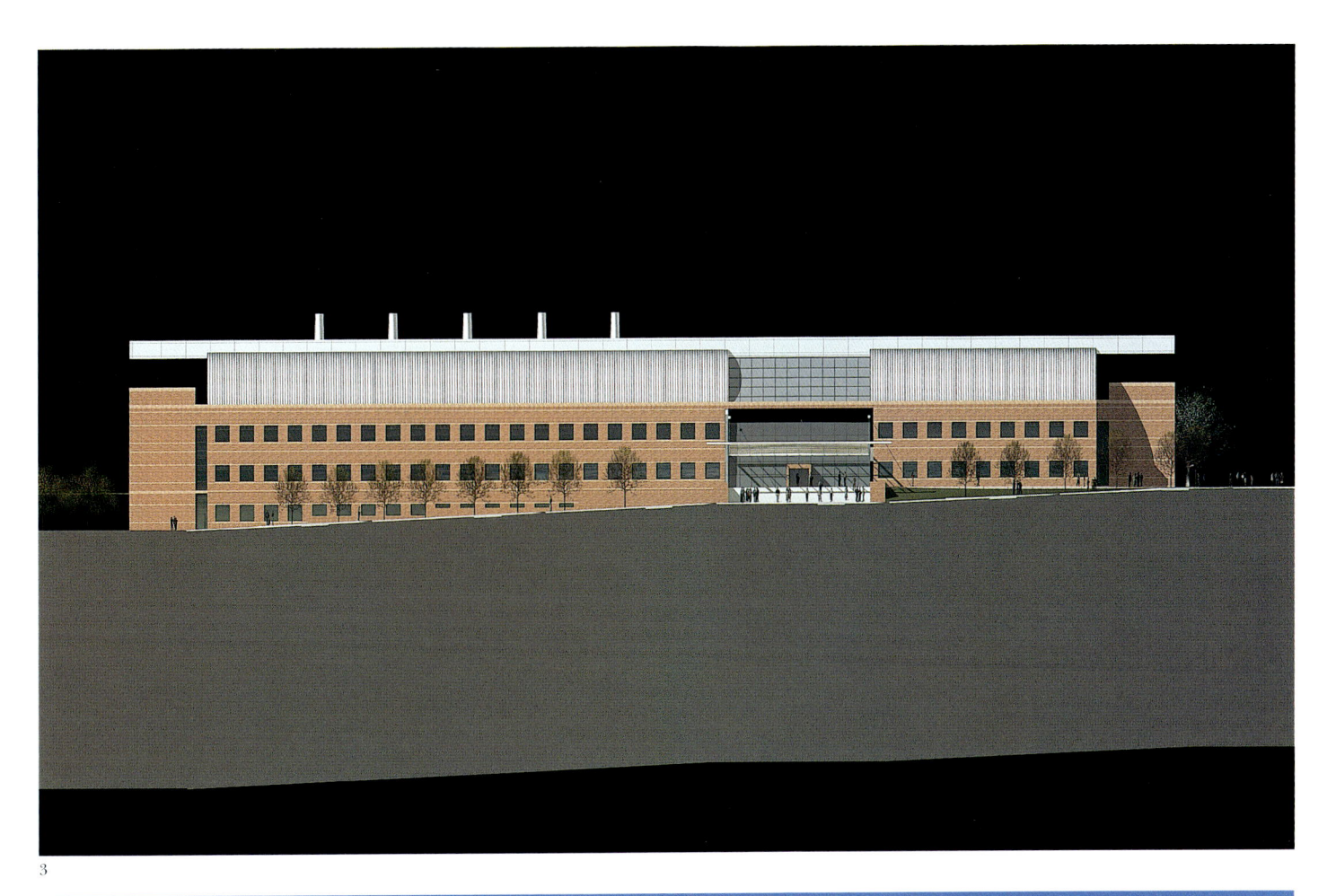

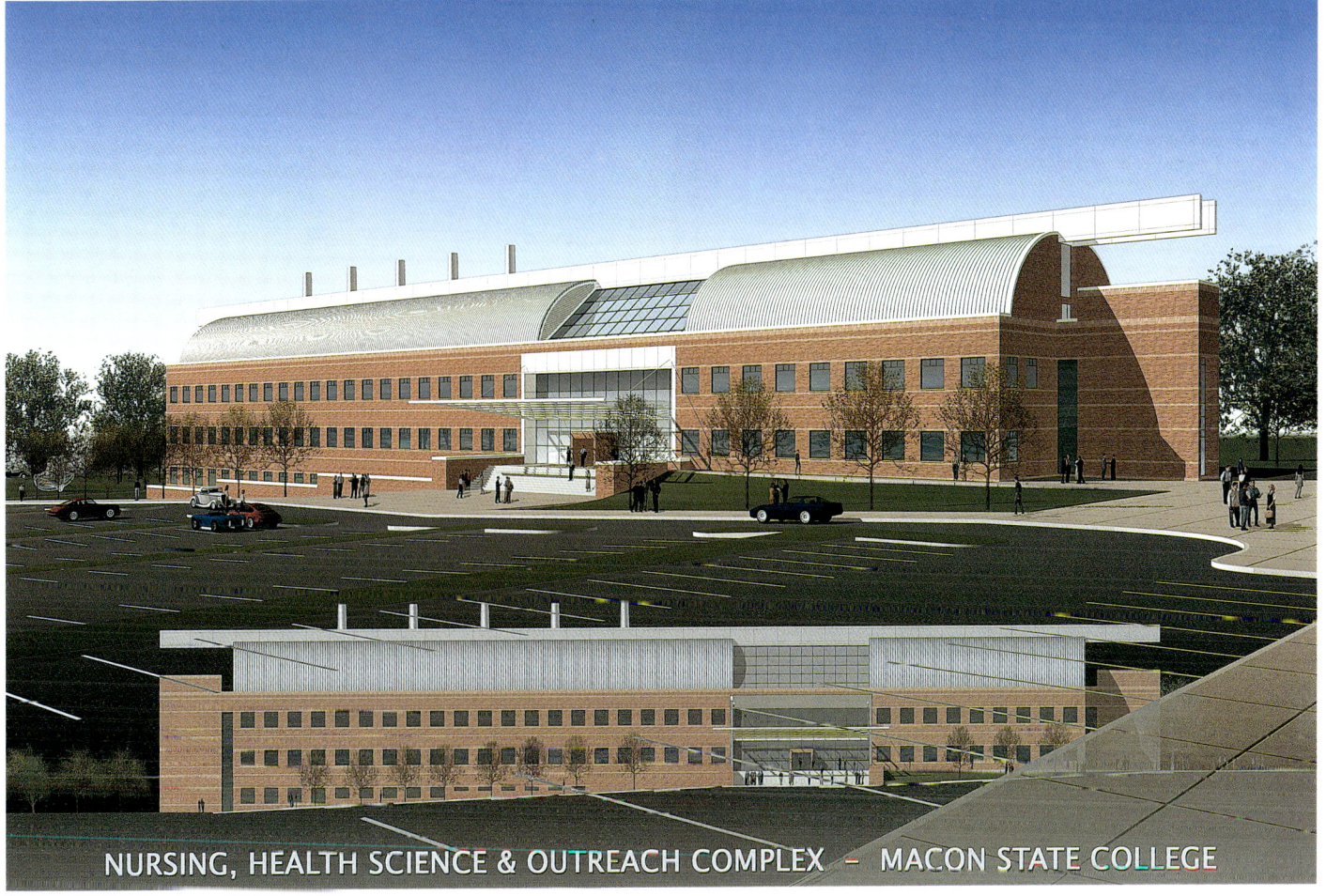

NURSING, HEALTH SCIENCE & OUTREACH COMPLEX — MACON STATE COLLEGE

Gwinnett Center Academic Building

Design/Completion 1998/2001
Lawrenceville, Georgia
Board of Regents of the University System of Georgia
10,408 square meters
Brick, metal, and glass

As the first building of a full college campus, the Academic Building sets the tone of the campus as a 'learning' center, not a teaching center. The client wanted the building to be a model for the integration of technology with education. It targets the new student—the embodiment of all ages, stages of education, and time constraints. The campus' mission is to become a learning laboratory, open around the clock, and focused on the evolving way education is delivered.

In response, the first building integrates all functions necessary to launch this new beginning. Classrooms, laboratory facilities, and faculty offices encircle the three-story central space that contains the library and research area. Student and faculty movement flows without containment throughout the building. A perimeter card-access system, cameras, and monitors apply new methods of securing the space so students can move freely.

High-tech solutions support a flexible environment. With education via broadband, the building provides network connectivity to every classroom seat and throughout the common areas. Classrooms offer complete audio-visual presentation capability and wiring to provide IP-based video-conferencing. The classrooms and labs are arranged with progressive teaching/learning concepts in mind and connectivity is stressed to allow students and professors the opportunity to interface with each other.

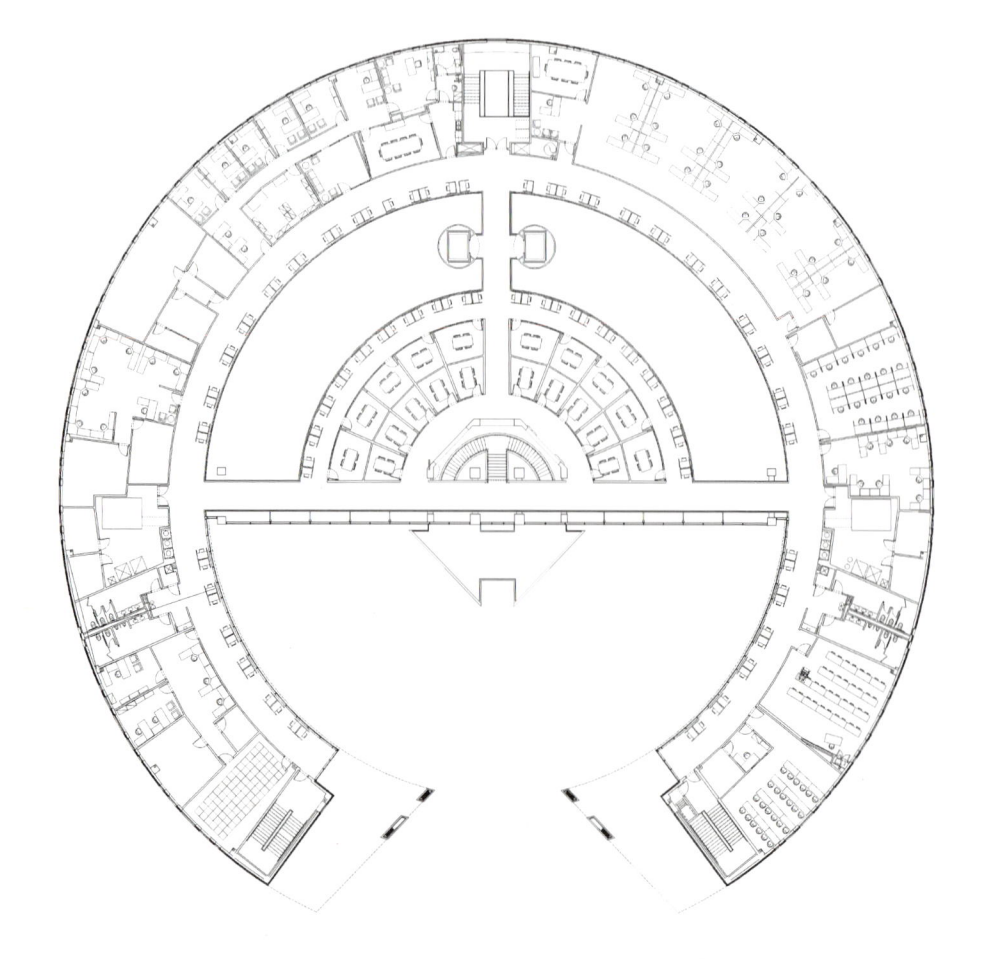

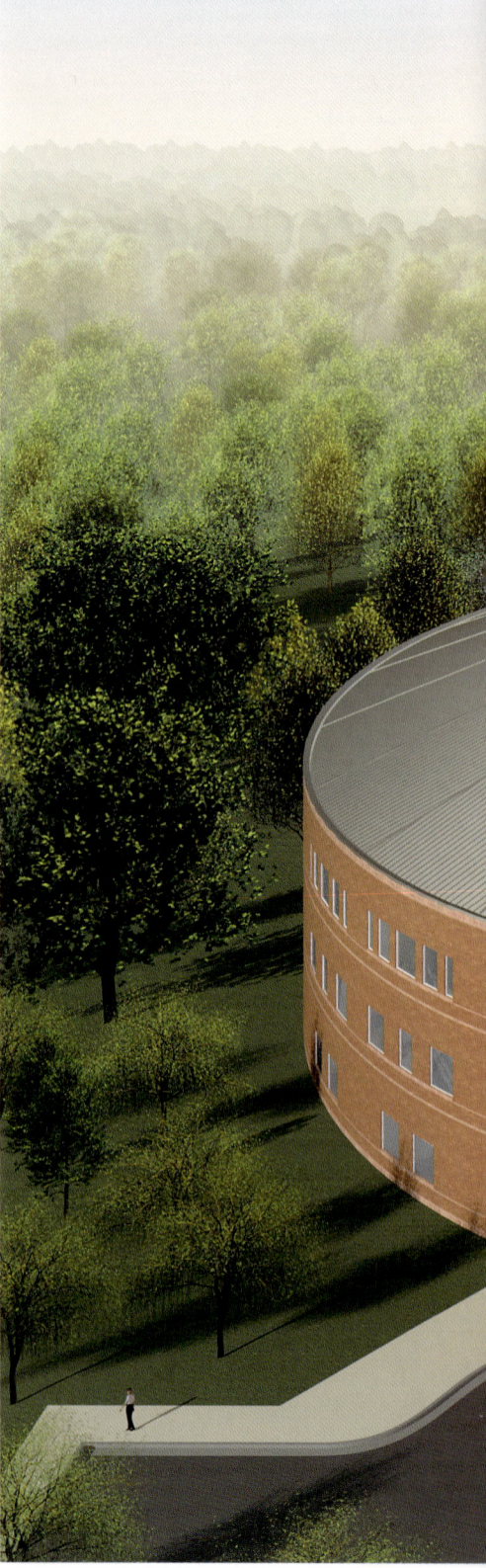

1 Third floor level plan
2 Aerial view rendering looking north

Gwinnett Center Academic Building 199

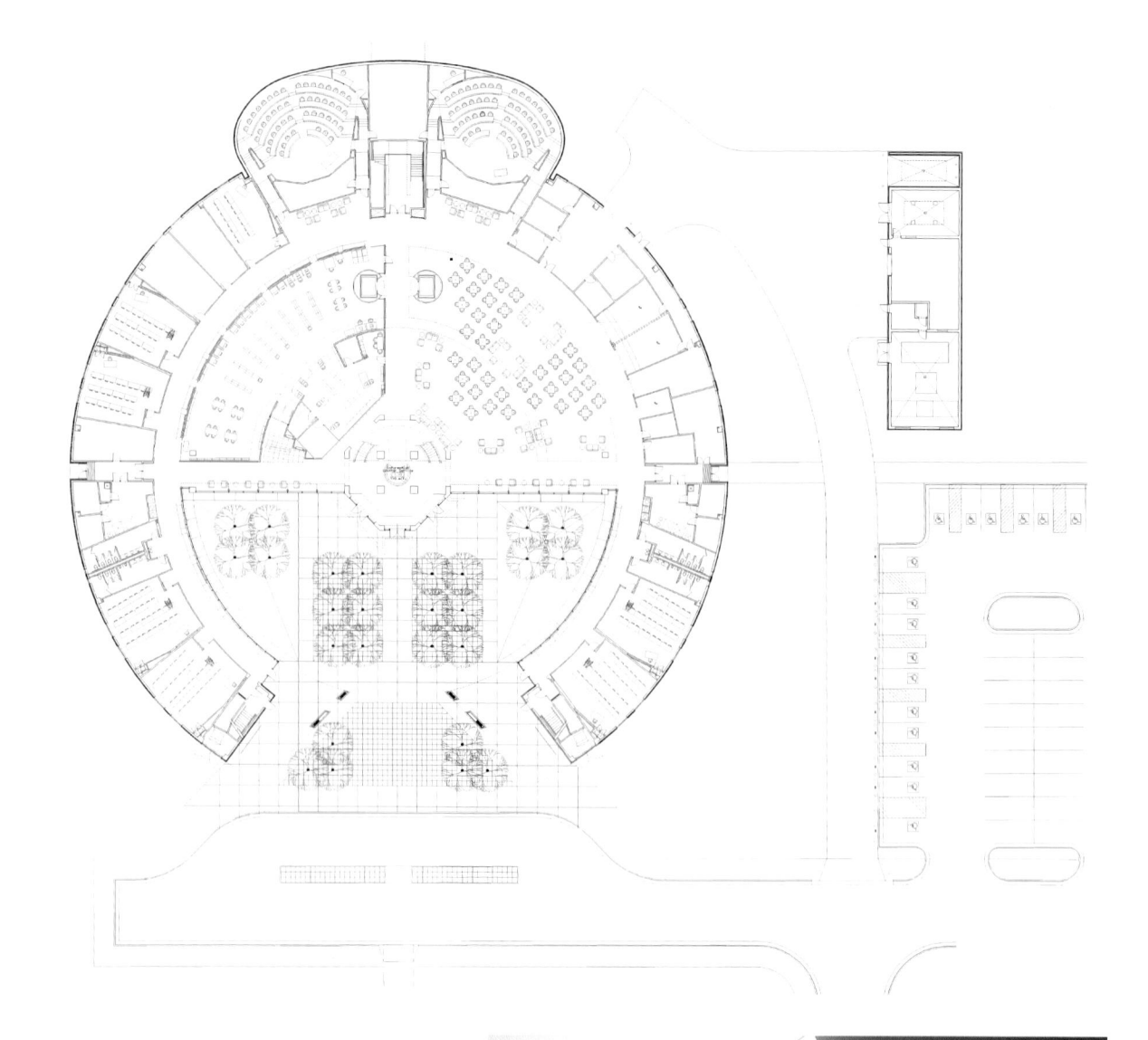

3 Ground floor plan
4 View of atrium skylight
5 Section through atrium
6 Rendering of front entrance

Gwinnett Center Academic Building 201

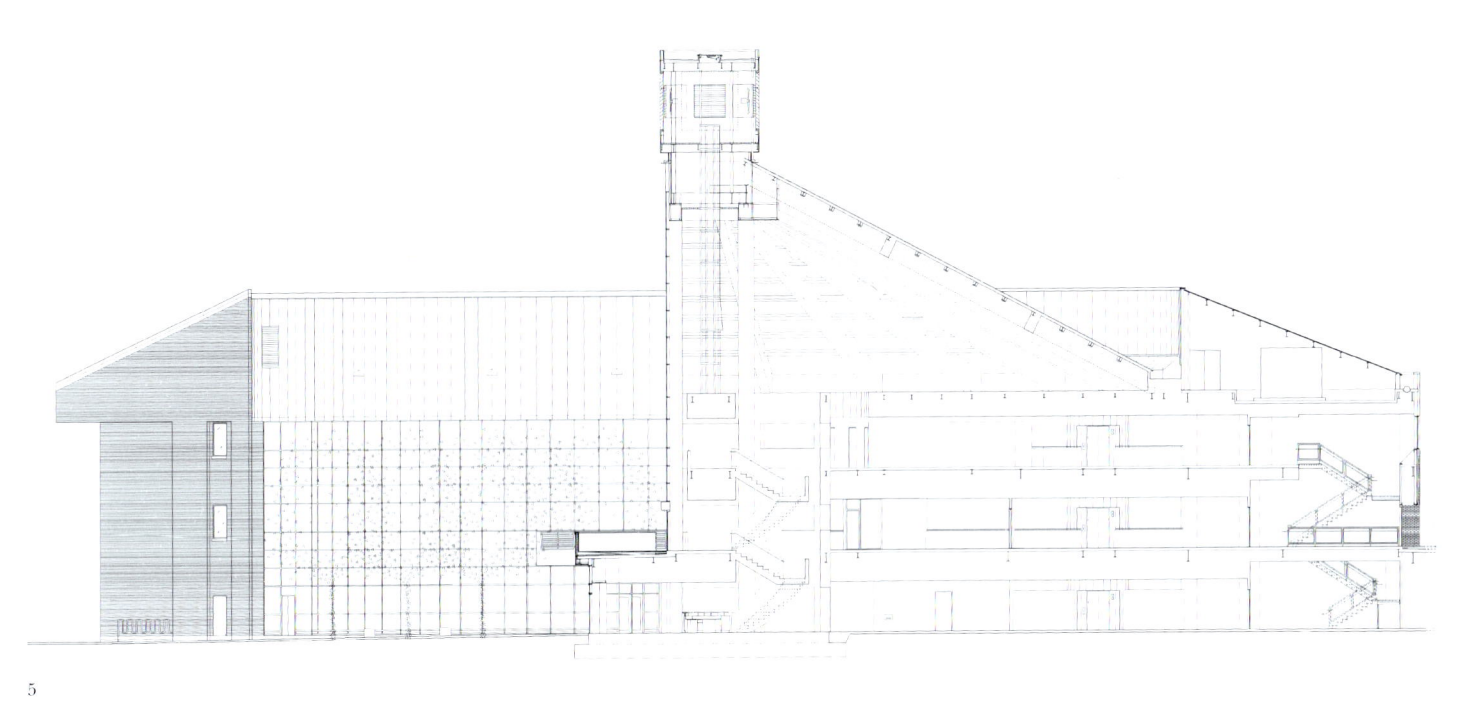

Indian School of Business

Design/Completion 1998/2001
Hyderabad, India
Kellogg Graduate School of Management, Northwestern University and
Wharton School, University of Pennsylvania
66,000 square meters
Concrete, sandstone, and glass

1 Site plan
2 Skyward view of Academic Center
3 View of tower at Student Housing Complex

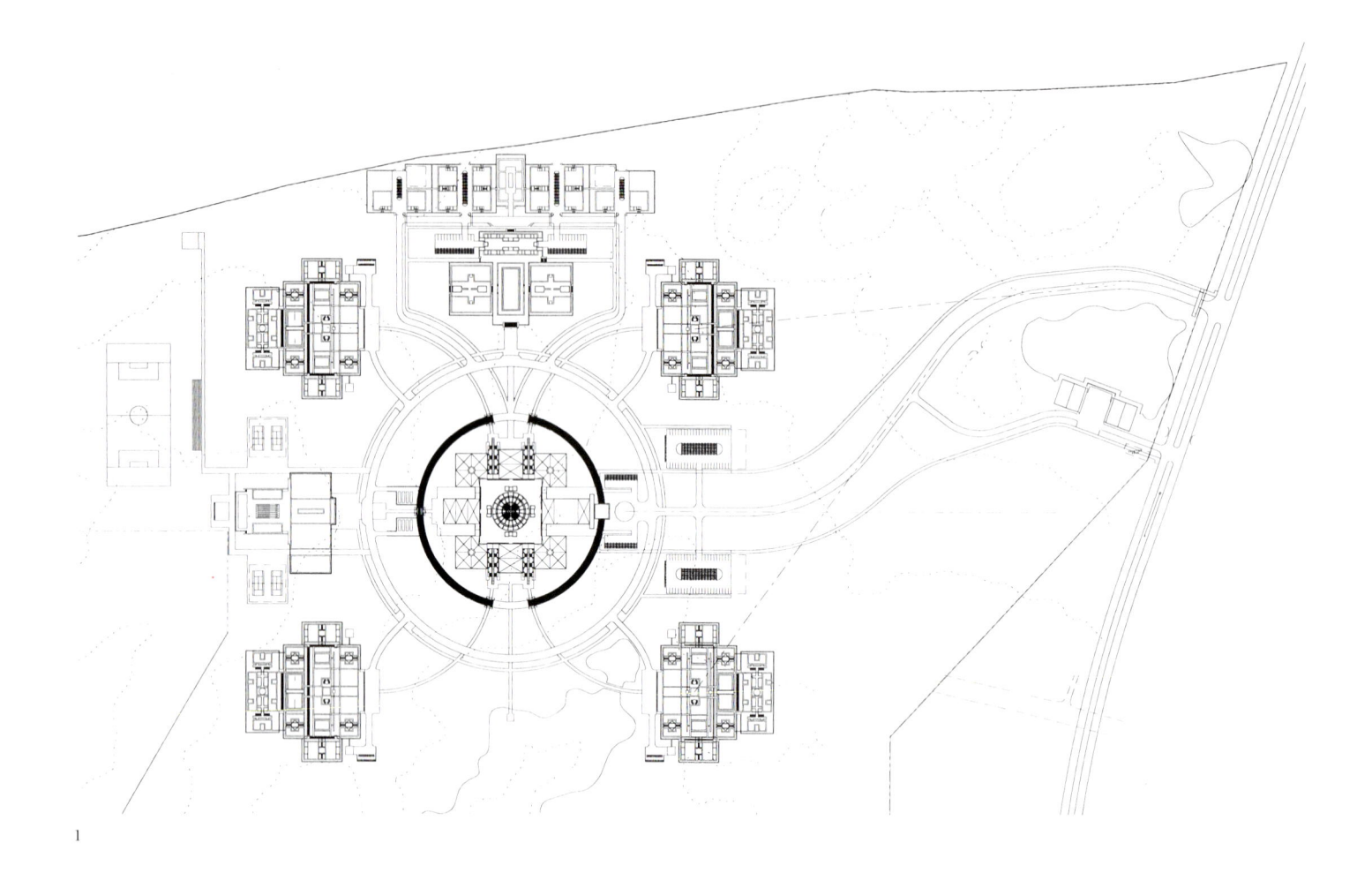

The design of the Indian School of Business attempts to address four criteria: the environment, the Indian character, interactivity, and information technology. The new 250-acre campus provides teaching facilities, offices, and a total living environment for faculty and 520 students. The project was fast-tracked to meet the school's ambitious opening schedule.

The campus is located in a semi-arid tropical setting, so design elements contrive to minimize the environmental impact on this fragile ecosystem. For example, runoff from the limited rainfall is captured for treatment and reuse. The architects also drew on symbolic and practical functions of traditional Indian architecture that had evolved in response to the region's harsh climate. The campus is inspired by the traditional nine-grid system found in the many mantras of Hindu temples. Sunscreens and arcades are used extensively in the design, and many buildings are elevated to enhance airflow, while water is used for its cooling effects. Although the campus is linked with India's culture, the architecture speaks to the future.

The school focuses on interactivity and communications, with the cylindrical library as the centerpiece. Social interaction as well as information technology is an important design goal. High-tech solutions support an environment that is flexible to allow for future change.

Indian School of Business

4 View from Executive Center reflecting pool
5 Elevation of Academic Center
6 View along Classroom Corridor
7 Plan of Academic Center and Recreation Center
8 View at entry of Student Housing Complex

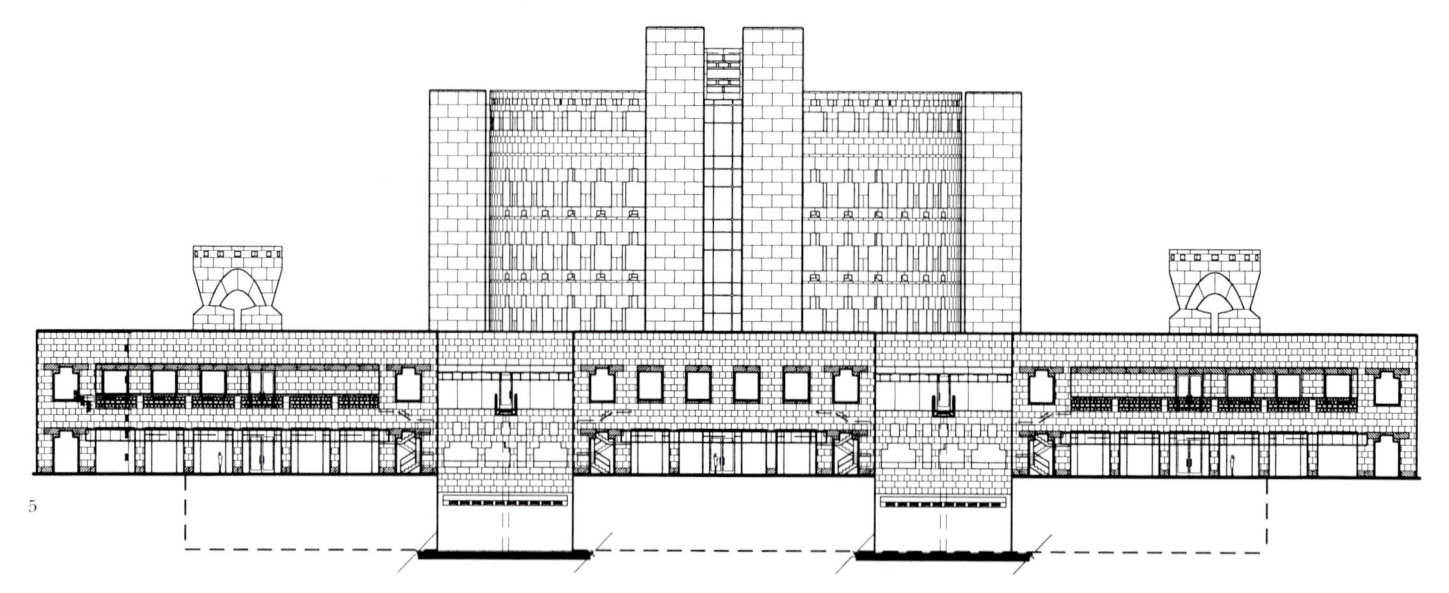

Indian School of Business 205

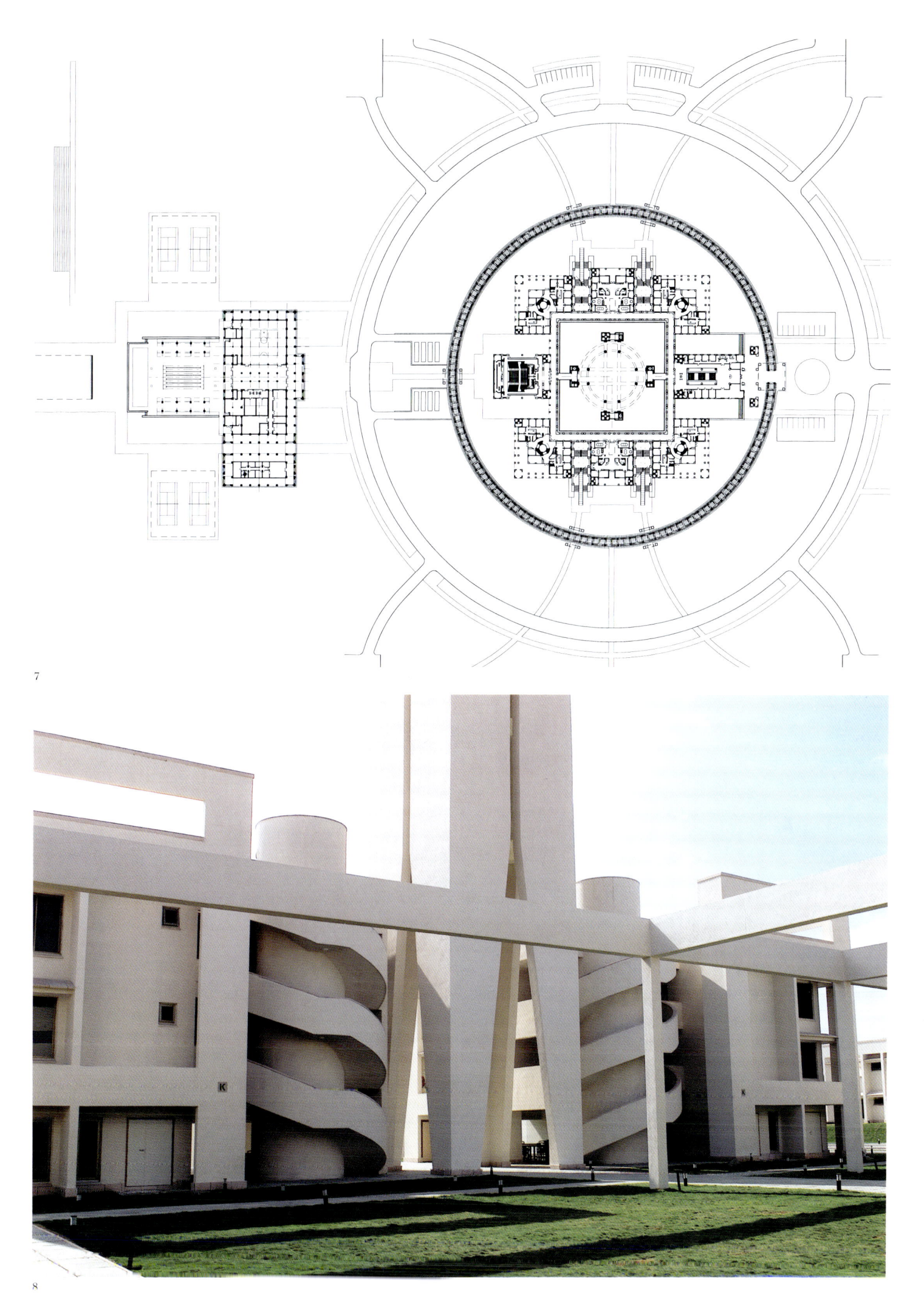

9   Section through Academic Center
10 View of Academic Center from Student Housing Complex
11 View looking north
12 View looking through courtyard
13 View of Academic Center courtyard
14 View of entry to classroom

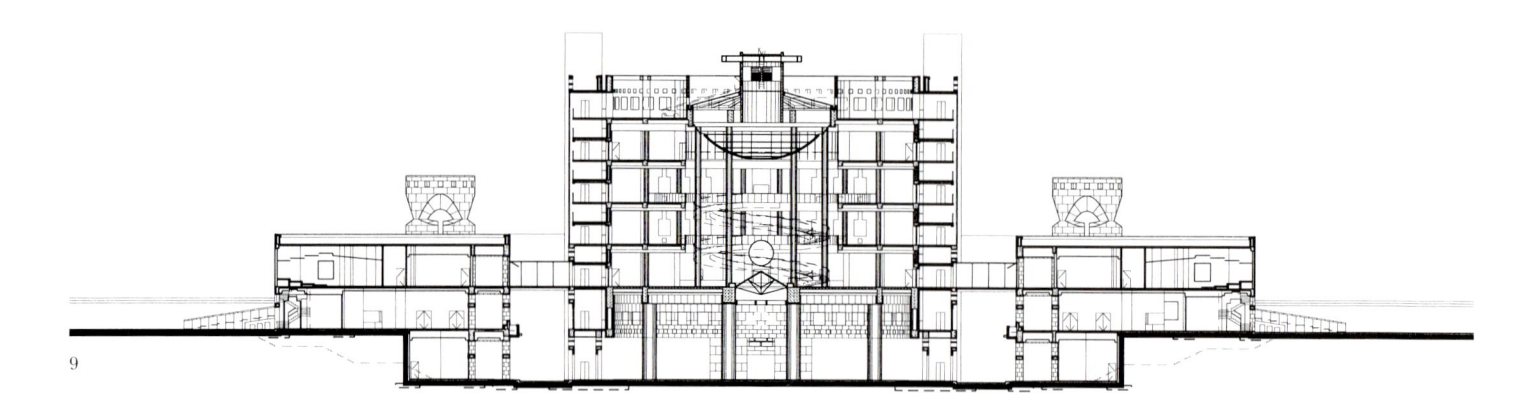

Indian School of Business 207

Rockefeller Center Promenade

Design/Completion 1962/1985
New York, New York
Rockefeller Center
20,000 square meters
Concrete, stone, and glass

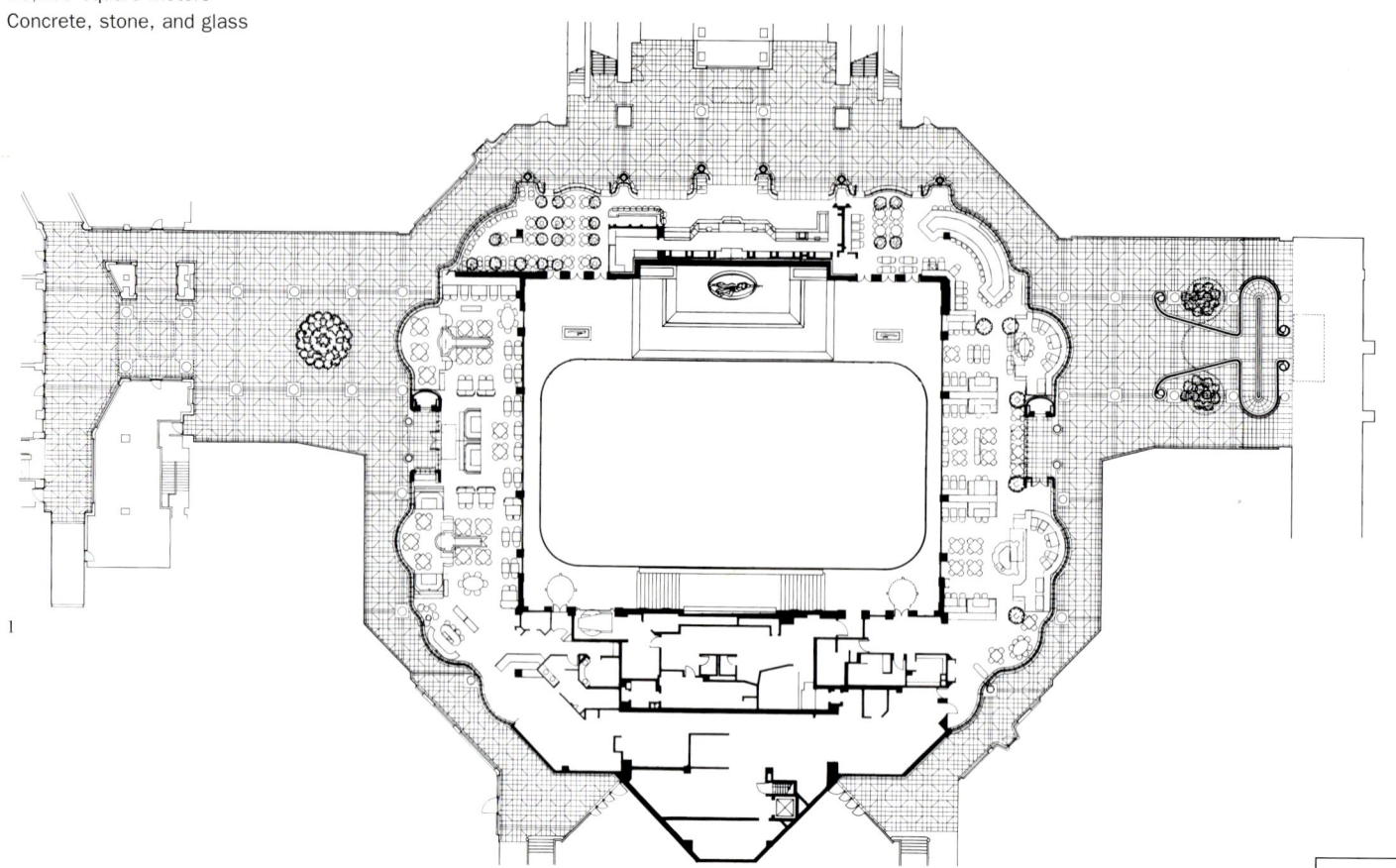

The Rockefeller Center Promenade Project is a renovation of the subterranean pedestrian concourse that surrounds the Rockefeller Center's famed stepped down urban plaza and ice skating rink, and links the Center's many buildings. The ice skating rink and the bronze statue of Prometheus have long been a symbol of New York City and its urban lifestyle.

The design thrust was to create a porous environment. By capitalizing on the daylight from the ice skating rink, which serves as a great central lightwell, light is brought into the Promenade Level. This was achieved by increasing the restaurant window wall surrounding the rink and by defining the restaurants' concourse elevation with an undulating glass and bronze screen-like wall. The public can view the rink through the restaurants, thereby bringing light deeper into the heart of the complex. The new concourse design further emphasizes lightness by utilizing white marble, bronze ornamentation, neon, and glass block skylights. Walking through the concourse, attention is focused back outside to Prometheus. Whether one enters the concourse from the towers or from the elevators housed on the street level in glass and bronze vestibules, the new renovation conveys and contributes to the culture and drama of the Rockefeller Center.

1 Plan at retail level
2 View of plaza and ice rink
3 Skyward view of entry vestibule
4 View of retail courtyard

Rockefeller Center Promenade

Entelechy I

Design/Completion 1962/1964
Atlanta, Georgia
Mr. and Mrs. John Portman, Jr.
1,091 square meters
Concrete, brick, and glass

The classic Greek word 'Entelechy' that the Portmans adopted for their home means 'that which realizes or makes actual what is otherwise merely potential'. Its design reflects many of the principles that have guided other works, yet Entelechy I also functions as the home in which their family was raised.

The house is both simple and complex. The geometry of circles and squares is dominant and reflects a strong sense of order in the design. The grid of 24 circular forms, which support columns, gives structure to the two-story dwelling. The columns have been 'exploded', or pulled apart, into segments that open the interior space to a variety of uses from circular stairwells, to powder rooms, closets, niches for art, and vertical and horizontal circulation. Additionally, their skylighted tops provide light, both day and night.

Space is pulled apart within the house, both vertically and horizontally. The entrance is at the upper level with communal rooms such as the living room and music room extending two levels. The integration of nature within the structure is evident in the extensive use of trees, plants, and water on the main level. A shallow pool separates the formal living area and creates a circular island in the dining room. A separate pool house beneath the swimming deck is immediately adjacent to the main house.

The plan's flexibility has enabled the family to change and adapt the space as the children have matured and left home.

1 Site plan
2 View of exterior patio
Opposite:
   View of dining room

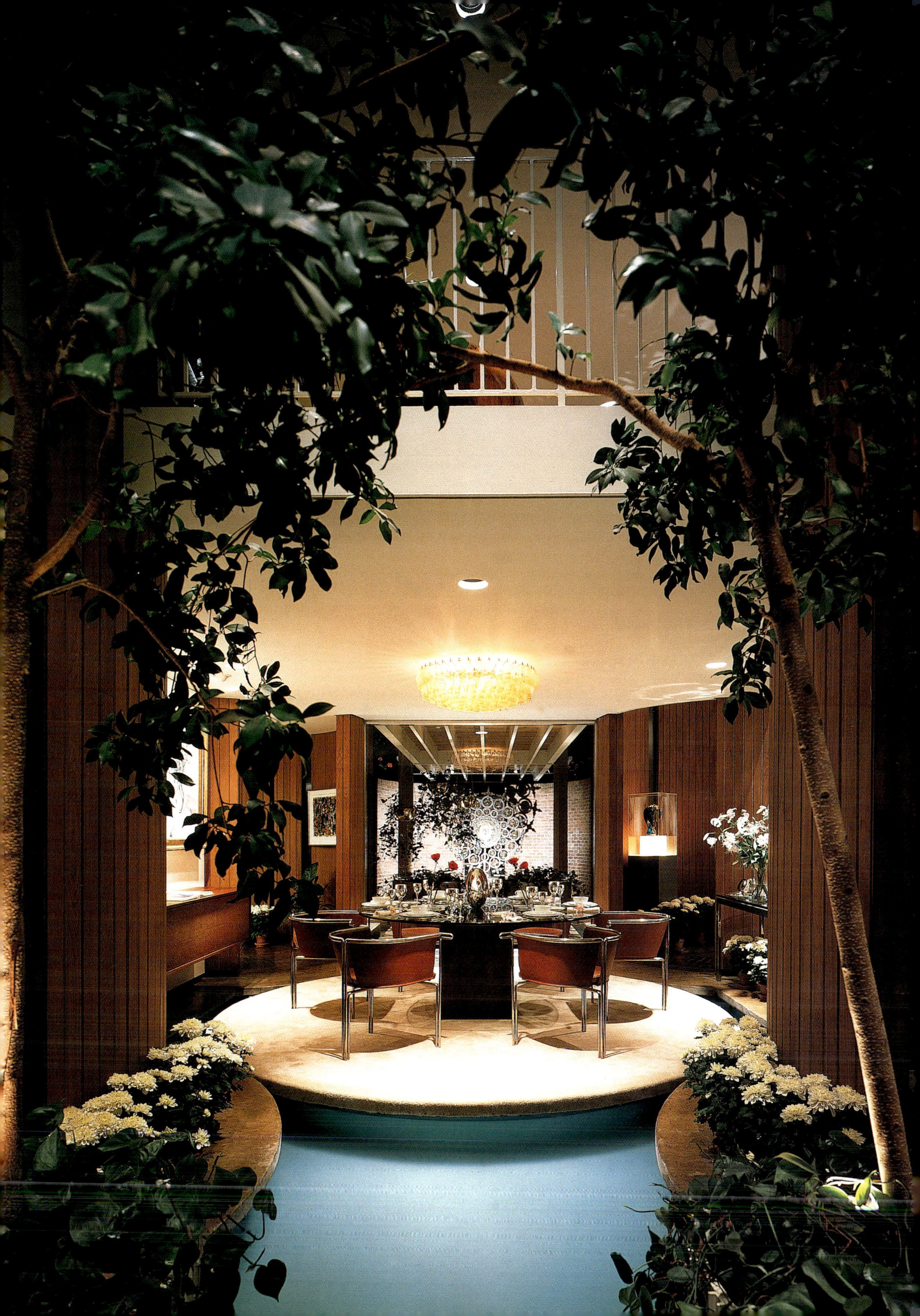

4

4 View of house from pool at night
5 View towards living room
6 Living room

Entelechy II

Design/Completion 1985/1987
Sea Island, Georgia
Mr. and Mrs. John Portman, Jr.
1,170 square meters
Concrete, stone, and glass

Entelechy II is Portman's own beach house and it is the most comprehensive and intimate insight into his architecture. Situated on the Atlantic Ocean, Entelechy II is a home/museum, a seaside retreat for his family, and a place to enjoy their extensive art collection.

Entelechy II is formed according to its own functional and environmental needs. The resulting form and space freely reflect the island and the sea. The house is literally penetrated by and wrapped in nature. In concept, the house is both simple and highly complex. Within the vine-covered walls that surround the site, 18 'exploded' columns support a large rectangular sunscreen, symbolic of the classic beach umbrella. Beneath the screen are the four enclosed living pavilions that comprise the house: a two-story entry wing; a cylindrical glass living/dining pavilion that springs from the large reflecting pool in the central interior courtyard; the single-level master suite suspended above the interior court terrace; and the lanai, a free-standing guesthouse facing the ocean.

Within the house, space is pulled apart vertically and horizontally to offer vast views of the ocean, intimate glimpses of a landscaped garden, or works of art. Gently sloping ramps link spaces and create paths that offer one an opportunity to see and use the house from changing perspectives. Sculpture abounds throughout, taking prominent positions in juxtaposition to the architecture. Being a project that is 'of the sea', water is another major design element, so pools and fountains, both large and small, are incorporated.

1   View from beach at night
2   Aerial view rendering towards ocean
3   Main entrance

Entelechy II 215

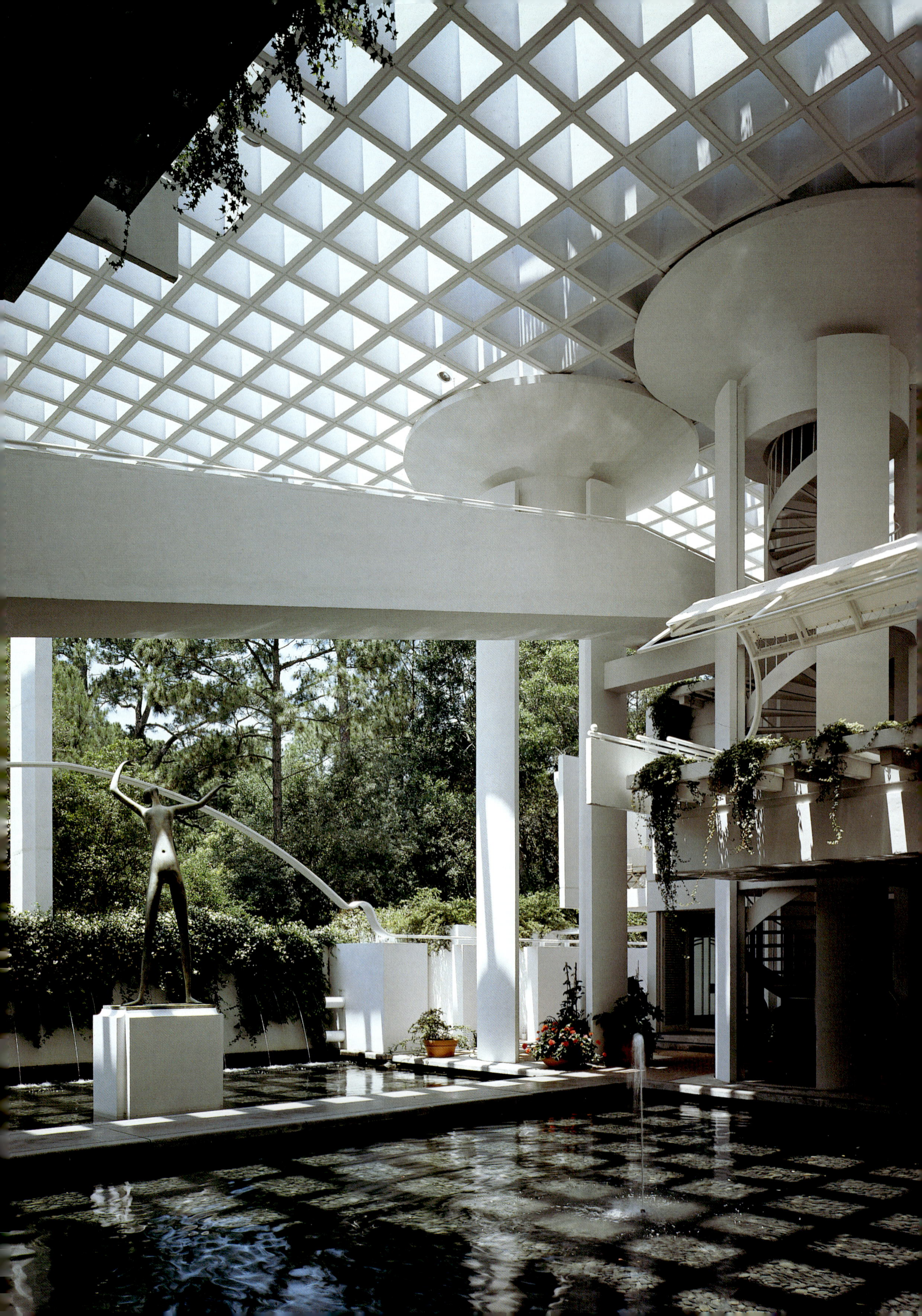

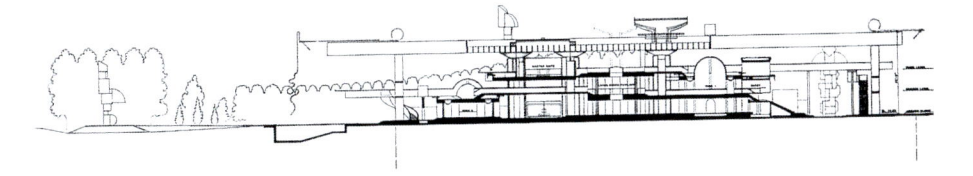

Opposite:
View of west wing courtyard
5 Longitudinal section
6 View of main entrance at dusk
7 Entry pavilion roof terrace
8 Interior courtyard looking northeast

9 View of pool towards ocean
10 Exploded column detail
11 Master suite living-dining room looking southeast
12 Interior courtyard
13 Master suite courtyard

12

13

Entelechy II 219

Furniture

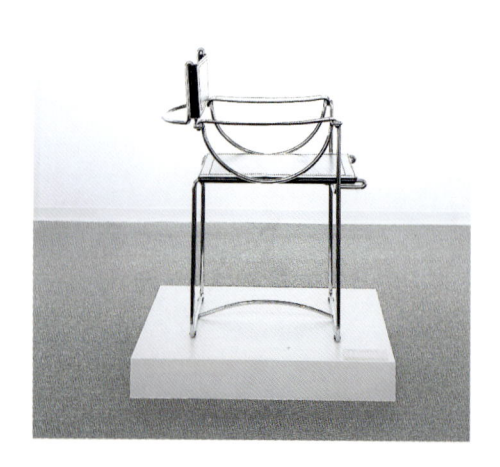

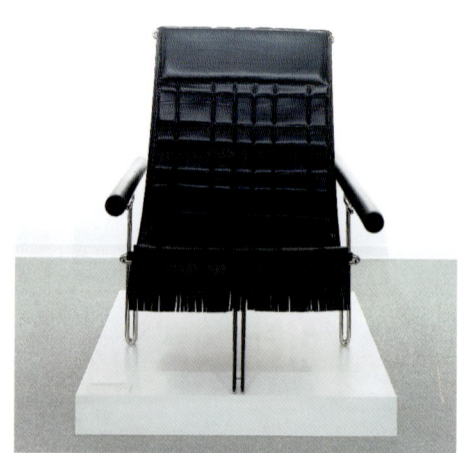

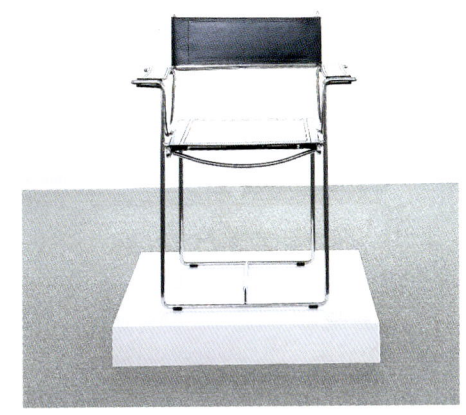

Furniture 221

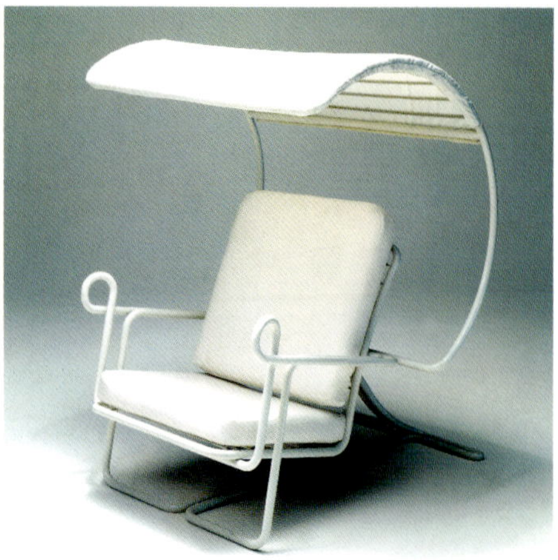
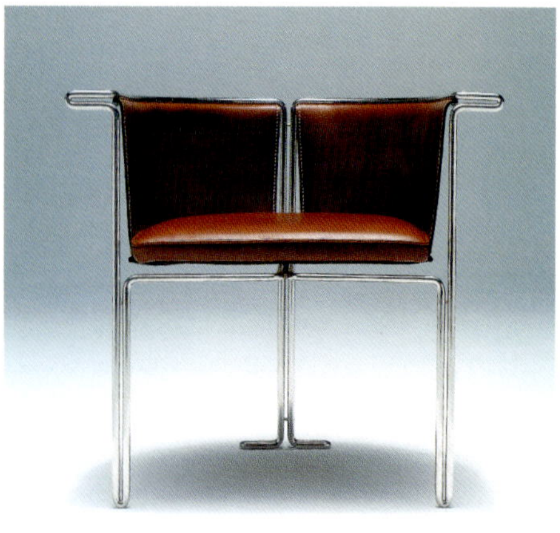
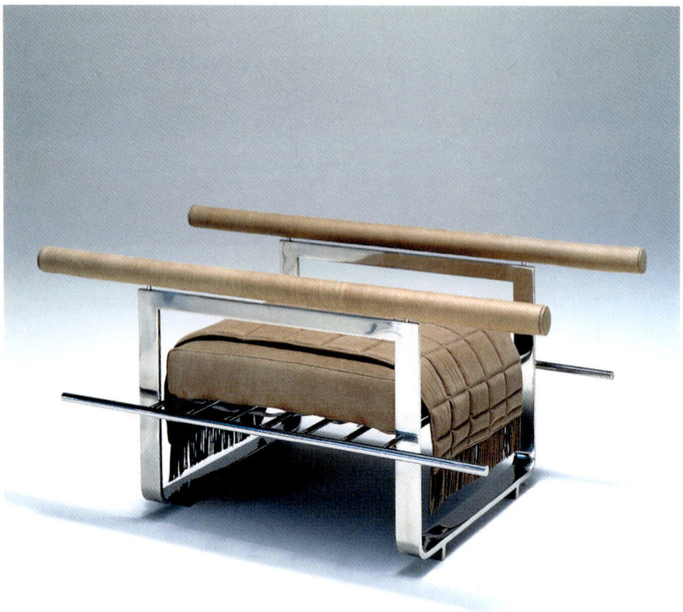
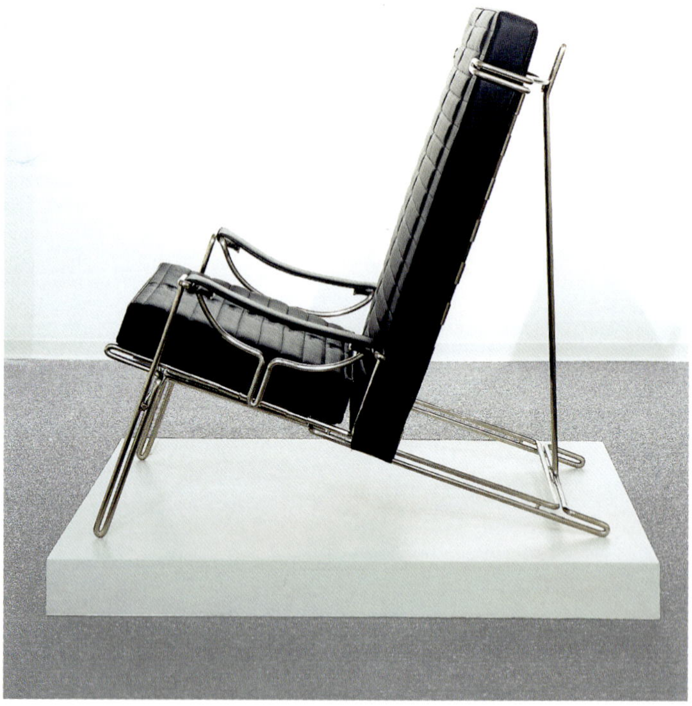
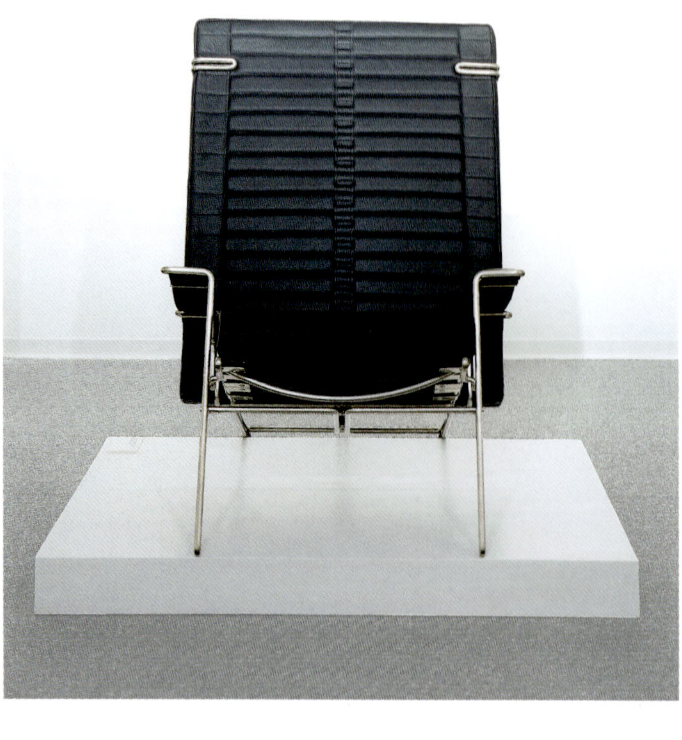
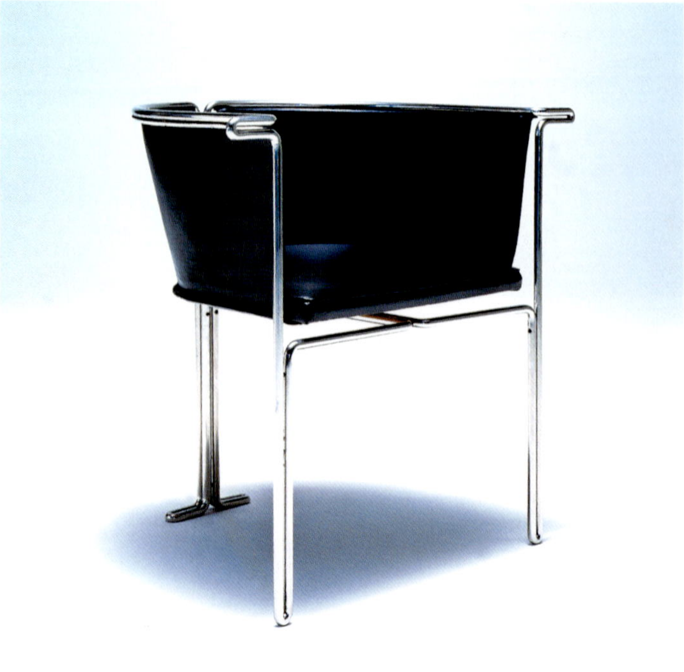

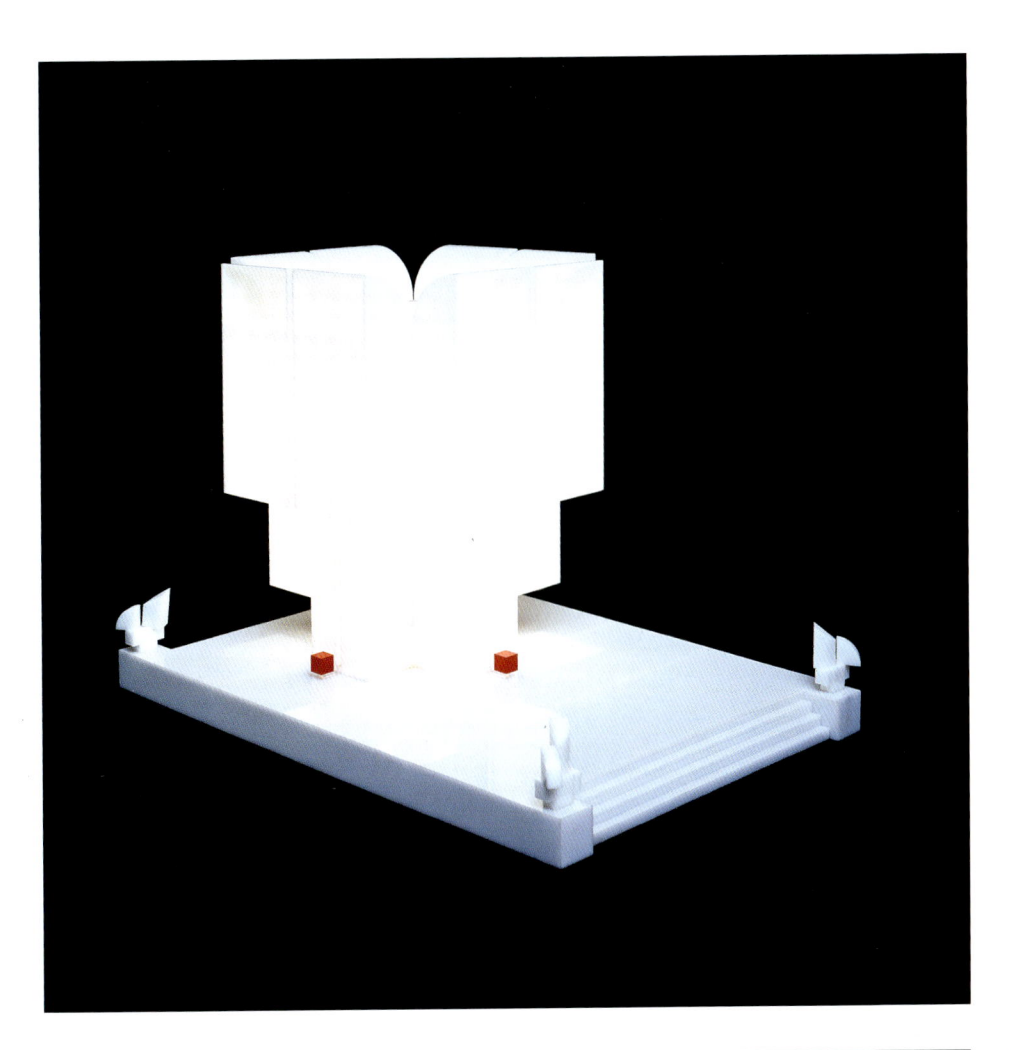

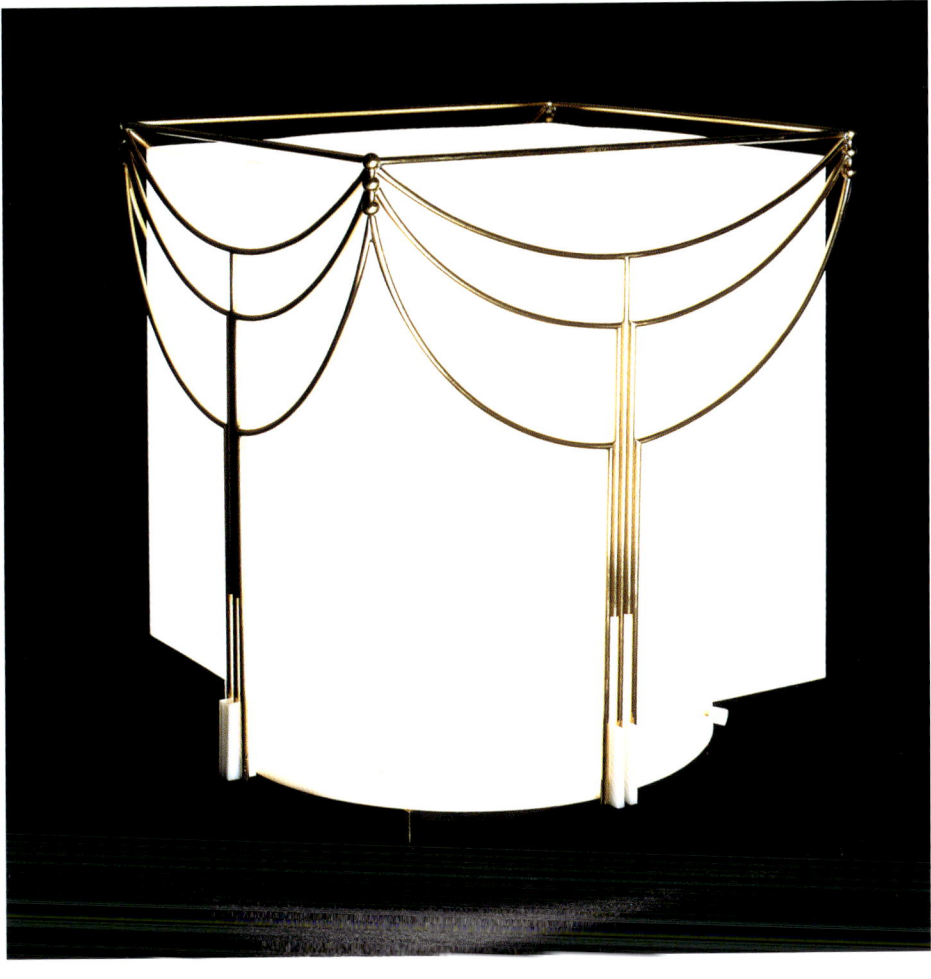

Furniture 229

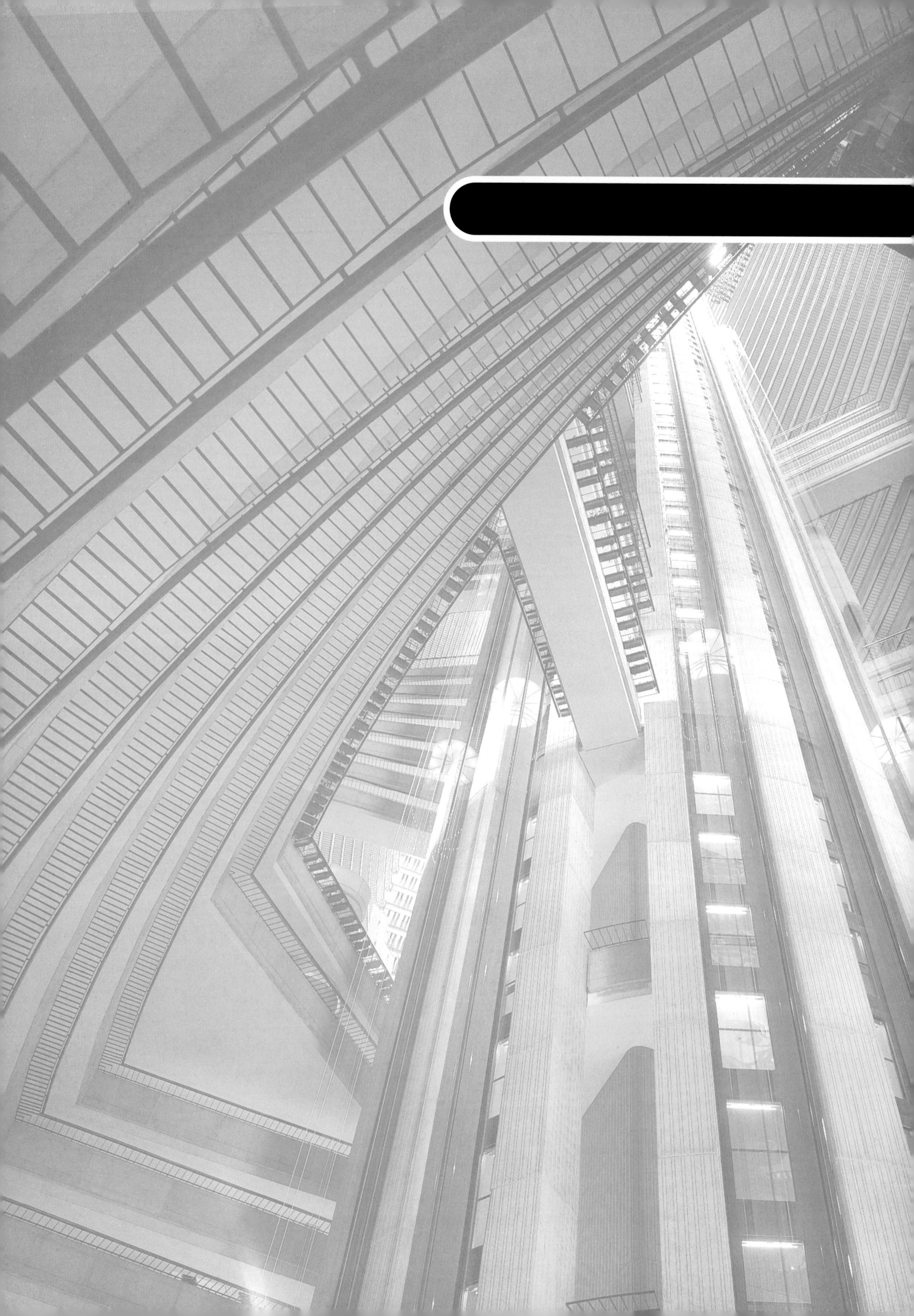

firm profile

The architecture of John Portman & Associates has demonstrated that quality design and economic viability can be simultaneously achieved. The architectural and engineering firm, which was established in 1953, specializes in mixed-use projects and is internationally recognized for its expertise in the design of office, hotel, retail, trade mart, and educational projects in cities throughout the world. John Portman & Associates is headquartered in Atlanta, Georgia, and has offices in Shanghai, Warsaw, and Mumbai (Bombay). The firm provides design services in master planning, architecture, structural engineering, and project management.

John Portman & Associates' focus is on people and their response to space. The firm has become well known for using space in new and innovative ways, especially in urban environments. They have also broadened the firm's knowledge base through participation in some projects as partners in the development process. Through a close working relationship with other Portman entities that develop real estate projects domestically and internationally, John Portman & Associates understands the importance of determining and addressing issues related to the financial feasibility of each project. This experience has brought an added value to all its clients in the process of achieving design excellence and economic viability.

Clients benefit from working with architects who are creative, yet pragmatic. Clients are always an integral part of the design process, working with the firm's team from concept through construction. The firm's broadened architectural knowledge base enables it to create effectively and efficiently constructed and operated projects that have a unique sense of place. Although John Portman & Associates strives to develop new and innovative solutions that respond to the uniqueness of each project, the work is always based on respect for human scale and the creation of space that appeals to the people who use it. Visually and functionally, John Portman & Associates projects are people-oriented.

Though the firm's projects span the world, they are not designed in satellite offices, but in John Portman & Associates' international headquarters, capitalizing on the firm's top talent. This assures clients that each project will be consistent with the creativity and quality associated with other Portman landmark buildings. From the 1960s, when the Hyatt Regency Atlanta introduced the concept of the large-scaled atrium hotel, to the year 2000, when Tomorrow Square changed Shanghai's skyline, the architecture of John Portman & Associates has a long history of redefining urban centers around the world.

The international work of John Portman & Associates began in Europe with the Brussels Trade Mart in 1975 and soon expanded to Southeast Asia with hotel and mixed-use projects in Singapore, Hong Kong, Indonesia, Malaysia, and India. The firm has had a major presence in China since the early 1980s with the design and development of Shanghai Centre. Its unparalleled success led to a large number of subsequent projects.

John Portman & Associates is experienced working with local architects, as well as a wide range of domestic and international consultants on projects with various codes, regulations, and governing agencies. Its talented international design staff in Atlanta mirrors the cultures where the firm works. They are sensitive to environmental issues and the importance of local culture in evolving architectural and planning solutions. John Portman & Associates has been recognized on numerous occasions for excellence in design, energy efficiency, and urban revitalization.

The firm strives to cultivate design solutions that enable the visitor/user to experience a strong 'sense of place', not just from the exterior but from the interior as well. The firm has delivered for its clients memorable and stimulating environments by taking innovative approaches to evolve dynamic new design solutions.

Principals Biographies

John C. Portman, Jr., FAIA
Founder and Chairman, John Portman & Associates

The founder of the firm is John Portman, whose vision, creativity, and entrepreneurial spirit has brought a fresh, new perspective to the practice of architecture. He has made a lasting impression on his profession by introducing the large-scaled atrium to modern architecture, creating pragmatic new concepts for mixed-use urban development, and combining the roles of architect and developer in order to expedite his design philosophy.

John Calvin Portman, Jr., whose home is Atlanta, was born to Edna and John Portman on 4 December 1924, while visiting in Walhalla, South Carolina. While growing up in Atlanta, his interest in architecture started in high school. During World War II he served in the U.S. Navy and attended the U.S. Naval Academy Preparatory School and the U.S. Naval Academy prior to earning a Bachelor of Architecture from Georgia Institute of Technology in 1950. Following his apprenticeship with Stevens and Wilkinson, a well-respected Atlanta firm, he quickly launched out on his own in 1953 with only one associate, John Street. In 1956 the firm merged with that of H. Griffith Edwards, a Georgia Institute of Technology professor who had taught Portman. The firm was known as Edwards and Portman until Edwards' retirement 12 years later when it became John Portman & Associates. During these early years the creativity and entrepreneurial spirit of Portman became apparent.

Through learning about real estate and business aspects of the building process, Portman demonstrated his commitment to projects that strengthened America's central cities, which were in decline due to urban abandonment. In the 1950s he controversially invested in and developed the Atlanta Merchandise Mart, now known as AmericasMart, pioneering the role of architect as developer. Subsequently his developments continued in office buildings, hotels, and other trade marts. Ownership interest gives him a unique perspective on the economic aspects of the design process.

Travel also shaped his perspective of urban design. As the Atlanta Merchandise Mart was being completed, Portman attended the dedication of Brazilia, the new capital of Brazil. To him, the newly created environment was austere and uninviting, focusing on form and not enough on the people of the city in reference to daily living and the environment created. Subsequent travel in Sweden found that the satellite cities of Farstav and Valanby worked well because of their strong pedestrian environment, orientation, and emphasis on surrounding greenspace. In the decades that have followed, his work emphasizes rebuilding existing cities by focusing on the scale and lifestyle of the city and making buildings more responsive to human values. Understanding the human response to environmental circumstances is intrinsic to his work.

Portman has always taken an active civic role, particularly in Atlanta. From 1970-1972 he served as President of Central Atlanta Progress, a coalition of downtown businesses that produced the first Central Area Study that gave downtown Atlanta a master plan for its growth and the development of its infrastructure. As a founding member of Action Forum, he took a leading role in human rights and the peaceful integration of the city in the 1960s and 1970s. Through ownership of the trade marts and his work with the Atlanta Visitors and Convention Bureau, he is acknowledged to have played the major role in the development of Atlanta as one of the nation's leading convention cities. In 1984 the Urban Land Institute presented Embarcadero Center, which he designed and developed in San Francisco, with its prestigious Award of Excellence in recognition of a large-scale project that 'exemplifies superior design, relevance to contemporary issues and needs, and resourceful utilization of land while improving the quality of the living environment'. Internationally, his contributions have also been recognized. The Queen of Denmark bestowed upon him the Royal Order of the Knights of the Dannebrog, First Class, in 1983, and the King of Belgium made him an Officer of the Royal Belgian Order of the Crown in 1975.

Portman has a passionate love of the arts. His work as architect, painter, sculptor, and furniture designer has been recognized by the National Academy of Design in New York and Accademia Internazionale d'Arte in Moderna, Italy. His work is primarily held in private collections and can be seen in some of his development projects such as SunTrust Plaza, SunTrust Plaza Garden Offices, Peachtree Center, Embarcadero Center, and others.

Some of John Portman's honors include: the American Institute of Architecture's Silver Medal for Innovation in Hotel Design, the Elsie de Wolfe Award from the American Institute of Interior Designers, the Exceptional Achievement Award from Georgia Institute of Technology, the Gold Plate Award from the American Academy of Achievement, the Horatio Alger Award, the Outstanding Humanitarian Award from the National Jewish Hospital, and an Honorary Doctorate of Letters from Emory University. He serves on the boards of numerous civic, cultural, and business organizations, including 30 years of service as the Honorary Consul of Denmark. John Portman is a Fellow of the American Institute of Architects and a member of the National Council of Registration Boards.

John C. Portman, III, RA
Chief Executive Officer, John Portman & Associates; Vice Chairman, Portman Holdings

John C. (Jack) Portman, III is Chief Executive Officer for John Portman & Associates, the architectural and engineering company of Portman Holdings, and is the Vice Chairman of Portman Holdings, the land and property development company. Mr. Portman is responsible for the international development activities.

After Mr. Portman graduated from Georgia Institute of Technology in 1971 and obtained his Master of Architecture from Harvard University in 1973, he began his career as an apprentice architect for John Portman & Associates. From broad experience in the architectural firm, he moved into working with the domestic arm of real estate development and then the international arm. He later helped establish Portman Overseas to pursue international real estate development and property management.

Seeing the tremendous potential in the Pacific Rim, Mr. Portman established the first Portman Asian office in Hong Kong in 1979, living there until 1982. He led the firm's projects, including housing in Hong Kong and mixed-use developments in Singapore, Malaysia, Indonesia, and Thailand.

In 1980, with the firm's entry into China, he provided the groundwork for the design and development of Shanghai Centre, the largest foreign investment project in China. The extraordinary success of the project spawned increased activity for the firm in China, Malaysia, Indonesia, and Singapore.

In early 1993 he opened the firm's office in Shanghai. In 1995 he moved to Shanghai full time, heading all international work for the firm and providing the groundwork to establish an office in Mumbai (Bombay) and cement an architectural practice in India. In 1998, while still responsible for the firm's international activity, Mr. Portman returned to Atlanta to lead all operations of John Portman & Associates on a global basis.

Principals Biographies continued

Richards M. Mixon, RA
President, Architectural Design,
John Portman & Associates

Since joining John Portman & Associates in 1978, Richards Mixon, participating directly with John Portman, has played a leading role as director of design. His extensive experience and interest in designing urban and suburban, high-profile projects has helped the firm build a talented architectural design team.

Prior to joining John Portman & Associates, Mr. Mixon worked for the firm of I.M. Pei in New York, he was Project Design Architect for the National Center for Atmospheric Research facility and the Des Moines Art Center. He also worked on such projects as Place Ville Marie in Montreal, the Redevelopment Plan for the Boston Waterfront, the Canadian Imperial Bank of Commerce in Toronto, and Dallas City Hall.

As a patron of the arts, Mr. Mixon strives to acknowledge the importance of a broad context in design. He also has a keen interest in math and science that creates a challenging approach to designing high-density environments. His awareness on highly competitive commercial projects displays the firm's ability to match economic viability and design excellence.

Mr. Mixon earned his Bachelor of Science in 1955 from Georgia Institute of Technology. After service in the U.S. Navy he returned to Georgia Institute of Technology for his Bachelor of Architecture in 1959.

H. Warren Snipes, AIA
Vice President, John Portman & Associates

Mr. Snipes brings to the leadership of Portman's organizations a wide range of experience as an architect, construction manager, and developer. He serves as a liaison between the design and development arms to facilitate project coordination for the client.

After serving in the U.S. Navy, Mr. Snipes began his architectural career in 1970 with Heery & Heery, focusing on construction management and specializing in scheduling and implementing cost control techniques. In 1977 he joined the Irvine Company, a major owner and developer of mixed-use communities in Southern California. He held the position of Director of Development with complete responsibility for planning and development of various type projects. Mr. Snipes left the Irvine Company in 1986 to return to Atlanta as Senior Director of Development for Portman Properties for three years prior to moving into key management positions with John Portman & Associates.

Mr. Snipes earned his Bachelor of Architecture from Georgia Institute of Technology in 1967 and his Master of Business Administration from National University in San Diego in 1976.

Rene J. Ferandel, RA

Vice President, John Portman & Associates

Mr. Ferandel is responsible for the financial operations of the firm, combining his architectural and business training. He joined John Portman & Associates in 1985 upon graduation from Georgia Institute of Technology where he represented the university in national and international competitions, and acquired professional experience working for Tarriba and Associates Inc., Mexico City.

At John Portman & Associates, he quickly demonstrated his talents and determination, participating in all phases of the architectural process for the Northpark Town Center and SunTrust Plaza projects. Mr. Ferandel has a broad range of experience from project management to business administration. He has demonstrated exceptional ability to manage complex projects, assuring adherence to schedule and budget.

His ability to communicate effectively with the client, design teams, and consultants has enabled him to meet the project's functional and financial requirements to the client's satisfaction. Similarly, Mr. Ferandel's experience in working with city agencies and public constituencies has helped build a solid working relationship with clients throughout the world.

Mr. Ferandel earned his Bachelor of Architecture from Georgia Institute of Technology in 1985 and his Master of Business Administration from Georgia State University in 1991.

Walter N. Jackson, RA

Vice President, John Portman & Associates

Mr. Jackson has been Chief Representative of John Portman & Associates' Shanghai Representative Office since 1993 and has been involved in the design of China projects since 1979. He was chosen to go to China because of the depth of his design experience, his ability to work well with clients, and his knowledge of China.

Much of his career since joining John Portman & Associates in 1973 has focused on the Pacific Rim. He relocated to the firm's Hong Kong office from 1981-1983 to coordinate the design activities and preparation of construction documents for John Portman & Associates East Asia Ltd. From 1985-1987 he was assigned to work with Kajima Corporation's architectural design division to direct the design review process during Kajima's preparation of construction drawings for Shanghai Centre. Since January 1993 he has lived full time in Shanghai.

He is a talented designer who understands and appreciates the practical business aspects of the design process. His attention to detail and the conscientious manner in which he communicates with the Atlanta office enables the John Portman & Associates design team to work effectively together.

Mr. Jackson earned his Bachelor of Architecture from the University of Illinois in 1968.

Principals Biographies continued

Ellis Katz, RA
Vice President, John Portman & Associates

As Director of the Hospitality Studio, Mr. Katz works closely with clients and coordinates the team of architects and consultants that serve them. Ellis Katz has repeatedly demonstrated the results of team leadership. Dedicated and energetic, he has successfully managed large-scale architectural projects in which he showed a clear understanding of the technical requirements of the project as well as being sensitive to the design issues. His communication skills and personal demeanor make him an excellent team player. His organizational skills and conscientious follow-through help keep his team focused.

By gaining his education through the Co-op Program at the University of Cincinnati, Mr. Katz was able to work for a wide range of architectural firms in cities such as Cleveland, Baltimore, Burbank, Cambridge, and Chicago. His talent was recognized with the Co-op Achievement Award, a student honor scholarship, and the prestigious Voorheis Honor Scholarship.

Prior to joining John Portman & Associates as a Project Director, Mr. Katz was an Associate with Loebl Schlossman & Hackl Inc. in Chicago. His work included design, master planning, and project management, with responsibility for complete project coordination through tenant move-in.

Mr. Katz earned his Bachelor of Architecture at the University of Cincinnati in 1984.

Walter Miller, RA
Vice President, John Portman & Associates

Mr. Miller directs the Education Studio for John Portman & Associates, working with schools and universities throughout the world to address new concepts relating to university design, to campus life and its educational purpose. His urban design and planning experience has evolved into his concentration on educational facilities, applying programming and design principles that focus on both the aesthetic and functional aspects of campus design.

Prior to joining John Portman & Associates, he joined the firm of Cesar Pelli & Associates in 1981, where he became a Senior Designer with responsibility for schematic design and design development of the World Financial Center (New York), the Society for Savings Tower (Cleveland), the Yale University Center for Molecular Medicine (New Haven), and the Tower for Yerba Buena Gardens (San Francisco).

Mr. Miller has traveled and studied extensively in Western Europe under the University of Illinois' Versailles Program and a Paris Prize Fellowship. His studies also included travel in Japan, Thailand, India, and Nepal on an Edward L. Ryerson Fellowship and a European Museum study through a Francis J. Plym Fellowship in 1990.

Mr. Miller earned his Bachelor of Architecture from the University of Illinois in 1975 where he subsequently taught and served as a Visiting Instructor in undergraduate design studios.

R. Don Starr, RA

Vice President, John Portman & Associates

Mr. Starr has been part of the Portman design team since the conception of the firm's first hotel, the Hyatt Regency Atlanta, in 1967. Since joining the firm upon graduation from Georgia Institute of Technology he has consistently played a key role in the organization.

As the firm focused on the hospitality industry, so developed Mr. Starr's expertise in hotel design. He has participated in the design of practically every hotel designed by John Portman & Associates, from large-scale convention hotels in mixed-use complexes to smaller properties for a segmented market. His understanding of the industry is strong and he excels in programming the various functions and designing back-of-the-house space, effectively and efficiently meeting the operators' design objectives. By staying abreast of changes in the industry, he assists by incorporating systems and products that provide the competitive advantages hotels must maintain in today's marketplace.

Mr. Starr earned his Bachelor of Architecture from Georgia Institute of Technology in 1963.

Grace A. Tan, RA

Vice President, John Portman & Associates

Ms. Tan returned to John Portman & Associates' Atlanta office in 2000 as liaison for Asian design after serving seven years in the Shanghai office. She was chosen to co-head the Shanghai office because of her extensive international design experience. Her career began in the Philippines working with multi-national design teams on international mixed-use projects that required an understanding of indigenous materials, local construction practices, and an appreciation of local culture and customs as they related to and influenced design.

Since joining John Portman & Associates in 1985, she has served as Project Architect for a number of projects and has demonstrated exceptional ability in using the CAD system to effectively present project documents. She is a talented designer with a keen understanding of the importance of context and culture on the design process. Fluent in Chinese, she interfaces well with the firm's Chinese clients and John Portman & Associates' affiliated architects in the local design institutes. Her language skills coupled with solid design and production expertise are a major asset to serving clients in China.

Ms. Tan earned her Bachelor of Architecture from the University of Santo Tomas in 1982, Master of Architecture from Ohio State University in 1984, and Master of Urban Studies from Harvard University in 2000.

Collaborators and Consultants

Collaborators

Bank of China: Zhejiang Real Estate Group Design and Research Institute

Bank of Communications: Shanghai Institute of Architectural Design & Research

BSD New Town: Doxiasis Associates

Capital Square: Jurubena Bertiga International Sdn.

College of Education Building: The Woodhurst Partnership

Dream Lake Mountain Villas: Zhejiang Province Architectural Design Institute

East Seaport Apartment and High Rise Hotel Addition: Zhejiang Real Estate Group Design and Research Institute

Indian School of Business: 23 Fortune 500 companies & Haseez Contract

Lot 6: Lot 8 S.P. Tao

Marina Square: DP Architects

Moscow Centre: Soviet Institute of Knowledge, American International Group

New Asia Center: East China Architectural Design & Research Institute

Shandong Hotel & Conference Center: Zhejiang Province Design Research Institute

Shanghai Centre: East China Architectural Research

Silver Tie World Trade Center: China Electronics Engineering Design Institute

Songdo Daewoo Town: Shanghai Institute of Architecture

The Regent Singapore: BEP Akitek

Tomorrow Square: Shanghai Institute of Architectural Design and Research

Village of Schaumburg Convention Center, Performing Arts Theater, and Convention Headquarters Hotel: HNTB Architecture (Convention Center); Daneil P. Coffey & Associates (Performing Arts Theater)

Wellington Mews: Raja Aederi Consultants Ltd.

Westin Hotel Charlotte: Odell Associates

Westin Hotel: Skanska Architect

Westlake International Hotel: Zhejiang Province Building Design & Research Institute

Zhong Xing City: Zhejiang Province Design & Research Institute

Consultants

The work of John Portman & Associates is produced through a team effort with outstanding consultants from around the world and from a wide variety of disciplines. The following are the major firms with whom the firm has worked most extensively. Their talent, expertise, and commitment have added to the success of the design process.

Arnold Associates

Artec Consultants Inc.

Auerbach Associates

Ballentine Walker Smith Inc.

Bennett & Pless Inc.

Bentley Engineers

Bilkey Llinas Design

Bolt Beranek & Newman

Bouraccorsi & Associates

Britt Alderman Associates

Cerami & Associates

Chastain & Tindel

Chermayeff & Geismar Associates

Chris Jaffe

Cini-Little International Inc.

Citadel Consulting Inc.

Costing Services Group Inc.

Curtain Wall Design Consulting Inc.

Daroff Design Inc.

Davis Langdon & Seah Ltd.

Diclemente-Siegel

Don Ashton Asia Designers Ltd.

EDAW

Edwards & Zuck P.C.

Flack & Kurtz Consulting Engineers

Gleeds

GNA Design Associates Inc.

Graelic Inc.

Graphic Systems International

H.M. Brandston & Partners Inc.

Hanscomb Associates Inc.

Harold Neilsen & Tamer Uzan

Hauser Associates

HDC & Associates

Heitmann & Associates Inc.

Herman & Lees Associates

Hilliker Associates

Hirsch Bedner Associates

Humble Arnold

J.R. Ballentine & Associates

Jack Cermak, Colorado State University

Jacob L. Friesen & Associates

Jerde Partners

John Dinkins

John Grissim & Associates

Jordan Jones & Goulding Inc.

Juru Ukur Bahan Malaysia

Law Engineering and Environmental Services Inc.

LeMessurier Consultants Inc.

Lerch, Bates & Associates Inc.

Lorenc + Yoo Design

Meyers Consulting Services

Moreland Altobeelli Associates Inc.

Morris Harrison & Associates

Muhlfausen Design & Associates Inc.

Newcomb & Boyd

Oreon Construction Company

Ove Arup & Partners

PHA Lighting Design Inc.

Piedmont Geotechnical Consultants Inc.

Planning & Parking Consultants

Post, Buckley, Schuh & Jernigan

Pran Inc.

PRC Sdn Bhd

Project Time & Cost Inc.

R.A. Heintges Architects Consultants

Rainbow Services

Raymon Noya

Reid, Cool & Michalski

Richard Frieson

Richard Poulin

Rider, Hunt & Bailey

Roger Morgan

Rolf Jensen & Associates Inc.

Rowan Williams Davies & Irwin Inc.

Roy Ashley & Associates Inc.

Sasaki Dawson & DeMay

Schiff & Associates Inc.

Shopworks

Sizemore Floyd Associates

Soil and Material Engineers

Spiker Baldwin Associates Inc.

Syska & Hennessey

T.Y. Lin & Associates

Thompson Engineering Inc.

Thornton-Tomasetti Engineers

URS/John Blume & Associates

W.L. Jorden & Company Inc.

Walker Parking Consultants

Waller-Davis Associates

Waveguide Consulting Inc.

Weems Doar Engineers

Weidlinger

Wet Design

Wilbur Smith Associates

William Hobbs Ltd.

William Lam & Associates

Wilson & Associates

Wilson, Ihrig & Associates

Chronological List of Buildings and Projects

1953	Fraternal Order of Eagles, Atlanta, GA
1954	Doctor's Office Building, Atlanta, GA
1955	Lemer Residence, Atlanta, GA
1956	Midway Elementary School, Decatur, GA
1961	Atlanta Merchandise Mart, Atlanta, GA
1961	Georgia Tech Infirmary, Atlanta, GA
1961	Atlanta Decorative Arts Center, Atlanta, GA
1962	Hawthorne Elementary School, Atlanta, GA
1963	Sequoyah High School, Doraville, GA
1964	Entelechy I, Atlanta, GA
1964	Trailways Garage and Parking Deck, Atlanta, GA
1965	Greenbriar Shopping Center, Atlanta, GA
1965	Atlanta School Service Center, Atlanta, GA
1965	Peachtree Center Office Building, Atlanta, GA
1965	Antoine Graves Home, Atlanta, GA
1965	Agnes Scott College, Dana Fine Arts Center, Decatur, GA
1965	Herndon Elementary School, Atlanta, GA
1965	Greenbriar Rich's, Atlanta, GA

1965	Greenbriar Theater, Atlanta, GA
1966	Spalding Drive Elementary School, Atlanta, GA
1967	Hyatt Regency, Atlanta, GA
1967	C.W. Hill School, Atlanta, GA
1967	Henderson High School, Chamblee, GA
1968	Gas Light Tower, Peachtree Center, Atlanta, GA
1968	Trailways Bus Terminal, Atlanta, GA
1968	Midnight Sun Restaurant, Atlanta, GA
1970	South Tower, Peachtree Center, Atlanta, GA
1971	J.F. Kennedy School & Community Center, Atlanta, GA
1971	Hyatt Regency, Chicago, IL
1971	Hyatt Regency Addition, Atlanta, GA
1971	Blue Cross Blue Shield Office Building, Chattanooga, TN
1971	Alfred Blalock Elementary School, Atlanta, GA
1971	Park Central Office Building I, Dallas, TX
1971	Park Central Office Building II, Dallas, TX
1971	Security Pacific National Bank, Embarcadero Center, San Francisco, CA
1974	Cain Tower, Peachtree Center, Atlanta, GA

Chronological List of Buildings and Projects continued

1974	Hyatt Regency, Embarcadero Center, San Francisco, CA
1974	Levi Strauss Building, Embarcadero Center, San Francisco, CA
1974	Texas American Bank Building (formerly Ft. Worth National Bank), Fort Worth, TX
1975	Peachtree Center Shopping Gallery, Atlanta, GA
1975	Brussels International Trade Mart, Brussels, Belgium
1976	Three Embarcadero Center, San Francisco, CA
1976	The Westin Peachtree Plaza Hotel, Atlanta, GA
1976	Harris Tower, Peachtree Center, Atlanta, GA
1976	Renaissance Center (Phase One), Detroit, MI
1977	The Westin Bonaventure, Los Angeles, CA
1979	Atlanta Apparel Mart, Atlanta, GA
1982	The Regent Singapore (formerly The Pavilion Intercontinental), Singapore
1982	Kwai Chung Condominiums, Hong Kong
1983	Emory University Physical Education Center, Atlanta, GA
1985	Rockefeller Center Renovation, New York, NY
1985	Atlanta Marriott Marquis, Atlanta, GA
1985	New York Marriott Marquis, New York, NY
1985	Marquis One Office Tower, Atlanta, GA

1986	Entelechy II, Sea Island, GA
1986	Emory University Student Center, Atlanta, GA
1986	Northpark 400 Office Tower, Atlanta, GA
1987	Marina Square: Hotels (Marina Mandarin, The Oriental Singapore, Pan Pacific Singapore) and Shopping Mall, Singapore
1987	The Portman-San Francisco (renamed The Pan Pacific Hotel), San Francisco, CA
1988	Marquis Two Office Tower, Atlanta, GA
1988	Embarcadero Center West Office Tower, San Francisco, CA
1988	Park Hyatt Hotel, Embarcadero Center West, San Francisco, CA
1989	Peachtree Center Athletic Club, Atlanta, GA
1989	Northpark 500 Office Tower, Atlanta, GA
1989	Inforum, Atlanta, GA
1989	Riverwood 100 Office Tower, Atlanta, GA
1990	Shanghai Centre, Shanghai, China
1990	San Francisco Fashion Center, San Francisco, CA
1991	Hung Yuan International Hotel, Taipei, Taiwan
1992	Atlanta Gift Mart, Atlanta, GA
1993	One Peachtree Center (renamed SunTrust Plaza), Atlanta, GA

Bibliography

Articles

'10,000 Hotel Rooms a Year.' *Progressive Architecture* (June 1988), pp 96-98.

Abalos, Iñaki & Juan Herreros. 'Interview with John Portman.' *Arqui 290 Tec Tura* (1992), pp 101-107.

'A Controlled Explosion in Entelechy.' *INTERIOR* Nanjing, China: Interior Design+Construction (October 2000), pp 18-25.

'A Courtin' on Times Square.' *Architectural Forum* (September 1973), p 16.

'A Few Minutes with John Portman.' *Atlanta Business Chronicle* (19 July 1987), p 1A.

'A Good Idea whose Come Again.' *Progressive Architecture* (September 1971), pp 122-127.

Anason, Dean. 'Portman's ADAC starting TV Show.' *Commercial Real Estate* (3-9 December 1993), pp 2B-16B.

Anderson, Kurt. 'Fast Life along the Skywalks.' *Time* (1 August 1988), pp 72-73.

'An Interview with John Portman.' *AIA Journal* (September 1991), p 19.

Anthony, Margaret. 'Portman pays "culture rent" with New Building's Art Works.' *Commercial Real Estate* (3 October, 5 November 1992).

'Antoine Graves Home for the Aged.' *Architectural Record* (January 1966), p 137.

'Architect and Entrepreneur.' *World* Peat, Marwick, Mitchell & Company (Winter 1971).

'Architect/Developer.' *R.I.B.A. Journal* (December 1977), pp 504-513.

'Architecte-promoteur.' *Architecture D'Aujourd'Hui* (October 1977), pp 48-61.

'Architecture '86: Marquis, Broadway's Newest Baby.' *Theatre Crafts* (December 1986), pp 22-23, 56-61.

'Architecture for People and not for Things.' *Architectural Record* (January 1977), pp 133-140.

'Art Works by John Calvin Portman.' *INTERIOR* Nanjing, China: Interior Design+Construction (September 2000), pp 48-51.

'At Home with John Portman—Circles in the Square.' *Interior Design* (March 1982), pp 160-167.

'Atlanta: Peachtree Center Plaza Hotel.' *Interior Design* (July 1976), pp 84-97.

Baldinger, Pam. 'Grinning and Bearing It.' *The China Business Review* (March/April 1990), pp 40-43.

'Bank of Babylon.' *Interiors* (July 1967), pp 68-77.

Baraban, Regina. 'A Theatrical Dining Design.' *Food Management* (March 1987), pp 174-180.

Barnett, Jonathan. 'John Portman: Atlanta's one–man urban renewal program.' *Architectural Record* (January 1966), pp 133-140.

Baxter, Lynn. 'Signing a Landmark.' *Signs of the Times* (May 1987), pp Z46-Z53.

Birney, Don. 'In the Lap of Luxury.' *Restaurant & Hotel Design* (November 1988), p 30.

Blankenhorn, Dana. 'Pioneer in an Urban World.' *Business Atlanta* (May 1987), pp 88-91.

Bolt, John. 'Personal File-Portman.' *Associated Press* (8 April 1988).

Bolton, Phillip & Phillip Campbell. 'Banks team with Portman to build Worldwide Empire.' *Southern Banker* (August 1987), pp 20-23.

Borcover, Alfred. 'Grand Hotel.' *Chicago Tribune* (11 October 1987), p 5.

Breckenfeld, Gurney. 'The Architects want a Voice in Redesigning America.' *Fortune* (November 1971), pp 22-24.

'Broadway gets a Flashy Marquis.' *Engineering-News Record* (23 February 1985), pp 26-29.

Bueno, Jacqueline. 'A Metropolis of his Own.' *Atlanta Business Chronicle* (30 July-5 August 1993), pp 1A-17A.

Canty, Donald. 'Evaluation: Rockefeller West? John Portman's San Francisco Colossus is complete for now.' *A.I.A. Journal* (October 1982), pp 56-63.

Capelin, Joan. 'Dialogue for AIA Dallas Practice Conference: what commands the respect of an architectural client?' *Architectural Record* (March 1985), pp 39-41.

Carmichael, Jane. 'Disneyland's for Adults: John Portman freely admits he's building for the man in the street.' *Forbes* (27 September 1982), pp 125-126.

Carrns, Ann. 'Bank picks One Peachtree.' *Atlanta Business Chronicle* (28 October-3 November 1994), pp 3A-36A.

Carter, Carol. 'Leaders in developing Atlanta.' (April 1998), p 87.

Casati, Cesare. 'Portman in Shanghai.' *l'Arca* Milano, Italy: l'Arcaedizioni (February 1996), pp 68-75.

Chaffin, Tom. 'Great Chest of Drawers Debate.' *Fulton County Daily Report* (31 May 1988), p 1.

Chaffin, Tom. 'Portman's Progress.' *Fulton County Daily Report* (24 May 1988), pp 1, 4-6.

Colgan, Susan. 'John Portman on the New York Marriott Marquis.' *Restaurant & Hotel Design* (November 1985), p 108.

Cowan, Joel. 'A Tale of Two Generations.' *Business To Business* (October 1999), p 70.

Craig, Robert. 'From Plantations to Peachtree.' *Southern Homes* (November 1987), pp 67-69.

Craig, Robert. 'Mythic Proportions: the Portman home.' *Southern Homes* (January/February 1988), pp 90-99.

Crane, Catherine. 'Ft. Worth.' *Interiors* (April 1972), p 124.

Credeur, Mary Jane. 'Portman designs Firm's International Expansion.' *Atlanta Business Chronicle* (14 June 2001), pp 7-9.

Crim, Sarah K.. 'Vertical Urban Centers may be Answer to Increasing Density.' *Mortgage Banker* (February 1975), pp 38-42.

Currimbhoy, Nayana. 'How John Portman maintains High Profile in East Asia.' *Interiors* (January 1987), p 204.

Cutts, Beau. 'I try to be Childlike: I see life as an adventure every day.' *Atlanta Journal & Constitution* (29 December 1989), p 14A.

Cutts, Beau. 'Portman shapes Buildings to fit his Soaring Dreams.' *Atlanta Journal & Constitution* (29 December 1989), p 1.

'Dana Fine Arts Center of Agnes Scott College.' *Architectural Record* (January 1966), p 138.

Davis, Douglas. 'Spaces for our Time.' *Newsweek* (24 December 1973), pp 49-53.

Dawe, Nancy. 'Atlanta's living Legacy.' *Atlanta Journal & Constitution, Atlanta Weekly* (6 September 1987), pp 8-14.

Dean, A.O.. 'Hotel Chain built upon an Architectural Concept.' *A.I.A. Journal* (July 1978), pp 64-71.

'Decorative Arts Center, Atlanta.' *Interiors* (January 1961), pp 66-73.

DeMarco, Edward. 'Atlanta becoming New York of the 21st Century.' *Atlanta Business Chronicle* (17 May 1992), p 1B.

DeMarco, Edward. 'World Trade Club off to One Peachtree.' *Atlanta Business Chronicle* (5 May 1993), pp 7-13.

Bibliography continued

'Development con arte.' *Architecttura* (May 1985), pp 374-375.

Dezzi Bardeschi, Marco. 'Big Void.' *Domus* Italy: (May 1980), pp 14-17.

Dishman, Laura. 'Paradise Within.' 'Portman's Legacy: buildings may never be the same.' *Orlando Sentinel* (1 May 1987), pp E1-5.

'Dixie Kid Socko on Great White Way.' *Architecture Plus* (August 1973), p 15.

Donner, JoAnne. 'CEO Insight: building on Atlanta's foundation.' *Business Atlanta* (September 1989), pp 40-42.

Donner, JoAnne. 'Portman on the Arts: a spiritual necessity.' *Business Atlanta* (November 1993), pp 16, 20.

Dorey, Guy. 'Developing Atlanta.' Dorey Publishing (January 1999).

Downey, Claire. 'Das Portman Hotel.' *Archithese* Zurich, Switzerland: Arthur Niggli Ltd. (February 1988), pp 19-25. (Marriott Marquis, Atlanta)

Downey, Claire. 'Entelechy II: a beach umbrella.' *l'Arca* Milano, Italy: l'Arcaedizioni (March 1988), pp 42-53.

Downey, Claire. 'John Portman: the Memorial Day interview.' *Artpapers* (July/August 1986), pp 19-21.

'Downtown Development.' *Architectural Forum* (April 1969), pp 42-47.

Duckworth, Michael. 'In Shanghai, a New Window opens to World Culture.' *The Asian Wall Street Journal* (December 1991), pp 13-14.

Dunn, John. 'The Shaper of Cityscapes.' *Georgia Tech Alumni Magazine* (Summer 1988), pp 18-25.

'Efficient Grandeur at 225 Peachtree.' *Interiors* (September 1971), pp 119-125.

Emerson, Bo. 'John Portman makes Top 10 of Architects.' *The Newsstand* (6 August 1991), p B5.

Feuerstein, Adam. 'Life at the Top.' *Atlanta Business Chronicle* (5 August 1991), pp 1B, 13B.

Finney, Paul B.. 'San Francisco Hotels.' *Travel & Leisure* (December 1987), pp 102-105, 162.

Florence, C.. 'MXD.' *A.I.A. Journal* (September 1977), pp 28-31.

Fox, Catherine. 'Mixed Blessing.' 'Punctuating Peachtree.' *Atlanta Journal & Constitution* (13 December 1992), pp K2, K4.

Fox, Catherine. 'Portman's Playhouse.' *Atlanta Journal & Constitution* (15 November 1987), pp J1-J2.

Freeman, A.. 'Introverted Trio of MXD's dominates Atlanta's New Downtown.' *A.I.A. Journal* (September 1977), pp 34-36.

'Ft. Worth National Bank.' *Architectural Record* (January 1975), pp 106-107.

Galphin, Bruce. 'John Portman of Peachtree Center.' *Atlanta Magazine* (August 1967), pp 33-36.

Gapp, Paul. 'A Space Revolution.' *Chicago Tribune* (February 1987), p 16.

Garrison, Webb. 'John Portman has pursued his own Vision.' *Atlanta Journal & Constitution* (12 July 1987), p H2.

'Genoa, We're with You all the Way.' *l'Arca* Milano, Italy: l'Arcaedizioni (December 1988), Editorial.

Gillam, Carey. 'Portman Trade Show Group poised for Deal with Mexico City Firm.' *Atlanta Business Chronicle* (18-24 February 1994), pp 3A-22A.

Goldberger, Paul. 'Architecture: John C. Portman, Jr.' *Architectural Digest* (December 1987), pp 98-111.

Goldberger, Paul. 'Buck Rogers in Times Square.' *New York Times, Magazine* (26 August 1973), Sec. 6, pp 2-7.

Goldberger, Paul. 'The Portman Formula in Miniature.' *New York Times, Travel Magazine* (10 January 1988), p 1.

Goolrick, Chester. 'John Portman, certain of his Urban Vision, tries it on New York.' *Wall Street Journal* (19 October 1981), p 14.

Goolrick, Faye. 'Visions in Glass and Steel.' *Atlanta Magazine* (June 1986), pp 67-70, 121-122.

Gove, Matt. 'Portman working on Major Rail Project in Taiwan.' *Atlanta Business Chronicle* (23-29 March 2001), p 11A.

'Grass grows tall, hair-raising talk.' *Architects Journal* (5 May 1982), p 34.

Grat, Roberta Brandes. 'Save the Helen Hayes.' *New West* (19 November 1985), pp 74-75.

Green, Lois Wagner. 'Dusky Drinking, Sunny Dining.' *Interiors* (March 1975), pp 66-69.

Green, Lois Wagner. 'The Portman.' *Interior Design* (June 1988), pp 266-277.

Grimes, Millard. 'Another Road Less Traveled.' *Georgia Trend* (January 1991), p 69.

Gueft, Olga. 'Detroit Plaza Hotel.' *Contract Interiors* (December 1977), pp 66-75.

Gueft, Olga. 'John Portman's Heaven under Glass.' *Interiors* (July 1976), pp 50-59.

Haddad, Charles. 'Fort Lauderdale Project Panel picks Portman.' (28 August 1990).

Harrison, Barbara. 'Hangzhou on a Georgian's Mind.' (12 August 1993), p 17.

Helgerson, Kay. 'Close-Up: John Portman.' *Go Magazine* (May 1988), p 60.

Hiskey, Michelle. 'Team to "develop a vision for Atlanta".' *The Atlanta Journal & Constitution* (1 October 1992).

'Hotel à Atlanta.' *Architecture D'Aujourd'Hui* (December 1976), p xxxii.

'Hotels: Building Fantasies for Travelers.' *Time* (8 March 1976), pp 54-55.

Huxtable, Ada Louise. '54-Story Hotel expected to revitalize Times Square.' *New York Times* (11 July 1973), pp 43, 50.

'Hyatt Regency, Atlanta.' *Architectural Record* (January 1966), pp 134-136.

'Hyatt Regency, Atlanta.' *Interiors* (November 1968), pp 122-135.

'Hyatt Regency Hotel.' *Global Architecture* (No. 28, 1974), pp 36-37.

'In Progress: Atlanta.' *Progressive Architecture* (May 1975), pp 42-43.

'In Progress: Portman's Projects.' *Progressive Architecture* (February 1978), p 41.

Iversen, Lance. 'S.F. Fashion Center provides Retailers New Spot to Shop.' *The San Francisco Chronicle* (16 July 1990), p C7.

Jodidio, Philip. 'Controlled Explosion.' *Connaissance des Arts* Paris, France: Connaissance des Arts (April 1988), pp 104-109. (Entelechy II)

'John C. Portman Jr.: who's who among metro movers and shakers in 1992.' *The Georgia Trend 100* (January 1991), p 40.

'John Portman: architecture is not a building.' *Art in America* (March 1973), pp 80-82.

'John Portman in London.' *Architects Journal* (5 May 1982), pp 38-39.

Bibliography continued

Johnson, Harriet. 'It's simply Symbiotic: offices, shops mingle.' *USA Today* (8 August 1986), p 4B.

Kalyk, Roni. 'San Francisco Memories by the Bay.' *B. International* (July 1988), pp 9-11.

Kasuga, Yoshiko. 'New York Marriott Marquis.' *Pronto* (Vol. 4, 1987), pp 20-23.

Katz, Ellis. 'Creating a Memorable Stay with the Latest Technology. *Lodging* (February 2000), pp 79-81.

Kennedy, Shawn G.. 'Architects now double as Developers.' *New York Times, Real Estate* (7 February 1988), p 1.

Kiener, Robert. 'John Portman: Architect/Visionary.' *Hospitality* (September 1975), 50-53.

Knack, Ruth Eckdish. 'A Bundle of Constructions.' *Planning Magazine* (April 1989), pp 28-32.

Kramer-Kabina, Margarete. 'Marriott Marquis Hotel, Atlanta, Georgia.' *Architektur+Wettbewerbe* (September 1986), p 20.

'La Fortezze di Vetro Degli Affari.' *Architettura* (January 1978), pp 522-523.

'La Hall Urbanizzata.' *Architettura* (February 1978), pp 592-593.

Lapidus, M.. 'Architect as Developer.' (book review) *Journal of the Society of Architectural Historians* (December 1978), pp 303-305.

'Learning from Atlanta.' *A.I.A. Journal* (April 1975), pp 33-45.

Leviton, Joyce. 'Architect John Portman: 'I violate Sacred Rules to create People Places.' *People Weekly* (11 August 1975).

'Living the High Rise Life.' *San Francisco Business* (December 1974).

'Los Angeles Bonaventure Hotel.' *Interior Design* (December 1977), pp 114-127.

Lueck, Thomas. 'Nine Forecasts on what's in store for the 1990's.' *New York Times, Commercial Property* (14 May 1989), pp 4-10.

Lundy, David. 'Portman moves without Tenants or Financing.' *Fulton County Daily Report* (24 May 1988), p 5.

Manghi, Luigi. 'One Peachtree Center Tower, Atlanta.' *l'Arca* Milano, Italy: l'Arcaedizioni (December 1989), pp 38-47. (One Peachtree Center, Atlanta)

'Marina Square: Portman's City from the Sea.' *Southeast Asia Building* (September 1987), pp 34-44.

Marlin, William. 'An Outside, Inside.' *Architectural Forum* (November 1973), pp 46-55.

Marlin, William. 'Urban Growth: Atlanta does it right.' *Christian Science Monitor* (19 May 1975), pp 14-15.

Marlow, Michael. 'Launching the Fashion Center: a talk with John Portman.' *WWD/San Francisco* (May 1990).

'Master Architects on Interior Public Space.' *Designers West* (November 1985), p 142.

McKnight, Kit. 'John Portman on Buildings and People.' *Bay Area Business Magazine* (Vol. 3, 1986), pp 28-32, 34.

McManamon, Kathleen. 'Building on a Building.' *Dixie Contractor* (5 June 2000), p 50.

Meltzer, Mark. 'Best in Atlanta Real Estate – the top deals of 1995.' 'SunTrust Expansion helps to shore up Downtown Market.' *The Atlanta Business Chronicle* (1-7 March 1996), p 4B.

Michaelides, Stephen G.. 'A New Service Orientation.' *Restaurant & Hospitality Magazine* (October 1988), pp 106, 108, 114, 116, 118.

Michaelides, Stephen G.. 'From Plaza to Portman: keeping the customer satisfied.' *Hospitality* (September 1975), R34-R37.

Michaelides, Stephen G.. 'The Other Side of John Portman.' *Restaurant & Hospitality Magazine* (October 1988), pp 118, 121.

'Modernism romps Home.' 'Art meets Acumen.' *Interiors and Lifestyle—India* Mumbai, India: Indian and Eastern Engineer Co. Ltd. (1997), pp 86-107.

'More than a Hotel—a Piranesian City.' *Interiors* (August 1971), pp 72-82.

Moriarty, Erin. 'India Business School mixes Technology with Tradition.' *Atlanta Business Chronicle* (8-14 September 2000), 3A-19A.

Muschamp, Herbert. 'The Thrill of Outer Space for Earthbound Lives.' (20 September 1992).

Muse, Vance. 'Lights dim on the Great White Way.' *Life* (December 1987), pp 84-91.

'National Trust, Portman and Gutheim to be Cited (AIA Medalists).' *A.I.A. Journal* (February 1978), p 12.

'New Life for Old in Downtown Detroit: a glittering preview of the riverfront.' *Detroit Free Press* (4 February 1973), pp 12-14.

Nolan, Martha. 'Can Portman wow them again?' *Georgia Trend* (November 1985), pp 2-68.

O'Neille, Harvard. 'What did he know, and, When did he know it? John Portman, Jr. As a Visionary & Prophet.' *Design News* (Winter 1998), pp 64-65.

'One Peachtree Center.' *Architecture and Urbanism* (November 1993), pp 52-59.

Oney, Steve. 'Portman's Complaint.' *Esquire* (June 1987), pp 182-189.

Pastier, John. 'Evaluation: San Francisco's Hyatt Regency Hotel as a Spatial Landmark.' *A.I.A. Journal* (October 1977), pp 36-43.

'Peachtree Hotel.' *Architectural Review* (May 1977), pp 265-267.

Pendley Koser, Karin. 'A Chat with the Architect of Atlanta's Hospitality.' *ACVB Industry Report* (13 March 1992), pp 47-49.

'People who made a Difference.' *Cornell H.R.A. Quarterly Anniversary Edition* (1985), p 122.

Picard, Maureen. 'Rooftop Revolution.' *Restaurant & Hotel Design* (September 1986), p 40.

'Platinum Circle Awards.' *Restaurant & Hotel Design* (February 1987), p 32.

'Portman: a new force for rebuilding the cities.' *Business Week* (17 February 1973), pp 58-63.

Portman, John. 'Atlanta must rediscover its Can-do, Will-do Spirit.' *Atlanta Business Chronicle* (12 June 1999).

'Portman Show to open on Broadway in 1977.' *Progressive Architecture* (August 1973), pp 23-24.

'Portman's Latest Core.' *Architectural Forum* (October 1997), pp 26-29.

'Portman's Most Animated Atrium Yet.' *Interiors* (October 1973), pp 78-93.

'Portman's Most Intensively Shared Space.' *Interiors* (November 1974), pp 96-103.

'Portman's Residence Atlanta.' *Architectural Record* (January 1966), p 140.

'Portman's Residence.' *Interiors* (April 1965), pp 92-99.

'Portman Theater's Uncertain Future.' *Progressive Architecture* (February 1978), p 25.

Bibliography continued

Pousner, Howard. 'City Sidewalks above Atlanta.' *Atlanta Journal & Constitution* (22 June 1986), p 1B.

Purnick, Joyce. 'Portman, thinking big, is unfazed by New York.' *New York Times* (7 October 1981), pp B1, B6.

Raine, Barry. 'Mr Portman builds his Dream Hotel.' *Avenue Magazine* (December 1988), pp 98-100.

Raskin, Betsy. '$40 Million says this Lady is no Tramp.' *Institutions/Volume Feeding Management* (15 June 1971).

'Record Houses of 1965.' *Architectural Record* (May 1965), pp 126-129. (Entelechy I, Atlanta)

Reis, Michael. 'Interview with Jack Portman.' *Contemporary Stone & Tile Design* (1999), pp 66-79.

'Renaissance Center a Detroit.' *Casabella* Milano, Italy: (April/May 1980), pp 36-39.

Riani, Paolo. 'A Compelling Landmark.' *l'Arca* Milan, Italy: l'Arcaedizioni (December 1988), pp 48-63.

Riani, Paolo. 'The Portman Hotel, San Francisco.' *l'Arca* Milano, Italy: l'Arcaedizioni (January 1989), pp 20-25.

Rice, Marc. 'Atlanta seeks a Towering New Image.' *Associated Press* (4 September 1988), p 5.

Ross, M.F.. 'Star for Tinseltown: Bonaventure Hotel, Los Angeles.' *Progressive Architecture* (February 1978), pp 52-56.

Ross, Stan. 'China, the New Frontier.' *Urban Land* (January 1994), pp 29-33.

Rubinger, David. 'Portman nabs First Japanese Deal.' *Atlanta Business Chronicle* (1992), p 3A.

Sailer, John. 'Bringing Stone to the People: exclusive Portman interview.' *Stone World* (May 1988), pp 17-18, 20, 22, 24.

Salome, Lou. 'Portman Company in the running for Project in Israel.' Tel Aviv, Israel: (20 July 1990).

Saporta, Maria. 'Portman's Peachtree "Evolution".' *The Atlanta Journal & Constitution* (1992), 3B.

Schonbak, Judith. 'The Men who built Atlanta.' *Business Atlanta* (March 1985), pp 50-71.

Schulman, James. 'The Portman Companies roll out the Red Carpet for Democratic Convention.' *Presenting The Season* (Summer 1988), pp 72-74.

'Seven Works: John Portman.' *Architecture and Urbanism* Tokyo, Japan: A+U Publishing Co. Ltd. (1993), pp 36-52.

Sharpe, Anita. 'The Importance of being John Portman.' *Atlanta Business Chronicle* (1 August 1988), pp 1A, 18A.

Sharpe, Anita. 'The Portman Papers.' *Atlanta Business Chronicle* (1 August 1988), p 27A.

Shipp, Bill. 'Builder will stay on Top.' *Marietta Daily Journal* (9 September 1990), p 7.

Shipp, Bill. 'Has revitalized Atlanta forgotten its debt to Portman?' *Atlanta Journal & Constitution* (21 January 1987), Editorial.

Shipp, Bill. 'The Art of Portman Bashing.' *Atlanta Magazine* (December 1987), pp 45-47.

Shipp, Bill. 'The Lion in Winter.' *Georgia Trend* (September 1995), pp 20-23.

Showley, Roger M.. 'Developer puts People in Forefront.' *San Diego Union* (6 March 1988), pp 2F, 8F.

Shropshire, Terry. 'Portman Architecture now shaping Charlotte's Skyline.' *Atlanta Business Chronicle* (September 2000), pp 13B-14B.

Singhal, Rashmi. 'Designs on India.' *The Economic Times* (25 April 1997), p 4.

Slavin, Maeve. 'Portmania.' *Interiors* (October 1984), pp 118-127.

Slutsker, Gary. 'Faces behind the Figures.' *Forbes* (21 April 1986), p 140.

Smertz, Mildred. 'Prometheus rebounded.' *Architectural Record* (September 1986), pp 126-131.

Smith, Gordon. 'Can City Scape win the Battle of the Blands?' *San Diego Tribune* (25 February 1988), pp 1D, 3D.

Smith, Starr. 'Atlanta Superstar Hotel another Southern Coup.' *Sunday Montgomery Advertiser* (24 June 1990).

Sotto, Cindy M.. 'I've never been a Loser.' *Atlanta Business Chronicle* (7 October 1991), pp 1B-2B, 14B, 22B.

Stanton, Cathy. 'Portraits: John Portman, Architect Plus.' *A.I.A. Journal* (April 1975), pp 60-61.

Stark, Al. 'The Atlanta John Portman.' *Detroit News* (9 January 1972), p 4B.

Stein, Karen D.. 'China Lights.' (February 1994).

Stephens, Suzanne. 'Introduction: leaving the natural behind.' *Progressive Architecture* (February 1985), p 45.

'Sul Futuro Dell'Architettura: Riposte a un questionario.' *Casabella* Milano, Italy: (November/December 1985), pp 97-98.

'The Atlanta Marriott Marquis Hotel.' *l'Arca* Milano, Italy: l'Arcaedizioni (March 1987), pp 32-37.

'The Challenge and the Reality: how Renaissance Center was born.' *Detroit News* (24 June 1973), p 6.

'The Life of Metal—Partial Presentation of Mr. Portman's Furniture Design.' *INTERIOR* Nanjing, China: Interior Design+Construction (November 2000), pp 78-83.

'The Midnight Sun Restaurant.' *Architectural Digest* (Summer 1969), pp 24-26.

'The Most Influential People in Georgia.' *Georgia Trend* (February 1990), p 47.

'The Portman Style.' *Newsweek* (23 July 1973).

'The Space of Things to Come.' *New West* (28 March 1977), pp 66-70.

'They made a Difference.' *Meetings & Conventions* (June 1986), p 43.

Thompson, Elizabeth Kendall. 'Dramatic Space for a New Hotel in San Francisco.' *Architectural Record* (September 1973), pp 145-152.

'Times Square Revival Gains Momentum with Portman's Hotel— plus' *Interiors* (August 1973), pp 6, 10.

'To San Francisco with Love.' *Architectural Forum* (March 1967), p 94.

'Trademark Atrium intended for Atlanta Hi-Tech Inforum Mart.' *Building Design Journal* (July 1984), pp 1, 23.

'Twelve who run Georgia.' *Georgia Trend* (February 1987), p 75.

'Viewpoint: Post Modernism and the future of Architecture.' *Georgia Tech* (August 1988), p 23.

Walker, Susan. 'Controversial Portman builds back Atlanta.' *Gwinnett Daily News* (24 July 1988), p 1D.

Walker, Tom. 'Peachtree Plaza gets a New Splash of Color.' *Atlanta Journal & Constitution* (February 1987), pp 1C, 8C.

Bibliography continued

Welch, Mary. 'Calls from a few still get it done Downtown.' *Power Broker* (16 July 1990).

'What to do for an Encore?' *Architectural Record* (June 1976), p 103.

Whitten, Kaye. 'The Victorious Atrium.' *OAG Frequent Flyer* (May 1987), pp 72-77.

'Who's Who in Metro Atlanta.' John C. Portman Jr., *Atlanta Business Chronicle* (21 February 1992).

Wilbert, Tony. 'Portman to develop Downtown.' *Atlanta Business Chronicle* (5-11 December 1977), p 7.

Williams, R.. 'Putting the Show Together.' (Architects as Developer, R.I.B.A. Lecture, 27 April 1982.) *R.I.B.A. Journal* (June 1982), p 24.

Wright, B.N.. 'Megaform comes to Motown.' *Progressive Architecture* (February 1979), pp 57-61.

Wright, Gordon. 'Moderately Sized Hotel bears John Portman's Imprint.' *Building Design & Construction* (April 1988), pp 48-54.

Xue, Qiuti. 'Shanghai Centre in Focus.' *China Daily* (16 June 1992), pp 5-6.

Zielinski, Bob. 'Portuguese Marble graces San Francisco's Portman Hotel.' *Dimensional Stone* (April 1989), pp 22-26.

Zwingle, Erla. 'Atlanta: energy and optimism in the New South.' *National Geographic* (July 1988), pp 2-29.

Books

Baraban, Regina. *Successful Restaurant Design*. Van Nostrand Reinhold, 1988.

Bedner, Michael J.. *The New Atrium*. New York: McGraw-Hill, 1986. (Hyatt Regency Atlanta; Hyatt Regency San Francisco; Peachtree Plaza, Atlanta; Apparel Mart, Atlanta)

Binder, Georgia. *Tall Buildings of Asia & Australia*. Victoria, Australia: Images Publishing Group Pty. Ltd., 2001. (Capital Square, Kuala Lumpur; Shanghai Centre, Shanghai; Tomorrow Square Marriott, Shanghai)

Black, David, Pam Baker & Virginia Parker. *Atlanta, the Making of a World Class City*. Montgomery, Alabama: Community Communications Inc., 1999. (Hyatt Regency Atlanta; SunTrust Plaza, Atlanta; Peachtree Center, Atlanta; Peachtree Plaza, Atlanta; John Portman; Atlanta Marriott Marquis; Merchandise Mart, Atlanta)

Bofinger, Helge & Wolfgang Voigt. *Helmut Jacoby, Master of Architectural Drawing*. Frankfurt am Main: Deutsches Architektur Museum, Exhibition Catalogue, 18 August-21 October 2001. (Embarcadero Center, San Francisco)

Dupre, Judith. *Skyscrapers*. New York: Black Dog & Leventhal Publishers, 1996. (Peachtree Plaza Hotel, Atlanta)

Futagawa, Yukio & Paul Goldberger. *GA 1970-1980, Global Architecture*. Tokyo: A.D.A. EDITA, 1980. (Hyatt Regency San Francisco; Peachtree Center Plaza Hotel, Atlanta; Bonaventure Hotel, Los Angeles; Renaissance Center, Detroit)

Futagawa, Yukio & Paul Goldberger. *GA 28, Global Architecture*. Tokyo: A.D.A. EDITA, 1974. (Hyatt Regency Atlanta; Hyatt Regency O'Hare, Chicago; Hyatt Regency San Francisco)

Futagawa, Yukio & Paul Goldberger. *GA 57, Global Architecture*. Tokyo: A.D.A. EDITA, 1981. (Peachtree Center, Atlanta; Bonaventure Hotel, Los Angeles; Renaissance Center, Detroit)

Greissman, Eugene. *The Achievement Factors*. Dodd, Mead, 1987.

'Hotels,' in *Encyclopedia of Architecture: Design, Engineering and Construction* (Vol. 2, 1989), pp 806-808.

'John Calvin Portman, Jr.' in *Contemporary Architects* St. James Press (1987), pp 708-709.

'John C. Portman,' in *Encyclopedia of Architecture: Design, Engineering and Construction* (Vol. 4, 1989), pp 2-3.

King, Carol Soucek. *Designing With Spirituality, The Creative Touch*. Glen Cove, New York: PBC International Inc., 2000. (Entelechy II)

King, Carol Soucek. *Designing with Tile, Stone and Brick*. New York: Rizzoli International Publications Inc., 1995. (Entelechy II)

Marder, Tod A.. 'Renaissance Center.' in *The Critical Edge*, MIT Press, 1985, pp 175-187.

Mescon, Michael & Timothy Mescon. 'Making Practical Idealism Work.' in *Showing Up For Work and Other Keys to Business Success*. Atlanta: Peachtree Publishers Ltd., 1988. pp 79-85.

Portman, John C. Jnr. & Jonathan Barnett. *The Architect as Developer*. New York: McGraw Hill, 1976.

Portman, John C. Jnr., Paolo Riani & Paul Goldberger. *John Portman*. Milano, Italy: l' Arcaedizioni, 1990.

Portman, John C. Jnr., Robert M. Craig & Aldo Castellano. *John Portman: An Island on an Island*. Milano, Italy: l'Arcaedizioni, 1997.

Rutes, Walter A., Richard H. Penner & Lawrence Adams. *Hotel Design, Planning and Development*. New York: W.W. Norton & Company, 2001.

Rutes, Walter A.. *Hotel Planning & Design*. New York: Watson-Guptil Publications 1985, pp 43, 58, 134, 165, 181.

Sailer, John. *The Great Stone Architects*. Oradell, New Jersey: Tradelink Publishing Co., 1991.

Saito, Gen Takeshi. 'The Portman San Francisco.' in *American Hotels And Their Restaurants*. Shotenkenchiku-sha Co. Ltd., 1988. pp 15-24.

Saxon, Richard. *Atrium Buildings, Development and Design*. London: The Architectural Press, 1983. (Antoine Graves; Apparel Mart, Atlanta; Bonaventure Hotel, Los Angeles; Ft. Worth National Bank, Fort Worth; Peachtree Plaza Hotel, Atlanta; Renaissance Center, Detroit; Times Square Hotel, New York)

Skyme, Ronald. *Hotel Specifications International*. London: Pennington Press, 1986. pp 7-16.

Skyme, Ronald. *Hotel Specifications International*. London: Pennington Press, 1988. pp 18-19.

Snyder, Stuart D.. 'Building Interiors' in *Plants & Automation*, Prentice Hall, 1989, Dedication Page.

Sproiregen, Paul. 'Portman, John (Calvin, Jr.).' in *Contemporary Architects*, New York: St. Martin's Press, 1985. pp 638-639.

Zaknic, Ivan, Matthew Smith & Dolores Rice. *100 of the World's Tallest Buildings*. Victoria, Australia: Images Publishing Group Pty. Ltd., 1998. (SunTrust Plaza)

Awards

Legends of Atlanta Business
Business to Business
John C. Portman, Jr.
Atlanta, Georgia
2000

Georgians of the Century
Georgia Trend
John C. Portman, Jr.
Atlanta, Georgia
2000

Shanghai Excellent Project Design Award
Bank of Communications
Shi Liu Pu Building
Shanghai Construction Commission
Shanghai, China
John Portman & Associates
1999

Lu Ban Award
Bank of Communications,
Shi Liu Pu Building
National Construction Commission
Shanghai, China
John Portman & Associates
1999

Lifetime Achievement Award
Design Build Institute of America
Dallas, Texas
John C. Portman, Jr.
1999

Most Influential Atlantans
Atlanta Business Chronicle
John C. Portman, Jr.
Atlanta, Georgia
1999

Hospitality Hall of Fame
Atlanta Convention & Visitors Bureau
John C. Portman, Jr.
Atlanta, Georgia
1999

Urban Land Institute
Atlanta District Council Award
John C. Portman, Jr.
Atlanta, Georgia
1998

Academician of the National Academy
Museum & School of Fine Arts
New York, New York
John C. Portman, Jr.
1997

FIABCI Award of Distinction
Capital Square Menara Multi-Purpose Building
Award for Commercial Development
John Portman & Associates
Kuala Lumpur, Malaysia
1997

Accademia Internazionale d'Arte Moderna
Elected Member of the Senate
Angel Orensanz Foundation
John C. Portman, Jr.
Italy
1996

Best in Atlanta Real Estate Award
SunTrust Plaza – Office Category
Atlanta Business Chronicle
John Portman & Associates
1995

Award for Excellence in Design
SunTrust Plaza
The American Institute of Architects, Georgia
John Portman & Associates
1994

Citation Award for Lighting Design
International Association of Lighting Designers
SunTrust Plaza
John Portman & Associates
Atlanta, Georgia
1994

Award for Excellence in Urban Design
SunTrust Plaza
Atlanta Urban Design Commission
John Portman & Associates
1993

Honorary Professorship
Shenyang Architectural & Engineering Institute
Shenyang, China
John C. Portman, Jr.
1993

Martin Luther King
'Salute to Greatness' Award
John C. Portman, Jr.
Atlanta, Georgia
1993

Award for Excellence in Energy Design
SunTrust Plaza
Georgia AIA and Georgia Power Company
John Portman & Associates
Atlanta, Georgia
1992

Service to the Profession Award
AIA Atlanta
John C. Portman, Jr.
Atlanta
1992

ACI Concrete Structure Award
American Concrete Institute, GA. Chapter
John Portman & Associates
Atlanta
1992

Doctor of Fine Arts
Honorary Degree
Atlanta College of Art
John C. Portman, Jr.
1992

AD 100 Architects
Architectural Digest
John C. Portman, Jr.
Los Angeles, California
1991

Building of the Year Award
Northpark Town Center
Atlanta Building Owners & Managers Association
Atlanta, Georgia
1991

Horatio Alger Award
Horatio Alger Association
John C. Portman, Jr.
Chicago, Illinois
1990

Shaping of the City Award
The Atlanta Convention & Visitors Bureau
John C. Portman, Jr.
1988

Platinum Circle Award
Restaurant & Hotel Magazine
John C. Portman, Jr.
1987

Awards continued

Exceptional Achievement Award
Georgia Institute of Technology Alumni Association
John C. Portman, Jr.
Atlanta, Georgia
1985

Award for Excellence
Urban Land Institute
Embarcadero Center, San Francisco
John Portman & Associates
1984

Silver Medal Award
Innovations in Design
American Institute of Architects
Atlanta Chapter
John Portman & Associates
1981

Archdiocesan Medal
Excellence in Design
Congress of the Greek Orthodox Church
John C. Portman, Jr.
Atlanta, Georgia
1980

AIA Medal
National American Institute of Architects
Innovations in Hotel Design
John C. Portman, Jr.
Washington, D.C.
1978

Los Angeles Headquarters
City Association Award
Los Angeles Bonaventure
Los Angeles, California
John Portman & Associates
1976

Elsie de Wolfe Award
American Society of Interior Designers
New York Metropolitan Chapter
New York, New York
John Portman & Associates
1976

Officer, Royal Belgian Order of the Crown
Appointment by the King of Belgium
Brussels, Belgium
John C. Portman, Jr.
1975

Royal Order of Knights of Dannenborg
Appointment by the Queen of Denmark
Copenhagen, Denmark
John C. Portman, Jr.
1975

Design in Steel Award
American Iron and Steel Institute
John Portman & Associates
1975

Golden Plate Award
American Academy of Achievement
John C. Portman, Jr.
1968

College of Fellows
American Institute of Architects
John C. Portman, Jr.
Washington, D.C.
1968

Ivan Allen Award
American Institute of Architects
North Georgia Chapter
John C. Portman, Jr.
Atlanta, Georgia
1964

Outstanding Young Man of Georgia Award
Georgia Junior Chamber of Commerce
Architectural Leadership and Civic Improvement
John C. Portman, Jr.
1959

Exhibitions

National Academy of Design
Architects of the Academy Exhibit
Entelechy II, Portman Beach Home, Sea Island, Georgia
New York, New York
30 January-14 April 2002

Global Atlanta 2000
International Architecture Exhibit
World Day of Architecture
SunTrust Plaza Garden Offices
Atlanta, Georgia
2-8 October 2000

National Academy of Design
Recent Accessions 1997-1998
Portfolio of Four Architectural Projects
New York, New York
9 May-4 July 1999

John Portman: A Retrospective Exhibition
Exhibit of Portman works of art, sculpture, lighting and furniture designs
SunTrust Plaza, Atlanta, Georgia
14 January-15 April 1999

Atlanta International Museum
Culture and Construct
American Architects Abroad
Sponsored by AIA Georgia and Historic Preservation Center
Atlanta, Georgia
18 July-27 December 1997

American Institute of Architects
Going Global
Exhibit of John Portman & Associates International Projects
SunTrust Plaza Garden Offices
Atlanta, Georgia
15 July-15-August 1996

Atlanta Historical Society
The John Portman Collection
Renderings of Architectural Projects
Architectural Model of Entelechy II, Portman Beach Home, Sea Island, Georgia.
July 1991 to Present

University of Wisconsin-Milwaukee
Fine Arts Gallery—Architectural Exhibit
Visionary Architecture
Entelechy II, Portman Beach Home, Sea Island, Georgia
16 October-22 November 1988

Acknowledgments

The work of John Portman & Associates over a span of 48 years is not just the effort of a few but the endeavor of a large, talented, and dedicated team of professionals. I would like to express my sincere thanks to those individuals.

Special appreciation goes to my long-time senior associates John Street and Mickey Steinberg, to my son Jack Portman for his untiring efforts with our work in Asia, China, and India, and to my son Michael Portman, whose photography has enhanced the pages of this book.

I would like to express my sincere thanks to the following people for their many years of loyal dedication:

Nasim Akhtar
Lell Barnes
Barry Barsh
Fred Benckenstein
Greg Botsch
Bill Bradfield
Tom Bray
Marvin Brewer
Tom Carter
Timothy Cent
Mary Chib
Rohit Chib
Emilio Coirini
Weiping Dai
Mike Delvin
David Doar
Jim Drury
Housh Farhadi
Earl Hartle
Tom Hughes
Norris Hunt
Walt Jackson
Rick Jewett
Bill Johns
Herb Jolly
Bob Jones
Scott Jones
Ellis Katz
Leland King
Fey Lau
Steve Lin
Sam McPhaul
Bill Miller
Walt Miller
Richards Mixon
Jose Oscar Flores Moreno
John Nipaver
Hershel Owens
Pat Pharr
Charlie Prince
Housh Rahimzadeh
G.P. Reddy
David S. Robertson
Doug Robinson
Raffie Samach
Ekapong Sarindu
John Schlenkert
Andrew Simmons
Vernon Smith
Simon Snellgrove
Warren Snipes
Don Starr
Louie Stokes
Rolf Stute
Grace Tan
Erin Uesugi
Tani Winata
Jean Wu
Kin-Ka Wong
John Yang
Roger Zampbell

I also wish to gratefully acknowledge the extraordinary contributions of Richards Mixon, my close design conferee and my executive assistant, Judy Perry-Jones, for her dedicated efforts and contributions for more than 30 years.

John C. Portman, Jr., FAIA
Chairman

Special acknowledgment is given to the following people for their contribution to this publication: Dannie Martin for her contribution to the text, Richards Mixon for his supervision, Andrew Simmons for coordination and selection, and the administrative staff of Lauri Martin, Judy McGowan, Judy Perry-Jones, and Katy Richardson. I also wish to give special thanks to the editorial staff at The Images Publishing Group.

Photography Credits

Michael Portman: Cover image; 17; 18; 19; 20 (1, 2); 21; 22 (2); 23; 24 (4); 32 (2, 3); 33; 35 (7); 37; 38 (1); 39 (3, 4); 40; 41 (6, 7); 44 (1); 45; 47 (6, 7); 48; 49 (10); 50 (12, 13); 51; 52 (1); 53; 55 (1, 2); 56; 57 (5); 58 (6); 59; 61; 62; 63 (4, 6); 64; 66 (1, 2, 3); 67; 73 (2); 74 (2); 75; 76; 77 (5); 81; 88 (2); 89; 101; 137; 140 (1, 3); 141; 143; 144; 145 (8, 9); 146 (2); 149 (6); 150 (1); 167; 168 (5); 170; 171; 184 (1); 185; 186 (2); 189 (6, 7); 190 (2); 191; 202 (2); 203; 204 (5); 205 (7); 207 (10); 209 (4); 210 (2); 211; 212; 213; 214; 215 (3); 216; 217 (6, 7, 8); 218; 219

Alexander Georges: 16 (2); 26 (2); 52 (3)

Timothy Hursley: 24 (5); 34; 35 (8, 9); 24; 25 (5); 34; 35 (8, 9); 46 (5); 187; 188

Kevin Ames: 27

Kevin Rose: 132 (1); 133

Jaime Ardiles-Arce: 29; 30 (3, 4, 5, 6)

Rion Rizzo: 25 (6)

Richard Sexton: 49 (11)

Clyde May: 70 (3); 71; 83 (4, 5); 84 (2); 87; 93; 117; 118 (1); 120; 121 (7); 124 (2); 125 (7); 126 (2); 127; 131 (10, 11)

Jennifer Almand: 73 (4); 84 (1)

Bo Parker: 136 (2); 138; 208 (2); 209 (3)

Dennis O'Kane: 139 (6, 7)

Letia Boutet: 99 (4)

Andrew Simmons: 151 (3); 152 (5); 153; 206 (9)

Provided by John Portman & Associates: 16 (1); 22 (1); 25 (7); 26 (1); 28; 31; 32 (1); 35 (6); 36; 38 (2); 44 (2); 46 (4); 47 (8); 52 (2); 57 (4); 58 (7); 60; 63 (5); 70 (5); 74 (1); 77 (6); 80 (12); 82; 86 (1, 2); 88 (1); 91 (5, 6); 92 (1, 2); 96; 97; 102 (1); 105 (4); 106; 109 (5); 110 (1); 111 (2); 112 (4); 114 (1); 116 (1, 2); 119 (3); 121 (6); 124 (1); 126 (1); 128 (4); 129 (6); 132 (2); 134 (2); 136 (1); 139 (5); 140 (2); 142 (5); 146 (1); 149 (5); 152 (4); 154; 156 (1); 158 (1); 159 (5); 160 (1); 163 (2, 4); 166 (2); 169; 178 (3); 182 (1); 184 (2, 3, 4); 186 (1), 189 (5); 191 (3); 196 (1, 2); 198 (1); 200; 201 (4); 202 (1); 204 (4); 205 (6); 206 (8); 208 (1); 210 (1); 217 (5)

Rendering Credits:

John Yang: 42 (1, 2, 3); 43; 105 (5); 107; 108; 109 (4); 111 (3); 112 (5, 6); 113 (7, 8); 114 (2); 115; 118 (2); 122; 123; 132 (3); 157; 158 (2, 3); 159 (4); 162; 163 (3); 197 (3, 4); 199; 201 (5)

Dan Harmon: 68-69; 70 (4); 72; 73 (3); 78; 79 (10); 80 (11); 85; 86 (3); 90; 92 (1); 98 (1, 2); 99 (3); 100 (1, 2, 3); 115 (4, 5); 128 (5); 129 (7); 130; 131 (9); 150 (2); 155; 166 (1); 167 (4); 174 (2); 175 (3, 4); 178 (2); 179 (4); 182 (2); 183 (3, 4); 215 (4)

David Hartley: 77 (7); 79 (9)

James Cagle: 83 (3); 134 (1)

Andrew Simmons: 103; 104; 105 (6, 7); 160 (2); 161

Ekapong Sarindu: 135

Chuan Wang: 178 (1); 179 (5)

Mark Geyer: 190 (1)

Provided by The Jerde Partnership: 132 (4)

Provided by Land Use Consultants, Inc.: 174 (1); 175 (5)

Provided by Zhejiang Province Building Design & Research Institute: 164; 165

Index

Agnes Scott College, Dana Fine Arts Center 234

Alfred Blalock Elementary School 235

AmericasMart (see Peachtree Center)

Antoine Graves Home 234

Apparel Mart (see Peachtree Center)

Athletic Club (see Peachtree Center)

Atlanta Decorative Arts Center 234

Atlanta Marriott Marquis (see Peachtree Center)

Atlanta School Service Center 234

Bank of China 172-173

Bank of Communications 174-179

Blue Cross Blue Shield Office Building 235

Brussels International Trade Mart 236

BSD New Town 182-183

Cain Tower (see Peachtree Center)

Capital Square 66-67

Chong Qing 98-99

C.W. Hill School 235

Doctor's Office Building 234

Dream Lake Mountain Villas 186-187

East Seaport Apartment and High Rise Hotel Addition 170-171

Embarcadero Center 44-51

Hyatt Regency, San Francisco 236

Levi Strauss Building 236

Park Hyatt Hotel 237

Security Pacific National Bank 235

Three Embarcadero Center 236

West Office Tower 237

Emory University Physical Education Center
(see George W. Woodruff Physical Education Center)

Emory University Student Center (see R. Howard Dobbs University Center)

Entelechy I 210-213, 234

Entelechy II 214-219, 237

Facilities for the Airport Terminal Complex—Jing An 116-117

Fort Worth National Bank (see Texas American Bank Building)

Fraternal Order of Eagles 234

Gas Light Tower (see Peachtree Center)

Gateway City 90-93

George W. Woodruff Physical Education Center
(Emory University) 188-189, 236

Georgia Tech Infirmary 234

Gift Mart (see Peachtree Center)

Great Park 180-181

Greenbriar Rich's 234

Greenbriar Shopping Center 234

Greenbriar Theater 235

Guangzhou Daily Cultural Center 120-123

Gwinnett Center Academic Building 198-201

Harris Tower (see Peachtree Center)

Hawthorne Elementary School 234

Henderson High School 235

Herndon Elementary School 234

Hotelero Business Monterrey 160-161

Hsinchu Regional Master Plan 184-185

Huading Mansion 118-119

Hung Yuan International Hotel 237

Hyatt Regency, Atlanta (see Peachtree Center)

Hyatt Regency, Chicago 235

Hyatt Regency, San Francisco (see Embarcadero Center)

Il Porto Vecchio 68-71

Indian School of Business 202-207

Inforum (see Peachtree Center)

J.F. Kennedy School & Community Center 235

Jin Mao 132-137

Kwai Chung Condominiums 236

Le Meridien Hotel 86-87

Lemer Residence 234

Levi Strauss Building (see Embarcadero Center)

Lot 6 138-139

Marina Square 54-59, 237

Marquis One Office Tower 236

Marquis Two Office Tower 237

Merchandise Mart (see Peachtree Center)

Midnight Sun Restaurant 235

Midway Elementary School 234

Moscow Centre 88-89

New Asia Center 102-103

New Ci Hou Plaza 104-107

New York Marriott Marquis 142-145, 236

Nile Center 84-85

Northpark 400 Office Tower 237

Northpark 500 Office Tower 237

Nursing, Health Science and Outreach Complex 196-197

One Peachtree Center (see Peachtree Center, SunTrust Plaza)

Pan Pacific San Francisco, The (formerly The Portman Hotel) 146-151, 237

Parcel 8 130-131

Park Central Office Building I 235

Park Central Office Building II 235

Park Hyatt Hotel (see Embarcadero Center)

Pavilion Intercontinental, The (see Regent Singapore, The)

Peachtree Center 16-43

AmericasMart 18-19

Apparel Mart 18, 236

Athletic Club 237

Atlanta Marriott Marquis 28-31, 236

Cain Tower 235

Gas Light Tower 235

Gift Mart 18, 237

Harris Tower 236

Hyatt Regency, Atlanta 22-25, 235

Inforum 20-21, 237

Merchandise Mart 18, 234

Office Building 234

Shopping Gallery 236

South Tower 235

SunTrust III 42-43

SunTrust Plaza (formerly One Peachtree Center) 32-37

SunTrust Plaza Garden Offices 38-41

Westin Peachtree Plaza Hotel 26-27, 236

Portman Hotel, The (see Pan Pacific San Francisco, The)

Regent Singapore, The (formerly The Pavilion Intercontinental) 152-155, 236

Renaissance Center 52-53, 236

R. Howard Dobbs University Center (Emory University) 190-193, 237

Riverwood 100 Office Tower 237

Rockefeller Center Promenade 208-209, 236

Sampoerna Tower 140-141

San Francisco Fashion Center 237

Security Pacific National Bank (see Embarcadero Center)

Sequoyah High School 234

Shandong Hotel & Conference Center 72-75

Shanghai Art Center 112-115

Shanghai Centre 60-65, 237

Shanghai Daewoo Business Center 94-97

Silver Tai World Trade Center 108-111

Songdo Daewoo Town 124-129

South Tower (see Peachtree Center)

Spalding Drive Elementary School 235

SunTrust III (see Peachtree Center)

SunTrust Plaza (see Peachtree Center)

SunTrust Plaza Garden Offices (see Peachtree Center)

Texas American Bank Building (formerly Fort Worth National Bank) 236

Three Embarcadero Center (see Embarcadero Center)

Tomorrow Square 76-83

Trailways Bus Terminal 235

Trailways Garage and Parking Deck 234

University/Olympic Apartments (Georgia Tech) 194-195

Village of Schaumburg Convention Center, Performing Arts Theater, and Convention Headquarters Hotel 166-167

West Office Tower (see Embarcadero Center)

Westin Bonaventure (Los Angeles) 236

Westin Hotel (Charlotte) 164-165

Westin Hotel (Warsaw) 168-169

Westin Peachtree Plaza Hotel (see Peachtree Center)

Westlake International Hotel 156-159

'W' Hotel and Residences 162-163

Zhong Xing City 100-101

Every effort has been made to trace the original source of copyright material contained in this book. The publishers would be pleased to hear from copyright holders to rectify any error or omissions.

The information and illustrations in this publication has been prepared and supplied by John Portman & Associates. While all reasonable efforts have been made to ensure accuracy, the publishers do not, under any circumstances, accept responsibility for errors, omissions and representations express or implied.